THE UNKNOWN COUNTRY

THE UNKNOWN COUNTRY

A LIFE OF
IGOR STRAVINSKY

Neil Tierney

LONDON
ROBERT HALE LIMITED

ISBN 0 7091 6092 5

Robert Hale Limited
Clerkenwell House
Clerkenwell Green
London EC1R 0HT

PRINTED IN GREAT BRITAIN BY
CLARKE, DOBLE & BRENDON LTD,
PLYMOUTH AND LONDON

CONTENTS

FOREWORD 9

ACKNOWLEDGEMENTS 11

THE LIFE

1   In the Beginning 15
2   City of the Bronze Horseman 25
3   Diaghilev stages *The Firebird* 36
4   Scandal in Paris 54
5   War and Exile 69
6   *Pulcinella*—A Discovery of the Past 87
7   More Conquests in Paris 94
8   London and *The Sleeping Princess* 102
9   The Death of Diaghilev 115
10 Gide Helps to Create *Perséphone* 133
11 Stravinsky becomes an American Citizen 149
12 Homecoming of an Exile 165
13 The Character of a Genius 184
14 Journey's End 194

THE MUSIC

15 Preparation for the Journey 203
16 The Green Pastures 207
17 The Hills and the Valleys 222
18 The Flowering Desert 247

NOTES 259

BIBLIOGRAPHY 265

INDEX 267

I will sing with knowledge
And all my music shall be for the glory of God
My lyre and harp shall be
For this holy fixed order
And the flute of my lips
I will raise
In this just circle

Translation by Millar Burrows from
the Dead Sea Scrolls

ILLUSTRATIONS

Between pages 112 and 113

1   Igor Stravinsky
2   The Maryinsky Theatre
3   A Russian Ballet poster, showing Stravinsky standing beside Nijinsky
4   Tamara Karsavina as the Firebird
5   Diaghilev with his old nurse, from the painting by Bakst, 1903
6   Alexandre Benois in 1896, from a pastel by Bakst
7   Vaslav Nijinsky as Petrushka
8   Drawing by Picasso for the cover of *Ragtime*
9   Stravinsky with Pierre Monteux
10 Lifar and Picasso
11 Original gouache by Marc Chagall commemorating the Stravinsky-Chagall-Balanchine production of *The Firebird* in 1949
12 Backcloth for Apollon Musagète painted by André Bauchant
13 Raimund Herincx as Creon in *Oedipus Rex*
14 Katherine Pring as Jocasta

Between pages 208 and 209

15 Karsavina, Diaghilev and Lifar with the unfortunate Nijinsky on the Opéra stage
16 First page of the manuscript score of *Agon*
17 Drawing of Stravinsky by Laszlo Krausz
18 Stravinsky at rehearsal
19 Stravinsky enjoying a joke with Mstislav Rostropovich
20 Stravinsky being greeted by Ekaterina Furtseva, the Soviet Minister of Culture
21 Stravinsky rehearsing the Moscow Conservatory Orchestra
22 A painting by Gloria Brown of Igor and Vera Stravinsky
23 Stravinsky with his wife Vera and George Balanchine

24 A water hearse carries Stravinsky's coffin across Canal San Giovanni and Paolo

25 The funeral service for Stravinsky

PICTURE CREDITS

Popperfoto/United Press International : 1, 20, 21, 23, 24, 25
Ivan Domherr : 3
J. W. Chester Ltd : 8
Erich Auerbach : 9, 18, 19
Hutchinson Publishing Group Ltd and Editions René Julliard : 10, 15
Martin Riskin : 11
Wadsworth Athenaeum, Ella Gallup and Mary Catlin Sumner Collection : 12
Reg Wilson : 13, 14
Boosey & Hawkes Ltd : 16

FOREWORD

On 6th April 1971, in the bedroom of a New York hotel, Stravinsky died. He was eighty-eight years old. My daughter, hearing the sad news on the radio, telephoned me at my office and said, as if announcing the collapse of civilization itself, "Stravinsky is dead." Shocked and unhappy, I thought fleetingly of Petrushka, the immortal puppet, and the face I saw was that of its creator. This book, which had grown prodigiously during the few weeks preceding his death, suddenly kicked inside me like a child struggling to be born.

The biographical scope of existing books about Igor Stravinsky is to a large extent restricted by the very thoroughness with which the authors carried out their segment-by-segment analysis of his music. Occasionally, in the tapestry of the book, the bright threads of Stravinsky's life are hidden or dimmed by the glitter of the music. *The Unknown Country* presents that life—a strange and wonderful one, indeed—as a single, dominating entity, mentioning the compositions as episodic events, rather than as a vast field of research for the musical scholar. Instead of interrupting the narrative with extensive library data and complex analyses, I have discussed the music separately at the end of my book. More searching assessments there undoubtedly are, and they provide a richer treasury of information than could possibly be added in this appendix. Yet the chapters I have written about the music give a detailed and explicit account of Stravinsky's creative output, setting the various compositions in the context to which they belong. My comments seek to convey the spirit, as well as to expound the structure of the work being discussed. They form an indispensable adjunct to "The Life".

Stravinsky, probably the greatest and certainly the most exciting composer of the twentieth century, moved like a Renaissance prince against a gripping and tumultuous panorama of people and events. The romantic aura of his own life contrasted vividly with the cool, transparent, almost sexless purity of much of his music. He fought battles of principle, routing the adversaries of stuffy and outmoded tradition. He mingled with a host of musicians, writers, painters, dancers, and others whose names belong not merely to posterity, but to history itself. His wit, his insatiable hunger for new artistic experiences, his wisdom, and the compassion which he hid so jealously from the prying eyes of the world, more than compensate for the wolflike rapacity with which, at times, he clawed and rent his enemies. There was in Stravinsky a sweetness of character that, like his beautiful *Apollo* music, could be savoured only by those who, in imagination, walked beside him. I have attempted, in *The Unknown Country*, to paint a three-dimensional picture of a titanic figure whose true significance and greatness may not be realized until many decades have passed. In doing so, I have necessarily dwelt at some length upon the outstanding men and women—Diaghilev, Karsavina, Nijinsky, Debussy, Monteux, Satie, Picasso, Gide, Balanchine, and others—who shared the limelight in the huge and inexhaustible drama of his life; for, as Donne reminds us, "no man is an island . . .".

NEIL TIERNEY

ACKNOWLEDGEMENTS

I am greatly indebted to Madame Tamara Karsavina, Madame Romola Nijinsky, Mr John Pritchard, Mr Raimund Herincx, Professor Gordon Green, the late Mr W. H. Auden, Miss Gloria Doyle Brown, Mr Junius Rochester, Mr Laszlo Krausz, Mr Martin Riskin, Mr William Roerick, Miss Naomi Galinski, Miss Andrea L. Craig, Mr Fritz Spiegl, Mr Ivan Domherr of Barnum Archives, Miss Helen Salomon, Mr David C. Rosenfield, Mr Christian Bourgois, Miss Margaret T. Vincent and Miss Anne Rives for reminiscences and material supplied to me during the preparation of this book.

To The Sadler's Wells Opera (now The English National Opera), The Grolier Society, Ltd, William Collins, Sons and Co., Ltd, Publishers, United Press International (U.K.), Ltd, Mr Erich Auberbach, *The Liverpool Daily Post and Echo*, Ltd, Fleetway Publications Ltd, *The Gramophone*, The Welsh National Opera, The Library and Museum of the Performing Arts, Mrs Harry B. Gibbs, *Miami Herald,* Mr Sydney J. Harris, *The New York Times Book Review*, Mr Gerald A. Ahronheim, René Julliard of *Ma Vie*, J. W. Chester, Ltd, Boosey & Hawkes, Ltd, Mr John N. Vincent, *Harper's Magazine*, Mr Goddard Lieberson, *Music and Musicians,* Victor Gollancz, Ltd, Faber and Faber, Ltd, *Musical America*, Eric Glass, Ltd, *Art News*, Burke Books, Hutchinson and Co. (Publishers), Ltd, and The Wadsworth Athenaeum for permission to use certain photographic or literary material, or for help in other ways.

To Mr Ates Orga, Mr Albert Howell, and Mr Anthony Hodges, former Music Librarian of Liverpool City Libraries, for their friendly advice and encouragement.

Finally, to Mr Chambré Hardman I express my thanks and admiration for his highly skilled services as a professional photographer.

FOR
JOAN, KATHY, AND JANE

THE LIFE

1
IN THE BEGINNING

At the ripe age of 111, Stravinsky's great-grandfather Ignatievich died as the result of a fall while climbing a fence to avoid being imprisoned, as a safety measure, by his children. Igor Fedorovich Stravinsky, a mere eighty-eight years old when he died on 6th April 1971, had been scaling fences all his life: not the sturdy, horizontal planks around a typical nineteenth-century Russian homestead, but the sharply pointed stakes of detested tradition. Unlike the hoary escapologist before him, he hardly ever put a foot wrong—not even in *The Rite of Spring*, which shocked and scandalized a Paris audience at its first performance in May 1913. For critics and public alike now recognize that *The Rite*, with its monumental grandeur, its violent evocation of the northern spring—the bursting earth and the splintering ice—is one of the universally great works of music. The creator of this provocative and seminal piece, vaulting the fence of what he regarded as outworn romanticism, soon found himself in that Unknown Country which, as Hilaire Belloc remarks in his essay, "stands out as clear as does a sudden vision from a mountain ridge when the mist lifts after a long climb and one sees beneath one an unexpected and glorious land".[1]

It was to Paris, the progenitor of so many liberating cults and crusades, that this vision would eventually lure Stravinsky. Only a few decades previously France had made tremendous artistic as well as social changes: the fall of the Bastille, opening up a highway for early nineteenth-century Romanticism, had crushed the concept that only the titled rich were fitting subjects for brush or pen. Man rediscovered his own image; the mighty were forgotten, and in music, painting and literature the meek inherited the earth. It was the age of Fennimore Cooper and Chateaubriand, of Meyerbeer and Ponchielli, who played their humanistic themes with a fustian eloquence. Not for long, however; since, at the dawning of a new century, tradition would crumble once again as the rhythmically exciting and colourful music of Stravinsky infused new life into opera and ballet.

To understand his complex, hieratic, often prickly character, one is guided largely by Stravinsky's autobiography, coupled with the brilliantly

devised group of volumes recording his conversations with the American
conductor Robert Craft. The name Stravinsky comes from 'Strava', the
appellation of a small river, tributary of the Vistula, in eastern Poland;
but, when his forefathers owned lands in that country, it carried the
hyphenated prefix 'Soulima'. During the scarlet reign of Catherine the
Great the family moved to Russia. It was an age of bone-baring poverty
and orgiastic gluttony, of gleaming palaces and rat-plagued hovels. One
of Igor's great-grandparents (not the fence-hopping Methuselah) bore
the title 'Excellency'; but, more important, he was an ancestor of Diaghilev, who in three magnificent ballets—*The Rite of Spring*, *The Firebird*,
and *Petrushka*—gave immortal dimensions to Stravinsky's fondness for
colour and spectacle.

The composer was born on 17th June 1882, in Oranienbaum, a sleepy,
picturesque seaside village with an eighteenth-century palace. His autobiography, *Chronicle of My Life*, provides unforgettable glimpses of
country life there, with the sharp, resinous tang of freshly cut wood tingling in the nostrils and the sound of new leaves whispering as they unfolded. It depicts a huge, red-shirted peasant seated on a tree-stump, "on
his feet birch sandals, on his head a mop of hair as thick and as red as
his beard—not a white hair, yet an old man".[2] As Igor and his companions, breathless with excitement, squatted at the feet of this dumb, Dos-
toievskian apparition, the peasant clicked his tongue, then with strange,
two-syllable cluckings began to sing. Pressing the palm of his right hand
under his left armpit, he so manipulated it that the delighted boys heard
"a succession of sounds which might be euphemistically described as
resounding kisses".[3] Igor, subsequently imitating this erotic, though doubtless innocent performance, was rebuked for indecorous behaviour. What,
one wonders, would his critics have thought if, like the composer, they
could have survived until the spring season of 1913 in Paris, to witness
what, for them, would have been a most unseemly exhibition in the Opera
House. There, in a Bakst-inspired tableau that conjured up, to the music
of Debussy, the sexually potent gambols of fauns and nymphs, Nijinsky,
the capricious and unpredictable, suddenly used a too intimate, audacious
gesture that drew horrified gasps from the audience.

Another of Stravinsky's childhood recollections was of a great company
of women from a neighbouring village singing in unison as, irradiated
by the soft glow of the setting sun, they returned home after the day's
work. These women sang the tune in octaves, their shrill, high, unharmonious voices reminding the boy of a gigantic swarm of bees. When he
repeated it in his own home, imitating their rustic mannerisms, he was
complimented on the trueness of his ear. From domestic incidents
as fragmentary as these, Stravinsky, reared in a land which still liked to
parade in national costume, acquired the sense of pageantry and of rhythmic differentiation that colours his early ballet music. It guided him

magnetically to the treasure-house of native art : to Russian folk-tales, dances, songs, and *pribaoutki*, or country ballads. For although he absorbed all the age-old culture of the West, from Monteverdi to Schoenberg, from Raphael to Paul Klee, transmuting and extending it, he also, like the poet Pushkin, developed a peculiarly Russian-flavoured universality of spirit.

Stravinsky's parents had gone to Oranienbaum a month before his birth. Dreading the gaunt grey wolf of tuberculosis which, from as far back as the Tsar's 'Council of Thirty', had stalked the family, they seized every health-giving opportunity. The composer himself periodically fell victim to this marauder, notably in 1939, when he spent five months in the sanatorium at Sancellemos. After his christening, Igor's parents moved to St Petersburg, where his father Feodor was principal bass at the Imperial Opera House; there, on one splendid occasion, the boy heard him singing the role of Farlaf in *Russlan and Ludmilla*. The family occupied a Victorian-type flat, furnished, as the composer recalled, with "the usual bad paintings, the usual mauve upholstery, but, exceptionally perhaps, with an unusual library and two grand pianos".[4] Napravnik, the conductor, lived next door. Although there was music in the house, the children, relegated to the nursery heard it only from a distance. The room shared by Igor and his brother Goury was like Petrushka's cell. In winter the cold pressed down hard upon the land, the frost transforming the birch trees into beauty like that of the iconastasis in the church. Igor, thin and frail, was allowed outside the house only after being anxiously scrutinized by his parents; also, while out, he must not play games or sports.

Did he, one wonders, sometimes defy adult strictures and indulge in the pranks and escapades common to boys everywhere? He certainly fell hopelessly in love with a girl called Lidia during his adolescence. Stravinsky, who always disliked inward-looking sentimentality, introduced few childish reminiscences into his autobiography. Perhaps, like other youngsters, he watched the fat, wood-carrying barges moving sluggishly along the canal that curved through St Petersburg to join the River Fontanka, though, when it froze in the winter, his prudent parents would scarcely permit him to skate on it. And there was always the fascination of a house on fire, which to a Russian of that period was irresistible. Often the local fire-station would have a watch-tower with a sentry walking around the parapet. For the children it was a blood-tingling spectacle to see the firemen in all their glittering array, brass helmets, bugle blowing, issue forth at the alarm and tear down the streets, four horses at the gallop.

One also imagines him, on some bright winter's day, isolated in the mysterious fairy-tale existence of boyish dreams. He must have glimpsed with particular vividness the dazzling snow on the roofs and the sparkling silver caps of the fence poles. Doubtless he strolled far into the country, staring at the black filigree of apple boughs in the orchards, watching the linnets planing in the flushed sky, and the goldfinches pecking at the turnip-tops in search of seeds. How much of this must have been absorbed and recollected. *The Rite of Spring* was conceived, not in the warmth of red plush and gilt, the comfort of downy couches and silken curtains, but in the crystalline intensity of images evoked from life. In this unique work are the profound convulsions of nature, the dynamic throes of prehistoric birth; but also there, one believes, are the gentler sounds of panting cattle, chirping chaffinches, and babbling streams which Stravinsky heard as a boy.

His father, a self-righteous autocrat whose peremptory outbursts remind one of the Barrett and Sitwell dynasties, not only possessed a flourishing ego, but regarded his own musical ear to be an organ of almost Papal infallibility. Feodor Stravinsky, fearsome in pride and temper, dominated those around him, his power, like that of the newly-crowned Boris God-unov, seeming to be absolute. On one occasion, walking beside his son, then about twelve years old, in a Bad Homburg street, he peremptorily ordered him to return to his hotel room. The boy, humiliated, sulked instead of obeying, whereupon his father, fairly trumpeting with rage, caused a public scandal. Yet, when Igor was ill, this *grand seigneur* of the family radiated immense kindness, particularly when, at the age of thir-teen, the boy developed pleurisy, with, for him, a lifelong tubercular legacy. Ezra Pound, that poet of sunlight and shadow, uttered a profound truth when, in one of his *Cantos*, he wrote: "Nothing matters but the quality of the affection".[5] It seems that when death claimed Feodor Stra-vinsky the spark of nobility inside him suddenly burst into flame. After a fall on the stage of the Opera House he developed cancer and died, with stoical dignity, a year and a half later. "His death brought us closer to-gether," declared his son.

Igor's feelings towards his mother were of duty rather than love, and, although fond of his brother Goury, he found in Bertha, his docile, unde-manding nurse, a pillar of strength and a refuge. Since she knew no Rus-sian, the language in the nursery was that of Germany, her native country. Thus, the Stravinsky children probably never heard nursery-rhymes like "Ladoushki, Ladoushki, we went to Baboushka", which Russian nannies often sang to their charges; nor, perhaps, while the birch logs spluttered in the fire at night, did they listen to spine-chilling tales of Buka and other horned, hoofed, taily creatures only in the dream-world of the very young. Bertha survived long enough to tend Igor's own children and served the family for forty years before dying in Morges in 1917. "I mourned her,"[6] said the composer, "more than I did later my mother."

A succession of governesses came to the Stravinsky household and pre-sided over the destinies of the children, with varying degrees of success. One of these, an "aggressively ugly spinster" from Switzerland, as Igor described her, many years later, showed an unnatural interest in seeing the boys into the bathtub. Her sexual appetite having been noticed by the parents, she was replaced by Vinogradova, who discharged her duties with an almost sadistic efficiency, glaring when the progress of her teaching came under interrogation. Igor subsequently referred to her as the least feminine woman he had ever seen. She chewed her finger-nails, had unsightly damp, red hands, and arranged her hair in a *bubikopf*.

His memories of his older brothers were mostly of how they bantered, teased; or otherwise annoyed him; but he felt immensely proud of handsome Roman, the law student, envying him when the village girls winked as he passed. Unhappily, at eleven years of age Roman caught diphtheria and, a decade hence, died of a weakened heart. Youry, an architectural engineer, was never really close to Igor; the gap widened, and shortly before the German invasion of the First World War, while domiciled in Paris, he, too, died. Goury had a fine baritone voice, studied with Tartakov, a famous St Petersburg singer, and sang professionally for three years in a private theatre in that city. He died of scarlet fever in Rumania, in April, 1917, leaving Igor desolate, for he loved this brother, who had been his companion so often. The composer wrote his Verlaine songs for Goury. These lines from *"La Sagesse"* describe "the great black sleep of despair" that engulfed Igor as, increasingly alone, he sensed the enormity of his loss; they speak poignantly of the "hand in the hollow of a crypt" reaching across the irrecoverable past towards him :

Je ne vois plus rien
Je perds la memoire
Du mal et du bien . . .
O, la triste histoire!

Je suis un berceau
Qu'une moin balance
Au creux d'un caveau . . .
Silence, silence!

After Feodor Stravinsky's death, Igor mentally spread his wings, breathing in great gulps the sweet, exhilarating air of that Western sophistication which, for him, represented superiority over factors, cultural and domestic, alien to his true stature. On one occasion, goaded by his mother's delight in tormenting him—almost certainly a pathetic symptom of deprived love —he fled from home, leaving a recriminatory note and lodging with a friend. After a few days, however, his mother became ill and he returned, to find a more congenial atmosphere.

Despite parental oddities and his own gnawing unrest, Igor, as a child, knew moments of intense happiness. At the age of seven or eight he saw *The Sleeping Beauty* and was moved to rapturous tears—"I applauded with all my strength". And one day, taken to a theatre for a performance of *A Life for the Tsar* he heard an orchestra—Glinka's own—for the first time. From that moment his gratitude to 'the father of Russian music' bubbled over, for the superb balance of tone, the instrumentation "so distinguished and delicate" which he found in Glinka's music represented for him "a perfect monument of musical art". Later he also heard a gala performance of Glinka's fairy-tale opera *Russlan and Ludmilla*, whose voluptuous Oriental atmosphere held him spellbound; at the same time he saw, in the foyer, that idol of the Russian public, Peter Ilyich Tchaikovsky, who, a fortnight later, was to die of cholera. This fragmentary glimpse of the living Tchaikovsky became a priceless memory.

Since Stravinsky was too young to coalesce bits of gossip, legend, and actual experience into a canvas of future reminiscences, he painted no Degas-like picture of the Russian ballet as it flourished in the Imperial Theatres of St Petersburg and Moscow when he was a boy. When Tamara Karsavina was a budding ballerina in Moscow at the close of the nineteenth century, the artistic inheritance of past decades had not been wholly spent. Soon the great Anna Pavlova would restore to the Russian stage the forgotten glory of the Romantic ballet of the days of Taglioni; meanwhile, anacreontic and mythological works, with a liberal splash of allegory and the traditional apotheosis of gods hoisted by means of a trap-door into a cloudy refulgence, still dominated the repertoire. Yet the balletomanes had their share of riches: the performance of *Swan Lake*, with Fokine and Siedova; Guerdt's ballet *In the Kingdom of Ice*; Gorsky's *Don Quixote*, and other favourites. In the Chinese Theatre of Tsarskoe Selo, a gem of beautifully lacquered panels, red and gold rococo chairs, and glittering chandeliers, built in 1778 by order of Catherine the Great and standing among pagoda-like fir trees, performances were given in the presence of the imperial family and the Court. In this environment the artistic seeds of the young Stravinsky, the musical genius of the twentieth century, slowly ripened.

With Uncle Ielatchitch, who owned vast farms and forests east of the Volga, the young composer made four-day trips on the river, drifting lazily between banks gaily ribboned with green and fragrant with the scent of pines. In his autobiography he described the places he saw: "Rybinsk (literally 'fish-town'), a white and gold city, with monasteries and glittering churches,—it looked like a set of *Tsar Saltan* as one came upon it round a sudden bend in the river; Jaroslav, with its blue and gold churches, and Nishni-Novgorod, where, surrounded by mendicant monks, one would walk to little booths to buy and drink kumiss (mare's milk)."[7]

It was Uncle Ielatchitch who, unaware that posterity stood outside, fingering the bellpush, introduced Igor to piano duet arrangements of Brahms's quartets and Wagner's *Ring*, which the boy studied fervently. This delightful uncle extolled the purity of classicism as ardently as he

praised the richness and diversity of romanticism, in music. He also adored
Beethoven, displaying a copy of the Waldmuller portrait on his walls. Not
so the ageing Igor Stravinsky, who scathingly asked, apropos of the first
movement of the *Choral* symphony : "How could Beethoven have been
satisfied—if he *was* satisfied—with such quadrilateral phrasing and pedantic development (cf. bars 387–400), such poor rhythmic invention?"[8] Igor
also detected banality in the octave violin passage of the early *Malinconia*.
It seems odd that, although contemptuous of these Homeric nods, all his
life he revered the music of Tchaikovsky, with its occasional padding and
triteness, though he was, of course, attracted largely by the nationalistic
merits, rather than the grandeur, pathos, and tenderness of that neurotic
individualist.

As to why Beethoven was satisfied with the particular musical idioms
and phrases he chose for expressing his thoughts and emotions, this is perhaps like asking why the architect of the Taj Mahal delighted in marble
domes and minarets, why Ernest Dowson crammed his nostalgic passion
for Cynara into a four-stanza poem, or why Leonardo da Vinci fastened
such a tantalizing smile on the face of the Mona Lisa. An artist
who fashions a masterpiece selects the language, whether of words, paint,
stone, or sound that, however imperfect, seems to fulfil his expressive
purpose. If Beethoven had composed in any other way, a supreme miracle
would have been lost to posterity.

When Stravinsky was nine years old his parents gave him a piano
teacher, a woman of impregnable bad taste, unimpeachable keyboard
brilliance, and a marked, almost obsessional dislike of Chopin. The boy,
who quickly learned to read music, browsing hungrily through the opera
and piano-vocal scores in his father's library, delighted to improvise, but
Mlle Kashporova reproached him for wasting his time; not surprisingly,
Stravinsky described her to Robert Craft as "a blockhead". These impro-
visations, he claimed, did nothing but good; they "contributed to my better
knowledge of the piano, sowing the seed of musical ideas". Stravinsky
quoted the remark which Rimsky-Korsakov made when, as a serious,
knowledge-seeking youth, he became his pupil : "Some compose at the
piano, and some without a piano. As for you, you will compose at the
piano."[9]

Stravinsky postulated that direct contact with the physical medium of
sound is better for a composer than working in the abstract realms of the
imagination. Doubtless that other twentieth-century musical genius, Ben-
jamin Britten, would have agreed; indeed, a framed, inscribed photograph
showing him composing beside his piano stands, in silent confirmation, on
the mantelpiece of my lounge.

Did Stravinsky treat his teacher unfairly in the matter of improvisation?
Doubtless every young man with a highly creative, but undeveloped gift
in music longs to improvise, to explore his own imaginative processes, to

project his own personality. For Stravinsky, the individualist and potential rebel, plagued by repetitive scales and exercises, the temptation to throw off the shackles put on him by Kashperovna was overwhelming; but improvisatory freedom is profitable only when it is based upon technical mastery, upon knowledge and understanding. As Rabindranath Tagore pointed out in *Gitanjali* "That training is the most intricate which leads to the utter simplicity of a tune." The music teacher, recognizing the truth of this dictum, as well as, presumably, the merits of her pupil, saw to it that he received thorough and disciplined instruction. Considering the marvellous precision and order in the mature Stravinsky's music, we may be thankful that she did so.

One of Kashperovna's topics of conversation was her own teacher Anton Rubinstein, and to this Igor listened attentively. Had he not seen the great pianist in his coffin, an imposing black-maned figure, with hands folded over a cross, immaculate in evening dress, as if ready for a performance—perhaps to play the B flat minor Piano Concerto the score of which his brother Nikolai had, figuratively speaking, flung contemptuously in Tchaikovsky's face? The boy had also seen the dead Emperor Alexander III lying in State in the SS. Peter and Paul Cathedral; a yellow waxen doll festooned with glittering decorations and orders. These macabre, ceremonial spectacles lodged in his memory, feeding that fondness for ritualistic drama which runs, like a purple thread, through much of his music.

> *Abrupt as when there's slid*
> *Its stiff gold blazing pall*
> *From some black coffin lid. . . .*

Kashperovna could not have been wholly repressive, since she taught Stravinsky to play the Mendelssohn G minor Piano Concerto, as well as sonatas and other pieces by Haydn, Beethoven, Schubert, and Schumann. They also tackled Rimsky-Korsakov's operas together, four hands. Her dislike of the aristocratic, dreamy-eyed Chopin was possibly the result of inferiority arising from her complete failure to understand his music. The piano teacher's only real idiosyncrasy seemed to be in forbidding Stravinsky all use of the pedals; he had to sustain with his fingers, like an organist. As he was never a pedal composer, this helped, rather than stunted, his development. Her greatest contribution to *The Rite of Spring* ethos was to ferment the bitterness inside him, until, in his mid-twenties, he revolted from her and from every constricting demand imposed by his studies, his schools, and his family. For Stravinsky childhood, illuminated by brief moments of bliss, was a period of waiting until he could "send everyone and everything connected with it to hell".[10]

He attended a government school, the Second St Petersburg Gymnasium, which he left at fourteen, entering the Gourevitch Gymnasium, a

private school where Youry had been before him. The Gourevitch estab-
lishment was situated eight miles from his home in a district called *peski*,
'the sands', and travelling there kept Stravinsky constantly in debt. Too
late to catch a tram in the mornings, he took a *fiacre*, paying forty or fifty
kopecks. But he liked those *fiacre* rides, particularly when school was over,
driving at a spanking pace along the Nevsky Prospect, with the steaming
horse kicking up a cascade of dirty snow, then, safely home, roasting himself in front of a big white porcelain stove.

Stravinsky studied history, mathematics, Latin, Greek, Russian, and
French literature in the Gourevitch school. "I was, of course, a very bad
pupil," he confessed in his autobiography, "and I hated this school, as I
did all my schools, profoundly and forever."[11] This is hardly surprising,
for at least two of the professors were drunkards. One of them, mocked
cruelly by the boys, took furtive nips from a bottle carried in his coat
pocket: a subject satirized, not without compassion, by the Russian novel-
ist Sologub. The other dipsomaniac, Woolf, an ex-Hussar officer who
taught mathematics, was, at least, a good Samaritan: knowing that Stravinsky composed, he helped, protected, and encouraged him. In the words
of Matthew Arnold:

> To the just-pausing Genius we remit
> Our worn-out life, and are—what we have been.[12]

The evolution of a great composer, especially one whose ways are mysterious and who walks alone, is an odyssey of alternating despair and revelation. How much bitterness Stravinsky absorbed in his childhood to
constrict and dry up the shallow stream of poetry inside him is a matter
for conjecture; happily he did not always practise his own dogma that
music should be nothing but a system of ordering sounds and that the
beauty which motivates such ordering must be untainted by specific emotion. Not only in the prismatic *Firebird* does one find a more tender
susceptibility, but in such passages as the voluptuous cello melody of the
pas de deux in *The Fairy's Kiss*, the self-effacing sincerity of the Mass,
the breathlessly plaintive quality of the fisherman's melody in *The
Nightingale*, and that winged passage in the *Canticum Sacrum* where the
baritone soloist calls for the gift of faith in support of his unbelief ("*Credo,
Domine, adjuva incredulitatem meam*").

The ethnic background of a creator must inevitably influence his outlook, and the recrudescences of Stravinsky's early Russian affinities with
Rimsky-Korsakov, Glinka, and Mussorgsky may be glimpsed in much of
his music. They appear in the golden ornamentation of the Piano Sonata
of 1924, in the beautiful Cadenza-Finale of the Serenade of 1925, in the
dazzling baroque figurations of the Concerto for Two Pianos written a
decade later, and in the postlude to the Requiem Canticles of 1967, with
its glinting timbres of bells, celesta, and vibraphone. What we experience

in music like this is not only the theatrical splendour, the gem-studded magnificence of a Russia steeped in the glory of Byzantium, but the encrustations of a peasant-flavoured past gleaming through the patina of Western sophistication.

This mingling of the jewel-bright ritualism of Russian orthodoxy with the dramatic austerity of Stravinsky's constructional thinking gave his music a singular depth and vividness, for true perspective rests upon contrasts. The composer looked back to the Russian Spring as the most wonderful event in every year of his childhood—"the violent Russian Spring that seemed to begin in an hour and was like the whole earth cracking".[13] That concept of "the Christ of seasons" might well serve to describe his own musical genesis.

CITY OF THE BRONZE HORSEMAN

Uncle Ielatchitch came into young Stravinsky's life like a benevolent Drosselmeyer to open up a glittering realm of make-believe. Nothing was commonplace any more; it had only seemed so. In Russia before the turn of the century many books from abroad suitable for young people were available in translations for those who could afford them—stories by Jules Verne, Fennimore Cooper, Hoffman, and other masters of that type. The boy had his share of them. Doubtless his uncle, blending fantasy with reality, talked enthusiastically about the marvels he had seen : the masked balls at the Salle de la Noblesse at St Petersburg, graced by lovely women; the frescoes of the Last Judgement under the arcades of the old Nikolsky Market, terrible in their gloomy and sinister gospel; the fragile grace of Nikitina, the *prima ballerina assoluta*, floating like a swan in moonlight through a misty *Les Sylphides*; the wild horses with streaming blonde manes and phantom riders that roamed the steppes beyond the city. A seed germinating in the dark earth, watered by the kindly influence of this enlightened uncle, the creative mind of Stravinsky slowly began to put forth shoots.

The St Petersburg he knew as a child was a city of large open piazzas filled with indelible sounds and images : the rattle of droshkies' wheels on the wooden paving, the harsh cries of street vendors, the clanging of the church bells on High Easter, and the tingling aroma of spices, coffee beans and incense. In the cultural 'theatre' to which Uncle Ielatchitch belonged, and in which Igor Stravinsky sat like some wide-eyed child watching his first *Nutcracker* with astonished wonder, the cults and dogmas of the day paraded themselves in balletic sequence. They included the scythe-bearing atheists and the sanctimonious adherents of Tolstoy's inflexible brand of Christianity, those who worshipped science and those who spat defiance at tyrannical government, as well as a warm-hearted sect extolling the rights of man. A passionate interest in folklore, flavoured by a predilection for the works of Mussorgsky, infused most of their cultural tastes, and nationalism in music, painting, literature and the dance flaunted its picturesque banner. Yet these enthusiasts found time for symphonic music : the masterpieces of Brahms and Bruckner, the heavy academic pieces of Glazunov, adopted son of 'the Five', the lyrical out-pourings of Tchaikovsky, the flaming epics of Borodin, or the glowing tone-poems of Rimsky-Korsakov.

Thanks to Uncle Ielatchitch and the friends who shared these artistic creeds, Igor Stravinsky came to know the great German composers. Although the school curriculum restricted such pleasures, he attended symphony concerts and recitals given by famous Russian or foreign pianists. The precise and fastidious playing of Joseph Hofmann so delighted him that he redoubled his zeal in studying the piano. Chaliapine, in his memoirs, wrote thus of Hofmann as a child prodigy : "He was a meagre, slender, and, so to say, not very noticeable child; but when he sat down at the piano and began to play he fairly made me look around in astonishment and noncomprehension, such were the force and tenderness of the sounds which fell on my ears. It seemed as though some magician were exhibiting a masterly sleight of hand." Other celebrities who excited Stravinsky were Sophie Mentner, Eugene d'Albert, Reisenauer, the pianist Anna Essipova, wife of Lechelitzky, and the violinist Leopold Auer.

He greatly admired the conductor Napravnik, who, immaculate in evening dress and white gloves, directed many of the concerts promoted by the Imperial Music Society and who, contemptuous of meretricious antics on the rostrum, seemed to Igor the very zenith of perfection, although Chaliapine disliked this maestro intensely, describing him as a cold, morose, and uncommunicative man. Napravnik had a flair for picturesque speech. When the young Stravinsky's close friend Vladimir Vassilievich Stassov, a disciple of Glinka, died, and the bearers carried his coffin into the street, Napravnik, who was present with Stravinsky, turned to his companion and said: "They are taking out a piece of history."[1] Stravinsky also subsequently came under the spell of Hans Richter, who, visiting St Petersburg to conduct the Wagner operas, displayed the same iron discipline as Napravnik, the same infallible ear and memory, the same clarity and objectivity in performance.

Sir Adrian Boult, in *Thoughts on Conducting,* spotlights Richter's omniscience by relating an incident which occurred at rehearsal during his London triumphs of the 1880s : "A grumpy German muttering in his beard, with a piercing eye that missed little, there seemed nothing about him that could endear him to anyone, and orchestras (a good deal tougher in those days) disliked him more and more. One day at rehearsal he presumed to tell a horn player in some detail how to play a certain passage. 'It can't be done that way, doctor,' was the risky reply. 'Ah, so, indeed; please pass me your instrument.' Richter then played the passage to the great discomfiture of the owner of the horn, and indeed of the whole orchestra, who all now wondered if he could play *their* instruments as well as the horn, and weren't going to put it to the test."[2] It used to be said that if all the Wagner scores were to be burnt, Richter could write them out from memory. Small wonder that the young Stravinsky revered this pedagogue of the baton, acknowledged in his day as the supreme interpreter, not only of Wagner but also of Beethoven and Brahms.

Stravinsky's regard for Mussorgsky, one of the nationalist heroes of Russian music in those days, is hardly surprising, for his compositions have the grandeur of an essentially religious act. The man who had been a salon fop, strutting about in the spruce uniform of a Guards officer, amusing society women by strumming operatic titbits on the piano, came, through some transmogrification of the spirit, to serve music as Dostoievsky did literature. Mussorgsky's dictum, "Music must continue to reflect our human evolution or die", fingerprinted nearly everything he composed. Stravinsky, a ritualist by nature, responded warmly to this priestly and apostolic figure. Much of his music, though fundamentally different in style and structure, exhibits the same vibrant, absolving, and fiercely ani-malistic involvement in the joys and tragedies of humanity.

It was not only Mussorgsky to whom the young Stravinsky looked for inspiration, but also a group of composers who flourished under the patronage of Mitrophan Belaiev, the music publisher and a promoter of many symphony concerts. The group included Liadov, Tcherepnin, the brothers Blumenfeld, and Solokov; but the leading figures were Rimsky-Korsakov and Glazunov, whose music Stravinsky admired tremendously. In his own early efforts at composition, which included a song for bass and piano with the curious title "The Mushrooms Going to War", he sought to imitate Rimsky's indisputable virtues.

The compositions of the mature Stravinsky are, according to some critics, completely devoid of the delicate sheen, the golden sensuality, and the scintillating beauty of the great impressionists; they equally lack the pulsating appeal of the master romanticists. His music, if we are to believe these myopic pessimists, is cubical and mechanistic, with thin metal-lic masses of tone, shining in girders of melody that stand up in rigid angularity. This glib assessment ignores the rhythmic energy that rises, like a youthful sap, in much of his music, setting up its own lunging and beating dance-routines; cold and lovely as moonlight filtering into a bare, darkened attic. But it also invites wonder that the rich, throbbing inspira-tion of Rimsky-Korsakov should have touched and ignited the boy com-poser's very soul.

Through a charming, highly cultured young friend, Ivan Prokovsky, young Stravinsky 'discovered' other significant figures in the world of music, including such French composers as Gounod, Bizet, Délibes, and Chabrier. Prokovsky, a thin, phthisical youth with an untamed shock of hair, who died of his disease at an early age, taught Igor such pieces as *Coppélia*, *Lakmé*, and *The Tales of Hoffman* by playing them four hands with the boy. His eager protégé noted a certain affinity between the style of the French composers and that of Tchaikovsky, comparing their different harmonic methods and conception of form with what he had learned already from the Belaiev group, and, in the process, starting along the path of his own emancipation—a journey which was to occupy many difficult years.

After matriculating at school, Stravinsky went to university and there met the youngest son of Rimsky-Korsakov, who, at that time, barely knew of Igor's existence. During a summer vacation at Heidelberg, he consulted his fellow-student's illustrious father about his ambition to become a composer. Rimsky made him play some of his first attempts, and after a discouraging reaction persuaded Igor to continue his studies in harmony and counterpoint, suggesting some of his own brilliant pupils as teachers, so that the youngster might acquire a complete mastery of technique. At least Igor fared better than the young doctor who, after a similar audition, was told by Rimsky "Excellent! Continue to practise medicine."

Stravinsky did follow the advice given, although the death of his father in November 1902 and other circumstances prevented him from working regularly. His friendly contacts with the great composer's family increased; they resulted in meetings with many scholars, painters, scientists, and musicians holding advanced opinions. One of them was Stepan Mitoussov, who later collaborated with Stravinsky, writing the libretto for *The Nightingale*. The two young men shared a passionate interest in all the cultural events of St Petersburg. Some of these events would vitally affect Stravinsky's own destiny.

A year after Igor's father died the inimitable Petipa, choreographer of *The Sleeping Beauty*, *The Nutcracker* and other immortal ballets at the Maryinsky Theatre, perpetrated the first real artistic fiasco of his notable career. He was eighty-four, and the authorities, looking around for younger blood, seized the opportunity to dismiss him, even refusing the broken-hearted old man admittance at the stage door. The change they sought came largely through a little group centred around a brilliant art-student, Alexandre Benois. A set of progressive, well-connected enthusiasts, including Walter Nouvel and Leon Bakst (his real name was Rosenberg) rebelled against the current nationalistic trend—even harlequinades were abolished at that time—and the realism of painters inspired by Repin. They founded a magazine *Mir Iskusstva* (*World of Art*) which flaunted the propagandist rosette of symbolism and illustrated new movements in Germany, London, and Paris. Those who supported it included artists of standing like Serov, Roerich, and Vrubel, all products of the St Petersburg Academy.

The editor of *Mir Iskusstva* was a breezy, fresh-faced young man from central Russia, Serge Diaghilev. He had struggled hard to be a musician, but Benois introduced him to painting and to the ballet. Diaghilev fructified as an impresario even at so early an age by successfully organizing a huge exhibition of portraits in the Taurida Palace. For a few stormy months he held an official post at the Maryinsky, but a sharp difference of opinion with Prince Serge Mikhailovich, the Director of the Imperial Theatres, forced his resignation. The influence of the group survived, however, when Bakst and Benois started to work for the theatre, their new ideas being reinforced by a revolutionary youngster, Mikhail Fokine. This magnificent dancer, full of cultural interests and restless, far-ranging ideals, infused fellow-pupils like Pavlova and Karsavina with a startlingly original and vivid concept of theatrical art. Under his tutelage, foreign ballerinas no longer migrated, at colossal expense, to the Maryinsky, for the fledglings at the *barre* were slowly spreading their wings. A thin girl, Anna Pavlova, dazzled audiences with her fragile grace; at twenty-six she danced a solo arranged for her by Fokine—*The Dying Swan.* A lovely dark-eyed child, Tamara Karsavina, was working her way up from a brown serge dress, through the pink, to the coveted white which signified the very summit of the class; and she kept an admiring eye on a boy in the junior class, Vaslav Nijinsky. A tough, resilient boy from Poland, and a champion boxer, he used to play a game with other boys in which they lashed each other's bare bodies with belts.

At that time Stravinsky's friends Prokovsky, Nouvel, and Nurock founded a musical society called Soirées of Contemporary Music for the propagation of new trends in that art. Diaghilev, through his review *Mir Iskusstva* added fuel to the 'revolutionary' flames, which the reactionary conservatives in the Academy and the Imperial Society for the Encouragement of Art sought by their scathing public protests to douse. Rimsky-Korsakov and Liadov tempered their disapproval with some courage and finesse. When Stravinsky asked Rimsky what he thought of Debussy's music, the old man replied, "Better not listen to him; one runs the risk of getting accustomed to him, and one could end by liking him." Debussy himself showed similar generosity of spirit after hearing *La Bohème* for the first time. "If one did not keep a grip on oneself, one would be swept away by the sheer verve of the music."

The artistic hub of St Petersburg in 1903 was the Maryinsky Theatre (now called the Kirov Theatre) which has been described by experts as the loveliest in the world—probably with truth, for the sky-blue and gold decorations are exquisite. There, guided by an imposing, richly liveried *kapelldiener* wealthy patrons entered the cosy ante-rooms of their boxes, where they tidied their hair and smoothed their clothes, before presenting themselves to public view. Between St Petersburg and Moscow there had existed for many years a ceaseless and bitter rivalry, with the inhabitants of both cities trying to surpass each other. The people of St Petersburg were inordinately proud of their River Neva, sweeping majestically between broad and picturesque quays, of the Summer Garden with its exotic splashes of colour, of their corps-de-ballet, reputedly the finest anywhere, and of their tradition and culture. As for the Muscovites, they pointed proudly to the fairy-tale spires and domes of the Kremlin, the St Basil Cathedral, where some religiose Van Gogh seemed to have caught eternity with a brush, the teeming icon-festooned churches, and the *avant-garde* spirit that looked courageously to the future.

At the turn of the century the Maryinsky Theatre always opened its season with Glinka's patriotic opera *A Life for the Tsar*, and always on the first Sunday of September the ballet commenced. There had been a period when many Russian aristocrats and upper middle-class regarded the ballet with a bantering scepticism and classed its devotees as eccentrics. But as the twentieth century dawned, ballet, no longer the Cinderella of the stage, sat on a throne of near-idolatry. To obtain a ticket for any performance one had to submit a petition to the Chancery of the Imperial Theatres; but success came only to the favoured few, and tickets changed hands at grossly inflated prices. Occupying the first row of the stalls was like penetrating the Royal Enclosure at Ascot; new faces were eyed with suspicion or open hostility, and the stranger arrived there only through the influence of one of the regular 'balletomanes'.

Once, as a child, Stravinsky saw the Tsar moving in a stately procession towards the Maryinsky Theatre; there, as the climax to an important State visit, a gala performance took place to honour the Shah of Persia. Igor watched the cavalcade from the first-floor window of a hairdresser's. The Nevsky Prospect—where Tchaikovsky contracted his fatal cholera—and the adjacent streets, decorated with flags and streamers in the bright colours of Russia and of the Romanov dynasty, seemed to smile at the wide-eyed, excited boy. Imperial guards, coaches with grand dukes, ministers, and generals inside, and a great concourse of cavalry, swept past, with the Tsar and the Shah following in an isolated car. The cheers rose in deafening crescendo waves as the Tsar, lifting his right hand towards his temple, saluted the multitude—including Igor Stravinsky, who, before long, as one being initiated for a sacred, lifelong vocation, would sit inside the magnificent theatre now opening its doors to royalty.

Indeed, little did the audiences of the Maryinsky Theatre, exacting and rapacious in their conservative standards, realize that the pale, ascetic-faced youth who bore the name Stravinsky, and who watched, in breathless wonder, the delicate movements of the solo dancers and ballerinas, would one day dazzle the entire world with his *Firebird*, and *The Rite of Spring*. Any new venture was heresy to them; like the hounds of the old Spanish Inquisition they ruthlessly sniffed out the nonconformists. If a passage was brilliantly executed the whole theatre rang with applause; but a dancer who stumbled, or showed too much originality might, as happened to one soloist, be dubbed 'a flying turkey' and have to bear the ugly sobriquet for many months to come. The jewels of the Maryinsky Theatre glittered in the boxes, and the critical claws twitched in their sheathes.

At least the balletomanes were enthusiastic. They seldom missed a performance, and when a favourite *prima ballerina assoluta* went to dance in another city the faithful often followed her. It was not only the wealthy who worshipped at the Maryinsky shrine, but also the rouble-counting throng in the gallery and pit. While the stalls and boxes clapped decorously to the rhythms of the music, the gallery roared its approval. One by one the lights expired in the auditorium; the safety curtain, sliding down, thudded gently against the stage; the attendants brought in the dust sheets —and the starry-eyed patrons close to the roof still shouted in delirious joy.

Isadora Duncan ridiculed the Maryinsky tradition. She herself danced like an intensely vital flame and could not respond to the cool, exquisite ritualism of classical ballet. Yet, as Stravinsky demonstrated in his music, the magic of all art is its diversity. The work of Béjart, Alvin Ailey, and others like them is invigorating; but God forbid that, like priests of Baal, they should require us to fall down before them in some Terpsichorean temple. A few *avant-garde* critics seem, by the lip-curling extravagance of their prose, to demand precisely that.

Isadora Duncan ridiculed the Maryinsky tradition, and Balanchine, who collaborated with Stravinsky years later, ridiculed Isadora Duncan. She went to Russia in 1922 at the age of forty-four to establish, at the invitation of Commissar Lunacharsky, a Duncan school of the dance. Balanchine, who regarded Isadora as ludicrous and incompetent, described her thus in an interview published by *Horizon* : "To me it was absolutely unbelievable—a drunken, fat, woman who for hours was rolling around like a pig. It was the most awful thing." That was how he saw her performance.

What classical ballet at its highest level has to offer, and will continue to provide, is not a rigid choreographic routine, an archaic fusion of stylistic anachronisms; but a vivid concept of make-believe and fantasy that satisfies an ageless human need. Not only the grand scenic effects but also the finesse and atmospheric appeal of the music, which at times almost defies description, make *The Sleeping Beauty* a firm favourite with audiences. The dark, glimmering wood, silent and enchanted, where "bats with baby faces in the violet light whistle and beat their wings", the handsome prince climbing the turret to wake Beauty on her brackeny bed, the triumphant wedding ball, with the happy couple performing superb arabesques and variations—here is an artistic miracle that outlasts every pseudo-cult and precept. In such balletic soil did Stravinsky's genius first take root.

Strangely, for such a fiercely independent and progressive soul, he

cherished a lifelong admiration for romantic make-believe, though he
often pretended—not altogether convincingly—to despise it. In 1921,
when the Russian Ballet was in London, Stravinsky wrote to Diaghilev
in these words :

> It gives me great happiness to know that you are producing that
> masterpiece *The Sleeping Beauty* by our great and beloved Tchaikov-
> sky. . . . It is further a great satisfaction to me as a musician to
> see produced a work of so direct a character, at a time when so many
> people who are neither simple nor naïve nor spontaneous seek in their
> art simplicity, 'poverty', and spontaneity. Tchaikovsky in his very nature
> possesses these three gifts to their fullest extent. That is why he never feared
> to let himself go, whereas the prudes, whether *raffinés* or academic, were
> shocked by the frank speech, free from artifice. Tchaikovsky possesses the
> power of melody, centre of gravity in every symphony, opera, or ballet
> composed by him. It is absolutely indifferent to me that the quality of his
> melody was sometimes unequal. The fact is that he was a creator of melody,
> which is an extremely rare and precious gift. . . .[3]

The paths of Stravinsky and Diaghilev, that finally came together in
the green pastures of the Unknown Country crossed more than once during those early days in St Petersburg—Peter the Great's fabulous 'window
on the west'; days when the dreamy youth felt deeply moved, and knew
not why, as he watched the soaring flight of gulls. Perhaps the sight of
those pale, floating wings aroused in him the same kind of exhilaration
that he would one day experience through the magnificent and unique
productions of the Russian Ballet. He and Diaghilev used to visit Alexandre Benois, the painter, in his rooms in the Vassilievsky Ostrov, or take
a boat to one of the island nightclubs, or dine in the Leiner restaurant on
the Nevsky Prospect, where the future impresario, regal and dignified
like the princess in Chekhov's tale, bowed to people right and left. After
concerts the worldly, sophisticated man and the slightly nervous, introspective boy visited a little sawdust delicatessen to enjoy marinated fish, caviar,
Black Sea oysters, and mushrooms.

Having, with much difficulty, composed a full-sized sonata for piano,
Stravinsky visited Rimsky-Korsakov in the country towards the end of
the summer of 1903 and stayed with him a fortnight. The old master,
richly endowed with the musico-descriptive faculty, fanned the tiny flame
of genius in his young pupil by expounding the principles of sonata form.
He also taught him the compass and registers of the different instruments
used in contemporary symphonic orchestras, and the elements of large-
scale instrumental composition. Rimsky would give the boy some pages
of *Pan Voivoda*, the new opera he had just finished and invite him to
orchestrate them. When the youngster had completed a section, the old
man would show him his own version of the same passage and ask "Why

have you done it differently?" Thus began a fruitful pupil-and-teacher relationship which lasted three years.

Rimsky-Korsakov had much in common with his protégé. He too had had a fairy godfather—'Uncle Pipon'—who, when the boy was collecting old songs, contributed some of the most haunting tunes in Russian music. Both *Maid of Pskov* and *Tsar Saltan* owe much of their thematic inspiration to Uncle Pipon. There was in Rimsky-Korsakov, as in Stravinsky, a devout love of singing. He used to hear and marvel at the organ-like chanting of the monks in the Monastery of the Blessed Virgin which faced his house across the river; the bells of this beautiful sanctuary chimed years later in his 'Russian Easter' Overture. He heard the vigorous, earthy singing of the peasant women of the province, summoned by the monks each summer to help with the haymaking, and grew up steeped in the folklore and ritualistic traditions of a typical Russian village.

"I like Canille very much," wrote Rimsky-Korsakov as a boy of one of his own teachers, "he makes the lesson interesting and not dry."[4] This feeling the old man undoubtedly evoked in Stravinsky, who, given pieces of classical music to orchestrate—largely parts of the Beethoven sonatas and of Schubert's quartets and marches—found the subsequent post-mortem as fascinating as any medical student discovering, through some Whitman-tongued professor, that the human body is "miracle enough to stagger sextillions of infidels".[5] Rimsky was not only a superb teacher, but a self-effacing one, who could listen sympathetically as well as talk. A tall man, who stooped over his scores while conducting, waggling the baton in the direction of his knees, he had a quaint habit during rehearsals of wearing two pairs of blue-tinted spectacles, one perched on the bridge of his nose, the other resting on his forehead. Stravinsky copied this idiosyncrasy years later.

Behind the sober, uncracked face of Rimsky-Korsakov lay a sensitive, poetic imagination fed and stimulated by a dream-world of fantasy where historical and supernatural creatures mingled grotesquely,—warrior princes and despotic tsars, fabulous snow maidens and swan queens, peasants and village dancers, sea kings and mermaids, gusli players, minstrels, woodcutters, devils, and witches. They schemed and battled, loved and hated, against a vast panorama of rolling steppes and wintry forests, birds flitting through glade-filtered sunlight, nightingales, golden fish, and swarms of bees. This love of fantasy manifested itself in his music, and as early as 1867, two years after he had completed his first symphony, he composed a symphonic poem *Sadko*, based on the legend of the famous gusli player of Novgorod, expanding the idea, later, into one of his most successful operas. In the tone poem Sadko's ship is becalmed at sea, until the minstrel is flung overboard with his gusli to placate the Sea King. At the bottom of the sea a great festival is in progress, celebrating the marriage

c

of the Sea King's daughter to the Ocean. Sadko plays his gusli so
eloquently that the king and all his court dance wildly, ruffling the ocean
into a raging tempest. Only when the minstrel breaks the strings of his
instrument does the dancing stop and the sea resume its calm.

Rimsky wrote his 'Russian Easter' Overture after attending an Easter
morning service in a great cathedral of the Russian Orthodox faith, and
the comments he made as to what he sought to achieve in this exotic work
persuade me that if, by some miracle, he had survived, with intellect un-
tarnished, to hear Stravinsky's pagan-inspired *Rite of Spring* in 1913 he
would have responded to it sympathetically :

> The capering and leaping of the Biblical King David before the ark,
> do they not give expression to a mood of the same order as the mood
> of the idol-worshippers' dance? Surely the Russian Orthodox chime is
> instrumental dance-music of the church, is it not? And do not the waving
> beards of the priests and sextons clad in white vestments and surplices and
> intoning "Beautiful Easter", in the tempo of *Allegro Vivo*, etc., transport
> the imagination to pagan times? And all these Easter loaves and twists and
> the glowing tapers—how far a cry from the philosophic and socialistic
> teaching of Christ! This legendary and heathen side of the holiday, this
> transition from the gloom and mysterious evening of Passion Saturday to
> the unbridled pagan-religious merry-making of the morn of Eastern Sun-
> day is what I was eager to reproduce in my Overture.[6]

Like Igor Stravinsky, the boy he taught so patiently, Rimsky, when
dealing in his music with the gorgeousness of ancient ritual and mystical
celebration, felt the blood course hotly in his veins, and the youngster's
enthusiasm for these aspects of his art stemmed largely from his early
contact with this nationalistic genius.

The gifted old man had a warm, forgiving nature. Diaghilev fancied
himself, unjustifiably, as a composer, and sought the expert opinion of
Rimsky as to his merits and prospects. Rimsky, shocked by Diaghilev's
arrogance and condescension, did not feather the blow, but delivered a
frank and scathing assessment; whereupon the future impresario, red
with rage, stomped out of the room, slamming the door, and shouting at
the top of his voice "The future will show which of us two is considered
the greater in history!" Rimsky-Korsakov bore his impudent visitor no
grudge, attributing his conduct to youthful impetuosity, and afterwards
showed a friendly charm to Diaghilev, who, writing to him in 1907, spoke
admiringly of his "godly" nature.

Chaliapine was twenty-two when he first met Rimsky-Korsakov. He
described him graphically in his memoirs : "The magical composer impressed me by his extreme shyness and modesty. He was very unfashion-
ably dressed; his black beard, that grew unchecked, flowed over a narrow,
carelessly-knotted black stock; he wore a black frock-coat that was hopelessly out of date, and his trouser pockets were inset horizontally in the

manner of bygone days. . . . A deep crease between his brows gave him a melancholy look. . . . He was profoundly silent. . . ."[7]

Profoundly silent. . . . Well, in his dealings with the public that phrase could never be applied to Igor Stravinsky; for, whether in *Chronicle of my Life* or in many published interviews, his teeming ideas about life and music poured out of him "like water bubbling from a silver jar".

DIAGHILEV STAGES "THE FIREBIRD"

Stravinsky finished his university course in the spring of 1905, became engaged to one of his cousins, Catherine Nossenko, and married her on 11th January the following year. Since an Imperial statute forbade marriages between cousins, he had to find a 'corruptible cleric' who would tactfully refrain from asking for documents, and, after a frantic search, unearthed one in the village of Novaya Derevnya, near St Petersburg. The happy couple drove in two droshkies to the village; there, kneeling while Andrei and Vladimir Rimsky-Korsakov held a gold and velvet wedding crown over their heads, they began a relationship in which, to use Stravinsky's own words, they "came closer than lovers sometimes are". When they returned home after the ceremony, Rimsky met them at the door, blessed Igor, and presented him with a splendid icon as a wedding gift.

During the season of 1906–7 Stravinsky completed his E flat major Symphony and dedicated it to Rimsky-Korsakov, who, by then, stood almost *in loco parentis*. Igor described how the old man, sitting beside him and making critical comments, shepherded him through the première of this work: "This is too heavy; be more careful when you use trombones in their middle register," etc.[1] As the concert took place at noon, and as the audience was not a paying one, the young composer could not determine whether the applause he heard signified a success. The only bad omen was Glazunov, who approached him afterwards, saying "Very nice, very nice,"[2] but adding the barbed remark that he found the instrumentation heavy for such empty music. At least Stravinsky, years later, had his revenge on Glazunov for this kiss of death by describing him to Robert Craft as "the most disagreeable man I have ever worked with".[3] Glazunov, according to Stravinsky, was a hopelessly addicted drunkard who locked his door "for two-week binges on Château Yquem".[4]

Glazunov, in fact, greatly disliked Stravinsky, which is hardly surprising, since the rather cocky boy had called him "a Carl Philipp Emanuel Rimsky-Korsakov", and the remark, probably repeated with some malice, came to his ears. He treated Igor with frigid politeness or frank rudeness whenever they met, and even in 1935, when Stravinsky called on Glazunov at a rehearsal of his music in a room beneath a studio in the Salle

Pleyel, showed the same hostility, extending two fingers in a cold silence. Glazunov died the following year.

Stravinsky, like Rimsky-Korsakov, heartily detested the strange, maniacally conceited, but gifted composer Scriabin, who treated him and other music students with a detestably patronizing air. It is not likely that Stravinsky's appraisal of his music over the years carried any strong flavour of approval, for it seems, in many respects, the complete antithesis of what he sought to achieve. The music Scriabin wrote in the final span of his bombastic and idiosyncratic life, when he built his harmony not on scales but on the intervals of chords constructed from superimposed fourths, has a certain opalescent beauty; but it is as futile and insubstantial as an opium dream.

After the publication of the symphony, Stravinsky composed a song-cycle, *Faun and Shepherdess*, on three poems in the manner of Parny which Pushkin wrote as a schoolboy. The influence of Debussy flavours the music like a delicate enigmatic perfume, and the closing bars of the third song presage the coda to the finale of *The Firebird*. The song-cycle and the symphony were performed by the Court Orchestra in the spring of 1907 at a private hearing under the direction of its conductor, H. Wahrlich. A year later *Faun and Shepherdess* had its public première at one of the Belaiev concerts directed by Felix Blumenfeld.

At that time a cold dank wind blew through the pages of any musical composition which dared to explore paths not trodden previously by the well-shod feet of the conservative public and critics; so that Stravinsky, venturing into his Unknown Country, owed much to Rimsky-Korsakov for his role of a kindly St Christopher. That shy, meditative old philosopher had long ago resigned himself to the eyebrow-twitching censors. "Apparently the general attitude towards him," wrote Chaliapine in his autobiography, "is in no way better than towards an unimportant person like myself. I recollect how unceremoniously entire pages were struck out of the score of his opera (*The Night Before Christmas*), how he knitted his brows and protested, while with stony insistence it was argued that if the opera were not cut it would appear to the public to be tediously lengthy."[5] Yet one can hardly blame the scissor-snipping producers or musical directors; for to the Russian public, who liked foreign operas of the flavour of *Il Trovatore*, native composers were almost without honour in their own country.

Greatly encouraged by his master, Stravinsky started work on two important compositions, the *Fantastic Scherzo*, inspired by Maeterlinck's *Life of the Bee*, and the first act of his opera *The Nightingale*, the libretto of which, based on a story by Hans Andersen, he wrote in collaboration with his friend Mitoussov. After the première of the *Scherzo* in St Petersburg under the baton of Alexander Siloti, one critic commented dryly "Whether or not it is 'Fantastic' is up to us to decide!" The preliminary sketches of *The Nightingale* pleased Rimsky-Korsakov. Using verses by the young Russian poet Gorodetsky, Stravinsky also wrote two fine songs which later appeared in print under the titles *Spring (The Cloister)* and *A Song of the Dew*; and in 1907 he composed a song without words called *Pastoral*, a cool, exquisite piece which he dedicated to Nadia Rimsky-Korsakov. Both *Pastoral* and the two Gorodetsky songs were performed by the Soirées of Contemporary Music in 1908. Stravinsky wrote his *Four Studies for Piano* in the same year, dedicating them to E. Mitoussov, Nicholas Richter, Andrei and Vladimir Rimsky-Korsakov.

In the winter of 1908, while celebrating his birthday, Rimsky-Korsakov, gasping for breath, complained of his heart; some days later he had a sharp attack of *angina pectoris*. The end of a great man was approaching. The last time Stravinsky saw him was during a visit to his country home that year, when he discussed with Rimsky his new composition, a short orchestral fantasy called *Fireworks*, written to commemorate the marriage of the old man's daughter to Maximilian Steinberg. A few weeks later, when Stravinsky, in Oustiloug, was about to send him the completed score, Rimsky-Korsakov died. After a splendid service in the chapel of the St Petersburg Conservatoire, he was buried in the cemetery of the Novodevichy Monastery. This kindly man, who in music conjured up a strange, half-supernatural world glittering with colour and spectacle, who mingled truth and absurdity, painting his native creations with a Raphaelesque brush, always confessed his own limitations. "Don't you think you value me far too highly?" he said to Yastrebtsev. "Study Liszt and Balakirev more closely and you'll see that a great deal in me is—*not* me."[6] Be that as it may, his death left Igor Stravinsky immeasurably poorer at the loss of a friend, and infinitely richer for the teaching given to him.

Igor wept unashamedly as he saw Rimsky, with a serene look on his face, lying in his coffin. His tears changed to shocked anger and hatred when the widow approached, told him to dry his tears, and remarked: "We still have Glazunov."[7] In that moment Stravinsky loathed her with all the venom of which a hero-worshipping adolescent is capable. As a tribute to the great man, he composed a *Funeral Dirge*, the score of which subsequently vanished. Years later he could not remember the music, but recalled that all the solo instruments filed past the tomb of Rimsky in succession, each laying down its own melody as its wreath against a deep background of *tremolo* murmurings that simulated the vibrations of bass voices singing in chorus.

The score of *Fireworks*, which death snatched from the fingers of Rimsky-Korsakov, found its way to one of the Siloti concerts, where the magnificent orchestra of the Imperial Theatre gave a performance that infuriated Stravinsky. He complained bitterly that they treated the music with utter contempt, as if they were ridiculing it. There were whispered asides, derisive grunts, and chuckles which hurt and angered the young composer. The players, many of whom were professors in the Imperial Conservatory of Music, had a sedate attitude to their art, and the spluttering incandescence of *Fireworks*, with its cascade of sparks, its hissing and whistling mimicries, puzzled and antagonized them. The audience disliked the work, too; but for one man present it represented an exciting, blood-tingling experience. That man was Diaghilev, the progenitor of one of the most splendid epochs in the history of the dance.

Dancing, which, at its highest level seems almost to be identified with the name Diaghilev, is one of the most fluid and capricious of the arts, yet, as this visionary man so often insisted, it depends for its perfection upon a firm and inflexible discipline. In 1892, when the unfamiliar style of Art Nouveau fructified at the Folies-Bergère in Paris, through Toulouse-Lautrec's wonderful paintings and the brilliance of dancers like Loie Fuller, it must have seemed to the public of the day like some gay and daring innovation—one which, in the realm of dance, involved an astonishing freedom of line, sinewy contours, swift rhythmic flights across the stage, and expressive torso movements. Yet it called for a discipline as rigid as that of classical ballet. Diaghilev, twenty years later, procreated a similarly daring dance-tradition; he sustained it by imposing the loftiest, and often the most dictatorial of standards.

Before his Paris triumphs, Diaghilev was Official for Special Missions in the administration of the Imperial Theatres; as mentioned in a previous chapter, he relinquished the post after quarrelling with the Director, Prince Serge Mikhailovich, an aristocrat with a sixteenth-century beard and moustachios, who disliked his propensity for disobeying orders. The choreographer and dancer Fokine described Diaghilev from an early meeting with the impresario as handsome and young, with a white lock in his dark hair. His eyes drooped oddly at the corners, and he had a habit of plucking a handkerchief from his sleeve and of extending one foot, which quivered distractingly. Diaghilev possessed immense charm and knew how to inspire loyalty and devotion in others. To make a ballet, he used to bring composer, choreographer, designer, and poet together, pooling ideas and stimulating each other until a completed work of art arose from the ferment.

Thrilled with what he had heard at the Siloti concert, Diaghilev commissioned Stravinsky to write the music for *The Firebird*, a new production which he proposed to take to Paris, with a fairy-tale décor by Golovine, a gifted designer from the Maryinsky. The composer discussed his first sketches and basic ideas with Fokine, at whose request he broke up his national themes into short phrases corresponding to the separate moments of a scene, the individual poses and gestures. On one occasion, Stravinsky, having created a beautiful Russian melody for the entrance of the Tsarevich Ivan, sat at the piano, the mysterious *tremolos* of the music rippling from his fingers, while Fokine, interpreting the role of the prince, climbed over the piano—a substitute for the wall of the sinister Kastchei's garden—jumped down from it, and wriggled, fear-struck, across the carpet. Thus, in a living-room, the iridescent and winged *Firebird* was born.

At Diaghilev's invitation the French critic R. Brussel, who happened to be in St Petersburg at the time, heard Stravinsky play through the score of *The Firebird* in a house on Zamiatin Pereulok. He wrote: "The composer, young, slim, and uncommunicative, with vague, meditative eyes, and lips set firm in an energetic-looking face, was at the piano. But the moment he began to play the modest and dimly-lit dwelling glowed with dazzling radiance. By the end of the first scene I was conquered; by the last I was lost in admiration. The manuscript on the music-rest, scored over with fine pencillings, revealed a masterpiece."

Although the new ballet did not take to the stage until a year after the Diaghilev company arrived in Paris, preparations continued over the intervening months. The rehearsals progressed with difficulty, since the dancers, dismayed at the scarcity of clearly-defined melody in the music and its unlikeness to what they usually heard, regarded the piece as an oddity. Some boldly declared that it did not sound like music at all. Stravinsky attended most rehearsals, playing over the passages, and, according to some dancers, appearing to "demolish the piano". He proved irritatingly inflexible about the rhythms and used to pound them out with much violence, humming in a loud slightly discordant voice and hardly caring whether he struck the right note or not. His extraordinarily volatile temperament certainly inspired Fokine, who, to the joy and amusement of the company, invented some new and highly original steps.

The frantic efforts of the choreographer and technicians to give the illusions of this ballet credibility resulted, at one rehearsal of the Firebird's flight, in Karsavina being rolled in on a kind of saddle attached to a thick solid plank projecting through a cut in the stage floor. On this contraption, to pianissimo music, she was trundled out to a distance of a few feet, accompanied by loud squeaky noises. Then immediately she 'flew' backwards, a grotesque manoeuvre that repulsed all who saw it and was gladly discarded. Yet there were moments of wonder, as for instance when Fokine, for the first time, saw the Horseman of the Night, robed in a magnificent black costume, mounted on a noble black stallion, and presenting a vision of apocalyptic beauty.

Stravinsky sometimes exchanged cross words with Gabriel Pierné, the conductor, over some musical principle. Once, in front of the whole orchestra during a full rehearsal, Pierné cried out irascibly "Young man, if you do not want a *crescendo*, then do not write anything,"[8] referring to the fact that, at one place in the score, the composer had written *non crescendo*. Despite their clashes of temperament, Stravinsky greatly admired Pierné; not surprisingly, for this brilliant musician, who succeeded César Franck at the organ loft of Ste Clotilde, had a plethora of operas, chamber music, and symphonic poems to his credit.

At the Opera House, Paris, on 25th June 1910, *The Firebird* came memorably to life, with Karsavina dancing the title role, Vera Fokina the Princess Unearthly Beauty, and Alexis Bulgakov the evil Kastchei. Karsavina wore a brilliantly imaginative costume designed for her by Bakst and showing a woman's head and shoulders surmounting a bird-like body. It had a greenish bodice, with the top edge trimmed with soft feathers and the lower ending in a mass of swansdown, fitting close to the hips. She wore fine orange-gauze trousers that seemed to glow as they caught the light. A cap, decorated with curved feathers, covered her head; from beneath it hung two long plaits of hair that fell over her breast. The other costumes, based on native Russian dress, included fur-edged coats, stiff with gold and jewels, as well as high, richly embroidered leather boots. Golovine created a dream of a garden, sensuous, unearthly, with the castle of Kastchei, rising against a mysterious horizon, surrounded by trees.

The corps-de-ballet, filling the stage with Russian folklore monsters who crawled on all fours or leaped like frogs, were, by all reports, superb; the princesses, soft and supple in their movements, danced barefoot, slightly resembling Russian folk dancers; the feathered 'arms' of the bird, opening like wings, introduced a strange Oriental flavour; and the lovers, using no sign language to express their love, managed by looks and atmosphere alone to convey it.

One of the most magical moments in the ballet was the scene where an almost impenetrable gloom enveloped the stage, unrelieved except for a luminous space in the centre, where stood a small tree heavy with golden apples. The soft whirring of wings could be heard; it grew louder, and suddenly a figure radiating orange light flashed across the shadowy background. Then, gliding as swiftly as a bird, the feathered Karsavina, glowing with an orange brightness, darted upon the stage, flitted about the tree, and vanished into the darkness.

After the première the critic Henri Gheon wrote: "*The Firebird*, the result of the closest partnership between choreographer, composer, and painter presents us with the most miraculous and exquisite balance between sound, movement, and shape that has ever been dreamed of. The vermicular old gold of the fantastic background seems created by the same means as the coloured tissue of the music. And in the music one really hears the magician crying, the sorcerers and gnomes swarming and struggling. When the bird passes by it is carried by the music. Stravinsky, Fokine, Golovine,—no, there is only one creator."[9]

Stravinsky, in *Chronicle of My Life*, wrote: "The choreography of this ballet always seemed to me complicated and overburdened with plastique details, so that the artistes felt—and still feel, even now—great difficulty in coordinating their steps with the music." Nevertheless, after the first glorious flight of *The Firebird* at the Paris Opéra performance, Stravinsky's fame blazed out across Europe. Only a few days before the première Diaghilev, pointing at the composer, had said to Karsavina : "Mark him well. He is a young man on the eve of celebrity."[10]

The success of *The Firebird* gave Stravinsky not only widespread fame and happiness, but also ebullient self-confidence; henceforth he carried himself with an erect, slightly jaunty air. Yet those who knew him intimately at the time have testified that, for all his meretricious antics to strangers, it made no real difference to his character : he continued to show to his associates and friends the same courteous and unaffected regard.

Although precedence has been given in this book to the production of *The Firebird*, it was not the first ballet to be staged by the Diaghilev company in Paris; nor did the impresario choose the Opera House as his headquarters. Instead, the Russian Ballet settled in at the Châtelet Theatre, a huge, old-fashioned place owned by the City of Paris. On its great stage fantastic spectacles involving the most intricate and thrilling illusions had taken place. They included *Around the World in Eighty Days*, which unfolded with staggering scenic effects, fires on the stage, storms, and hurricanes. That the Châtelet survived the economic blizzards that howled around its doors over the years may be regarded as a minor miracle. When it first opened in 1862 a friend said to Holstein the manager : "What a unique position to be sure! This enormous house to ruin you, right across the bridge from the Tribunal de Commerce to file your petition, the Palais de Justice just across from that to sentence you, and at your very feet the Seine to drown yourself in!"

The huge auditorium, dark and dusty, seemed to throw out a silent challenge as Diaghilev wandered around the deserted aisles. Soon, however, a cacophony of banging, sawing, shouting, and disembodied chords filled the shabby old Châtelet. Carpenters began to spread a new and resilient pine floor on the chipped and dirty stage, covering over the orchestral pit and the first rows of stalls; decorators faced the columns and balustrades with expensive, rich velvet and transformed the foyers into exotic flower gardens; painters, working with fast, deft strokes, created some of the most beautiful scenery the Châtelet had ever known; and the famous Colonne Orchestra, under the charge of the Russian conductors Tcherepnin and Cooper, rehearsed night and day.

While the sweating carpenters, painters and technicians scuttled to and fro inside the huge theatre, the broad avenue of the Champs Elysées, bathed in spring sunshine, pulsated with endless movement, as a restless flow of traffic coursed between the Place de la Concorde and the distant Arc de Triomphe, poised, aloof and beautiful against the skyline, on the crest of the slope. Beneath the café awnings the talk swelled into a chattering chorus as the patrons, lolling in their seats around the coloured tables, watched the fashionably dressed people on the broad, shady pavements. Many of them undoubtedly talked about the strange invasion which had descended on the faded old theatre. Already, while the tapping of feet, the murmur of voices, and the hum of traffic swelled into the great symphony of springtime, billstickers were putting bright posters on the boards, splashing the news that the Russian Ballet would shortly open its first Paris season.

At the invitation of Astruc, the impresario, Jean Cocteau wrote and illustrated a booklet publicizing the marvels of the visiting company, whose praises Auguste Rodin, Marcel Proust, Reynaldo Hahn, Jean-Louis Vaudoyer, Robert Brussel and other Parisian intellectuals also sang eloquently.

While the crashing chords, the cries of the workmen, and the bleating of a flock of goats to be used in *Le Pavillon d'Armide* filled the theatre, a gleeful Diaghilev, fortified by epicurean meals trotted in from a *brasserie* opposite, moved from one group to another, praising, criticizing, advising, and co-ordinating, the magic of his personality transforming chaos into order. Behind him, like a Sultan's bodyguard, flitted the faithful Vassily, his valet. Erect and sinister, with a bushy copper beard, a closely cropped head, and a saturnine Mongoloid face, Vassily, a genuine Russian *moujik*, idolized his master and, at a word of command, would have tossed a bomb into any hostile audience if it had pleased Diaghilev. Hovering backstage and sneaking up silently behind some protective scenery, he gathered fragments of gossip more avidly than a crow gathers worms; these he pieced together with the most lurid and scandalizing results.

Maestro Enrico Cecchetti, that great teacher of the dance, presiding over a classroom filled with admiring French and Italian dancers, drove his pupils to the point of exhaustion, beating time—and them—with an indefatigable stick. Born in the dressing-room of a theatre, this awe-inspiring figure deserves more than a passing mention, for he contributed immeasurably to the success of the Russian Ballet. A man with whom Stravinsky worked in the most harmonious relationship, Cecchetti, who had been one of the greatest of male dancers at the close of the nineteenth century, took up the appointment of teacher of mime and *maître de ballet* to the Diaghilev company in 1909. On his shoulders rested the efficiency of the entire company. Growing weary of tours throughout Europe, he settled in London in 1918 and opened a school, although he continued to give lessons to the company and to appear with them during seasons in the capital.

"Maestro", as his pupils affectionately called Cecchetti, had a fine large, closely cropped head, broad shoulders, and ivory-coloured features. He looked, years later, rather like Mr Pickwick. Cecchetti had a fanatical regard for punctuality and was always the first to arrive for a class, being greeted by each ballerina with a kiss and returning it. He showed a profound and priestly reverence for the beauty of the human frame as revealed in the dance. Maestro had no use for people with inflated and pompous ideas about their own importance and looked scornfully on doting parents who pestered him with their infant prodigies.

His classes, like Toscanini's opera house, contained no 'stars',—whether his pupils were nervous, fumbling beginners or polished and experienced ballerinas, he treated them alike. "Whatever the difference in your status outside, here you are all my pupils and I shall make no distinction."[11] He would emphasize the time of a melody or a movement by tapping his cane vigorously on the floor. When a dancer executed a step or sequence to his liking, Cecchetti smiled like a Botticelli angel; but when he spotted a careless movement, Maestro pounced on the offender, fixing a glaring, bloodshot eye on him, and discharged a vitriolic flood of mingled Italian and Russian.

Sometimes his rougher side brought a sensitive pupil to tears, whereupon Cecchetti, patting her cheeks affectionately, would make noble amends. "I had to scold you because you danced badly," he would gently point out, "and if God himself were my pupil and His work did not please me, I should treat Him just the same."[12] He had a satirical, sometimes barbed sense of humour, and on one occasion snapped at a dancer: "I asked you for an *attitude croisée*, but what you are doing reminds me of a dog lifting its leg!"[13]

Serge Leonidovich Grigoriev, the *régisseur* of the Russian Ballet and Diaghilev's right-hand man, saw to it that all future performances, once the details had been arranged, ran smoothly and efficiently. He had to remember precisely all the music cues, and the tempo at which a particular number should be taken; how the costumes had to be worn, and the type of make-up required; the setting for each scene; the intricate and subtle lighting effects used during the production; and devote his attention to a host of other matters, including the packing, transportation, or storage of the costumes and set. Grigoriev was a superb mime himself: his Shahriar in *Schéhérazade* and his Bibulous Merchant in *Petrushka* were triumphs of characterization.

Diaghilev had a large technical staff under the leadership of O. Allegri, head of the scenic department of the Maryinsky; and E. Valz, the chief mechanic. Valz regarded the word 'impossible' as an archaic fallacy, and when told that he could not have two fountains playing in *Pavillon d'Armide*, because of a totally inadequate water supply, merely shrugged his shoulders and laughed disbelievingly. On the opening night two splendid fountains filled the stage with a delicate splashing sound.

Fokine, the inspired and inspiring choreographer of the Russian Ballet in those early days is rightly regarded as the father of modern ballet. He had tried, unsuccessfully, to introduce necessary reforms at the Maryinsky. It was he who devised for Anna Pavlova, then *première danseuse* at that theatre, the dramatically expressive solo dance *The Dying Swan* to the poignant music of Saint-Saëns. From 1909 to 1914 this brilliant young man was the sole choreographer for the Diaghilev company of all ballets other than the classical pieces included from time to time, and, through his imaginative creations, he swept away the stylistic cobwebs of centuries. Fokine, for all his artistic sensitivity, was a difficult, often craggy person to deal with, and, on one occasion, flew into a raging temper because he saw a ballerina talking to a stranger, who proved to be a distinguished dance critic.

Alexandre Benois and Leon Bakst, the scenic designers of the Russian Ballet, irradiated every set not merely with breathtaking, often exotic colours, but with the kind of atmospheric realism that brings paint and canvas, wood and plaster, into vivid, glowing life. Benois, a short, grave-looking man with a beard and moustache, wore a pince-nez. He had a charming smile and moved with a quiet gentleness. Bakst had curly red hair, which he kept neatly brushed, humorous eyes, and clean-shaven cheeks. He dressed elegantly, loved to sprinkle perfume on his clothes, and spoke with a curiously guttural accent.

Of the brilliant company of dancers whom Diaghilev gathered around him, and which included the lovely Ida Rubinstein, two are mentioned by Stravinsky with particular affection: Karsavina and Nijinsky. The composer praised Karsavina for her gentle and feminine grace. All her movements were soft, rounded, and beautiful to watch. Her dancing was neither sensuous nor coldly chaste, but simple, unaffected poetry, and she scorned such tricks of stagecraft as playing to the gallery, or flicking her hand to attract attention. It was in the Maryinsky Theatre in 1900 that Karsavina, then a young student at the Imperial Ballet School, sat in a box, enthralled by a performance of Tchaikovsky's *The Nutcracker*. She made one of her early appearances in the part of Clara on the stage of this famous theatre. Cyril Beaumont, quoting Gautier, described her eyes as being like two pieces of jet floating in a pearly sea. After her initial triumphs in the 1909 Paris season, people began referring to her as La Karsavina, and one French critic wrote of her: "Si grande virtuose qu'elle soit, elle ne sacrifie rien à ces traits extérieurs, qui surprennant plus qu'ils n'émeuvent. Elle a découvert le merveilleux mystère du lyrisme choréographique—tout en elle est poésie. . . ."

Much has been written about Vaslav Nijinsky, the supreme god of the dance, the silent, wide-eyed witch boy with the soft, feline step who made that famous leap through the window in *Le Spectre de la Rose*, seeming, as he executed a fantastically wide parabola, almost to float in the air. Stravinsky studied him closely, finding him a backward youth mentally under-developed for his age; yet with a superb gift for interpreting certain roles. Fokine, during his collaboration with the composer, never had to offer lengthy explanations to Nijinsky of the meaning of a particular dance. By demonstrating, say, a tricky Mazurka, dancing it in front of him, and making a few corrections, he stamped it indelibly on the youth's mind. Nijinsky's imitativeness, one of the secrets of his mastery of dance forms, caused him to transplant favourite gestures—the brushing away of a lock of hair from the face, for example, or the languid raising of one hand—from ballet to ballet.

Nijinsky was fastidiously neat. His costumes, dancing-shoes, and stocks of Leichner grease-paint were arranged in their respective places in his dressing-room with a precision and symmetry that suggested an impending military inspection. Not even Diaghilev could invade that sanctum with impunity. Nijinsky spent a full half-hour applying his make-up and executed the task with unerring artistry, sometimes calling upon Bakst or Benois for professional advice in the delineation of a new character. When he had finished making up, the hairdresser came in to glue his wig and head-dress on, so that his gazelle-like leaps could not dislodge them; then Maria Stepanova, the wardrobe mistress, plying needle and thread with incredible speed, effected any necessary repairs or alterations to his costume. While all these preparations went on, Nijinsky spoke not a single word; already, enveloped in a deep reverie, he faced the footlights, no longer the brilliant, slightly nervous *danseur noble* of the Russian Ballet, but a fictional character into which the magic of the theatre, and his own introspective genius, had breathed pulsating life.

He used small dancing-shoes made specially for him by Nicolini of Milan. His feet swelled when he danced, splitting the thin hide, and he needed two or three pairs of shoes for each ballet. Diaghilev's valet Vassily kept a reserve supply and, during performances, always stood in readiness with half a dozen pairs of shoes and a tray of resin where Nijinsky could scuff the soles.

Shortly after his arrival in Paris, Stravinsky formed a firm and profitable friendship with José Maria Sert, a dilettante painter, and his wife Misia. A flamboyant character with an affected manner, Sert, black-bearded, with a magnificent physique, played at being a Spanish grandee; but made amends for his idiosyncrasies with a bubbling sense of fun and a natural kindness which, for Stravinsky, resulted in frequent introductions to rich and influential people.

During that first glorious epoch of the Russian Ballet the composer also met Debussy, Ravel, Florent Schmitt, and Manuel de Falla, who looked like an ascetic courtier from some El Greco painting. Harriet Cohen described Falla as a slender man, modest and unassuming, "with eyes that alternated between a humorous, ironic twinkle and the burning look of a visionary".[14] Debussy's mastery of the piano, treating it now as an orchestra, now as a solo instrument, and creating exquisite nuances, commanded Stravinsky's admiration. "Lord! how well this man played the piano",[15] he wrote in his memoirs. Debussy himself greatly admired Stravinsky and subsequently, when the Russian composer visited Switzerland, wrote in a letter to Robert Godet, a Swiss journalist and life-long friend : "Do you know that right near you, at Clarens, there is a young Russian musician, Igor Stravinsky, who has an instinctive genius for colour and rhythm?" And, describing his music, he added "It is childlike and savage. And yet it is extremely delicate."[16]

It is probable that Stravinsky had the first really intimate meeting with Debussy at the French composer's home in the spring of 1913; although Debussy had previously visited him backstage after the première of *The Firebird*. Igor embraced Claude; then the two men sat down at the piano to play through a four-handed arrangement of *The King of the Stars*, a work of abstract splendour which he had dedicated to Debussy and which, exploring a richly impressionistic harmonic idiom, owed something to that composer. It was never performed, because of the difficulties of intonation which the choruses presented.

The more Debussy cultivated Stravinsky over the years the more he admired and, at times, venerated him; but certain prejudices or dislikes persisted, as can be discerned from a letter he wrote on 4th January 1916 to his friend Godet : "I have recently seen Stravinsky. . . . He says *'My Firebird*, my *Sacre* !' as a child would say 'my spinning top, my hoop'. And it is exactly that—a spoiled child, who sometimes puts his fingers into the nose of music. He is also a young savage, who wears loud ties and kisses women's hands while stepping on their feet. When he grows older he'll be unbearable—that is, he won't be able to bear any music, but at present he's terrific."[17]

This rather condescending manner of Debussy in no way implied harsh disparagement; he knew Stravinsky's value, but with Gallic shrewdness tempered approval with a slightly cynical appraisement. Debussy had good reason to like the Russian, since both had much in common.

It is true that the Frenchman drew most of his inspiration from the contemporary cult of symbolism and impressionism; but he also used the Gregorian modes, found magical influences in the Middle Ages, the music of the French and Italian Renaissance, and the pentatonic scales of the Far East. His was a searching mind clearly more exploratory than that of his coevals, Brahms or Strauss or Ravel, and, like Stravinsky, he grew into a phenomenon of his time.

One of the facets of Debussy's art that should have increased Stravinsky's affection for him was the wonderful neatness and delicacy of much of his scoring. One notices this particularly in *Pelléas et Mélisande*, which surely must cast a spell over any listener. This great work is put together like a film, or a pointillistic landscape—thousands of little separate pieces collated with infinite patience, with genius. When Pelléas and Mélisande, for instance, return to the cave in their vain search for the lost ring, we hear in the music first the calm sweeping of the water, then the cry of Mélisande when she sees the old beggars sitting side by side against the rock. All the tiny segments have to be put together by the producer, the conductor, and the singers with the utmost precision and insight.

Another feature of Debussy's writing in *Pelléas et Mélisande* that should have appealed to the creator of *The Firebird* was that his love writing is always *pianissimo*. In Wagner the love motives flood the opera house *fortissimo*, and this is the general tendency in such music; but Debussy, like Maeterlinck, cherished the idea of a gentle, silent love. Heavy romantic effusions did not appeal to Stravinsky any more than they did to the Frenchman. Nevertheless, he regarded *Pelléas et Mélisande* as "a great bore", in spite of its "many wonderful pages". Debussy, a dark-complexioned man with a double forehead, spoke in a low, quiet voice which sometimes muffled his phrase-endings. As his innocent remarks might contain booby-traps and stinging barbs, this, on the whole, pleased Stravinsky.

For all his spark-emitting and gay temperament, Stravinsky at this time looked slightly intimidating, even pompous. He wore striped blazers or sober, neatly-tailored suits, with or without plus-fours, and a flat peaked cap reminiscent of a respectable, middle-class Victorian. His manners were usually impeccable and he invariably showed courtesy to the opposite sex.

Stravinsky made the acquaintance of Ravel when he first arrived in Paris, and soon recognized the special quality in his music.

Ravel lived in a small cottage at Fontainebleu. The area was flooded in 1909, and when Walter Nouvel visited him the force of the water pushed up the floor-boards, an occurrence which seemingly did not worry Ravel, as he proceeded to expound the virtues of *Daphnis et Chloé*, or at least that part of it which he had completed.

Stravinsky spoke affectionately of Ravel as "a Swiss clockmaker", comparing the precision and polish of his music with that of the industrious craftsmanship practised by his family. Serge Lifar related how, in 1934, after a triumphant performance of *La Mer* and *Bolero* at the Théâtre des Champs-Elysées in Paris, the conductor Toscanini crossed the stage, and, seeing Ravel in the wings, approached him with smiling face and out-stretched hand. Ravel, pulling an old-fashioned watch out of his pocket, studied it and said phlegmatically "A minute and a half too fast". Then, turning on his heel, he strode majestically from the building. The two men never met again.

Stravinsky enjoyed a firm, but not extensive friendship with Florent Schmitt, a composer with a large output of minor works who also wrote *La Tragédie de Salome*, a ballet score which, published in 1910, presents a rich orchestral palette, capable of overwhelming climaxes and strong barbaric rhythms. It may well have contributed to the birth of *The Rite of Spring*.

The Rite—we may well wonder why, unlike *Tristan*, its sole rival in iconoclast fame, this great work has not procreated a whole new species in the floribunda of music, why its innovations were not seized on as an alternative when harmony seemed to have reached a dead end. It may be that the sheer audacity and colossal stature of Stravinsky's achievement numbed the responses of those who found his torch too heavy and bright to bear.

"Music exists when there is rhythm, as life exists when there is a pulse," Stravinsky jotted down in the sketches he prepared for "Dance of the Earth"—a remark which exposes the driving force behind much of his irrepressible art. The seed of *The Rite of Spring* consisted of a 'fleeting vision' which came to Stravinsky when he was finishing the last pages of *The Firebird* in St Petersburg. He saw in imagination a solemn pagan rite, with patriarchal elders seated in a circle, watching a young girl—chosen to propitiate the god of spring—dance herself to death. This vision so fascinated him that he described it to his friend Nicholas Roerich, a painter who had specialized in pagan subjects. Roerich, fired with enthusiasm, became his collaborator in the project and Diaghilev, when it was put to him, warmly approved, although subsequent events postponed its realization.

A mere ostinato chord, repeated 212 times throughout the "Dance of the Youths and Maidens" was gleefully acknowledged by Stravinsky as the first real musical idea that occurred to him for the score of *The Rite of Spring*. In the words of Pope, "what mighty contests rise from trivial things".

This musical idea, the genesis of an indisputable masterpiece, germinated slowly; meanwhile, Stravinsky, having dazzled Paris with *The Firebird*, began a period of wanderings. He visited in turn Switzerland, the Riviera, and Italy. It was at La Baule that he wrote his two Verlaine songs; steeped in mysticism, they rebut the charge that Stravinsky had no great depth of feeling. The tragedy and pain of humanity saddened and troubled him as much as they do any other sensitive composer; but, conscious of the weakening effect of sentimentality, he secreted much of his compassion until, through the filter of his music, it could be purified and given more perfect, lasting utterance.

During his travels, Stravinsky really 'discovered' his unknown country when, like a weird and ghostly dream, the story and the music of *Petrushka* fused inside him. He originally intended the work to be for pianoforte and orchestra, with the title *Burlesque*; but, searching about for a more picturesque title, he alighted on the subject of Petrushka, the immortal and unhappy puppet. Stravinsky finished *Petrushka* in Rome in May 1911, about a year after the glorious première of *The Firebird*. Unsettled by the malaise of a vanishing epoch, he sought in *Petrushka* to remove the sweet taste of epigonism from his work.

D

This barbaric tale, redolent of a Russia filled with Cossack-plagued peasantry, noisy fairgrounds, steaming samovars, troikas, and onion-domed churches, delighted Western sophisticates who found a refuge from reality in its wonderfully exotic though tragic make-believe. Stravinsky used the different instruments in the score with a touch of genius : the flutes bubbled like the reeds in a fun-fair organ; trombones and tubas, released from their Wagnerian servitude, filled exciting new roles as circus clowns; hurdy-gurdy tunes, churned out to the tinkling rhythm of triangles, infused a delicate flavour of irony into the music.

In composing *Petrushka* he drew upon his rich, almost inexhaustible memory. As a boy he had visited Yarmolintsy, a city in the middle of the great Ukrainian wheat-prairie, and seen the brightly dressed peasants taking part in the famous dancing contests. One of the dances Stravinsky watched was the *presiatka*, or 'heel dance', and this he used in the coach-man scene of *Petrushka*. He also incorporated the *kazachok*, or 'kicking dance', into the ballet, as well as the *trepak*.

A superb portrait is that of the Moor, whose part largely comprises barklike sounds, loud snarls, and bass pizzicato. Such exactness in the tone-painting of the character, such daring originality, makes nonsense of this criticism of Stravinsky levelled by a fellow composer, the late Rut-land Boughton, in 1929 :

Stravinsky, in his least pretentious works, shows that he is entirely un-able to formulate a musical idea of his own. As a member of a savage orchestra he might perhaps be allowed to play a recurrent theme upon a drum—as the only evidence of real form in his work is of that kind of primitive repetition which birds and babies also do very well. Stravinsky stands at the head of a movement which interprets much that is real and rotten in the modern world.

Boughton, one of the most pathetic figures in twentieth-century British music, hardly seems a suitable critic to pronounce judgement on so invig-orating and progressive a spirit as Igor Stravinsky. His dream of an English Bayreuth at Glastonbury was based on the misguided belief that his own music had the inner strength and originality to support a great festival single-handed as Wagner's had done.

In writing the story of *Petrushka* the composer enjoyed the collabora-tion of Benois, to whom Diaghilev entrusted the whole décor of the ballet, both scenery and costumes. During a sojourn at Beaulieu, serious illness, an attack of nicotine poisoning, interrupted work on the score; this caused Stravinsky grave worry, since the ballet had to be ready for Paris in the spring. He recovered in sufficient time to travel to Rome, where Diaghilev was giving performances at the Constanza Theatre during the International Exhibition. There, with Fokine as the choreographer, rehearsals took place, while Stravinsky completed the final pages of the score.

Fokine had to use a cellar for the Rome rehearsals, with the clank of machinery and the clatter of other commercial operations punctuating the music; but he created the scene of Petrushka, the Moor, and the Ballerina on the stage of the Paris Opera. He found the music, at times, almost unmanageable for choreography : the rapid changes of the counts at first eluded him, though he did, in the end, master them. Nijinsky had only slight musical knowledge; yet he grasped the movements with uncanny insight, bringing the role of Petrushka vividly to life. He worked in perfect harmony with Fokine, his only difficulty being to assimilate the music.

What I remember about *Petrushka* [Tamara Karsavina told me] is that it was utterly tempestuous. We had some very harmonious productions—like *Le Spectre de la Rose*—which were not interrupted by nerves. *Petrushka* was not like this. All was storm. . . .

We began rehearsals in Rome while we were doing a season there. At that time Fokine was overworked, and endlessly there were tempers because the Stravinsky score was not quite finished; at one time he threw the manuscript papers down and trampled on them. But of course one must remember that Fokine was one of those who believed in a little judicious rage. It was calculated uncontrol, so to speak, to get us up to hysteria level and keep us there. He thought that a ballet going smoothly was growing dull. Toscanini was rehearsing at the time in the theatre, and when he rehearsed you couldn't come near; you were supposed to walk on tiptoe even in the corridors. So somewhere else had to be found for us. We went to an old restaurant where unfortunately they did a lot of frying. A small piano was wheeled in and we began work among the smells of stale scampi and stale carpet.

Stravinsky was playing his own score. There was hardly another musician who could tackle it. Many of the rhythms were hard for us to follow, and he used to help us by counting it out with vehement nods. He had a woodpecker nose and it looked as if he were pecking the piano. It was a great labour and very hot—how much we sweated—and Stravinsky, too, got very heated, for he was so eager; we were deeply impressed by his beautiful manners, for he bowed to us, all of us in ragged clothes and dishevelled, and asked our permission to take his coat off.

Fokine, bullying and cajoling, drove his dancers to the point of exhaustion. Stravinsky described him—as he did Glazunov on a previous occasion—as "the most disagreeable man I have ever met", and the choreographer certainly tried the tempers of those who worked under him. Cecchetti, the ballet master, strongly disapproved of the sequence where Karsavina, joining in the cobbler's step, had to leap from squatting position right up on to her points. He rightly considered gymnastics of this kind as weakening for a ballerina's knees. Difficulties and clashes of temperament aside, it was, Karsavina told me with a smile, "an adorable ballet to work on".

She praised the costumes designed by Benois,—"an observer of life, full of humour, tremendously knowledgeable about the history of art and very affectionate about detail; he was the Olympian among us and we turned to him whenever perplexed". Karsavina, recalling some of the anonymous members of the company at that time, mentioned a woman who helped to make and fit the costumes. Although extremely gifted, she frequently appeared in a state of intoxication, behaved like a peppery field-marshal, crying "Allons! A nous!", and was rather unpunctual. "One of my costumes had to be pinned on me in pieces at the dress rehearsal", said Karsavina. "Of course the pieces became unpinned with movement. . . . She was really more of a sculptor. But how appreciative. Once she came backstage with paeans of praise, saying 'Do you know that you have a very beautiful back?' I determined that I must never turn my face forward again. . . . Somehow reminiscent of the Mikado's ugly sister of Gilbert and Sullivan, who proudly boasted that one day a week people gathered to admire her left shoulder blade".

It was the rotund, genial, walrus-moustached Pierre Monteux, for several years conductor of the Russian Ballet, who directed both the rehearsals and the première at the Châtelet Theatre on 13th June 1911, of this great work. Stravinsky wrote of him in his autobiography "Monteux knew his job thoroughly. He knew how to get on with his musicians. . . ."[18] Indeed he did, for Monteux belonged to that small group of conductors who are loved by the men who serve under them; his beat was clear and unambiguous, he knew how to 'read between the lines' of the score. Monteux regarded his job as being to communicate with the orchestra and to bring out the conception of the composer. An unfashionable concept in this era of airborne baton prima donnas!

Puccini, who died a decade later after an operation for cancer of the throat, visited Stravinsky at the Châtelet Theatre after one performance of *Petrushka*. He pleased the Russian composer by classifying his music as very talented, but spoiled the compliment by saying that he personally regarded it as horrible. Renato Simoni described Puccini as "straight, tall, with shoulders squared and hat at a slight angle, his hands in his pockets, his step slightly swinging, but strongly rhythmical, with his strong sunburnt face, his suggestion of rough shyness and his good nature—sometimes boyish and sometimes touched with compassion".[19] Puccini's compassion showed when he subsequently called on Stravinsky during a period of illness, expressing kindly concern. In one of his letters he remarked "Almighty God touched me with his little finger and said 'Write for the theatre,—mind, only for the theatre'."[20] His dislike of Stravinsky's music, with its glinting, raw-edged timbres and earthy ebullience, is understandable. Theatrical drama for him meant broad sweeps of melody, exquisite arias, pathos and exotic instrumental effects. He had a flair for utilizing the harmonic and orchestral innovations of others and, after that meeting at the Châtelet, even borrowed brilliantly from Stravinsky.

At the première of the ballet Nijinsky danced the title role, Karsavina the Ballerina, Orlov the Moor, and Cecchetti the Showman. For Nijinsky only the stage was real, and without the smell of resin and grease-paint to breathe life into his nostrils he had no vital spark to distinguish him from ordinary people. Through his own body he could translate the most beautiful visions of movement into fantasy and grace; but he could not create for others the same choreographical inspiration. Ansermet, the conductor, said of him : "As an instructor in ballet-dancing Nijinsky was entirely lacking in pedagogical gifts. When we resumed performances of *L'Après-midi d'un Faune* in Rio, I recall that he forced me to go over the beginning of the second movement, where the cellos have a *motif en triples croches* twenty-three times, because he could not make it clear to the artists what he wished them to do." Stravinsky fully confirmed this in a similar remark.

Those who met Nijinsky declared that he had no personality at all off the stage. "Nijinsky was a nonentity," said Prince Peter Lieven, writing of the dancer's social life, "an absolute and thorough nonentity. After five minutes in any society his existence was completely forgotten." And Misia Sert, according to Lieven, described this gifted creature as "an idiot of genius", which perhaps comes nearer the truth. He had the vague, partly developed mind of a sunlight-loving peasant boy. Physically he was abnormal, with no resemblance to the Greek god type that sets female hearts aflutter. He had a slightly Mongolian face, with high cheek bones and curiously slanting eyes. Nijinsky's unusually muscular thighs and over-developed, even bulbous calves made him seem rather clumsily built; yet on the stage he underwent a miraculous transformation, moving with the exquisite grace of a perfect *danseur noble*. Audiences everywhere awaited his appearance with breathless excitement. As a choreographer Nijinsky needed, more than anything, to be understood and encouraged; for his great creations were all in the dream-world of fantasy—*Le Spectre de la Rose*, *Petrushka*, the Gold Negro in *Schéhérazade*, to name three of the finest—and only the fragile and delicate really appealed to, and kindled his choreographic sense. There can never be another Nijinsky—his greatness as a dancer, characterized by the often divine or childlike simplicity of encroaching madness, as well as by his own imitative genius, made him unique.

4

SCANDAL IN PARIS

After his triumphant Paris season, Stravinsky returned to Oustiloug, the family estate in Russia, to devote all his creative energy to *The Rite of Spring*, although he did find time to write two songs with words by the poet Balmont. He travelled to Princess Tenichev's country estate near Smolensk to meet Nicholas Roerich and discuss the scenario of the new ballet. Rail services being infrequent at the time, Stravinsky undertook the journey—described in *Expositions and Developments*—not in the upholstered comfort of a passenger coach, but in a rattling, jolting cattle truck, watched menacingly by a stamping, slavering bull tethered insecurely a few feet away! The bull clearly had no respect for the dapper, expensively dressed interloper who, had he but known it, would soon procreate one of the supreme masterpieces of music.

Meanwhile the spectre of madness had not yet crossed Nijinsky's threshold and Diaghilev did his best to make him into a choreographer, inviting him to compose, under his own constant supervision, the classical tableau *L'Après-midi d'un Faune*, which depicted the erotic gambols of a faun importuning nymphs. Debussy wrote the music for it, but only after much pleading by Diaghilev, since he had no respect for Nijinsky as a producer and spoke more than once of his "perverse genius".[1] Nijinsky, as the Faun, wore a skin-tight body stocking and was painted a coffee colour by Bakst, with big brown spots; around his loins he had a garland of green leaves which ended in a small tail. His make-up, emphasizing the Oriental slant of his eyes, brought a slumbrous languor and a bestial line to his face which, with its high cheek-bones, lent itself marvellously to the transformation. Nijinsky's ears, elongated with flesh-coloured wax and pointed, seemed almost to twitch as he presented, or rather lived, the image of an adolescent Faun, half beast, half human. The other dancers, carefully instructed about their make-up by Bakst, gave themselves whitish-pink eyes, like those of a pigeon. Barefooted and looking like Greek statues in a frieze, they wore no tights and had nothing under their pleated, cream-coloured gauze tunics, which Bakst painted with the motif of Greek keys, some in light blue, some in apple green.

The staging of *L'Après-midi* at the Châtelet Theatre on 29th May 1912, resulted in a major scandal, for Nijinsky, carried away by the erotic nature of the subject, perpetrated one of the most intimate and audacious acts ever seen in the theatre. As the ballet ended one of the running nymphs dropped a scarf. Nijinsky picked it up and, gliding purposefully across the stage, spread it across a rock, then lay full length upon it. The implication was unmistakable.

An incredible uproar filled the theatre at the close of this choreographic poem. It consisted of wild applause from those who approved of what had taken place, and shouting, hissing abuse from those who regarded it as an obscene affront. After the performance Rodin, the sculptor, who had watched it all from a box, rushed round to Nijinsky's dressing-room and, clasping the dancer in his arms, cried in a voice choking with emotion "The fulfilment of my dreams. You brought it to life. Thanks." Next morning most of the critics praised *L'Après-midi d'un Faune* almost un-reservedly; but Gaston Calmette, owner of *Le Figaro*, published a tirade of condemnation that seethed with anger. "It is neither a gracious eclogue nor a profound production," he wrote. "We have a faun, incontinent, with vile movements of erotic bestiality and gestures of heavy shameless-ness. That is all. And the merited boos were accorded the too-expressive pantomime of the body of an ill-made beast, hideous from the front, even more hideous in profile. These animal realities the public will never accept."

Diaghilev was greatly shocked by Calmette's pious defence of the morality of Paris and disturbed, not only by the horde of sensation-hungry journalists who swooped upon him, but by the news that the Prefect of Police had been asked to stop the next performance of the ballet as an obscene spectacle. The issue split Paris like a Samurai sword; in the *salons* and clubs, the cafés, the newspaper offices, and the corridors of the Chamber of Deputies, the pro-Calmettes and the pro-Faunists argued furiously. An article in the *Gaulois* claimed that an apology was due to the public. Nijinsky, requested by the police to remove or change the incident of the Faun lying on a rock, refused, saying that he saw nothing objectionable. Then, answering Calmette, the titanic voice of Rodin spoke in the pages of *Le Matin*. His article ended with these words : "You would think Nijinsky were a statue when he lies full length on the rock, with one leg bent, and with the flute at his lips, as the curtain rises, and nothing could be more soul-stirring than his movement when, at the close of the act, he throws himself down and passionately kisses the discarded veil. I wish that every artist who truly loves his art might see this perfect personification of the ideals of the beauty of the old Greeks."

The sculptor's lofty and dignified defence resulted in a victory for Nijinsky and the pro-Faunists, for although Rodin and Calmette fought a duel of words and the Press published biting caricatures or satirical poems, the police, at last, conceded that the ballet contained nothing offensive, and the moralizing fuddy-duddies retired in utter defeat. Diaghilev realized that Calmette had rendered the Russian Ballet a priceless service in publicising one of his major productions.

Romola Nijinsky, wife of the dancer, declared, rather naïvely, that Debussy was delighted with the sensation that L'Après-midi created, and that he was "enthusiastic at the idea of collaborating with Nijinsky on a new composition".[2] This conflicts with the scorn which, in a letter to his friend Godet, Debussy heaped unreservedly on the Russian dancer.

Returning to Paris for the Diaghilev season, Stravinsky heard the ravishing score of Ravel's Daphnis et Chloé, part of which the composer had previously played to him on the piano. He described it as one of the finest things in French music; not surprisingly, for the luminous colours and dancing swing of the music, written for a Diaghilev ballet, display the rhythmic vitality which Stravinsky so much admired.

While working on the score of The Rite of Spring at Oustiloug, Stravinsky received an invitation from Diaghilev to join him at Bayreuth to hear Parsifal performed. Stravinsky had never seen this opera staged. When he reached Bayreuth all the hotels were filled to overflowing; but he and Diaghilev, his "dear portly friend", managed to find two servants' rooms. How did Stravinsky, one of the high priests of a new harmonic language, react as he passed through the unpromising, indeed forbidding exterior of the Festpielhaus that Wagner amazingly conjured into existence and saw for the first time that interior so unlike any other, astonishingly beautiful with its ranks of tall Corinthian columns receding towards the stage on either side and its great clusters of once gaslit globes? How, indeed! He found the whole atmosphere, its design and its setting, lugubrious. The building reminded him of a crematorium, "and a very old-fashioned one at that",[3] in which he half expected to see black-robed ushers chanting the praises of the departed.

As he sat there, with a frozen look on his face, the customary fanfare of trumpets rang out, seeming almost to herald the coming of a Pope, the globes slowly dimmed, and then from the invisible orchestra, under its shell, curled upward the opening phrases of Parsifal, steeped in the atmospheric theme of the Holy Grail. In such a place, hallowed by usage and tradition, the performers and musicians should seem like gods and heroes; but to Igor Stravinsky the grave and devout manner of the presentation and its reception by the audience, were utterly ridiculous. He regarded the whole concept as "unseemly and sacrilegious",[4] turning the theatre into a temple and, by its cult-like symbolism, degrading those who worshipped at the Bayreuth shrine. This, for him, was not an Unknown Country, but a farrago of nonsense.

Shocked and motionless, he sat with numbed limbs, not daring to ruffle the awed silence of the opera house; then, unable to bear it any longer, he changed his position with a noise that invited the horrified scowls of those around him. During the interval he was rewarded with sausages and glasses of beer; but the memory of that first pilgrimage to Bayreuth rankled in his mind for many years.

Despite the strictures which Stravinsky heaped upon Bayreuth, its magic remains as powerful as ever, for the Bayreuth sound alone—that tonal blend of silver and gold that Wagner dreamed of and knew how to create —is enough to coax disciples from every part of the world. The sets are often—not always—breathtaking. And few people can resist, for example, the delicate orchestral postlude which crowns Act II of *Die Meistersinger* and which, as a flood of moonlight descends upon the stage, captures the full poetry of that exquisite curtain.

Returning to *The Rite of Spring*, Stravinsky viewed with misgiving the prospect of working with Nijinsky. He admired his gifts as a dancer profoundly; but, alas, the poor boy knew nothing of music and could neither read it nor play any instrument. Yet Diaghilev, still hoping to make a Petipa out of Nijinsky and enthusing over his "plastic vision", insisted that the dancer should choreograph both *The Rite* and Debussy's *Jeux*. Not only did Nijinsky demand a fantastic number of rehearsals, but Stravinsky had to teach him the very rudiments of music—semibreve, minim, crotchet, quaver; bars, rhythm, tempo, and so on—before any progress could be made. Inevitably friction arose and, according to Stravinsky, the young Russian, saddled with a huge task beyond his capabilities, became presumptuous and unmanageable.

Stravinsky worked on the score of *The Rite of Spring* in a tiny room of a house at Clarens, in Switzerland, during the winter of 1912–13, interrupting his labours only when Diaghilev summoned him to first performances of *The Firebird* and *Petrushka* in different countries of central Europe where the Russian Ballet was on tour. At one performance of The *Firebird* in Berlin he met Richard Strauss, who ventured on to the stage, talked animatedly about his music, and offered this characteristic advice: "You make a mistake in beginning your piece *pianissimo*; the public will not listen. You should astonish them by a sudden crash at the very start. After that they will follow you, and you can do whatever you like."[5]

Well, the public did listen, and they have done so ever since; for the dark, flickering beauty of the introduction to *The Firebird* is irresistible. As for Richard Strauss, the progenitor of so many orchestral innovations and the *enfant terrible* of his own day, it is true that he upheld the principle of 'astonish them' with the stormy and brazen opening of his own tone-poem *Don Juan*. And yet how delicately he used some of the instruments in his scores, as, for example, in the Dance of the Seven Veils from *Salomé*, where the softly glowing flute runs up the scale to a high C sharp. Strauss, a rotund, worldly man, could be surprisingly insensitive.

Once, watching Fokine rehearsing Massine in a dance, he rudely interrupted the sequence with the remark "At this point, M. Fokine, there should be an elevation step to emphasize the crescendo in the music." He then leaped up and dropped on one knee. The outraged Fokine glared at him in silence, then told Massine to carry on as if nothing had happened.

During his Berlin visit, Stravinsky met Schoenberg, who invited him to an audition of his melodrama *Pierrot Lunaire*. Although the Russian paid tribute to the distinction of the scoring, he regarded this as a Beardsley-flavoured antiquity. As Oscar Wilde remarked, through one of his characters, "Nothing is so dangerous as being too modern. One is apt to grow old-fashioned quite suddenly".[6] Stravinsky noted Schoenberg's music as being chopped up into tiny breathless chunks, instead of moving in broad, continuous lines. He met the composer after the performance in the green room of the Choralion-saal, Bellevuestrasse, and described him afterwards as being short in stature; bald, with a fringe of black hair circling the rim of his pale, domed head, like a Japanese actor's mask. Stravinsky wrote of Schoenberg's large ears, soft deep voice, and mellow, Viennese accent. He had "protruberant and explosive" eyes, which radiated the whole dynamic force of his character. Shortly after the meeting Schoenberg left for St Petersburg to conduct his *Pelleas und Melisande*.

Stravinsky, when he visited Budapest, found the inhabitants openhearted, warm, and friendly. Once, during a sojourn in that city, he spent some time with Karsavina and her husband, Mr H. J. Bruce, who, before he died on 12th September 1951, wrote two charming books about her, *Silken Dalliance* and *Thirty Dozen Moons*. The dancer had rented a house on the highest vantage point of Buda, which is situated on the right bank of the Danube, facing Pest on the opposite bank. It was from this height that Bishop Gellért, who came to the city in the eleventh century to help convert the Magyars to Christianity, found a martyr's death when the unco-operative 'heathen' sealed him in a barrel studded with spikes and rolled him down the hill. The house commanded a breathtaking view of the Danube, a silver ribbon along which, like fat crawling beetles, drifted cargo-laden barges. Below stretched the rich tapestry of Buda itself, a priceless fabric of neo-baroque Lutheran churches, narrow, medieval alley-ways, Gothic arches, crumbling citadels, and houses with barrel vaults, stone stairs, and blackened oak doors. The whole fascinating spectacle, subtly impregnated with the heady throb of gipsy violins from cafés and restaurants, might have been some ghostly, idealistic illusion of the senses. In the evening, as dusk settled in a blue haze over the city, Stravinsky joined Karsavina and her husband. After dinner, Bruce sat with the composer in a room that looked directly down on the river. Hours passed without a word being spoken; hours in which Stravinsky

squatted like a small hunched Buddha, staring fixedly through the un-
curtained window. At last Bruce, who must have been ruminating on
whether his companion had actually expired, could no longer endure the
silence. "What are you thinking about?" he blurted out. For a long time
Stravinsky did not answer; then he slowly turned, a radiant, almost angelic
smile lighting up his face. "The river," he whispered, "the river . . . isn't
it . . . beautiful!"

Stravinsky loved Budapest, but Vienna shocked and disgusted him. He
had never before—not even when *Fireworks* had its première in St Petersburg—encountered such hostility as the orchestra showed him during
rehearsals of *Petrushka.* This hostility developed into open sabotage, with
such coarse remarks as *schmutzige musik* being flung at composer and
director. Much of the venom was reserved for the Prussian comptroller
of the Hofoper, who, in engaging Diaghilev and his company, had deeply
offended the Imperial Ballet of Vienna. Hurt and distressed by the vicious
attitude of the orchestra, Stravinsky took comfort from a kindly old man
with Franz Joseph whiskers whose task it was to raise and lower the curtain. "Don't let's be downhearted," said this good Samaritan, patting his
shoulder. "I've been here for fifty-five years, and it's not the first time that
things of that sort have happened. It was just the same with *Tristan.*"[7]

While completing the orchestration of *The Rite of Spring*, Stravinsky,
having read and enthused over a little anthology of Japanese lyrics, took
three of the verses and set them to music. The idiom of the last of these,
"Tsaraiuki", shows a surprising affinity with that of Schoenberg. He also,
some time later, completed *Three Little Songs* (*Memories of Childhood*)
for voice and piano. The gay diatonic tunes in these unpretentious pieces
are instantly appealing. At Clarens the composer played his *Japanese
Lyrics* to Ravel, who liked them so much that he decided to do something
similar, and, soon afterwards, reciprocated with a rendering of his own
delicious *Poèms de Mallarmé.* Stravinsky had a special affection for
Clarens, a quiet, sleepy village with superb views across the Lake of
Geneva and a place which Rousseau immortalized in his *Nouvelle Héloïse.*
The meadow-ground, covered with the snowy blossoms of the narcissi in
springtime, may well have sown in Stravinsky's mind the creative memory
of the old Greek legend of Persephone, who picked the flower before
descending into Hades; a legend which the composer one day set to spellbinding music.

It was in 1912, in the middle of the London season that Fokine, his
contract having expired, left the Diaghilev company. His departure
signified the end of a glorious era in the history of Russian dancing. The
responsibility for supervising rehearsals fell upon the *régisseur* Grigoriev,
who, with plans of his own maturing, protested vehemently, but to no
avail. He did, in fact, discharge his new duties with dazzling success.
Fokine returned to the Russian Ballet in 1914, but left after staging a few

productions, and Leonide Massine, then young and comparatively un-known, joined the company in the same year to begin his own glorious career as a dancer and choreographer.

Soon Diaghilev gave Stravinsky another commission, that of Mus-sorgsky's *Khovanstchina,* which he wanted to stage in the next Paris season. This work, like many others written by Mussorgsky, had been completed and revised by Rimsky-Korsakov, who often took too pedantic a view of his harmonic and rhythmic audacities. Diaghilev, dissatisfied with the 'ghosting' of *Khovanstchina,* invited Stravinsky to orchestrate such parts as the author had left only in simple thematic drafts and, from one of these drafts, to compose for the finale a chorus impregnated with a typically Russian flavour. In the event, Stravinsky, at his own request, shared the commission with Ravel, who joined him at Clarens, so that they could work together. Stravinsky rightly condemned Rimsky-Korsakov's tampering with a dead composer's work and wrote disparag-ingly of his Meyerbeerization of *Boris Godunov.* It is, indeed, a presump-tuous and unnecessary liberty to finish what the stiffening fingers of a great man were incapable of completing; whether the end product be the consummation of Schubert's "Unfinished" Symphony or a St Mark Passion fashioned, like an Identi-kit portrait, from the Eberhardine *Trauer-Ode* of Bach.

Preparations for the première of *The Rite of Spring* slowly fructified. In choosing Nicholas Roerich to design the sets for the new ballet, Stravinsky had acted wisely. Having seen and admired Roerich's sets for *Prince Igor,* he knew that the blond-bearded painter, who claimed descent from Rurik, the Russo-Scandinavian Ur-Prince and had the manner of a *grand seigneur,* would not apply too much colour and detail. In fact, the backdrop which Roerich created, a wonderful vision of steppes and sky, delighted Stravinsky and, with twelve lusty, flaxen-haired girls mak-ing a statuesque group in front of it, provided an unforgettable scene. His costumes, visually arresting as well as historically accurate, also pleased the composer.

In the spring of 1913 in Paris the Russian Ballet inaugurated the open-ing of the Théâtre des Champs-Elysées by staging a season which began with a revival of *The Firebird* and included the première of the now completed *Rite of Spring.* The complexity of Stravinsky's score had necessitated many painstaking rehearsals under Pierre Monteux, the "well-tempered avantgardist" as he has often been called. Little did the gentle Monteux realize, as he lifted his baton before a large and fashionable audience on 29th May that he was about to precipitate one of the most celebrated scandals in musical history.

Protocol at both French and Italian theatres had for many years been a restraining harness of tradition and chafed the sensitive soul of the foreigner unused to such ritual. Illustrative of this, Spike Hughes described the humiliation suffered by Stravinsky at the Teatro dell'Opera in Rome when, during a festival of modern music held there in the 1950s, he was barred from entry because he had neglected to put on a black tie. In 1913 at the Théâtre des Champs-Elysées a slightly different atmosphere prevailed. It carried with it the delicate flavour of a past when opera was conceived as an Italian or Stendhalian *salon*, where subscribers could exchange greetings and, popping from box to box, pay fulsome compliments to the ladies. In such an atmosphere *The Rite of Spring* opened its Dionysian floodgates. . . .

It was a lovely evening. The aristocracy, seated amid the Louis XVI garlands, on soft divans and cushions, fanned themselves, ogled their betters, and regaled each other with titbits of gossip; while the not-so-rich feasted their eyes upon the opulence below. A wave of respectful and pleasantly expectant applause greeted Pierre Monteux as, bowing, he turned and picked up his baton. Before long, however, while it seemed to the astonished music-lovers as if the foundations of the theatre were crumbling under the mountainous dissonance of the score, the brutality and strength of *The Rite* swept across the rows of seats and into the gilt-and-plush seclusion of the boxes. Whereupon the audience demonstrated so vehemently that it was often impossible to hear the music. Distinguished people, including the Austrian Ambassador burst into laughter; a lady in a box slapped the face of a man who was hissing; and the Princess de Pourtalès loudly exclaimed that "this horrible din" was nothing short of an insult. Florent Schmitt shouted "Taisez-vous garces du seizième" ("Shut up, you aristocratic bitches") at some of the most elegant ladies in Paris, and, to his eternal credit, Debussy, himself capable of an intense, white-hot rage, rose to his feet and begged the audience to listen.

In the wings Stravinsky, trembling with emotion, grabbed Nijinsky by the collar to stop him from rushing on to the stage and raving at the *canaille* who dared to pollute the holy atmosphere of a ballet. In the pit Monteux threw desperate glances towards Diaghilev, who, seated in a box, made signs for the orchestra to keep on playing. When the second tableau began a cacophony of screaming and shouting filled the theatre; no-one, except those in the front stalls, could hear the music. The players, fortified by Monteux's Gallic calm, plodded valiantly through the score. Finally, with every member of the audience exhausted, the tumult slowly subsided. The full extent of the disturbance which this historic score provoked may be realized from the fact that during the ensuing scuffle fifty people stripped themselves naked and, after being rounded up, landed in the Commissariat de Police on the rue Havre Commartin.

Jean Cocteau described the emotional scene that followed the storm:

At two o'clock in the morning Stravinsky, Nijinsky, Diaghilev and I crowded into a cab and got it to take us to the Bois de Boulogne. We

were silent; the night was cool and pleasant. . . . When we arrived at the
lakes Diaghilev, muffled in opossum, began to mutter in Russian; I felt
that Stravinsky and Nijinsky were listening, and, as the cabby lit his
lantern, I saw tears in the impresario's face. He continued to mumble
slowly and without tiring.

"What is it?" I asked.

"*Pouchkine.*"

There was a long silence, then Diaghilev uttered another short phrase,
and the emotion of my two companions seemed so great that I could no
longer resist interrupting them to ask the reason.

"It is too difficult to translate," said Stravinsky, "really difficult;
too Russian, too Russian. . . . It means approximately, 'Will
you make a trip to the Islands?' That's it; and it's very Russian
because, you see, with us we go to the Islands, just as tonight we go to
the Bois de Boulogne, and it is while going to the Islands that we first
conceived *The Rite of Spring.*"[8]

All his life Cocteau remembered that poignant scene in the cab, as
Diaghilev, his plump face streaked with tears, recited "*Pouchkine*".

After the première of *The Rite* all the critics who reviewed it, with the
exception of Emile Vuillermoz, one of the most distinguished of the
Parisian writers, resolutely disowned what to them was a hideous fire-
spouting monster. Vuillermoz wrote :

How can we explain the monstrous attraction of such a deliberately
extravagant work, so purposefully aggressive, so rich in new ideas, and so
opposed to our most respectable taste? *The Rite of Spring* cannot be
explained; one suffers it with horror or ecstasy according to one's own
particular temperament. Not all women take a crowning insult in the same
way. Music, generally speaking, accepts all crowning wrongs without distaste. The music bends the rows of dancers, passing over their shoulders
like a storm on a cornfield; it hurls them into the air, it burns the soles
of their feet. Stravinsky's interpreters are not merely electrified by a
rhythmical current, they are electrocuted! Their limbs shudder with
terrible convulsions. Confronted by the music's devastating effects, one
feels the futility of the choreographer's literary and pictorial preoccupa-
tions, as he attempts to display his memories of the museum. Nothing
could be less happily chosen than this indiscreet erudition!

Pierre Lalo, music critic of *Le Temps*, criticized *The Rite* in these
words : "The cult of the false note has never been practised with such
zeal and persistence . . . whatever note you expect, it is never the one
which comes, but the next one to it; whatever chord may seem to be
involved by a preceding chord, it is always another that follows . . . and
often gives an impression of sharp and almost atrocious discord."

During a Press interview in 1956, Pierre Monteux, then eighty-one
years old, expressed the view that the venom of the shouting, hissing
audience was directed, not at Stravinsky's music, but at the ballet itself.

"I suspected at the time that it was not the music, and so, a little while later on, determined that such a score should not be lost, I suggested to Stravinsky that we should play the music at one of the Colonne concerts. We did, and it was an enormous success and has remained so ever since. The fact that the music has survived, and has even gained in popularity, and that the ballet has died, proves my original judgement."

In my opinion it does not necessarily do so. Many masterpieces have provoked intense dislike, even apparent hatred at a first hearing; then, as public taste adjusted itself to the unfamiliar, have become established favourites. It is difficult to believe that, indecency aside—and none has ever been suggested of this production—an audience would respond to a new ballet with such vitriolic animosity. And let it not be forgotten that Montreux also wrote that, when Stravinsky played over the score to him on the piano, he was convinced that the composer was raving mad, adding, however, that while he was sure the music would cause a scandal among the public, musicians would delight in it.

True understanding and appreciation of Stravinsky's masterpiece came slowly. When Pierre Monteux and the Boston Symphony Orchestra introduced the orchestral suite of *The Rite* into America in 1924 the flame of antagonism still burned fiercely. One poetic wit sent the following to the pages of the Boston Herald :

> Who wrote this fiendish Rite of Spring?
> What right had he to write this thing?
> Against our helpless ears to fling
> Its crash, clash, cling, clang, bing, bang, bing!

On reading this piece of doggerel, the composer is said to have pointed out that there was one *bing* too many : *The Rite of Spring* begins with six, not seven notes on the bassoon.

By the time the ballet was mounted for the first time in the United States—at Philadelphia on 11th April 1930, with Leopold Stokowski—most music-lovers, critics included, were ready to recognize and admire the remarkable vitality, sense of excitement, and audacity of the score. And less than a decade later, when Walt Disney incorporated the music into the film *Fantasia*, to be heard by millions, the initial shock seemed completely to have evaporated.

Stravinsky was never wholly ignored, and almost before the printer's ink of the articles that condemned *The Rite of Spring* after the Paris première had properly dried, young men in all the arts extolled him as the chief protagonist in their bitter onslaught against smug tradition, complacency, and outmoded practices. In Italy the futurist Marinetti marched through the streets with a banner proclaiming "Down with Wagner! Long live Stravinsky!"

After another performance of *The Rite of Spring*—this time at the

Casino de Paris under the baton of Pierre Monteux in 1914—the famous
critic Georges Auric wrote :

> At the conclusion of the last bars of music a long clamour arose which
> went on and on interminably. Members of the audience, clinging to the
> ledges of balconies and boxes, were applauding, cheering and yelling at
> each other amid a terrifying tumult. And suddenly I spotted a little man
> who, almost panic-stricken by all this, was trying to get away, to steal out
> and escape from the frenzied crowd. A young man was with him whom I did
> not as yet know. It was Igor Stravinsky and Jean Cocteau,—and in this
> way I learnt of the friendship which bound Cocteau to the master, just as
> I had that day understood (to be always remembered) the important
> message which the master had conveyed to us.

Monteux died, aged eighty-nine, in 1964. The only orchestra he failed
to bring under the spell of his benign, undemonstrative genius was the
Vienna Philharmonic, who rebelled when he asked it to play *Petrushka*.
One of his reflections about rostrum exhibitionism appealed greatly to
Igor Stravinsky : "I have deplored the fact that many young conductors
of today employ their noble metier for self-aggrandisement. Many of them
seem to feel the need to make a sort of show of themselves. I think these
often erotic gyrations are an insult to their orchestra and, most certainly,
an outrageous disrespect to the music they are supposed to interpret. I
have been deeply offended for the composer and have felt like crying out
wrathfully 'Stop !' "[9]

Stravinsky is not the only twentieth-century composer to have suffered,
almost literally, the slings and arrows of outrageous fortune. At the 1960
Donaueschingen Festival, when Messiaen's *Chronochromie*, a wonderfully
descriptive piece, was performed before a supposedly intelligence audience,
it provoked a storm of howls and whistles. At Paris, in the spring of the
following year, passion erupted into actual violence. "I watched bearing
down on me," recalled Messiaen, "a horde of respectable ladies, clad in fur
capes and jewels, who had clearly been turned into Furies. They put out
their tongues at me and screamed at the tops of their voices 'Get out; you
dirty beast, get out !' " What annoyed Messiaen, as he confessed with a
wry smile, was that "they booed the nicest passage in the whole work".

The initial revulsion against *The Rite of Spring* undoubtedly shocked
and angered Stravinsky; but recollection of the unsympathetic treatment
of his *Fireworks* by the orchestra of the Imperial Theatre in St Petersburg
probably softened the impact. He must have realized by then that he had
a particular destiny and, with it, a cross to bear.

During his Paris phase, Stravinsky was not alone in his search for new
lands to conquer. Marc Chagall had come from Russia and, isolated by
his Oriental outlook from the other painters of Montparnasse, sat alone
on the terrace of the Dôme, dreaming of the goats, cows and soft-eyed

virgins of his native Vitebsk, while he subsisted on coffee and pieces of bread purchased from his dwindling resources. The international conclave on the Left Bank included Diego de Riviera, experimenting with Cubism before returning, in a cloud of fire, to rule and inspire Mexico. There was Modigliani, courageous under the burden of poor health and poverty, creating strange pictures of people with ovoid faces, the blank eyes child-like and resigned with suffering. In this heterogeneous community the art experts had 'discovered' Van Gogh, Gauguin, Matisse, and the supreme master Cézanne. The exotic Apollinaire occupied a kind of penthouse under the eaves of a high building in the Boulevard Saint-Germain, where, surrounded by masks, fetishes, weird sculptures, and a glowing plethora of paintings, he dominated the artistic life of Montparnasse. And in a huge studio with immense beams that looked more like a hangar, Pablo Picasso held court for poets, painters, critics, and others assembled to do homage to the Spanish genius who found enchantment in everything he saw and touched. His canvases, which at first were brilliant, cruel gropings in the style of Toulouse-Lautrec, passed through the Blue Period, with its pathetic, tenuous Jews and 'Maternities', through the succeeding Harle-quin and Pink Periods, massive and sculptural in their reddish-brown and pink shapes, to the profundity and mystery of a Cubism seemingly inspired by a scientific conception of artistic purity.

In the rue de la Grande Chaumière a swarm of models, crowding in from every corner of Paris, offered themselves for sale : they included bearded old men like Spanish grandees, huge big-breasted matrons, slender, dark-eyed beauties, negroes, fragile girls barely out of school. This was the Montparnasse where grass grew among the paving-stones, where artists—real artists—walked about in rope sandals, and where the army of sham poseurs had scarcely begun its insidious infiltration.

Stravinsky did not attend subsequent performances of *The Rite of Spring* or the première of the revised *Khovanstchina* because, a few days after that electrifying first night, he fell ill with typhoid and spent six weeks in a nursing home. He did, however, see Debussy's *Jeux* and admired the vivacity of the score. Nijinsky, in choreographing this piece, described tennis-players who lose their ball and play hide-and-seek. They sulk and quarrel, and then clasp each other in a fond embrace, when, suddenly, another ball is thrown by some mischievous onlooker. The score has a rather studied delicacy and, after a desultory existence, the ballet was abandoned by Diaghilev.

During his illness, Stravinsky's friends, including Debussy, de Falla, Ravel, Florent Schmitt, and Casella visited him regularly. Diaghilev also called, but, being afraid of infection, refused to enter the sick-room. Was it, one wonders, an act of self-preservation, or simply his reluctance to involve himself in the personal misfortune of others? He could be kind and considerate, as he chose to be so often with poor Nijinsky; but, as

E

Karsavina indicated, out of his artistic integrity, his dedication to the dance, sprang a disregard for others, a ruthlessness in discarding once cherished collaborators who no longer fitted into his plans.

And one person who fell from the starry firmament of Diaghilev's favour was Vaslav Nijinsky. On 15th August 1913, after finishing a London season, the Russian Ballet sailed from Southampton, without Diaghilev, in the liner *Avon*. It was a voyage made memorable not only by Baudelairean sunsets and moonlit nights, but, for Grigoriev, by the sudden and intimate association of Nijinsky with a young Hungarian dancer called Romola Pulsky. Hitherto the god of the dance had given companionship to practically no-one but Diaghilev; now the breath of romance —illicit for a 'star' under contract—blew through the close ranks of the company.

Shortly after the *Avon* berthed, the happy couple married, and the first bitter fruit of the union ripened at Rio when, during a South American tour, Nijinsky refused to appear in a performance of *Le Carnaval* in which he should have taken the part of Harlequin. In the absence of a doctor's note, certifying illness, the failure of a principal dancer to appear in a performance constituted, for Diaghilev, a grave, unforgivable misdemeanour. After he had been informed of the matter, the impresario sent Nijinsky a curt telegram of dismissal.

Stravinsky, recovered from his illness, returned to Clarens, intending to spend the winter there, and immediately received from the newly-founded Théâtre Libre of Moscow a request to finish the composition of *The Nightingale*, of which, at that time, only the Prologue existed. At first he demurred, afraid that his new 'musical language' would ill accord with the Prologue; but the theatrical sponsors insisted, and finally he agreed.

In the story of *The Nightingale*, by Hans Christian Andersen, the Chinese Emperor is told that only the little kitchen-maid already appreciates that the nightingale is a famous singer and its repute justly earned. There is also a fisherman who fulfils a kind of apocalyptic role. Summoned to Court, the bird gives a 'Command' performance, for which the Emperor awards a present of gold. The fashion of singing, inculcated by this feathered prima-donna, spreads among the courtiers. Then news arrives that the ruler of Japan has a still more remarkable nightingale which he begs the Chinese monarch to accept. The usurper has a rich coat of diamonds and a clockwork heart; it must be wound up before it can sing. During its *coloratura* 'flights', which the Emperor and his Court assume to be genuine, the real nightingale disappears. The monarch, infuriated, decrees that the offender shall be exiled. Finally, on his deathbed, the Emperor, troubled by remorse, invokes the healing spirit of music. The voice of the compassionate true nightingale, singing of Death's garden, floods the sickroom, and Death, moved by the bird's poetic imagery, gives the Emperor back to life. Happy that the music of his friend will be with him forever, the ruler cheerfully greets the courtiers glumly awaiting his death; while the voice of the fisherman is heard heralding a bright future.

Stravinsky, fascinated by the Oriental flavour of the story, tackled *The Nightingale* enthusiastically. He realized that the forest with its fluting bird, and the pure soul of the little girl who loves it so passionately, called for a musical idiom quite different from that needed for the Chinese court, with its bizarre customs, its opulent fêtes, its tinkling bells, glimmering paper lanterns, and metallic-voiced Japanese nightingale. Alas, after working on the score throughout the winter, Stravinsky received the news that the whole project of the Théatre Libre of Moscow had foundered. He was free to dispose of the opera as he wished. Diaghilev, who had watched Stravinsky working for another company with ill-concealed jealousy, seized the opportunity and decided to stage *The Nightingale* during his next season at the Paris Opera House. Benois designed exotic sets and costumes, Romanov created the choreography, Monteux conducted, and at the première on 26th May 1914, the opera, using singers from the production of Rimsky-Korsakov's *Le Coq d'Or*, another highlight of the season, was performed with great success. Unfortunately, the original production did not survive, for the superb costumes, which included a gorgeous robe sparkling with gold and jewels for the Emperor, perished in the store-room of Drury Lane during the 1914–18 war.

Soon after the première of *The Nightingale*, the composer met Ernest Ansermet, the conductor, at Clarens, and the two men became firm friends. Tall and spare, Ansermet, with his pale face, high brow, tapering beard, and magnetic eyes, had a dominating, energetic, and Svengali-like personality. It was he who, at a rehearsal, invited Stravinsky to take up the baton and direct a performance of his own first symphony, which was included in the programme. The composer did so, making his first real appearance as a conductor.

Ansermet clearly admired Stravinsky's music from the very beginning, and in later years acted in many concerts and recordings as a powerful advocate for it. Whether his purpose in presenting the first symphony— then comparatively unknown—at one of his concerts was inspired by a genuine regard for it, or by a desire to give *Musica Viva* a hearing, is debatable. Glazunov's criticism of "heavy instrumentation"[10] seems fully justified. The orchestra is a big one (including four horns, three trumpets, three trombones, and tuba) and the rousing tuttis which constantly burst out in the first and last movements are thickly scored. Any discerning listener can see the student bending over his manuscript pages, busy filling up all those empty staves. After the publication of this work, Stravinsky progressed by leaps and bounds. His own wise comment on the symphony was that it lacked personality, but showed technical proficiency.

At Salvan, in 1914, Stravinsky wrote *Three Pieces for String Quartet*, before spending short periods at Oustiloug and Kiev. He enjoyed his visits to Salvan, one of the most popular summer resorts of Switzerland. A winding road climbs up to the town by way of the Gueuros Bridge, the highest in Europe. The view of the valley it spans is breathtaking, and close by is the town of Saint-Maurice, whose great castle guards the Rhône. The cloister of this majestic bastion, founded in 515 by Sigismund, King of the Burgundians, has an antiquity not surpassed anywhere in Switzerland; the treasures stored there are priceless. Stravinsky loved beauty and seclusion, a magnet which on a number of occasions drew him irresistibly to Salvan.

There is at this time growing evidence of the nostalgia inseparable from his self-imposed exile from his own country. He read many Russian folk-poems. Captivated by the sweeping sound of their language, he visualized, for future use, themes involving Russian dancing scenes based on the folk poetry of Pushkin's age. This ethnical rebirth persuaded the composer, in some measure, to reappraise the instrumentation needed for its realization. In *The Rite of Spring* he had harnessed for his purpose a huge orchestra which in the past had been surpassed only by that used for Schoenberg's *Gurrelieder*; but now, possessed by the idea of a grand *divertissement*, or cantata depicting peasant nuptials, he discarded all allegiance to the Russian orchestral school. The tenuous concept of *The Wedding*, hidden deep inside him, began to take on a clearly defined and recognizable shape.

On his way from Russia, passing through Warsaw, Berlin, and Basle, Stravinsky encountered the tense atmosphere which preceded the outbreak of the 1914–18 war and, a fortnight later, while he was at Ansermet's house in Clarens, the dread proclamation came. Outside the Maryinsky Theatre, in which a patriotic audience had once sung the *Boie Tzarya Khrani*, the national anthem in honour of a visit by the Tsar, fierce-faced recruits drilled, prodding hay-stuffed dummies with their bayonets. At night the public, seeking distraction from the constant privations and scares, flocked as usual to the Maryinsky; but no more white uniforms, no white-dusted hair, or glittering diamonds, no obsequious *Kapelldiener* to guide wealthy patrons to their boxes. Before long, in Berlin, howling mobs, infected by the Nietzschean arrogance of Kaiser Wilhelm, rampaged along the Unter den Linden, where shop windows displayed national emblems and maps of the future German Empire.

Having been exempted from military service, Stravinsky had no need to return to Russia. Although he did not realize it at the time, he would never again see the country of his birth as he had known it.

WAR AND EXILE

Saddened by the news of war, and troubled by twinges of patriotism, Stravinsky steeped himself in Russian folk-poems. His delight in their crude, but vivid pictures, their capricious metaphors, and their syllables flowing like chiming cadences produced a distillation which he injected into three compositions: *Pribaoutki* (translated by Ramuz under the title *Chansons Plaisantes*) for voice and chamber orchestra; the Cat's Cradle Songs, also for voice, with three clarinets; and, lastly, *Four Russian Peasant Songs ('Saucers')*, for women's voices, *a capella*. In writing these pieces he also stored up these and ideas for *The Wedding*. Other compositions of the period 1914–15 were the *Valse des Fleurs* for two pianos, the manuscript of which subsequently disappeared, Three Easy Pieces for piano duet, with a simplified part for the left hand, and a rather brash march for piano entitled *Souvenir d'une Marche Boche*.

It is pertinent at this phase of Stravinsky's development to trace the direction of his footsteps into the Unknown Country. He had begun with the Symphony in C, by imitating the grandiosity of nineteenth-century Russian composers. *The Firebird*, although still rooted in a diatonic past, showed Stravinsky reaching out towards a 'wildness' which had its parallel in Bartok's attempts to unite the barbaric aspects of Hungarian folk music with the harmonic and contrapuntal style of Beethoven's final period. In *Petrushka*, finally parting company with the methods of Rimsky-Korsakov, he had, introducing street tunes (including one pumped out by a hurdy-gurdy in Beaulieu) depicted suffering humanity through a pathetic little puppet in variegated clothes, revealing a deepening involvement in people. In *The Rite of Spring* he had proved his virtuosity, and his genius, by creating a monstrous, awe-inspiring dissonance. Now, as *The Wedding* gestated inside him, conjuring up wild, compulsive dance-measures and orgiastic rhythms, he was rediscovering, with a stylistic elegance completely at variance with the brutality of *The Rite*, the irresistible vitality of a peasant-flavoured ritualism.

His odyssey, though concerned with new and exciting discoveries, carried with it a fondness for images of a ceremonial nature. Dvořák, subconsciously imitating the Czech custom of accenting each word on its first syllable, liked to launch his melodic themes on a strong beat without an anacrusis; and Stravinsky, influenced by the predilection of Russian folk-songs for tunes in 5/4 or 7/4, or patterns of 2/4 or 3/4, directed his musical thinking accordingly. Ritualism in music appealed to Stravinsky not only because it imposed a prescribed pattern of order upon the work itself, but because, in applying it to many of his own compositions which had their roots in the musical theatre, he provided a sparse but ceremonious structure of language accessible to the greatest possible number of people. And coupled with this was a patriotism that not even the bright sophistication of Paris could efface: "A man has one birthplace, one fatherland, one country—he *can* only have one country—and the place of his birth is the most important fact in his life."

Stravinsky's care for precision and simplicity, together with his fondness for the kind of ritualism which has a universality of appeal, makes it easy to assimilate almost everything he wrote since *The Rite of Spring*. He brought tremendous powers of concentration to every project he undertook

The Countess Sayn-Wittgenstein shrewdly observed of Liszt that what he lacked was *Sitzfleisch*—the capacity to stay put and work. No-one could have rightly accused Igor Stravinsky, the apostle of neatness and order, of such a deficiency. Ramuz, in *Souvenirs sur Igor Stravinsky*, described his scores as "magnificent" and showed him, in his study, prepared, like a latter-day Don Quixote, to do battle with the windmills of musical hieroglyphics.

His writing desk (at Morges) resembled a surgeon's instrument case. Bottles of different coloured inks in their ordered hierarchy had each a separate part to play in the ordering of his art. Nearby were indiarubbers of various kinds and shapes and all sorts of glittering steel instruments: rulers, erasers, penknives, and a roulette instrument for drawing staves invented by Stravinsky himself. One was reminded of the definition of St Thomas: beauty is the splendour of order. All the large pages of the score were filled with writing with the help of different coloured inks—blue, green, red, two kinds of black (ordinary and Chinese), each having its purpose, its meaning, its special use: one for the notes, another the text, a third the translation; one for titles, another for the musical directions; meanwhile the bar lines were ruled, and the mistakes carefully erased.

Stravinsky worked with the same consummate care on *The Wedding* during the winter of 1914–15, which he spent in a little villa at Clarens rented to him by Ansermet. In his moments of relaxation he formed a circle of friends, including Ramuz, the painter R. Auberjonais, the brothers Alexandre and Charles Albert Cingria, Ansermet, the brothers Jean and René Mora, Fernant Chavennes, and Henri Bischoff. Ansermet, who joined the musical staff of the Diaghilev company, subsequently acquired a great reputation, not only as a conductor, but as a fine interpreter of Stravinsky. He did not, however, like all of the composer's output, and stated during the course of two lectures in London in 1963 that he felt uneasy over the direction of Stravinsky's latest phase. Ansermet also shone as an advocate of Debussy, Ravel, Bartók, Berg and Hindemith, giving first performances of some of their works. At one time a professor of mathematics at Lausanne University, he had the kind of neat, methodical mind that appealed to Stravinsky and wrote extensively on the subject of the philosophy of music.

It is odd and yet typical of the twentieth century that in *The Wedding*, one of the noblest of ballets, that belongs in depth of characterization to such masterpieces of Russian art as *Boris Godunov, The Seagull,* or *The Brothers Karamazov* the composer had to use scraps of peasant gibberish, foolish proverbs, and banal exclamations as a base for the intensely solemn music. Here the concept of marriage is presented, not with a Victorian sweetness, but with something of the atmosphere of a funeral parlour. Did the audience of the Gaieté Lyrique in 1928 glimpse the strata of pure gold in *The Wedding*? Certainly H. G. Wells did when it was done at His Majesty's Theatre, London in 1926, and he wrote to the papers about it : "It was an amazing experience to come out from this delightful display with the warp and woof of music and vision still running and interweaving in one's mind, and find a little group of critics flushed with resentment and ransacking the stores of their minds for cheap trite depreciation of the freshest and strongest thing they had a chance to print for a long time." His letter of protest, issued as a throw-away reprint at subsequent performances in the same theatre, must have warmed Stravinsky's heart.

The composer had chosen Morges as an ideal place in which to continue work on *The Wedding* and Ramuz wrote an amusing description of his daily routine there :

Stravinsky had gone from the slate-roofed and turreted villa in the suburbs of Morges to the second floor of a fine, early nineteenth, perhaps late eighteenth century house near the outskirts of the town. It is still standing, an ornament to the place. Its enormous, well-laid-out rooms included a grand salon, with three windows, large enough to accommodate even his accumulation of furniture. A half-concealed wooden stair, shut off by three doors, led to a room he had fitted up as a study in the immense attic. We made a joke of it. Did the doors protect him from interruptions by his intimates—or them from his music? I incline to the latter.

Each day the music became more aggressive and noisy, each day less acceptable to the 'good connoisseurs', his neighbours, who could conceive of music only as 'sweet' or 'harmonious,' or at least *nuancée* in the sense that word has for members (active, passive or honorary) of our men's choruses, where art consists in the exact distribution of the *ff and pp*.[1]

The Wedding was the last of Stravinsky's purely Russian works, and although he returned to Russian themes in *Mavra* it was in an entirely new way. The ballet did not take to the stage until 13th June 1923, being presented at the Théâtre de la Gaieté-Lyrique, Paris. It was Bronislava Nijinska, sister of Vaslav, who created all the dances for it. Bronislava, who died in February 1972, was not only a fine choreographer, but a *prima ballerina assoluta* in her own right. According to Romola Nijinsky, "She had in her dancing the same quality as Vaslav : a marvellous technique, a great range of performance, chiselled down to perfection, as well as unusual strength and lightness. In her was combined something of the ethereal charm of a Pavlova, the technique of a Kshessinskaya, a great dramatic gift, and an inherent, overwhelming temperament."[2]

Goncharova's colourless costumes for the ballet emphasized the anonymity of the two families and their friends. The characters, gathered by Nijinska into epic groups, had the pulsating vitality of a windswept cornfield, and the finale, which sounded as if all the bells in Christendom were chiming, crowned the ballet with a touch of splendour.

It seems astonishing that Stravinsky, throughout the period in which he composed *The Wedding*, could tackle any serious work, since he worried constantly about his wife's health, the problem of supporting her and his children, and the task of arranging for the safe return to Russia of his mother, who had paid them a prolonged visit.

Diaghilev, a victim of the war like so many other artists, had seen the greater part of his magnificent company disperse and had to look around for fresh talent in order to stage new enterprises and recoup his dwindling resources. He tried to persuade his beloved Karsavina, then in St Petersburg, to join him; but, imbued with a strong feeling of patriotism, she preferred to remain in Russia. There, particularly in St Petersburg, a sense of impending tragedy impregnated the very air, and the sinister prophecies of the maniac Rasputin tainted the daily life of the people. They still flocked to the Maryinsky Theatre; the poets continued to write madrigals to their favourite ballerinas; Chaliapine sang loyal songs at concerts; but over all this hovered the malign spirit of Rasputin and his prophecy : "The end of me will be the end of the dynasty."

Stravinsky shared the gloomy forebodings; partly through a wish to commune with a friend, and partly because Diaghilev needed him so badly, he visited the impresario twice, once at Florence and once at Rome. On the second visit he joined Diaghilev at his furnished apartment in Rome, bringing with him the scores of the three new piano duets which he had composed at Clarens—a March, a Valse and a Polka, dedicated to Casella, Satie and Diaghilev respectively. When the pair of them played the Polka, the composer revealed that in writing it he had pictured Diaghilev as a circus-ring master in top hat and evening dress, cracking a whip as he urged on a rider. They both laughed uproariously at the joke.

Stravinsky certainly had a ripe sense of humour, and, although in many respects completely ascetic, he knew how to enjoy himself. Vera Newman, widow of the former music critic of the *Sunday Times*, related how, at a party in Paris in 1927, the composer sat next to her at dinner. Stravinsky caused much amusement by suddenly grasping her hand and, beginning with her fingertips, executing a glissando of kisses up her arm. Arriving at the elbow, he abruptly dropped her arm and exclaimed "Oh, I forgot, your husband doesn't like my music!"[3] According to Vera, he appeared on the strength of six hastily consumed vodkas to be tipsy.

It is interesting to note that, after hearing Stravinsky's *Symphony of Psalms* for the first time, Newman wrote: "The general effect was to make us wonder what has lately become of the man of genius who produced some of the earlier works of the same composer. . . . In the case of Stravinsky it has been a matter of failure due to a persistent attempt to assert himself in a kind of music for which he has the minimum of aptitude."[4] Newman did, however, change his opinion of this masterpiece after subsequent hearings; he maintained over the years a generally enlightened and perceptive appraisal of Stravinsky's music.

He did, nevertheless, indulge in ironic sallies which, to the extent that they are remembered, have turned against him. Only a musical eccentric would say, today, as he did then of the *Symphonies of Wind Instruments in Memory of Debussy* (1920): "I had no idea that Stravinsky disliked Debussy as much as this. If my own memories of a friend were as painful as Stravinsky's of Debussy appear to be, I would try to forget him. . . . His music used to be original; now it is aboriginal."

In Rome the ubiquitous Diaghilev had gathered a circle of friends around him; they included Gerald Tyrwhitt, who, as Lord Berners, later acquired fame as composer and painter, being commissioned by the impresario to write the music of the ballet *The Triumph of Neptune*. It is sad that the fine suite from this ballet has vanished from concert-hall programmes, and gratifying that we still enjoy, in odd revivals here and there, his music for the ballet *Les Sirènes*, which mischievously recaptures the qualities of 'high life' in the Victorian era.

Stravinsky also met Prokofiev, who had rushed to Rome to discuss the composition of a new ballet commissioned by Diaghilev, and found him in every way remarkable. Prokofiev, like Stravinsky, came to know the venom-spitting reaction of diehards opposed to any new artistic creed or trend, and one critic wrote that in his brilliant score for Fokine's ballet *Sur le Borysthène* "a sort of polyrhythmic agitation causes the music to give way under the dancers' feet like a quicksand. The texture is constantly torn, the themes change sharply without sustained development and without a continuous music from the wind instruments or the strings allowing the ballet master to unfold in harmonious fashion the logical sequences of movement and rest".

After spending a fortnight in Italy with Diaghilev, mulling over various projects, Stravinsky returned to Switzerland and, staying with his family in a hotel at Château d'Oex, he hunted for a music room in which to compose. A friendly music dealer provided him with a lumber room, cluttered with packing cases and opening out on to a chicken run, but, by the grace of God, containing a new, though badly tuned piano. The room was so cold that it might have been used by Mimi in *La Bohème*, and Stravinsky, fortified by a rug across his knees, muffled up in a great over-coat, tried vainly to work there. He looked around again, and in the village managed to rent a large comfortable room, where he installed a piano. There he not only continued work on *The Wedding*, but also tackled a new piece which subsequently became his *Reynard* suite. Both works have their origins in folk poems. *Reynard*, a burlesque scored for thirteen wind instruments and percussion (with male voices) appeared in two ballet versions in 1922 and 1929, after being commissioned by the Princess Edmond de Polignac. It represents a complete break with the romantic past that dominated Stravinsky when he wrote *Petrushka* and *The Rite of Spring*. Opened and closed by 'village-band' music for trumpet, cymbal and drum, and spiced by the falsetto swooping of the singers, *Reynard* has a pungent tone colour that heralded a new phase in Stravinsky's life.

At the suggestion of Diaghilev, the composer chose Michel Larionov to design the Reynard sets and costumes. A huge, blond man who looked more like a Russian serf than a painter, Larionov had an uncontrollable temper and once knocked the impresario down during a quarrel. He had —strangely for a man who sparked with violence—an incurable streak of laziness.

Diaghilev visited Stravinsky in Switzerland in the spring of 1915, renting a property at Ouchy, where, surrounded by an artistic coterie, including the dancer Massine, the painters Larionov, Gontcharova and Bakst, the dancing-master Cecchetti, the conductor Ansermet, and a troupe of dancers, the composer shared in the preparations then being made for a season in the United States which the impresario was negotiating.

Stravinsky was fond of the picturesque town of Ouchy, the port of Lausanne. With its tiny, steep little streets, and unreal, almost toyland atmosphere, it provided a perfect setting for his creative activities. There, at Vidy-Plage, the visitor finds the biggest and probably the most beautiful beach in Switzerland. In the vicinity of Ouchy are small villages, each with their ports, a profusion of plane trees, flowers, boats, and seagulls clustering around the stone jetty. The town can boast of some historical interest, aside from its association with Stravinsky. It was at the Hôtel de l'Ancre, now called the Hôtel d'Angleterre, that Byron and Shelley had to stay two days through stormy weather after boating across from Diodati, and there, in 1816, as a commemorative tablet proclaims, *The Prisoner of Chillon* was written.

At the time of Diaghilev's arrival, Stravinsky's youngest daughter had the measles and, not surprisingly, the impresario, who dreaded any contact with sick people, kept well away until the contagion had vanished. Stravinsky joined Diaghilev as soon as he could and played for him the first two tableaux of *The Wedding,* which the impresario immediately liked. The composer dedicated the work to him.

Stravinsky originally planned to use a large symphony orchestra for *The Wedding*; but, influenced by Schoenberg's *Pierrot Lunaire,* he decided instead to score the first two tableaux for a mechanical piano, a harmonium, and percussion. The needs of the music, however, subsequently persuaded him to change the grouping of instruments, and he substituted four pianos, timpani, bells, xylophone and percussion.

Serge Lifar, in his autobiography, paints a graphic picture of Stravinsky, years later, directing rehearsals of *The Wedding* at Monte Carlo:

> The first time I saw Stravinsky was in the low, dark, damp rehearsal-room of the Russian Ballet. I was astonished by his appearance. He was thin and he stooped. His head was rather bald and his great forehead betokened intelligence. I wondered who such a monkey could be—he wriggled about, thumped the keys, panted, made up for missing chords by kicks on the pedal . . . or to keep up the tempo he would bring his elbows crashing down on the piano.
>
> It was fascinating. Sometimes he would abruptly break off . . . and then the storm of sound would start up again louder than ever . . . it was very Russian, also. As the artists could make out only with difficulty the sounds and accents of the score, he had a barrel-organ sent down from Paris and on its rolls was inscribed the music of the ballet. We then had the extraordinary spectacle of an accompanist transformed into a mechanic and turning the handle![5]

How, one wonders, did the young Stravinsky appear to the other members of the artistic group gathered around Diaghilev in his Swiss retreat? Throughout his life there was something mystical and monarchistic about the composer, who loved to adorn his walls with ikons and portraits of the Emperor Nicholas II and his children. His colleagues must have found him a vivid and interesting personality; particularly the dancing master Cecchetti. The hot Italian temperament flowing in his veins, coupled with the irascibility and impatience of a strolling player, made Cecchetti an uncommonly picturesque figure, and he warmed to similar characteristics in others. As for the painter Bakst, he was a magician with a brush, able to reproduce the intimate, almost breathing lines of the human body on paper or canvas in the most vivid, arresting perspectives. He created many wonderful adjuncts for Diaghilev's productions, including the costumes of the Firebird and the Princess Unearthly Beauty, and the scenery for the one-act ballet *Narcisse*, set to Tcherepnin's haunting music.

The awe-inspiring vistas, the visions of transcendental beauty which the Russian Ballet presented in its productions may have dazzled audiences, but to the watchers backstage—including, on many occasions, Igor Stravinsky—it was the curiously segmented glimpses of the sets, and the paraphernalia behind the illusions, that proved spellbinding. A fragrance unlike any other, compounded of grease-paint, scarcely dry scenery and the different perfumes used by the dancers, hung in the air made vibrant by subdued whispers and the strange grating noise caused by a ballerina rubbing her shod foot in the resin-box. During a ballet performance the watcher in the wings feels caught up in the spectacle, as through the gap between each of two wings, chains of dancers in white ballet skirts flash past like swans skimming a lake. Other dancers, performing a *grand jeté* or a series of *petits tours*, glide into, or from the wings; and in the shadows, positioning herself for an entrance, another ballerina, sometimes bathed in the multi-coloured lights that flood the stage with paradisal tints, crosses herself and invokes God's blessing. Seen in close perspective the faces of the dancers, heavy with make-up, have a bizarre, insect-like appearance. Between the scenes wings glide swiftly upwards; others descend as if from heaven; loops and lines of rope, with sandbags for counter-balances, hurtle to and fro.

Not only the sheer mechanics of this balletic dream-world fascinated Stravinsky, but also the music that irradiated every facet of a production; for the whole success of a ballet depends largely upon the tempo at which the music is taken. If a dance is taken too slowly, the dancer must expand, or inflate the movements to fit the music; conversely, if it goes too fast, he must accelerate his movements to correspond. A bad conductor can make a dance-sequence that is intended to be noble and expressive turn into one that is merely fussy and irritating; he can also transform a sweetly humorous scene into one of shallow charm and ill-defined, elusive comedy. Stravinsky gave much to the Russian Ballet—his genius, his loyalty and his love; but he also gained a priceless insight into the unique, three-dimensional world of the theatre.

Diaghilev decided, before going with the Russian Ballet to America, to stage in the Paris Opera House for the benefit of the Red Cross a grand gala performance of a number of ballets, including Stravinsky's *The Firebird* and Massine's first choreographic creation *Le Soleil de Minuit*, based on excerpts from Rimsky-Korsakov's opera *Snegourotchka*. A kind of preliminary 'dress rehearsal' took place at Genoa; then, at the Paris presentation, Stravinsky made a successful conductor of his own *Firebird*.

He undoubtedly had a gift for conducting, but not a supreme one; for manipulating a baton intelligently before a group of experienced players confronted with a challenging score is as difficult and specialized a task as that of a master goldsmith. For the conductor there is a perpetual compromise between what is happening *now* and what, from his knowledge and instinct, he *wishes* were happening—it calls for an infallible, split-second reaction. Stravinsky may have had it; but he did not always use it. His own Symphony in C begins with repeated notes all over the orchestra written out in quavers with no dots on them. The idiomatic flavour of the music suggests that these should be played short, off the string; yet Stravinsky, when he conducted this work, played them on the string, as, in fairness, other maestros have done. It is, to me, the wrong way to perform the music; but this is one of those occasions when the critic grudgingly defers to the composer.

Diaghilev, an extremely poor sailor, embarked for America, deeply moved, not only at being separated from Stravinsky, but at the thought that he might never reach those hospitable shores. In the meantime Stravinsky, perturbed at the submarine danger to his friend, sought refuge from worry in his *Reynard* sketches and asked the Princess Edmond de Polignac to present the work as a drawing-room entertainment in her stately home, to which she readily agreed, although it was never actually performed there. Her salons were famous and, as the kindly and always approachable patron of the Russian Ballet, she helped to bring many great productions to the stage.

At Morges, in Switzerland, the composer, working hard on the score of *Reynard*, received a welcome visit from Nijinsky and his wife. Morges, a typical Swiss lakeside town with a famous line of ancient elms, a fine thirteenth-century castle, and a profusion of houses brightened by geraniums, zinnias and nasturtiums clustered around the windows or growing in the gardens, provided the tranquil atmosphere which Stravinsky needed at that time. Romola Nijinsky, in her brilliant biography of her husband, described Stravinsky, whom she was now meeting for the first time, as being dressed like a dandy, with excellent taste. He regarded his appearance as very chic and displayed a certain naïveté and conceit. According to her, Stravinsky spoke in a rather childish way about his own genius; there was nothing dignified about his confident self-assessment, yet it had a certain charm. In the company of Vaslav Nijinsky he poured out a torrent of words, explaining his compositions, his plans for the future, and his opinion of Diaghilev. "I am a composer, and sooner or later people will realize the value of my music," declared Stravinsky proudly. "Of course, Serge Pavlovich is a great help, and especially now that the war is on. In Russia, anyway, it is impossible to be played, if one has modern ideas. He can't crush me. His enmity against you I fully disapprove; but we must be just; he suffered terribly when he heard that you had married—he never imagined this possible."[6]

Stravinsky made friends with Vaslav and Romola Nijinsky's daughter, Kyra, and, according to her mother, showed himself to be tactful, kind, communicative, and an expert handler of children. When Nijinsky and his wife visited Stravinsky at his villa they found a beautifully furnished, but simple house that by imagination and artistry had been transformed into a type of dwelling found near Moscow; drawings by Stravinsky's eldest son, Theodore, a gifted artist, adorned the walls; an atmosphere of peace and contentment filled the rooms. Madame Stravinsky excelled in handicrafts; she embroidered, knitted, and painted superbly.

Romola Nijinsky described a heated discussion which arose between Stravinsky and her husband. The composer bitterly attacked Beethoven, Bach and other titans whom, a few years previously, he had respected; now dismissing them contemptuously as "the Boches". He again extolled his own genius. "Why should we show any regard towards these Boches, when my own publishers in Germany are not publishing me at present? God knows if they will go on distributing the compositions of Tchaikovsky and Rubinstein."[7] One evening Stravinsky came to the dancer and his wife in a raging temper, complaining of what he called "a dirty trick played on me by Diaghilev". The impresario had promised that, while in New York, he would arrange for an official invitation to be extended to Stravinsky so that he could go and conduct his own ballets at the Metropolitan and, in this way, present himself to the American public. Fascinated by the spectacles and opportunities of that great city, Diaghilev forgot his promise, or at least made no effort to fulfil it. Stravinsky, hurt and angry, shouted and wept, pacing up and down the room as he cursed the impresario. "He thinks he is the Russian Ballet himself. Our success went to his head. Where would he be without us . . . !"[8] The composer subsequently learned that Diaghilev had been greatly distressed at his failure to visit the Metropolitan on his behalf.

Before Nijinsky and his wife visited Stravinsky in Switzerland they had been caught by the war in Hungary and interned there. They owed their freedom to the loyalty and persistence of Diaghilev, who moved almost insuperable obstacles to obtain it.

While composing *Reynard*, for which he put *The Wedding* aside, Stravinsky succumbed to the magic of what was, for him, a new instrument, the Hungarian cimbalom. He first heard it at a little restaurant in Geneva, being played by Aladar Racz, a Hungarian (since recognized as a master exponent), and admired its full, rich sound, as well as the manner in which the performer, holding little sticks between his fingers, made direct contact with the strings. He managed, with Racz's help, to find an old Hungarian in Geneva who possessed a cimbalom; this he bought and, carrying it off to Morges in high delight, set about learning to play it. Soon he could manipulate the sticks so capably that he was able to compose a part for the instrument which he introduced into the score of *Reynard*.

He saw much of his friend Ramuz at this time and together they worked on the French translation of the Russian text of Stravinsky's *Pribaoutki*, Cat's Cradle Songs and *Reynard*. The composer expressed his astonishment at Ramuz's insight and intuitive gift for transferring the spirit and lilt of the Russian folk poems into a language so remote and different as French. He found his friend a lively and stimulating person, with a natural kindness which he poured generously on everyone except his own wife, whom he had been obliged to marry and whom he called Mademoiselle in a hard, rasping voice in front of his associates.

Diaghilev, on his way from America to Switzerland in the spring of 1916, arrived at Madrid in Spain. He sent word to Stravinsky, who hastened to join him. The impresario had figuratively died of fright many times during the voyage in an Italian ship filled with munitions and hunted by submarines; he embraced Stravinsky with even more affection than usual—"I have been waiting for you like a brother," he said. On crossing the Spanish frontier, the composer entered a new and unfamiliar world. It was spring. The distant sound of a *banda* playing a *passadoble* drifted into his hotel room; the sunlight dappled the pavements and the gaudy bazaars, making a scene worthy of the brush-strokes of Bakst. Two trips to Toledo and the Escorial gave Stravinsky a revealing glimpse of the profoundly religious temperament of the Spanish people, and the mystical depth of a Catholicism akin to the Orthodoxy of Russia. He spent whole evenings in picturesque taverns, listening to the strumming of guitars and the singing of native ballads.

A strange combination of royal grandeur with monastic austerity, the Escorial, sprawling across a gigantic square, contains sixteen courts, eighty-eight fountains, three chapels, fifteen cloisters and eighty-six staircases. The visitor is dazzled, as Stravinsky undoubtedly was, by its fabulously beautiful carpets, porcelain, and tapestries; its magnificent church, shaped like a Greek cross, with a priceless library of 40,000 rare books; and its exotic Pantheon, where repose nearly all the kings and queens of Spain.

Falla, whom Stravinsky met and admired, came from Southern Spain, and something of the mystery and brilliance of his music can be found in that of the Russian composer. One can imagine Stravinsky warming to the evocative, half Oriental manner of the Andalusian or Catalan regions, where Falla's parents were born; and to the curiously mixed components of Spain's musical tradition: the sixteenth-century religious classics, the theatrical *zarzuelas* and street music of the eighteenth and nineteenth centuries, and that wonderfully virile, earthy folk music which, for so long, has been inseparable from popular culture. Yet although Stravinsky paid tribute to the distinctive character of Spanish folk music, he confessed that he found no revelation in it. Debussy was fascinated by the Javanese music which he heard for the first time at the Paris World Exhibition of 1889; those exotic gamelans, coupled with the subtle virtuosity of the players, gave him new and ravishing auditory experiences. It is difficult to believe that Stravinsky did not feel, in some degree, the same tingling stimuli when he encountered at first hand the picturesque tunes and whirling rhythms of Spain.

At Madrid in 1917, the following year, Nijinsky rejoined the company. His presence proved as embarrassing as that of Gloria Swanson did in the Hollywood studio where, acting the part of an ageing film star of the silent screen, she found herself completely out of touch with the progressive flow of events. Nijinsky was still young, but he discovered a new galaxy of talent around Diaghilev, who had ceased to depend for success upon great names like those of Nijinsky, Karsavina and Fokine. Nijinsky might still be a superb dancer, but the shadows of insanity were already spreading crepuscular fingers over his life, and meanwhile Leonide Massine, another exceedingly gifted dancer, had succeeded Fokine as Diaghilev's chief choreographer.

"The King is dead, long live the King" seems to be an apt comment on the situation which Nijinsky encountered. As he brooded, like a deposed Emperor, upon the base ingratitude of those around him, his relationship and that of his wife, with Diaghilev became frayed beyond repair; and when the company moved on to Barcelona poor Nijinsky's nerves had come very close to breaking point. The screaming injustice and degradation of his downfall, as he saw it, created a paranoiac resentment that burned inside him like a huge, incurable cancer. His fame had been unparalleled. He had dazzled Paris, London, New York and Buenos Aires with his mastery of characterization, his sublime grace as a dancer and his incredible, almost superhuman gift for *elevation*, or rising, like Elijah, into the air. Now he found himself no longer a god, a myth, but simply a member of Diaghilev's company; respected, but on an equal footing with the other principals.

In Barcelona the public, doubtless lured by the magic of Nijinsky's name, flocked to the theatre, filling every seat. This might have pleased the neurotic dancer, but for the fact that Diaghilev's posters gave him no star billing, concentrating, instead, on the merits of the company as a whole. Nijinsky, convinced now that the impresario, having utilized his rare gifts for his own selfish ends, wanted to push him into the background, seethed with hatred; and one day, after a few performances had been given, prepared with his wife to depart from the scene of his ignominy. Unhappily for the couple, Diaghilev, passing the hotel where they had been staying, saw their luggage piled up in the doorway. He made enquiries and, learning of the impending desertion, called first on his lawyer, then on the governor of the city. Two policemen visited Nijinsky and, reminding him of his contract, ordered him to remain in Barcelona.

When the company left for a South American tour, the Nijinskys agreed to go only because Diaghilev, who feared sea travel, refused to accompany them. The wretched dancer, his mind now clouding with the malady that was to destroy him, moved into a paranoiac nightmare. He insisted on taking part in performances not provided for in his contract; when discouraged from doing so, and informed that he could not be paid for such unauthorized appearances, Nijinsky suspected the hatching of some diabolical plot. He ceased to smile; his eyes had a dreadful hunted look.

Matters reached crisis point in Buenos Aires where, imagining himself to be the victim of cunning hostility, he refused to step across the stage until someone had inspected the trapdoors or carefully scrutinized the boards to make sure that no projecting nails or broken glass awaited his unwary feet. Grigoriev, in his memoirs, brilliantly translated by Vera Bowen, related how Nijinsky, in the role of Narcissus, would refuse to be lowered through a trapdoor in case he was killed and, flinging himself on the floor, would lie there, trembling. During a performance of *L'Après-midi d'un Faune* he arrived late and in a tense, overwrought state; refused to take up his position on the Faun's rock; and, when the audience grew restive, had to be commanded, and practically forced, to obey the director's order. From that moment, tottering sanity gave up the unequal struggle. The last time he danced was at Buenos Aires on 26th September 1917, when, in *Le Spectre de la Rose*, he executed his famous, now final leap through the window, and when, in *Petrushka*, the vicious Moor sealed his death with a dagger blow.

Stravinsky's preoccupation with *Reynard*, and the task of adapting his friend Ramuz's translation to the notation, kept him busy at Morges in 1916; but also—to help amateurs unskilled in using the instrument—he wrote Five Easy Pieces for piano duet, with a simplified part for the right hand. Concerning the Three Tales for Children which he composed during this period (*Tilim-Bom*, amplified and orchestrated by Stravinsky at a later date; *Chansons de l'Ours*; and the *Berceuse* mentioned in a subsequent page of this book) one is conscious of a unique musicianship applied like a jeweller's cutting-tool to plain, but increasingly bright facets.

During the winter of 1916–17 some of Stravinsky's compositions, including *Reynard*, the *Pribaoutki*, and the Cat's Cradle Songs appeared in print, thanks to the generosity of friends who met the costs of publication. Shortly before Christmas he suffered a harrowing attack of intercostal neuralgia, which at times made it almost impossible for him to breathe. The illness persisted into the New Year, and by then his legs, partly paralysed, could scarcely support him; but the skill and devotion of Dr Demieville, a professor at Lausanne, brought him back from the shadows. Diaghiliv visited Stravinsky and discussed future projects. The composer, who wanted to create an orchestral symphonic poem of the second and third acts of *The Nightingale*, offered to place this at Diaghilev's disposal

F

as the basis for a ballet and, when the impresario agreed, promptly adapted a scenario from Andersen's fairy-story to serve his purpose. He worked on this and *The Wedding* as soon as he was fit enough to do so.

After the completion of *Reynard*, the Princess de Polignac presented Stravinsky with a cigarette-holder shaped like a pipe and made of ostrich feathers and gold. She subsequently wrote a warm-hearted account of her visit to Stravinsky's house at Morges,[9] admiring his wife; a striking figure—pale, thin, full of dignity—who, surrounded by her delicate, fair-haired young children, looked like a princess in a Russian fairy-tale. It was a clear, moonlit night when the visitor arrived, and the house, brilliantly illuminated like a starry Christmas tree, made her welcome, its bright interior, "decorated in the warm colours that the Russian Ballet had brought to Paris", seeming like a beneficent sanctuary. At dinner, served on a table with glimmering candles, she enjoyed a superb Russian cuisine with zakousky, borsch, tender sterlets coated in succulent jelly and served with a heavenly sauce, various dishes of fowl, and an incredible variety of sweets.

Meanwhile, in Russia the February Revolution swept away many of the cultural landmarks and customs that Stravinsky had known as a boy. The Tsar had abdicated and a provisional government of men with stern faces and resentful eyes ruled the country. In St Petersburg the splendid Maryinsky Theatre, shorn of its eagles and Imperial arms, with the attendants wearing dirty jackets instead of smart liveries, looked almost a different place. When the raging fires and the ruthless cannonades had ended, the soldiers went from house to house, reassuring the terrified inhabitants, and an uneasy optimism settled over the city, soon to be dispelled when the second phase of the Revolution thundered down upon them. The remote Front, a flimsy, ramshackle defence cracking before a hurricane, disgorged a flood of hungry, frantic deserters. Soon, millions of people, crawling like ants under self-imposed burdens, were on the move. In many of the villages the peasants demanded a fair division of the land, and factories that might have provided work and sustenance were strike-bound. Hostility and suspicion tainted the air; spy rumours passed from mouth to mouth until no-one felt safe; looters and murderers roamed the streets. The sinister prophecy of Rasputin—that victim of a gruesome assassination—came home to roost.

Stravinsky, summoned to Rome in 1917 by Diaghilev, who wanted him to conduct *The Firebird* and *Fireworks* at an Italian Red Cross gala performance at the Constanzi Theatre, could hardly, in these circumstances, open the programme with the customary National Anthem. The impresario chose as a substitute the famous Volga Boat Song, for which, alas, no parts were available for the orchestra. Throughout the night before the concert Stravinsky, seated at the piano in Lord Berners's apartment, scored the song for orchestra, while Ernest Ansermet, fortified with sheafs of music paper, wrote it down, note for note, as he dictated it. The performance next evening opened with the Italian National Anthem, followed by the Volga Boat Song in its new orchestral dress.

For the stage production of *Fireworks* the set was designed by Balla, who put what Stravinsky described as a few splashes of paint on an otherwise empty backcloth. It puzzled the audience, as well as the composer, so that when, at the close of the performance, Balla came out to bow, a chilly silence greeted him. This derived, not from hostility, but from a sense of bewilderment and the fact that the audience did not know who he was and why he should be bowing and smiling before them. To the astonishment and delight of Stravinsky, the resourceful Balla popped a hand into his pocket and, squeezing a rubber bulb, made his necktie do pantomime tricks. Alas, his boyish fun failed to titivate the audience, who remained silent. Stravinsky found Balla an immensely droll and likeable character.

The composer's autobiography has bequeathed to us no vivid word-pictures of the great theatres in which Diaghilev staged his ballets; but it is interesting to note that at least one of them, the Constanzi Theatre, where the Italian Red Cross charity event took place, had a tradition almost as splendid as that of the Maryinsky. Added to this, there had been, only thirteen years previously, a performance nearly as sensational as that of *The Rite of Spring* in Paris.

Built in 1880 by Domenico Constanzi to the design of the great architect Achille Sfondrini, it opened on 27th November of that year with Rossini's *La Semiramide*. The new theatre, lit by gas and seating 2,200 people, dazzled the citizens of Rome with its painted opulence. In 1887 electricity was installed. At the Rossini première an audience described as "youthful, beautiful and elegant", with a generous sprinkling of princesses, duchesses and countesses, filled the auditorium. The first tier of boxes contained the officers of the garrison regiment of Rome. As the orchestra burst into the *Marcia Reale*, the King and Queen entered their box. Apparently the performance surpassed for longevity even that of *Götterdämmerung* given sixteen years later at Bayreuth, since it ended at a quarter to one in the morning.

It was the performance of *Tosca*, staged on the night of 14th January 1900, that elicited the hot breath of scandal. Puccini, enthusing over the example of Mascagni in taking *Cavalleria* from a play presented to the public with the superb Eleonora Duse in the leading role, decided to adapt for the opera house the melodrama which had shown Sarah Bernhardt at the height of her powers. This, for some reason, caused resentment among a section of the theatre-going public. Puccini, after discussing *Tosca* with Sardou, and his own librettist Illica, in Paris, felt uneasy over the last act, disliking even the music he had written for it. "Questa é l'aria del paletot!" he exclaimed. ("This music will make the audience put on their coats and leave!")

On the night of the première, shortly before the curtain rose, Mugnone, the conductor, warned Puccini that a bomb might be thrown in the theatre, and the presence of an agitated Chief of Police seemed to confirm the possibility of this disaster. Mugnone had orders to play the *Marcia Reale* if a disturbance arose. The audience may have heard the sinister threat; the artistes clearly knew of it. As the curtain lifted, a hullabaloo filled the theatre. The patrons muttered, grumbled and, in some instances, vacated their seats, while the singers, upset and nervous, with a few women sobbing loudly, could hardly face the footlights. Shouts of "Ring down the curtain!" assailed them. Happily, both Mugnone and Puccini kept cool, and succeeded by their example in restoring sanity. The noise subsided and *Tosca*, staged without any more unseemly incidents, won the hearts of most of those who saw and heard it.

Work on rebuilding and improving this magnificent theatre began in 1926, and it became one of the most influential opera houses of the world; but at the time Igor Stravinsky conducted *The Firebird* and *Fireworks* there it had the Raphaelesque beauty and ambience which Sfondrini gave to it.

Stravinsky, accompanied by Diaghilev, Picasso, whom he had recently met for the first time, Massine, and other members of the company, spent a fortnight in Naples. They encountered, not the butter-yellow sunshine and azure blue of the picture postcards, but a dirty grey sky, with a dense mist hanging over the summit of Vesuvius. Stravinsky and Picasso wandered like delighted schoolchildren round the famous aquarium, which lies in the centre of the public park stretching between the Riviera di Chiaia and the sea. Opened by Dr Anton Dohrn in 1874 and probably the first of its kind, it has remained one of the great sights of Naples. The live octopus, hideous at one moment and beautiful the next, doubtless enthralled Stravinsky and his companion. Moving by a primitive system of jet propulsion, it ceases, on rising to the surface of the tank, to be a horrid tangle of probing tentacles and, as it floats upwards, folding its arms to its sides and gliding like a ballet dancer, displays the simple poetry of motion. Perhaps the sight of the rainbow-tinted fish in some of the other tanks evoked in Picasso those exquisite Baudelairean sensibilities which fructified so magically in *Fishing by Night at Antibes*.

I like to believe that Stravinsky and his companion also visited the exquisite church of S. Lorenzo, where Boccaccio first saw and loved his Fiametta; the lofty cathedral, built upon the site of a temple of Apollo, where the heart and blood of Saint Januarius are kept in a gorgeous chapel glittering with gold, silver and precious stones; the Castle of the Egg, created, so legend has it, by Virgil—a veritable wizard's fortress—rising majestic and uncouth against the skyline; and the dusty Piazza del

Mercato, where on an autumn day in 1268 the Hohenstaufen dynasty was extinguished in the person of a brave, sixteen-year-old boy, Conradin, killed at the instigation of the Papacy by Charles of Anjou.

Picasso must have found his association with Stravinsky and the Russian Ballet a rewarding one. Reticent and Spanish in appearance, the painter, when he began to explain anything, fairly shook with excitement. In cafés and restaurants he used to draw on table-cloths, on menu cards, and on Diaghilev's ivory walking-stick. Many of Picasso's friends, including Apollinaire and Braque, had been mobilized. It was Jean Cocteau who, rushing into his *atelier* one day, dressed as Harlequin, dragged him into a new and fascinating world—that of the theatre. Urged on by the enthusiastic Cocteau, the painter took Cubism on to the stage by designing sets and costumes for the ballet *Parade*. He went with the company first to Rome, then to Madrid and Barcelona, and finally to London, collaborating brilliantly with Goncharova, Bakst and Benois. In 1918 he married Olga Khoklova, a dancer in Diaghilev's company; the wedding took place at the Russian Church in the rue Darie, Paris, with the couple wearing crowns in the customary Orthodox ritual. Seventeen years later, already divided by their clashing temperaments, they separated. Olga, paralytic and eaten by cancer, died at Cannes in 1954.

After returning to Rome with his friends to spend a week with Lord Berners, the composer set off for Switzerland and, while crossing the frontier at Chiasso, fell foul of the military authorities, who clearly regarded him as a spy. The cause of the trouble? A portrait of himself which Picasso had drawn in Rome. Nothing could convince the interrogators that it was not a plan devised with devilish cunning and of strategic importance. The officials excitedly scanned the portrait; their faces hardened and their eyes narrowed; they whispered meaningfully together, then flung a voluble accusation at the bewildered and angry composer. "This is not a portrait. It is a plan. What have you to say?"[10] Stravinsky, never taciturn when prodded by some petty irritant, had plenty to say, and treated the officials to a prolonged and picturesque assessment of their stupidity. He assured them that, if plan it was, then it represented only the apoplectic face they saw before them. The officials smiled disbelievingly and, in the end, he had to despatch the portrait, in Lord Berners's name, to the British Ambassador in Rome, who subsequently redirected it to Paris in a diplomatic bag.

At Morges, in December 1917, Stravinsky composed a *Berceuse*, or lullaby for his little daughter Ludmila, known to the family as Mika or Mitoucha. Earlier in the year he had written his Canons for Two Horns, a gift and tribute to the kindly Swiss doctor who cured Ludmila of appendicitis and would take no payment from Stravinsky but music. 1917 also saw the first performance, at Geneva, of his Four Russian Peasant Songs (*Saucers*) for unaccompanied female voices, which he began writing in

1914. Stravinsky explained in his *Expositions and Developments* that choruses of this kind were sung by Russian peasants while fortune-tellers read their finger-prints on the smoke-blackened bottoms of saucers.

In the space of only a few months two crushing blows fell upon Stravinsky. The first was the death of old Bertha, the nurse of his childhood days, whom he had brought to Morges at the beginning of the war. In his *Expositions and Developments* the composer described Bertha as the "safest" person in his childish world and her voice the most loving he ever heard in those early days. She had played an almost maternal role in his affections, and the news of her passing, which followed the bursting of a blood-vessel, saddened him immeasurably. The second calamity was the death of his brother Goury who, fighting with the Russian Army on the Rumanian front, succumbed to typhus. They had explored diverse paths, but Igor loved him deeply. The visits of friends during this tragic period helped to console him. He continued working on the final scene of *The Wedding* and also wrote a piece for the pianola, which he subsequently orchestrated under the title *Madrid*.

6

"PULCINELLA"—A DISCOVERY
OF THE PAST

Throughout this period, towards the end of 1917, Stravinsky found himself in choppy financial waters, likely at any moment to sink. The pitifully small income which had trickled into Switzerland from his own land suddenly dried up as the Revolution swept like a prairie fire across Russia. Machine-guns rattled in the streets of St Petersburg; barricades, fencing in the Winter Palace Square, created a cemetery for the bodies that sprawled there; grim-faced soldiers, with bayonets and a lust to kill, searched houses and flats for 'traitors', while the blood of the Russian royal family seeped into the crevices of the cellar in which they had been butchered. Lenin, with a greasy cap for a crown, sat on the throne, and all over Russia the word 'comrade' served as a talisman when Death knocked at the door.

Not only did the Revolution deprive Stravinsky of a country, but also, as he believed, of a nationality; and World War I, breaching the fortress of Diaghilev's finances, thus raised a new signpost for the composer in his Unknown Country. Seeking to produce a fresh source of income, Stravinsky and his friend Ramuz conceived the idea of establishing a little travelling theatre that could be transported easily from one place to another. They discussed this crazy venture, as it then seemed, with Ansermet, chosen to direct the orchestra, and with Auberjonais, who agreed to design the sets and costumes. All they needed was a wealthy patron to subsidize the project, and luckily Werner Reinhart of Winterthur, a man noted with his brother for generosity to the arts, came to the rescue.

The gallant enterprise concentrated for its productions on Afanasyev's famous collection of Russian tales and, in particular, on the cycle of legends dealing with the adventures of a soldier who deserted, and the Devil who came to carry off his soul. Both Stravinsky and Ramuz felt a deep human compassion for the unhappy soldier, and out of this *The Soldier's Tale* was born. In spite of Stravinsky's own reservations about it, the work not only satisfied the artistic criteria relevant to what he termed "a total experience" but also proved to be a financial success. In this early example of his post-war retrenchment, he began the dissolution of certain old musical traditions by substituting narration for singing, and adding dance. Written on and for a shoestring budget, when the composer scarcely knew where to turn for sustenance, *The Soldier's Tale* is the ideal choice for those seeking to provide good entertainment cheaply.

Stravinsky and his friends worked hard at *The Soldier's Tale* throughout the first half of 1918, the year in which he also wrote a trifle called Duet for Two Bassoons. The music of *The Soldier's Tale*, humble and demotic in style, was scored for seven solo instruments. He used in it an Argentinian tango, a Viennese waltz, American rag-time (which the soldier plays to the sick princess) and a Bach-like chorale which, in tones recalling Luther's mighty hymn, expresses the victory of faith and unity over dark, demoniac forces. Yet, characteristic of the sadness which impregnated Stravinsky's own soul at this time, it is the Devil who finally triumphs, carrying the soldier to Hell against a background of ironically percussive and brutalistic music.

Stravinsky believed in drama, and in later years often talked about them to his mystical friend Aldous Huxley, in whose memory he wrote his deeply moving *Variations*. He confessed of *The Soldier's Tale* that the violin music came to him in a dream in which he saw a woman sitting with a baby on her knees and playing a violin to amuse it. He remembered the music next morning.

The highly successful première of this work, given in a small Victorian theatre at Lausanne on 28th September 1918, with professional actors and university students filling the stage parts, owed much to the discerning musicianship of Ansermet, whom Stravinsky warmly praised. Over the years this great conductor championed many contemporary composers— Debussy, Ravel, Bartók, Berg, Hindemith and others—who needed a sympathetic advocate to overcome prejudice or indifference. He had an intellect of the finest calibre.

René Auberjonais, a Swiss painter and intimate of Ramuz, designed the sets. A veil depicting two fountain jets, with a boat rowing on top of each one, served as the outer stage curtain. For the tiny inner stage Auberjonais created painted oilcloths showing vivid pictures purposefully unrelated to the text. The Princess wore bright red stockings and a fluffy white tu-tu; the narrator a dress-coat, and the soldier looked smart and handsome in the uniform of a 1918 Swiss army private. Wearing suitable costumes, the Devil appeared successively as a lepidopterist, a French-Swiss cattle merchant, an old woman, and, returning to his true self at the end of the play, with forked tail and pointed ears. Some years later Massine produced *The Soldier's Tale* as a dance diversion at Covent Garden for himself and Lydia Lopokova.

Alas, just as the Devil came for the unhappy soldier in Stravinsky's dream-composition, so disaster, in the guise of Spanish influenza, called first upon one member of the Russian Ballet, then another. This humble, but merciless contagion, spreading across Europe, not only kept Stravinsky to his bed for a lengthy period, but also completely destroyed the little travelling theatre enterprise. It did not, however, prevent him from succumbing to another and more kindly epidemic—that of jazz, whose popular appeal and freshness did much to brighten his outlook. A pile of jazz music sent to Stravinsky by Ansermet inspired him at Morges in 1918 to compose his *Ragtime* for eleven instruments, wind, string, percussion and—one is hardly surprised at the choice—a Hungarian cimbalom.

How he loved this prima-donna of gypsy instruments, with its bright tinkling sounds. One is reminded of the boyish delight which Tchaikovsky showed when, in 1891, shortly after he had commenced work on the Waltz of the Snow-Flakes for *Casse-Noisette*, he stopped at Paris, on his way to America, and was introduced to a celeste by Victor Mustel, a well-known maker of musical instruments. Tchaikovsky had never seen or heard one before. He raved over its "heavenly" timbre, and immediately recognized its delicate, fairy-like quality as being ideally suited to the new ballet. He had one sent to St Petersburg with great secrecy. "I am afraid," he wrote, "that Rimsky-Korsakov and Glazunov might acquire one and use the novel effect before me. I expect this new instrument will produce a tremendous sensation."[1]

Stravinsky invited Picasso to design a cover for *Ragtime* and the painter did so, drawing six figures, each from a single, uninterrupted line, one of which he selected for publication. It appeared under the imprint of the Editions de la Sirene, Paris. The composer dedicated the work to Artur Rubinstein, hoping to encourage him to play contemporary music, and received 5,000 francs from the pianist.

If *Ragtime* did not seduce the critics, it added greatly to the composer's reputation when, some years later, he conducted it at one of Koussevitzky's concerts in the Paris Opera House. This music, though it may appear as merely a postscript to the devilish jazz fiddle-music of *The Soldier's Tale*, does introduce an attractive new element in the prominent concertante part given to the cimbalom. The glinting texture and chirpy regularity of metre which the work displays may disguise the existence of a heart, but they also transpose the self-consciously blithe or soulful manner of the Negro-inspired 'rag' into a musical experience more rational than that of the minstrel background from which it erupted.

After composing *Ragtime*, Stravinsky occupied himself with arranging certain fragments of *The Firebird* in the form of a suite, and with the creation of Four Russian Songs on folk poems translated by Ramuz. He wrote the Piano-Rag Music, which he dedicated to Artur Rubinstein. It sprang from his delight in the percussive possibilities of the piano, and with its clusters of "added" notes, has an earthy, swinging vigour. Stravinsky also composed the Three Pieces for Solo Clarinet, dedicating them to Werner Reinhart, who sponsored *The Soldier's Tale*. He visited Paris and met Diaghilev, who responded coldly to his enthusiastic account of the success of *The Soldier's Tale*. The impresario regarded any artistic triumph achieved by his colleagues outside the sphere of the Russian Ballet as a kind of defection or treachery. He overworked the members of his company, set them impossible tasks, and demanded an unquestioning deference to his wishes; yet music and the poetry of movement saturated his being and, for all his faults, he was a faithful, loving friend to those who served him.

Diaghilev, pleading with Stravinsky to return to the Russian Ballet, coaxed him, unsuccessfully, with new projects, but managed to interest him in the music of Pergolesi as the inspiration for another ballet. In *The Good-Humoured Ladies,* a brilliant new addition to the company's repertoire, the music had been adapted from Scarlatti's; and, as Diaghilev had collected some unpublished Pergolesi music from Italian libraries, he felt confident that Stravinsky could use it for a ballet based on a Neapolitan *commedia-dell'arte* plot. Stravinsky, tempted by the exotic Spanish flavour of Pergolesi's music, swallowed the bait, though he took some time to digest it.

For Stravinsky the task of creating *Pulcinella* involved frequent trips to Paris, lengthy conferences—sometimes ending in stormy scenes—with Diaghilev, Picasso and Massine, his collaborators. In the meantime, at Geneva, on 6th December 1919, Ernest Ansermet conducted the first performance by the Orchestra de la Suisse Romande of *The Song of the Nightingale* (the symphonic poem based on the last two acts of *The Nightingale* which Stravinsky wrote at Morges in 1917).

Massine, who choreographed *The Song of the Nightingale* for the ballet performed by the Diaghilev company at the Opera House, Paris on 2nd February 1920, with Ansermet conducting, chose the great painter Matisse to design the sets and costumes. He visited him at Nice shortly before rehearsals began and found him living in a penthouse flat. A giant birdcage, filled with hundreds of exotic birds from all over the world, occupied one of the best rooms. Matisse was so proud of his birds that he carried on his person an official affidavit testifying to the vocal range of his favourite nightingale. During a subsequent trip to Paris, he and Massine went to the Cluny Museum; standing in front of a Chinese warrior, the painter sketched it from different angles. For the ballet he reproduced the costume of the warrior, in his own inimitable way, for the costumes of the Emperor's bodyguard. Using the minimum of decorative detail, he designed a set imbued with all the charm and delicacy of Hans Andersen's imaginary Chinese court. Three friezes, with black-painted, scalloped edges, overhung a white backdrop. The dying Emperor, danced by Grigoriev, wore a black mantle; he loosened it, as he came to life at the end of the ballet and, flowing down, it covered about sixty square feet of the stage with its magnificent vermilion lining. Massine himself, striving to imitate the tiny segmented movements which he had seen in Chinese silk and lacquered screen paintings, created superb Oriental-flavoured dances. He chose Karsavina to play the real nightingale. In his own words "she floated on to the stage in a filmy white dress and danced the song of the nightingale, which saved the Emperor's life, with ethereal lightness and a haunting atmosphere of pathos. At the end of her dance she was joined in a lovely *pas de deux* by Sokolova, who danced the part of Death, vanquished by the thrilling song of the true nightingale".[2]

Stravinsky gave himself unstintingly to *Pulcinella*, finding yet another dazzling vista of his Unknown Country. Writing of this work, years later, in *Expositions and Developments*, he called it "my discovery of the past, the epiphany through which the whole of my late work became possible. It was a backward look, of course,—the first of many love affairs in that direction—but it was a look in the mirror, too. No critic understood this at the time, and I was therefore attacked for being a *pasticheur*, chided for composing 'simple' music, blamed for deserting 'modernism', accused of renouncing my 'true Russian heritage'. People who had never heard of, or cared about, the originals, cried 'sacrilege': 'The classics are ours. Leave the classics alone.' To them all my answer was and is the same : 'You respect, but I love.' "

And whatever Stravinsky loved he sought to possess. Ramuz said to him in 1929 : "What you love is yours, and what you love *ought* to be yours. You throw yourself on your prey—you are, in fact, a man of prey." Stravinsky acknowledged the truth of this, describing his idiosyncrasy—or perhaps virtue ?—as a rare form of kleptomania.

Well, Mozart had no truly progressive ideas of his own and his music, though beautiful, repeats many of the clichés of indifferent eighteenth-century composers. Since the ability to compose is not only a gift, but also a legacy—the handing on of certain melodic, stylistic and organic principles which have passed into common use—it is natural for any composer to profit by his inheritance. Stravinsky's creative thoughts and stylistic trends to the eighteenth century was, admittedly, his *Pulcinella* commission. For this ballet he turned fragments and finished pieces by Pergolesi into a wonderfully entertaining theatrical score. Yet the *Pulcinella* thesis has been grossly exaggerated by many writers. Stravinsky had, from his early days, a taste for contrapuntal discipline and traditional form, so that even without the nudging encounter with Diaghilev and the ghost of Pergolesi he would, sooner or later, have dabbled in 'neoclassicism', as the new venture was quickly called. Constant Lambert, who usually criticized Stravinsky harshly, said that the first performance of *Pulcinella* constituted a date of historical importance equal to that of Debussy's *Pélleas et Mélisande*. It took place at the Opera House, Paris, on 15th May 1920. For this production Picasso filled part of the huge stage with a three-dimensional view of a street in Naples, with a glimpse of the bay and Vesuvius in the distance. Massine, who wore red socks and tie, a sugar-loaf hat and a Petito mask, presented Pulcinella as a typical Neapolitan extrovert and a bit of a rascal. As he danced, he used every possible flourish, twist and turn to convey the roguishness and ambiguity of Pulcinella's character. Massine executed a series of flirtations, or *pas de deux*, first with Tchernicheva as Prudenza, then with Rosette, played by Nemchinova, and finally with Pimpinella, danced by Karsavina. Later the jealous lovers of the three ladies glided on to the stage and stabbed him with their swords, leaving him apparently dead; but in a grotesque ritual dance the Magician brought him back to life. The ballet, unfolding at an exhilarating pace, delighted the audience.

Stravinsky at this time was feeling very unsettled, conscious that some of the landmarks of his glorious *Firebird* phase were disappearing, one by one. He had been saddened two years previously by the death in Paris, on 25th March 1918, of Claude Debussy, who a decade ago had shown symptoms of the grave illness that, possessing his body like an evil spirit, finally destroyed him. Stravinsky had found him gentle and courteous, devoid of arrogance, generous in praising others; and so he was—but not always. A big man, broad in the shoulder, with black hair and beard, he could be terrifying in his sudden outbursts of temper. The universal notion of Debussy as being invariably shy and charming seems ludicrous when one recalls that, during a rehearsal of *Pélleas et Mélisande*, he rounded on the accompanist, who was playing for Maggie Teyte, the Mélisande, and, white with rage, nearly pushed him off the piano stool. On another occasion, after four distinguished musicians had performed his *Quartet*, he snapped viciously at the leader "You played like a pig!"[3]

Yet his virtue, like his courage, triumphed in the end. He shared with Stravinsky a fanatical love of order and precision, which dominated every piece of music he wrote. Debussy could not bear to see a scrap of paper, or a thread of cotton, on the carpet or the furniture; they had to be scooped up immediately, so that the room presented once again a clean, unruffled perfection. In his music every note that dissipated the beautifully soft impressionistic effects, or the flashing drama which he sought to achieve, must be ruthlessly purged. He had a visionary courage, and while shells exploded in the streets near his home, during World War One, penned these words: "I want to work, not so much for myself, but to give proof, however small it may be, that even if there were thirty million Boches French thought will not be destroyed!"[4]

Debussy had a sensitive and finely-tempered judgement which enabled him to recognize not merely the value, but also the universal relevance of music by other composers. When thanking Stravinsky for his gift of the score of *The Rite of Spring*, he wrote: ". . . it is not necessary to tell you of the joy I had to see my name associated with a very beautiful thing that with the passage of time will be more beautiful still. For me, who descend the other slope of the hill, but keep, however, an intense passion for music, for me it is a special satisfaction to tell you how much you have enlarged the boundaries of the permissible in the empire of sound".[5] He delivered this brilliant appraisal in a letter written in November 1913, only a few months after the stormy première of *The Rite of Spring* in Paris.

Debussy's death from cancer at the age of 55 probably contributed to the decision which Stravinsky made in June 1920 to leave Morges with his family and settle in France. Before doing so, they spent a happy summer at Carantec in Brittany, where Stravinsky composed not only his *Concertino*, a one-movement piece for string quartet, but also a choral work which subsequently became the closing section of the Symphonies for Wind Instruments, dedicated to the memory of Debussy. There, looking back over that part of the Unknown Country which he had already explored, the composer knew that he had reached a point of no return.

7

MORE CONQUESTS IN PARIS

Throughout his life Stravinsky's profound and penetrating interest in every possible aspect of culture, resulting in a wide, specialized, but never pedantic knowledge, seemed a direct reflection of his greatness. I am reminded of how the famous conductor Fritz Busch once asked a now equally famous, but then much younger and comparatively untried maestro, John Pritchard, "How long is it since you looked at Renaissance paintings?" To John's astonished "Why?" Busch replied "Because you will improve your conducting by looking upon great things,—do not become narrow." John Pritchard, taking his advice, spent months feasting his eyes upon the magnificent paintings of the High Renaissance and, in the opera houses of Italy and Germany, steeping himself in the wisdom of the world's finest interpreters. He developed an uncanny insight on the rostrum which produced some of the most authoritative readings I have heard.

Paris, to Stravinsky, was the Shangri-la of culture, the idealistic sanctuary where, immune from the germs of a decadent Romanticism, he might acquire the radiant glow of a progressive outlook. It widened and enriched his own personal vision, so that, like John Pritchard, he gained a universality of spirit. There, like a benevolent Father Perrault, the indefatigable, inexhaustible Diaghilev, during the Paris seasons of the Russian Ballet, directed and inspired the community he served. That community included Cocteau, Apollinaire, Massine, Picasso and the baffling musical jester Erik Satie. It is necessary, if the reader is to measure the intellectual dimensions of these giants, and to relate them, in perspective, to the mental stature of Igor Stravinsky, that he should know something about their activities.

Jean Cocteau, pioneer poet of the first half of the twentieth century, who died in 1963, descended in a cloud of fire upon the European theatre and cinema to create and present masterpieces or failures that ranged from the mundane to the mythical. Obsessed by the legends of Greece, and dominated by his favourite hero Orpheus, he displayed a sensitivity to mystery and wonder that may keep some of his plays, films and poetry alive and fresh for many years to come.

This former darling of the gossip-writers was barely twenty-two when opportunity came his way to collaborate with Diaghilev, Bakst, and other composers and artists who formed that select company. One of his first published drawings, the poster showing Nijinsky and Karsavina in *Le Spectre de la Rose*, proved so successful that it established his fame overnight. Carried away by the novelty and excitement of the Diaghilev "circus", which he described as "gaily-coloured like the fair of Nijni-Novgorod", he possessed, as did the Russian impresario, the rare quality of a catalyst, or animator, able to impose a magical influence on others—but, with it, Cocteau had a streak of creative genius.

His first book of poems, favourably reviewed by André Gide and Henri Ghéon, showed a fascinating originality. Cocteau knew the Diaghilev productions intimately. He had seen Nijinsky land in the wings, like a panting gazelle, after the last leap in *Le Spectre de la Rose*, there to be revived with hot towels and vigorous massage. He watched and silently criticized every performance, and Tamara Karsavina described him thus: "Like a mischievous fox-terrier, he bounded about the stage and had often to be called away: 'Cocteau, come away, don't make them laugh.' Nothing could stop his exuberant wit; funny remarks spluttered from under his voluble tongue." His antics reminded her of "fireworks, Roman candles, vertiginous catherine wheels of humour".[1] The bantering, comic sense in Cocteau, coupled with a flair for caricature, or irony, may be glimpsed in his own verbal portrait of Diaghilev: "His dancers called him 'Chinchilla' because of a white streak in his hair which was dyed deep black. He wrapped himself up in a pelisse with an opossum collar, and sometimes fastened it with safety pins. He had the face of a bulldog and the smile of a baby crocodile, with one tooth sticking outside. . . . And his moist eyes as they looked downwards were curved like Portuguese oysters."[2]

Cocteau, who, at the opening in 1953 of the Picasso exhibition at the Eden Theatre near Rome, was to make an impromptu speech which uncovered profound truths about the Spanish painter not then fully realized, accepted Picasso as a close friend and a master-influence from their very first meeting. For the rest of his life he tirelessly and intelligently extolled Picasso's genius. It was he who introduced the painter to Diaghilev.

The astonishing Satie, surely the oddest figure in the history of music, won the admiration of Cocteau with his *Morceau en forme de Poire*, which, composed in 1903, showed traces of the anti-Impressionist reaction valued so highly by the poet. Satie, both during his lifetime and since, has been held up to ridicule by the stupid and undiscerning, who have failed to detect behind the jester's mask the penetrating vision of the seer. The humorous comments and bizarre titles which he attached to so many of his works deflect from the rhinoceros hides of some Anglo-Saxon musicologists who mistake the mask for the man; yet these absurdities, as Cocteau shrewdly observed, were put there, not as tokens of buffoonery, but "to protect his works from persons obsessed by the sublime".

"Monsieur Ravel has refused the Legion of Honour, but all his music accepts it"—only Satie, perhaps, could have said that. He hated simply being regarded as a *farceur*, but knew his own limitations as a composer and fell back on writing brittle pieces with grotesque titles—a diversion in which Rossini had indulged. Satie loved to pose as a dandy, dressing immaculately and adopting the odd habit of polishing his hands with pumice stone and sporting gorgeous handkerchiefs and umbrellas. Darius Milhaud movingly described how, when Satie was ill, he expressed a childlike craving for these things.

In the last two decades of his life Satie existed in a tiny, dismal room in the Parisian suburb of Aroueil, a room that even his friends never entered until after his death. It contained two shabby upright pianos, denuded of mechanism and strings; about two hundred umbrellas; and an assortment of shirts, both new and soiled, that littered the floor. There was no running water. Instead of lighting a fire, which he could not afford, Satie used an improvised heating system. He had sewn his bed-sheets together in such a way that they held, in pockets, a number of hot-water bottles. On a cold night he heated water over a primus stove and poured it into the bottles to keep himself warm throughout the night. The bedclothes were filthy, not having been changed for twenty years.

Debussy, like Stravinsky, had a high opinion of Satie, since he took the trouble to orchestrate two of the *Gymnopédies* and conduct them himself. The two men sustained a curious and sometimes unhappy association which, described by Debussy's biographer Louis Laloy as "stormy, but indissoluble", lasted for thirty years. Finally, the two friends drifted apart. When Debussy lay dying, Satie, hurt by the older man's apparent indifference, sent him a bitter letter of reproach; this he subsequently regretted and, indeed, the memory of what he had done caused him indescribable anguish.

Some of Satie's music, including the three *Sarabands* (1887) is ravishingly beautiful. His *Gymnopédies* (1888), in the marvellous orchestral version, exhale a strange, almost mystical fragility, their cool, transparent harmonies and lilting rhythms conjuring up some graceful, bare-footed dance under an early morning Mediterranean sky. It was with the *Trois Gnossiennes* (1890) that he began to write the kind of music that has endowed him with a unique reputation for peculiarity and flamboyance; music characterized by such oddities as the suppression of time and key signatures, and bar-lines, as well as by the addition of a verbal running commentary superimposed upon the music. In these he gave full play to his puckish imagination and often Surrealistic fantasies.

Stravinsky must have warmed to this Till Eulenspiegel of French music who, in divesting it of the trappings it had accumulated through the ages, had also, like himself, caused it, with the imperious wave of a magician's wand, to undergo the most exciting transformations. He described Satie as one of the most rare and consistently witty persons he had ever encountered, and was touched by his sudden and mysterious death. Towards the end of his life Satie had embraced religion and found solace in attending Communion. The Russian composer had visited Paris in 1917, when his friend Diaghilev was about to stage the ballet *Parade* at the Théâtre des Champs-Elysées, and had made a point of seeing it. Satie wrote the music for this work and Cocteau the scenario, while Picasso devised the décor and Constructivist costumes. The ballet, a masterpiece in its genre is—largely because of Satie's profoundly original score—a landmark in the history of the theatre. Like Stravinsky's own *Rite of Spring*, it created, though on a much smaller scale, something of a scandal at its première on 18th May 1917.

The scenario which Cocteau wrote for this ballet concerned the biblical David, and included a 'parade' of dancers and acrobats who performed before the king. Cocteau and Massine, who had succeeded Fokine in the Russian Ballet, worked together on the choreography, which presented a simpler, more everyday tableau. After seeing Picasso's brilliant sketches, which were pure Cubism transferred to the stage, they decided, as a means of providing a 'superhuman' element and a contrast with the dancers and acrobats involved, to introduce three Managers who, fortified by megaphone voices spoken by actors sitting in the orchestra, would organize the publicity. Finally the megaphone voices were discarded and superseded by the sound of steps without music, a "fugue of footsteps", as it was called.

Parade, designated by its authors a *ballet réaliste*, consisted of 'the gestures of life' amplified and magnified into dancing, and rejected all the conventional means of translating a story into choreographic steps, poses and mime. There was, in fact, no story to translate; the *parade* included turns for a Chinese conjuror, a couple of acrobats, and a Little American Girl. Outside a fairground booth a music-hall parade is held, giving a sample of the more splendid events inside. The Managers, realizing that the crowd mistakes the parade for the show itself, try in their clumsy voices to make them understand this; but nobody goes in, and the Managers, exhausted by their efforts, collapse in a heap. Finally, the conjuror, the acrobats and the little girl rush out of the empty theatre and, seeing the Managers on the floor, unsuccessfully try to explain to the crowd that they should go into the theatre.

It was a very uneventful scenario and Satie's music, stripped of any grand orchestral excitement, confined its appeal to subtle and unsophisticated beauties; although Cocteau insisted on adding to it certain 'Cubist' sound effects : dynamos, typewriters, sirens, aeroplanes and Morse-tapping apparatus. Apollinaire wrote an enthusiastic programme note, extolling

G

"l'esprit nouveau" and interpolating a sadly commercial flavour with the words "The typewriters heard in the orchestra are *Underwood* machines."

The première of 1917 had been a huge and ghastly fiasco. The names of Picasso and Cocteau, coupled with that of Diaghilev, led the audience to expect some dazzling entertainment; instead, they found themselves deflated by a complete anticlimax. Most of the sound effects had been suppressed, partly because they seemed incongruous and partly because the typewriters could not be heard; the music-hall turns seemingly had no relevance to a ballet and the Managers, ambling about like creaking robots in their square, built-on costumes, provoked uproarious laughter. The audience, too, failed to apprehend what the Little American Girl, caught up in racehorse riding, dancing to ragtime and buying a camera, was supposed to be doing.

Diaghilev raved at their diehard imbecility and the loud, inescapable remark "If I'd known it was going to be like this I'd have brought the children!" According to Cocteau, the crowd looked as if it was about to lynch him, together with Picasso and Satie. The reviews next day were scathing. "The unharmonious clown, Erik Satie," wrote *La Grimace*, "has composed his music on typewriters and rattlers. . . . His accomplice, the dabbler Picasso, speculating on the eternal stupidity of mankind . . . Guillaume Apollinaire, poet and naïve visionary, managed to get all the critics, all the habitués of Parisian first nights, the scoundrels of the *Butte* and the drunkards of Montparnasse, to witness the most extravagant, the most senseless of the lucubrations of Cubism. . . . " Another critic described the authors of the alleged outrage as "Boches", to which Satie, displaying a masterly command of the vernacular, replied with a string of insulting postcards. The enraged critic reported Satie to the police and the composer cooled his ardour in prison for a week before a friend intervened and obtained his release.

Stravinsky, who had already played the music of *Parade* on the piano, seen the costumes and sets, and read the scenario, admired its freshness and originality. He recognized in Satie a kindred spirit who, governed by a desire for simplicity of outline and brevity of utterance, did not react against the excessive preciosity and complexity of the Romantic and Impressionist schools, but sought only to reintroduce a fundamental purity and directness of vision which had been overlaid by the accretions of tradition and highly developed techniques. These men belonged to a renaissance of youthful thought and action which was about to sweep like a hurricane across Europe, carrying away the cobwebbed façade of the past. In the ballet, in the dazzling hallucinatory music of Stravinsky, in the brilliant décors of Bakst and Benois, in the wild leaps of Massine, successor to Nijinsky, the younger generation had discovered an echo of its own exuberance.

In 1920, for a performance in Paris, Massine, with Stravinsky's full approval, choreographed a new production of *The Rite of Spring*. The dances, which Nijinsky devised for the Paris première of May 1913, created irreplaceable memories for those who saw them. One of the supreme moments of the ballet came in the second 'picture', where young girls danced in a circle, shoulder to shoulder, with what André Levinson called "the angelic airs of Byzantine saints", and where a sudden convulsion seized Marie Piltz, the Chosen One, as she stood in a trance, projecting her body sideways and causing her, as if burned and consumed by a white-hot ecstasy, to writhe fantastically, then shrivel at the stiffening touch of death. It thrilled and overwhelmed the spectator, as did Roerich's décor, depicting the strange face of primitive humanity as seen through the ritualism of pagan Russia still dominated by the elemental forces of nature.

Massine, in the new version, incised with the cutting edge of a surgeon's knife the magnificently human basis of the work, stripping the action of all historical reminiscences. His dances, pared of expressive tumult and appearing, by contrast, impoverished in design, seemed to many observers, including Levinson, to have no dramatic unity, no compelling *raison d'être*. Nijinsky set his dancers writhing and twisting to the rhythm of Stravinsky's music, but Massine used that rhythm, on the whole, ineffectually and with a semblance of artificiality. Although Sokolova executed the final death-dance, a supple variation with a series of *grands jetés en tournant*, superbly, she could not match the terrible and frightening spasms that made Marie Piltz's beautiful body appear to disintegrate in a prolonged, explosive agony.

In the spring of 1921 a Paris music hall persuaded Stravinsky by the sweet blandishments of the owner, and against his better judgement, to create a few pages of music for a small, unpretentious sketch within the tastes of the audience. He orchestrated four pieces from his collection of Easy Duets, using an orchestra of chamber-music dimensions. To his horror and indignation, the "pitiful band",[3] as he termed the body of players entrusted to perform the music, reduced it after a few desultory renderings to a travesty of the original, removing some instruments and replacing others. He decided never again to risk this kind of artistic mutilation.

Diaghilev, engaged for a season that spring at the Royal Theatre, Madrid, induced Stravinsky to participate by conducting *Petrushka*, the King's favourite ballet. Alfonso and the two Queens attended all the performances, with every seat in the theatre filled. The King also saw *Parade*, staged specially for him; he loved it, and laughed uproariously at the capriciously prancing horse who not only jumped alternately on its front and hind legs, but also sat down. He attended rehearsals. Arriving late on one occasion, he remarked, after apologizing to the waiting company, "Je viens d'accoucher d'un nouveau gouvernment."

Stravinsky went with Diaghilev to a theatre to hear Pastora Imperio, a gypsy singer from Cadiz and the idol of Spain. To their dismay a fat, middle-aged woman walked on to the stage from behind a simple curtain; she looked faded and nondescript. Then she began to sing, using body movements as well as castanets for added appeal. Her voice would not have thrilled any classical concert agent, but it vibrated with her personality, her dramatic genius, her subtle and varied artistry. With gesture and mime she uncovered something of the fascinating history and the soul of Spain. Stravinsky and his companion, bobbing about in their seats like restless, excited children, applauded, laughed and cried as this intensely vital performer evoked one mood after another.

He and Diaghilev spent Easter at Seville, mingling with the crowds at the famous processions of *La Semana Santa*. This wonderful and unique city, unlike Paris, Venice, Florence and Siena does not pulsate with life. Proud and beautiful, it resembles a dead Infanta reposing beneath a richly embroidered pall of history. So, presumably, did the Russian composer find it, as he strolled with Diaghilev through its ancient highways, where Goya boys with dirty faces padded bare-foot beside donkey caravans, and sad-eyed people flitted about their business. For the two men, steeped in the exotic Byzantine tradition of their own distant land, Seville also represented a treasure-house of rare and exciting art.

Whatever Stravinsky thought about the citizens of Seville, he thrilled to the pageantry and ritualism of *La Semana Santa*, referring to it nostalgically in his memoirs. Seville is rich in churches and from these, on the Thursday before Good Friday, spill two hundred penitents wearing high conical head-dresses that mask their faces. Walking in silent procession, they move slowly towards the great cathedral, second only to the basilica of St Peter's for size and, with its lofty Giralda bell tower, one of the most magnificent in Christendom.

Many of the groups hold aloft an image of the Virgin, wearing a halo of jewel-studded gold and robes of opulent, embroidered silk; others carry superbly carved tableaux depicting the last days of Jesus on earth. The most popular of the statues is 'La Macarena', the Virgin of Hope, who, as the guardian of poor people and of bullfighters, has a special place of honour in the procession. Behind these people walk priests in their vestments and cherubic acolytes swinging censers.

Suddenly in the silence, broken only by the shuffling of many feet, rises a high-pitched wailing note—a song of lamentation called a *saeta* (from the Latin *sagitta*), or an 'arrow of prayer' shot towards heaven. The dark pomp of Our Lord's death, speared by wild chants like these, reminds the foreign tourist, as well as the people of Spain, that it was through death and torture that Christ redeemed the world. Perhaps Stravinsky, following the procession, thought of *Boris Godunov* and the newly-crowned Tsar moving like a golden, jewel-encrusted statue in the centre of the boyars and clergy. He loved spectacle, and the dimly-lit cathedral, soaring to a height of 170 feet, provided it. To stand before the immense altar, with its forty-five biblical scenes and its gleaming sacramental vessels, is to stand, like Gerontius, before the Supreme Judge. Did the faint glow of Stravinsky's anthem *The Dove Descending Breaks the Air*, which he wrote many years later, touch his imagination as he glimpsed the "timeless, branching wonder" of that great roof? In the words of Herbert Read :

> A pallid rout stepping like phantoms
> beneath the arching boughs
> have come with angel hands and wretched voices
> to the valley and this choir of perish'd stones.
>
> Valid was my anguish—as though a turbulent dove
> had scattered the leafy silence.
> Now in airless vistas, dim and blind my limbs will loiter
> while the senses stray to vast defeats.[4]

For Igor Stravinsky, however, there were few real defeats and many noble victories as he travelled further into his Unknown Country.

8

LONDON AND "THE SLEEPING PRINCESS"

The year 1921 was a troubled one for Stravinsky: firstly, because the brilliant choreographer and dancer Massine, having signed a contract for South America, left the Russian Ballet; and secondly because of a distressing incident which took place in London, Massine not only departed for fresh artistic pastures, but he coaxed some of Diaghilev's company into following him. The impresario was enraged; he had no great choreographer to replace Massine and, faced as he was with important touring commitments, the defection of part of his flock embarrassed him. Soon, however, he began to look around for a new choreographer. He chose a young dancer named Slavinsky and instructed Larionov to coach him and help him to stage a ballet called *Chout* (*The Buffoon*). Although Picasso painted the scenes and Prokofiev wrote the music, it was not a success. Based on an old legend, the ballet presented one of those tortuous, typically Russian tales whose involved drollery kindles no responsive spark in English or Continental breasts.

The salvoes of praise that now surround Prokofiev's music make it hard to remember that between 1918, when he put Russia behind him in disgust, and 1933, when he returned there, a voluntary sacrifice to the bitch-goddess of success, the Soviet authorities condemned nearly everything he wrote, including *Chout*. Although, like Stravinsky, clear-minded in his artistic principles, he was a strangely ferocious, egocentric man. When, during the Russian 'trials' of 1934–36, his friend the producer Meyerhold was executed and his wife hideously murdered, Prokofiev took refuge in his work and the popular cry 'it's none of my business'. But it became his business, ultimately, for the bloody scythe of Russian politics destroyed first his marriage then his career.

The incident that upset Stravinsky occurred during the London visit of the Russian Ballet. With some diffidence he yielded to Koussevitzky's request to permit him to conduct the first performance of the Symphonies of Wind Instruments. Stravinsky slightly denigrated this work, regarding it as a piece of austere ritualism without any throb of passion or dynamic sparkle; and, indeed, its highly finished metronomical systems give it a splendid machine-tooled finish that for the average listener is tantamount to the pleasure of riding in a new Rolls-Royce. Yet he hoped that the cantilena of clarinets and flutes that take up and sing the liturgical dialogue might delight at least those members of the audience who shared his own dictum about composers, that "we have a single duty towards music, namely to invent it".

Alas, the concert in the Queen's Hall on 10th June 1921, seemed to be doomed from the outset for Koussevitzky, with singular ill judgement, prefaced Stravinsky's austere work, scored for only twenty players, with the marches of *Coq d'Or*, exuding a sumptuously decorative flow of melody. Nothing could have been more calculated to give it an anti-climactic flavour. As the deafening applause for the marches died away, Stravinsky, to his horror, saw three-quarters of the instrumentalists move nimbly from their seats, leaving, between the conductor and the twenty still in their places, an area that might have accommodated a whole corps-de-ballet. How, wondered the composer, was Koussevitzky, gesticulating across this huge space, to make the intimate and subtle contact with the players which his work needed. How, indeed! The performance was a fiasco and the audience, chilled by the frigidity of the orchestral response, must have welcomed the coffee interval more than usual.

When *The Times* dismissed the piece as "nothing but senseless ugliness", Stravinsky pointed out that it had not been written to gratify or excite the passions : "It is an austere ceremony which revolves in brief litanies among different families of homogeneous instruments."

Koussevitzky was a sensitive, astute and progressive conductor and this error of judgement must not be counted against him. Born in Russia of a poor Jewish family, he left that country filled with a sense of the cultural mission he must discharge for the wellbeing of humanity. Even in Russia, as a young man, he enjoyed fame as one of the most forward-looking personalities in the world of music. He founded a symphony orchestra in Moscow and took it on extensive tours throughout the country. Astonished peasants saw bearded and moustached musicians in heavy fur coats and hats boarding a Volga steamer, and men carrying contrabasses, harps, cellos and other instruments moving in procession up the gangplank. This was Koussevitzky's orchestra going down the Volga to play in all the towns from Nijni-Novgorod to Astrakhan. He founded the first publishing-house in Russia where composers, treated as equal partners in the enterprise, received a more generous share of royalties than other publishing-houses would have given them. Notwithstanding the contretemps that attended the performance of his Symphonies of Wind Instruments, Stravinsky held him in high regard.

In 1921 the composer also wrote eight little piano pieces for children called *The Five Fingers*, in which " the fingers of the right hand, once on the keys, remain in the same position for an episode and sometimes even for the whole length of the piece, while the left hand accompanies the melody with a harmonic or contrapuntal design of the utmost simplicity".

Bronislava Nijinska, who had left the Russian Ballet at the same time as her brother, rejoined it in 1921 as a choreographer. One day in London the impresario remarked jokingly to Grigoriev that he wished he could produce a ballet which, like the musical comedy *Chu Chin Chow*, would run for ever. He scorned Grigoriev's suggestion of *Coppélia*, but, because of it, he announced, shortly afterwards, that he proposed to revive *The Sleeping Beauty* under the title *The Sleeping Princess*. Diaghilev invited Nijinska to choreograph some new dances for this ballet. She discharged her task brilliantly. The impresario asked Stravinsky to help him—not surprisingly, for the composer revered Tchaikovsky and once said of him : "he was a creator of melody, which is an extremely rare and precious gift. . . ."[1]

The melody which Tchaikovsky created in *The Sleeping Beauty* served as his own 'kiss of life' at a time when good fortune seemed to have expired. He had already written *Swan Lake* in Moscow in 1887, but it was crudely, unimaginatively staged and proved a dismal failure. Tchaikovsky thought his music was to blame, but twelve years later Vsevolozhsky commissioned *The Sleeping Beauty*. It was a tough assignment, even though the great choreographer Petipa dictated almost bar by bar requirements; the first performance at the Maryinsky in 1890 received a standing ovation, however, and the Tsar murmured to Tchaikovsky "Very nice!"

During the London season which saw the birth of *The Sleeping Princess*, a brilliant company of creative artists met in Diaghilev's suite after a splendid meal at the Savoy Grill. It included Stravinsky, Prokofiev, Edith Evans, Arnold Bax and Harriet Cohen. Stravinsky regaled his companions with wise, droll comments about life and music; but Diaghilev and Prokofiev provided healthy competition with their iconoclasms. Bax described the Bach suites as "sewing-machine music";[2] while Diaghilev, shocking everyone by his intemperance, spoke of Beethoven as "a mummy, a corpse",[3] dismissing the whole of the Violin Concerto as "music from the morgue".[4] In more serious vein, he and his colleagues discussed *The Sleeping Beauty* and their plans for the forthcoming revival.

Following the Maryinsky première of 1890 this magnificent ballet unaccountably suffered years of neglect. Riccardo Drigo had conducted the first performance, when, with Tchaikovsky's consent, he made certain cuts in the music to meet the requirements of the choreographer. In the original production Enrico Cecchetti created two roles : Carabosse, the harpy-like fairy who arrived in Act I in a conveyance drawn by two rats, and the contrasting one of the Bluebird. The role of the Lilac Fairy was introduced by Petipa's wife Marie; Carlotta Brianza and Gerdt danced the Princess

Aurora and Florimund. Although greeted with warmth by the critics, nobody regarded the music as the work of a genius. The ballet continued to appear in Russia for some years, but it was not seen elsewhere until Diaghilev conceived the brilliant idea of staging it in London.

Those parts of the score which Drigo expunged existed only in the piano arrangement and, since Diaghilev wanted to stage a full-scale ballet, he entrusted Stravinsky with the task of orchestrating them. For this production Nicolas Sergueev created, or resuscitated his choreography from a form of notation set down years before by Vladimir Stepanov. Two of the items in Act III were omitted and were replaced by the Danse Arabe and the Danse Chinoise from *Casse Noisette,* and the music included Stravinsky's fine orchestrations. Spessiva danced the Princess Aurora, with Vladimirov as her partner, Lopokova as the Lilac Fairy, and Carlotta Brianza, the Princess of 1890, filling the role of Carabosse.

Diaghilev's publicity agents worked indefatigably before the première of the new production, so that when the opening night arrived everyone was talking about the fabulous ballet to be staged at the Alhambra. This was the restless, post-war London of 1921, with its short skirts, blasé manners, long cigarette holders, convulsive Charleston and blaring jazz. The pessimists might, in that phase of trumpery, short-lived values, be excused for prophesying a poor response to anything so romantic as *The Sleeping Princess,* but, in fact, people young and old scrambled for first night seats, and on 2nd November, long before the doors opened, an immense queue formed outside the box-office, at the gallery entrance. As dusk settled over the city, a magnificent *Sleeping Princess* sign flashed into brilliance, cheering those who waited hopefully outside the theatre. Meanwhile, at the Savoy, Stravinsky, Diaghilev, Bakst, Kochno and others, their faces lined with anxiety and fatigue, sat down to caviare and smoked salmon, toasting the health of the 'Princess' in champagne.

Those who stood for long hours on aching feet and managed to gain admission to the Alhambra had their fortitude and patience rewarded when, as the music of Tchaikovsky filled the house, the curtain rose on a scene of breathtaking splendour, the Palace of the King and Queen at the birth of Aurora. Superbly fashioned columns soared into the sky; on the gleaming steps of marble staircases that curved majestically into what seemed like infinity stood the scarlet and gold Negro guards of the King's household, grouped symmetrically in tier upon tier of finely proportioned and dignified figures. As the music changed to a march and ballerinas in white tutus executed a dazzling series of *pas de deux*, a panoply of glittering costumes swept across the stage as the fairies and nobles brought their gifts for the baby Princess in her golden cradle.

The lissom, dark-eyed Tchernicheva looked radiant in the white and scarlet costume of the Mountain Ash Fairy, while the fair-haired Sokolova had a sweet-faced fragility in the role of the Cherry Blossom Fairy. Bronislava Nijinska, as the Humming Bird Fairy, danced with a grace and delicacy that must have reminded many in the audience of her famous brother. Carlotta Brianza, who, at the very birth of *The Sleeping Beauty* at the Maryinsky Theatre in 1890, had danced as Aurora before the Tsar and all the élite of the old Russian nobility, now hid her faded beauty beneath the hideous, wrinkled make-up of the wicked fairy Carabosse. The scene, one of the most wonderfully contrived pieces of stagecraft that London had ever witnessed, ended with an exquisitely fashioned dance by Lopokova, the Lilac Fairy.

To Olga Spessiva fell the honour of dancing the role of Aurora on this legendary night. Wearing a shimmering pale gold wig, she appeared like a lovely vision in her deep rose-coloured tutu and a bodice laced with gold, seeming unearthly, unreal when, as the curtain lifted on the second scene, she floated into the dazzling lights. Alas, after she left the stage, the malicious poltergeists that lurk in the darkness behind the illusion at pre-mières like this crept into action. First the mechanism that worked the Lilac Fairy's spell unaccountably jammed; then, when the curtain came down, it obstinately refused to rise again; finally, the whole complicated stage machinery creaked to a halt. While the audience grew restive and the nervous worried dancers fidgeted behind the scenes, technicians and stagehands battled with the invisible gremlins, eventually succeeding, like the toy soldiers in *Casse Noisette*, in restoring order.

To Stravinsky, the precise and calculating master, who regarded a single blot or erasure on a virgin sheet of music paper as an obscenity, the contretemps, causing the ballet to run nearly an hour late, could hardly be endured. This was a ballet set to music by his revered Tchai-kovsky; moreover, the 'reconstituted' score bore his own creative finger-prints. Yet the scenes of the Enchanted Palace and of the Awakening made all who saw them gasp at the sheer magic of the genius who designed them. In a room bathed in deep shadow, a shaft of milky light shone on the golden-haired Princess, asleep on a huge canopied and cobwebbed bed guarded by two enormous spiders. Bakst's imagination really touched the heights in the closing scene, that of Aurora's wedding, where vast colonnades, with fluted pillars of white and gold, entwined with flowers, created a fairy-like setting of limitless space and beauty.

To an audience accustomed to a simpler, more austere type of ballet, Diaghilev's production presented an unbelievably colourful and romantic spectacle. There was a Mandarin who made love to two blushing, fan-fluttering Porcelain Princesses, and a gorgeously costumed Scheherazade carried in a kind of Persian sedan-chair, while the Shah and his brother, bearing upraised scimitars, watched jealously. The magnificent first scene of the Christening has already been described; with its Marshal of the Court greeting the guests, its slim and beautiful pages, its Dumas-like aristocrats in silks and satins, it constantly dazzled the eye. And Carabosse's sinister black coach brought a whiff of Edgar Allan Poe into the Versaille opulence of the palace. At the end of the second act, when the Lilac Fairy conjured up from the ground a climbing net of tendrils with purple blossoms, floods of lilac light issued from above and below the swiftly rising plants. Through the transparent green and lilac haze the dancers moved like ghosts in the distance. After the grande finale at the close of the ballet a crescendo of applause filled the theatre, rising and falling in seemingly endless waves. Even Diaghilev, who had been pale with anger at the technical hitches, smiled happily as the curtain lifted again and again on the bowing, or curtsying dancers.

Diaghilev's incomparable artistes, coupled with the gorgeous costumes and sets of Leon Bakst, made the production of *The Sleeping Princess* at the Alhambra Theatre in 1921 an outstanding success. Nevertheless, although the public raved over the ballet, the first night critics, irritated by the unfortunate delays, treated it rather coldly and *The Sleeping Princess* never recovered from its bad start. The impresario had confidently expected that this brilliant spectacle would cast an unbreakable spell upon the British public; but, alas, they were accustomed to one-act ballets, and a full-scale performance, which included a long prologue, taxed their powers of endurance. When, after a run of some months, there were more and more empty seats in the theatre, Diaghilev withdrew the production.

While orchestrating the piano parts for this ballet, Stravinsky, sharing with Diaghilev a revival of enthusiasm for Pushkin, started work on his newly-conceived opera *Mavra*, taken from the great poet's rhymed story *The Little House in Kolomna* and set to a libretto by Boris Kochno, who later became Diaghilev's assistant and secretary. On returning to Biarritz in 1922, where he and his family stayed for three years, Stravinsky resumed his composition of this gem, which had been interrupted by the Tchaikovsky assignment. He also established a connection with the Pleyel company, who wanted him to make a transcription of his works for their Pleyela mechanical piano, a device in which punched paper, or wafer-thin metallic rolls, rotated by clockwork, reproduced pre-ciphered music. He undertook this task with enthusiasm, regarding it as a method by which the wishes of a composer concerning the performance of his own music could be precisely registered. To carry out the Pleyel commission he paid regular visits to Paris, where, at the Opera House, thanks to the patronage of Princess Edmond de Polignac, his *Mavra* and *Reynard* would shortly be staged by Diaghilev.

The name of Pleyel is not, of course, known solely through the mechanics of the piano which it immortalized. Ignaz Pleyel, the founder of the firm, composed some delightful music, including the Sinfonia Concertante No. 5, which, with its rococo elegance and bubbling gaiety, deserves a more frequent hearing than concert promoters allow.

Stravinsky visited Monte Carlo, where Bronislava Nijinska was creating

Reynard. He found this playground of the rich utterly captivating, with its deep blue sea, its mimosa, its flowered hillside and quaint, twisting streets, its café terraces and bright, sometimes gaudy shops, and its magnificent opera house.

What the members of the Russian Ballet did not see was the more seamy side of this lovely old town, where 20,000 loyal subjects of His Highness Prince Louis lived in dignified Mediterranean poverty. Diaghilev frowned on the gambling rooms of Monaco and dissuaded Nicholas Nabokov from patronizing them. Yet the *desperadoes*, or addicts of gambling, as they were called, with their hopeful, bulging eyes and black moustaches, looked as melodramatic as those members of the Pre-Raphaelite brotherhood in painting, who sported sombrero hats and Spanish cloaks; they must surely have appealed to any practitioner of the graphic arts.

In certain rooms of the Théâtre du Casino, known officially as 'His Princely Highness's Opera and Ballet Theatre of Monaco and Monte Carlo', situated in the same building as the Casino, they could have seen some peculiar objects used by certain patrons of the last two centuries. These included a very ornate and complicated love chair built in the 1880s, so legend has it, for the Prince of Wales, but monopolized by the virile and impatient Russian Grand Dukes. And there was a beautifully carved bed in the shape of a swan. This had been 'prepared' for Louis II of Bavaria, who, with his adulation of Wagner must have found the *Lohengrin*-inspired opulence of the management in excellent taste.

Stravinsky used to dine with Diaghilev, Prokofiev, Picasso and other members of the Diaghilev 'court' at Giardino's restaurant at the top of the hill in Monte Carlo. This was a well-known haunt of famous people, with a mouth-watering cuisine. Always an epicure, even in those early days, Stravinsky ordered the best foods and the best wines; fortified by these, he proved to be a witty and stimulating companion. He had a passion for clear, precise and pithy language. After browsing through a book, he turned to a friend and remarked "The sexual organ is a formation peculiar to living beings, who delegate to it a special role in the act of procreation,—isn't that a superb definition!"[5] Once a cold troubled him and he complained "I have a change purse in my larynx."[6] Seeing someone in a hurry, he exclaimed "Why do you hurry? *I have no time to hurry.*"[7]

Meetings with the late Aga Khan, then a slim and fastidious young man with a debonair, sophisticated manner, produced a real friendship, which the Aga subsequently acknowledged with pride; but not the financial windfall which Diaghilev sought and for which Stravinsky, prodded along by the impresario, delicately fished. The young prince, screened by his dark glasses, listened politely, but showed no desire to swallow, or even notice the dangling bait. He did, however, take a keen interest in the ballet.

Nijinska, in creating *Reynard*, was the first woman to specialize and excel in work of this kind. She was also the first to unite form and emotion, so that, under her direction, gestures became signs or symbols. Nijinska was a superb artiste, but also something of a slave-driver, with a gift for barbed invective; Serge Lifar, who trained at her school in Russia, related in his memoirs how, after an entrance test, she wrote opposite his name on the report prepared for the judges the one word "Hunchback!"

The first performance of *Reynard* was given at the Paris Opera on 18th May 1922, and in the same theatre on 3rd June the Russian Ballet also staged the première of *Mavra*. Designed by Charles Garnier at a cost of thirty-six million francs, the Opera House, with its façade richly decorated with sculptures, its dome surmounted by Millet's noble statue of Apollo, its white marble and onyx stairway, and its foyer ablaze with glittering chandeliers, might seem to some people hardly the place to stage works which did not, in any sense, partake of its opulent tradition or atmosphere. The busts of famous composers, the comical sculptured groups of young ladies blowing down silent, antique instruments proclaim the dedicated role of this intimidating opera house. In their respective programmes, which contained large-scale, spectacular works, the unpretentious *Mavra* and *Reynard* appeared rather like pieces of farm-house cheese sandwiched between slabs of rich fruit cake. The performances, although brilliantly directed, and with Nijinska herself playing the part of Reynard, fell completely flat. Otto Kahn, whom Diaghilev hoped to cajole into taking *Mavra* to America, reacted unfavourably by saying "I liked it all, then 'poop' it ends too quickly!"

During that Paris season Diaghilev had his revenge on Massine for having deserted the Russian Ballet. Massine, who had not been doing very well as a free-lance, implored the impresario, through a Monsieur Rouché, to take him and all his dancers into the company. While the anxious Massine waited outside the Opera House for his answer, Diaghilev gazed inscrutably at Rouché and said in icy tones : "I will send him my answer in a few days' time. It will be in the negative!"[8]

Stravinsky, disgusted with the diehard reaction of the critics, began, at Biarritz in 1922, to compose his Octet for Wind Instruments. He later wrote of this work : "The Octet began with a dream. I found myself in a small room surrounded by a small number of instrumentalists who were playing some very agreeable music. I did not recognise any of the music they played, and I could not recall any of it the next day, but I do remember my curiosity—in the dream—to know how many the musicians were. I remember too that after I had counted them to the number eight, I looked again and saw that they were playing bassoons, trombones, trumpets, a flute and a clarinet."[9] Stravinsky finished the Octet in May, 1923; the following autumn he conducted the first performance at a Koussevitzky concert at the Paris Opera.

The choice of instrumentation had always been a perplexing problem for Stravinsky in any work he undertook. Now, since Diaghilev wanted to stage *The Wedding* at last, he returned to the task of scoring it, and decided on four pianos, timpani, bells, xylophone and a number of percussion instruments. "This sound combination resulted directly from the needs of the music itself and was not inspired by any desire to imitate the sounds of some such popular fête. . . . In this spirit I also have composed my music and nowhere have I used any folk songs with the exception of the theme of a factory song which reappears several times in the last tableau. . . . All the other themes, motifs and melodies are my own original ideas."[10]

Various chronicles of the period indicate that Stravinsky was a monarchistic and bourgeois aesthete who loved to adorn the walls of his home, or hotel bedroom, with icons and pictures of the Emperor Nicholas II and his children. How much this visual tribute to Christian and royalist ideals derived from a natural, though occasionally dormant faith, and how much to his infatuation with the more exotic and mystical aspects of Russian life, it is difficult to assess. Certainly, during those formative years, the composer had a closer relationship with God than the polite, nodding acquaintance which pantheism provides; but he also found inexhaustible delight in exploring the rich treasure-house of Russian nationalism.

While Stravinsky, in imagination at least, rejoiced in the sweet, cleansing breeze of a progressive outlook, the winds of fortune that caressed Diaghilev and his company at that time had the teeth of an Arctic blizzard. The impresario's money drained away faster than he could replace it; he looked around for fresh fields—or rather patrons—to cultivate. His eyes rested once again on the oasis-like vision of Monte Carlo and, in particular, on the daughter and son-in-law of the new Prince of Monaco, who worshipped the arts and had a special regard for the Russian Ballet. So, after the signing of a contract with the Casino, the company established themselves at Monte Carlo, there to collaborate with the resident Italian company, whose director, Monsieur Offenbach, a descendant of the composer, held out a hand of friendship.

It was in 1923 that Serge Lifar, travelling from Russia, joined the Russian Ballet at Monte Carlo. He was then a mere boy, and Diaghilev remarked of him, as of other recruits who arrived with him, that he hardly seemed worth the trouble and expense of being brought so far. For the eighteen-year-old Lifar the boundless view of Monte Carlo, with its mimosas, palms and orange-trees bathed in sunlight—the paradise of *la dolce vita*—represented an exhilarating freedom after the hell of Russia, where the Bolshevik machine-guns rattled, and the dancer, caught in the blast of an exploding shell, had fallen to the ground in a pool of blood. Lifar did not find Monte Carlo as Utopian as it at first appeared, especially when, one dreadful day, Nijinska, watching him exercise, scowled dis-approvingly and remarked "Tell me, Lifar, can you really dance?"

On another occasion the awe-inspiring Diaghilev, seated on a flap-chair in the middle of the studio used by the company, demanded to see the newcomers, including Lifar, performing their exercises. After the sweating, nervous youngsters had complied, his face darkened, he rose to his feet, slamming the chair seat back, and, in a dead, clammy silence, left the studio. They heard him in the distance bawling at the top of his voice to Nijinska "Crass ignorance . . . you've fooled me . . . let them go back to Russia!"[11] When he had calmed down, however, he returned to the studio to watch another session of exercises. For the trembling Lifar there was a glorious, unbelievable surprise when Diaghilev, staring at him intently, said to Nijinska "I've got faith in this boy,—he'll be a dancer."[12]

Inspired by the trust placed in him by this strange, inaccessible divinity, kindly and irritable by turns, Lifar sought to please him and to establish himself as a dancer. It was a superhuman task, for Diaghilev drove his company with implacable ruthlessness. The impresario sometimes ordered the same steps to be repeated twenty times; the youngsters, lonely and bewildered, so far from their native land, shivered with apprehension. The first ballet Lifar had to study was Stravinsky's *The Wedding*; a tough assignment for unfledged dancers, but one made easier by the com-poser, who, directing rehearsals, managed to inject into the company his own pulsating excitement and creative power. The première of *The Wedding* at the Gaieté Lyrique Theatre in Paris on 13th June 1923, with Ansermet conducting, met with remarkable success, and Lifar felt like an uncrowned king with a destiny to fulfil. At this performance the frame-work of the set, consisting entirely of backcloths, with details of a Russian peasant cottage interior painted upon it, proved surprisingly effective.

Diaghilev, who liked personally to adopt promising dancers, at first resented Lifar's rather shy and diffident nature. One day he buttonholed him and said angrily "If I stopped you, young man, and if I want to speak to you, it is not in my own interest, believe me, but in yours. I have been noticing you for some time now, and you've got more talent and enthusiasm than your comrades. I want to help you to develop that talent, but you won't recognize this and you shy away from me like a wild animal. Take your choice. Do not imagine that I'm going to implore you? You are making a mistake, young man. Well, what are you waiting for? You can go home!"[13]

Lifar did not go home. He survived the reproaches, the jeers, the goad-ing, driving, but benign dictatorship of Diaghilev to become not merely a superb *danseur noble*, but also a choreographer who, honoured by Pope Pius XII and General de Gaulle, helped to make French culture a univer-sal symbol of excellence. A firm, altruistic friendship grew between him and Diaghilev, and although horrible, unseemly quarrels jeopardized their relationship (once, because he fell in love with Karsavina, the impresario grabbed him by the hair and accused him of debauchery) it persisted until death intervened.

In June 1923, when Diaghilev, having revived Prokofiev's *Chout*, invited the composer to Paris to play the score of *The Love of Three Oranges* for him, Stravinsky attended the audition, but did so in a waspish mood of criticism, refusing to listen after Prokofiev had finished playing the first act. Prokofiev, probably stung by this unfriendly, intolerant attitude, censured Stravinsky for his new trend towards what he called "Bach on the wrong notes"; whereupon Igor reminded him of his own Classical Symphony, only to be told that it had been written 'on the side', while Stravinsky's latest foible was the strongest characterization of his current output. "After this meeting," Prokofiev said, "for several years Stravinsky adopted not so much a malevolent as a critical atitude towards me, and there was a definite cooling off in our relationship."[14] Influenced by Stravinsky's judgement, Diaghilev also expressed his disappointment in *The Love of Three Oranges*.

During the autumn of that year Stravinsky visited Weimar to attend a great exhibition of modern architecture which included, as a side attraction, a series of concerts at one of which the audience warmly applauded *The Soldier's Tale*. In Weimar he met Ferrucio Busoni, who was to die a year later. The famous pianist-composer, a romantic whose work and personality seemed the antithesis of Stravinsky's own, completely won over the Russian by the sincere feeling of admiration which he revealed while listening to the concert performance of *The Soldier's Tale*. Stravinsky had a very high regard for Busoni's own musical vision, retaining a lifelong affection for *Doktor Faust*; he also considered his head, glimpsed in profile, as one of the noblest and most beautiful he had ever seen.

For all his faults, Busoni was an intellectual giant. Some musical interpreters can make a work sound greater than it actually is and Busoni, who played even short Chopin preludes in the grand manner, was one of them. He took scrupulous care over detail. In his transcription of the Bach Chaconne he even put a bracketed sharp against the F in the final chord, as it is not clear from the open D of the violin version whether Bach himself sensed a D major or a D minor conclusion. His brilliance as a pianist retarded and, to some extent, prevented his recognition as a composer.

Stravinsky, anxious to explore the possibilities of piano technique, planned a Concerto for piano and wind orchestra. This he wrote at Biarritz in the autumn and winter of 1923–24, putting the finishing touches to it in Paris. The composer became something of an *aficionado* and a staunch patron of the *corrida* while living at Biarritz. He and Artur Rubinstein, the pianist, attended a tragic *corrida* at Bayonne, where an enraged bull, dislodging a *banderilla*, sent it flying through the air, trans-

Igor Stravinsky

The Maryinsky Theatre

A rare photograph of a Russian Ballet poster, showing Stravinsky standing beside Nijinsky. The inscription on the poster is to William (Fakhnovsky) Fox, a great and almost legendary sculptor and ballet artist, as well as a close friend of Nijinsky. This poster was smuggled out of a Siberian prison-camp more than a decade ago and sent, via Finland-Canada, to Ivan Domherr

Tamara Karsavina as the Firebird

Diaghilev with his old nurse, from the painting by Bakst, 1903

Alexandre Benois in 1896, from a pastel by Bakst

Vaslav Nijinsky as Petrushka

Drawing by Picasso for the cover of *Ragtime*

Stravinsky with Pierre
Monteux

Lifar and Picasso

Original gouache by Marc Chagall
commemorating the Stravinsky-
Chagall-Balanchine production of
The Firebird in 1949

Backcloth for Apollon Musagète
painted by André Bauchant

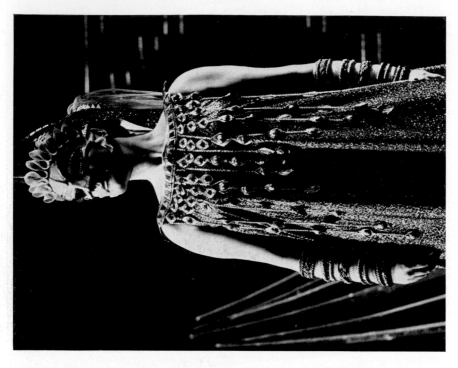

Raimund Herincx as Creon in the Sadler's Wells Opera production of *Oedipus Rex* and (*right*) Katherine Pring as Jocasta in the same production

fixing and killing the Consul-General of Guatemala, who had been standing by the railing.

Shortly before the completion of the Concerto, Koussevitzky, to whose wife the work is dedicated, visited Stravinsky and suggested that he should play the solo part himself. The composer hesitated at first; not surprisingly, since the gruelling and repetitive practice which a concert pianist undertakes reminded him of shortcomings known only to himself. A professional pianist cannot play for an audience until he can forget about his instrument; he is like a skiing champion who cannot expect to win unless he has complete command over the two pieces of wood attached to his feet. Technical perfection being the *sine qua non* of a virtuoso, Stravinsky set out to acquire it and began by loosening his fingers with Czerny exercises.

His doubts vindicated themselves in a fleeting loss of memory at the first public performance of the Concerto given at the Paris Opera on 22nd May 1924, at a Koussevitzky concert. Understandably, he suffered from 'stage fright' in the early phase of his career as a concert pianist, and mastered his terror of facing a staring, silent, critical audience only with the greatest difficulty. After performing the first part of the *Concerto*, he raised his hands to launch the piano solo which opens the Largo, when to his horror he realized that he had forgotten it. He whispered this in a distressed voice to Koussevitzky, who, hardly blinking an eyelash, glanced rapidly at the score and hummed the first notes to him. Stravinsky, now smiling confidently, attacked the Largo with spirit and determination.

His memory faltered on another occasion, when, playing the same work, he became obsessed by the notion that the audience was a collection of dolls in a panopticon. The reflection of his fingers in the glossy wood at the edge of the keyboard caused a lapse of memory at another performance, and at one concert, while moderately inebriated, he found the fumes of alcohol clouding his clear recollection of the score.

Nerves and forgetfulness—or even hallucinatory disturbances—are certainly not confined to the inexperienced. Dame Myra Hess confessed, shortly before her death, that, after years of fame as one of the greatest pianists of the age, she still trembled with fright and felt her mouth go dry as she crossed a concert platform to sit down at the piano before an audience. And I recall how, in November 1968, during a performance of Richard Strauss's *Burleske* at the Philharmonic Hall, Liverpool, the conductor, Sir Charles Groves, had to stop the Royal Liverpool Philharmonic Orchestra because the soloist, Shura Cherkassky, forgot several bars of the music and made a false entry.

Constant Lambert attacked the lyricism of the Largo movement of Stravinsky's Concerto, failing to realize that the fragmentation of line and disintegration of rhythm represented one of the finest spanned lyrical periods in the music of that time. Lambert, for all his virtues, which included witty polemics about his art and the creation of music impregnated

H

with sensuous appeal, could be surprisingly insensitive. His ridiculous description of Ravel's melodies as "synthetic" highlights the extreme fallibility of his judgements. "Burly, pink and scornful," wrote Richard Buckle the dance critic, "Lambert looked more like a sporting clubman than a musician. . . . There was a touch of patriotic pride which amounted almost to insularity in his artistic outlook . . . one divined a mistrust of foreign nonsense, a determined belief that native craftsmanship could compete with exotic glamour."[15]

9

THE DEATH OF DIAGHILEV

Although 1924 was a year of intense hard work and unrelenting pressures, Stravinsky managed, during the last few months of his stay at Biarritz, to write a sonata for solo piano, which he dedicated to the Princess Edmond de Polignac, at whose Paris house, patronized by famous and gifted people, many private auditions of his works had been given prior to public performance. The Sonata is a magnificent piece whose staccato and legato effects revivify Baroque contrasts of texture and whose classical tonal simplicity and grace foreshadow Britten.

Stravinsky met Hindemith for the first time in 1924 at a concert in Amsterdam given by the Amar Quartet, which the German composer founded and in which he played the viola. A short, stocky, nearly bald man, with a cherubic, yet slightly impish grin, Hindemith, like Stravinsky, wanted "music that would live its own life, governed by its own laws and its own logic, free from the superficial idioms and thoughts of the romantics". During the Nazi regime his music was blacklisted by Hitler's ideological thugs and labelled as 'degenerate art'—a high honour, indeed, for any sensitive artist surrounded by that viper's nest of cruel and perverted values! Hindemith and his wife, clad in white linen shorts, used to go for early-morning runs, and these athletics reminded Stravinsky of the German composer's setting-up-exercise concertos. The two men became good friends, although Stravinsky found some of Hindemith's music as indigestible and tasteless as cardboard.

Joseph Szigeti met Stravinsky at the Blüthner piano store at Leipzig in 1924, after a prolonged and very Russian lunch that followed the Furtwängler rehearsal for the Gewandhaus performance of the master's Piano Concerto. Szigeti had his violin with him, since Stravinsky had asked him to perform Bach's Solo Sonata in A minor; but the Russian composer played his own sonata twice in succession, then, turning to his companion, remarked "Tchistaya rabota!" ("Clean work!"). He meant, not his own rendering, but the taut, beautifully contrived contrapuntal texture of this gem of his neoclassic period.

Twenty years later, Stravinsky met Szigeti again, at his home in Southern California, where they performed the Duo Concertante together, and the violinist noted his partner's humility and pride. "C'est extrèmement travaillé," remarked the composer of the first movement of this work, which, though stemming from 1932, belongs to the same phase of neo-classicism—a movement described by Virgil Thompson as "an achievement unique in history". Stravinsky's enthusiasm for his own music resulted, during preparations of the Duo Concertante for recording and for concert performances, in his producing with a childlike spontaneity a set of interpretative signposts. He classed one movement as "monolithic", an important theme as "Bachlike", and the rhythmically ebullient Eclogue No. 1 he regarded as a *Kazatchok* (Cossack Dance). Coming, in his descriptive odyssey, to the first Trio of the Gigue, he swung round on the piano stool, leaped to his feet and, speaking in faultless German, declaimed, danced, hummed and mimed this refrain from Johann Strauss's *Die Fledermaus* :

> *Glücklich ist*
> *Wer vergisst*
> *Was nicht mehr*
> *Zu ändern ist*

At Biarritz Stravinsky suffered increasing irritation from the howling gales that, sweeping across the Atlantic, battered mercilessly against the coastline. Towards the end of 1924, unable to stand it any longer, he moved to Nice; there he completed a Serenade in A for piano, which he dedicated to his wife.

Although he did not realize it at the time, a new star had begun to shine in Stravinsky's firmament when George Balanchine joined the Russian Ballet at the end of 1924 and gradually won the approval and friendship of the exacting Diaghilev, who at first chided the choreographer for spoiling the splendid, sometimes beautiful episodes he created in his ballets with false, crude and disappointing effects. "You are like someone who prepares an elegant and delicious meal," said the impresario, himself a noted epicure, "and then, when the guests are waiting for just the right wine to go with it, brings them a big jug of water."[1]

Balanchine, christened Georgi Melitonovich Balanchivadze at his birth, which took place in St Petersburg on 22nd January 1904 (he changed his name to 'Balanchine' at Diaghilev's request when he joined the Russian Ballet) inherited his physical characteristics—black hair, intense, almost burning, dark eyes, hawk-like face, and lithe, spare frame—from his Georgian ancestors. From them he also probably derived much of his fiery artistic temperament. Neither of his parents could claim aristocratic lineage, so that unlike many of the Russians he met in exile, Balanchine had no princes or counts to display proudly on his family tree. Yet his father, Meliton Balanchivadze, mingled with artists and intellectuals; a moderately successful composer, he wrote an opera with the intriguing title *Tamara the Wily,* numerous choral works, a mass, and other church services.

Even at an early age, Georgi had a fond, discerning eye for feminine beauty—an indispensable attribute for a future choreographer—and, as a very young boy, he succumbed to the charms of a twenty-year-old woman dentist in the village of Lounatiokki, close to where he and his family lived. The pain she caused him by yanking out, or drilling a decayed tooth vanished like a dark cloud in a blaze of sunshine when, writhing in the chair he noticed the swanlike arch of her neck, the exquisite line of her arm, or the lovely tilt of her wrists as she grasped the instrument of torture. A visit to the dentist was, for him, not simply an ordeal, but also an acutely ambivalent experience. After being auditioned by the famous *prima ballerina* Olga Preobrajenska, he was accepted as a student at the Imperial School of Theatre and Ballet; so, inauspiciously, began a distinguished career whose path would eventually lead him into Stravinsky's Unknown Country.

From the very beginning, Diaghilev treated his prodigy with respect and indulged in a smile of vindication when, in June 1925, Balanchine's new version of Stravinsky's *The Song of the Nightingale* had a successful début in Paris. It was a magnificent production which captured all the enchantment of the fairy-tale libretto and the mysterious, even mystical lyricism of the music. Alicia Markova, then only fourteen years old, danced the role of the Nightingale, her fragile beauty and grace so dazzling the critics that she leapt, or rather floated into fame overnight and became, in her own words, "the first baby ballerina discovered by Balanchine".[2]

Some time later, when Markova suddenly became ill, Balanchine himself filled the role of the Nightingale and being, at one hundred and forty pounds, what Bernard Taper called "a great hulk",[3] filled it more than adequately. Clad in a ridiculous costume, sewn together in frantic haste backstage, poor Balanchine, who had been almost press-ganged by Diaghilev into deputizing for the fragile, winsome Markova, just managed to squeeze into the cage. With his bulging muscles threatening to burst the cage asunder, he looked, according to one witness, more like an ape behind bars than a nightingale. The maidens of the Emperor's court, catching sight of this apparition, tittered uncontrollably. Grigoriev, the company director, who was playing the dying Emperor, hissed at them under his breath; then, glimpsing the caged Balanchine, nearly choked with laughter. Having been virtually forced into this humiliating exhibition, Balanchine, seeing Diaghilev rolling about with mirth in his box, must have felt like strangling him.

The master of a classical vocabulary inherited from Petipa through his training at the Maryinsky School, he was not only Stravinsky's gifted collaborator, but the most potent of all influences upon American choreography. At the time of Diaghilev's death in 1929 other fine choreographers, including Kostov, Fokine, Bolm and Mordkin, had founded important schools in New York, Chicago, San Francisco and Los Angeles; while, under the sponsorship of the impresario Sol Hurok, the Russian Ballet of Monte Carlo maintained a decade of tours which, notably in America, brought inspired productions and performances to ballet audiences. Balanchine himself created a School of American Ballet at the invitation of Lincoln Kirstein and Edward Warburg, starting the enterprise in a small way at Hartford, Connecticut, then transferring it to Isadora Duncan's former studios in New York. From the Balanchine School sprang an American style of classical dance and a chain of companies which developed into the New York City Ballet.

Just as Ashton is linked in posterity with Sophie Fedorovich, Tudor with Hugh Stevenson, MacMillan with Nicholas Georgiadis, Jerome Robbins and Leonard Bernstein with Oliver Smith, so, as regards the American phase of his life, Stravinsky is forever associated with Balanchine. In setting various texts, Stravinsky often subordinated the words to the music. So he must have rejoiced at finding such a pliant collaborator, for Balanchine stands out as a brilliant example of the type of choreographer whose usual starting point is the music. He was, indeed, a master of the difficult art of translating music, primarily intended to be heard, into visual images which do not have the motivation of narrative or mood. Birgit Cullberg wrote of him : "He allows the dance patterns to dissolve and come together again like rings of water in a wide, never-ending flow. He has the gift of revealing the symphonic character of the music in choreography. . . . But he is no slave of music. He builds his ballets in accordance with the aesthetic laws of choreography."

In January 1925, Stravinsky, then aged forty-three, visited America for the first time. He personally directed performances of a number of his works, and appeared at Carnegie Hall with the New York Philharmonic Orchestra under the baton of Willem Mengelberg, as the soloist in his own Piano Concerto. Most of the critics cooed like turtle-doves over this visit by the most revered and provocative composer of the day; but at least one of them, Olin Downes, the distinguished critic of the *New York Times*, was not over-awed : "There is little question that the bewildering rise of Igor Stravinsky from apparent creative nonentity to the position of composer of *The Rite of Spring* has been followed by a decline fully as rapid and destructive of the high hopes of those who believed that in him there was a prophet of a new age. The trouble is that Stravinsky appears to have been precisely the opposite of a prophet of a new age; he seems to have succumbed utterly to the aimlessness, the superficialities and pretensions of this one."[4]

Yet at the concert Downes, like the rest of the critics, found much to admire in Stravinsky's Piano Concerto and in the composer himself as, seated at the keyboard, he performed the solo part with incredible speed, power and precision. A number of people laughed out aloud at some of the tonal grimaces and apparent distortions of the music; but the critic of the *New York Times*, more cautious than hitherto, noted that the concerto had "stirred a majority of the audience". He found beneath some of the rhythmic abandon of the music the bold confidence of the master and commented of Stravinsky ". . . one thing is certain; he will have more to say before the end comes".

Stravinsky met George Gershwin in New York in 1925 at the home of Paul Kochanski, who, since Gershwin could speak only a few words of Russian and knew no French, acted as interpreter. Gershwin impressed Stravinsky as a nervous, energetic man. "At that time," said the Russian composer, "I hardly knew who he was, and I was totally unacquainted with his music."[5] Gershwin played the *Rhapsody in Blue* and other pieces for him at the piano. Shortly before Gershwin died, Stravinsky met him again at a party given by Edward G. Robinson, and attended by Charlie Chaplin, Paulette Goddard and Marlene Dietrich. His popularity and fame had not spoiled him. Gershwin is supposed to have bumped into Stravinsky in Paris and said, "How much will you charge to give me lessons?"; whereupon, so the story goes, Stravinsky asked the American how much he earned, and, on being told $100,000 a year, replied, "Then I should take lessons from you." Stravinsky, with a snort of contempt, repudiated this anecdote as being completely false.

Gershwin, a dominating figure with intense black eyes set in a large forceful face that somehow reminded one of a ram, tried painstakingly to keep himself as fit as an Olympic Games runner. He played golf regularly, took long walks with his adoring wire-haired terrier, and usually played tennis every week with his Beverly Hills neighbour Arnold Schoenberg. His efforts availed him nothing. After a period of increasingly hideous headaches, when he felt strangely listless and, on one occasion, insisted that he could smell burning rubber, poor Gershwin died, at the age of thirty-eight, of a brain tumour.

In September 1925, while at Nice, Stravinsky set off for Venice to perform his Piano Sonata there. He had a nasty suppurating abscess on his right forefinger, and afterwards related how, in a little church outside Nice, kneeling before an old and 'miraculous' icon, he prayed that his injury might be cured. Stravinsky departed for Venice only half believing in the efficacy of his prayer, and fully expecting that the concert might have to be cancelled. With his finger still apparently festering and certainly causing him pain, he walked on to the stage of the Fenice Theatre and, addressing the audience, apologized in advance for, as he saw it, the inevitable faulty performance. Seating himself at the piano, Stravinsky removed the bandage, then, suddenly aware that the pain had vanished, found the finger completely healed. The composer felt that a miracle had occurred, although in recording the incident he wrote "the fact that I took it for a miracle is at least as significant . . . I do, of course, believe in a system beyond Nature."[6]

In the same year he orchestrated four piano duets (Andante, Napolitana, Española and Balalaika), which subsequently appeared in print as the Suite No. 1. As mentioned in a previous chapter, he had already, in 1921, orchestrated the other four pieces from the same group of piano duets to meet the request of a Paris theatre, which needed incidental music for a vaudeville sketch.

Throughout his life, Stravinsky, while challenging or repudiating any political or artistic creed which inhibited his freedom of outlook accepted the dogmas and discipline of the Church with a cheerful acquiescence. For years he conformed wholeheartedly to the practices of the Russian Orthodox Church but some time after his second marriage he switched his allegiance to the Roman Catholic Church. In 1926 he wrote an *a capella* setting of the *Pater Noster*, which sprang from his deep piety. Perhaps because of the childlike faith that inspired it, the *Pater Noster*, influenced by his recollections of the singing and services to which he was taken as a boy, uses only a few mildly dissonant harmonies, contains no suggestion of counterpoint, and must have appeared very un-Stravinskian at the time of its publication. After his 'transfer' to Roman Catholicism, the composer expunged the Russian words not only of the *Pater Noster*, but also of the *Credo* (1932) and *Ave Maria* (1934), replacing them with Latin texts.

It was in September 1925, that the idea of *Oedipus Rex*, prompted five years previously by Stravinsky's awakening desire to compose a large-scale dramatic work, began to develop. During a short stay at Genoa, the scene of his fifth wedding-anniversary celebrations, he found in a book-stall a life of St Francis of Assisi, which he read avidly the same night. It gave him the idea that by transposing a sacred text into a secular one —a reversal of the normal procedure—he could endow it with a monumental character, a universality of spirit untouched by the passage of time. After considering various Greek myths for the 'still-life' drama he envisaged, Stravinsky decided to compose a work on the tragic play of Sophocles. He had greatly admired Cocteau's *Antigone*, for which Honegger provided a superb musical setting; but, having recently quarrelled with the poet, felt diffident about discussing the *Oedipus* project with him.

One day, after they had become reconciled, the two men were travelling in a sleeper near Villefranche. The composer asked his companion to write the libretto of *Oedipus Rex* and, to his joy, the other promptly agreed. Stravinsky lived at that time at Mont-Boron with his wife and sons. There was a wonderful trip to the mountains, which February had covered with rosy trees. Stravinsky brought along his son Theodore, and a chauffeur whom Cocteau re-christened Tiresius for his habit of speaking in oracles with one finger pointing up. The poet read his *Orphée* to Stravinsky, who liked it and expounded to Cocteau the music he was composing for *Oedipus Rex*. "I want to write music as curly as Jupiter's beard",[7] he chuckled. Cocteau took to Stravinsky passages of the text as he wrote them. They enjoyed fishing trips in the dazzling sunlight and walked together, admiring the superb scenery.

The first draft submitted by the poet, a music drama in meretricious prose, disappointed the composer. Stravinsky abhorred *verismo*, and in *Oedipus Rex* he wanted to leave the play, as a play, far behind and, with the text translated into Latin, to make a purely musical dramatization the focal point of interest. Cocteau patiently endured his criticisms and editorial clippings; he re-wrote the book twice and, when all seemed complete, saw Stravinsky again snip ruthlessly at the text. A brilliant cartoonist and master designer, he would discuss the costumes and masks he proposed to create, then with incredible speed sketch the designs on paper. The speaker device which Cocteau introduced remained inviolate, as did his recommendation that the speaker should wear a dress-coat and conduct himself like a *conférencier*, though in a more dignified and priestly rôle.

Time alters everything and the composer came, as the years passed, to detest the speaker, who destroyed the dramatic tension by his constant interruptions; and he regarded some of the speeches as tiresome, classing the line: "And now you will hear the famous monologue 'the divine Iokaste is dead' ", as a piece of intolerable snobbery. The music he adored —even the Messenger's fanfares, which to him suggested the braggadocio trumpets of early 20th Century Fox films. Jean Daniélou, a friend of Cocteau, tackled the Latin translation of *Oedipus*, expunging any 'ecclesiasticism' from the libretto and delivering a strong Ciceronian version. The première of the work as an oratorio, staged by the Russian Ballet and conducted by the composer, took place at the Théâtre Sarah-Bernhardt, Paris, on 30th May 1927. It made little or no impact on an audience which, excited at the prospect of hearing new music by Stravinsky, found *Oedipus* strange and even depressing. The first performance of the work as an opera, in Vienna on 23rd February 1928, also gained few critical plaudits.

Presented as an opera-oratorio, *Oedipus* failed to seduce an audience at the American première given at the Metropolitan Opera House, New York in the winter of 1930, by the Philadelphia Orchestra under Leopold Stokowski and involving the Harvard University Glee Club, the stage designer Robert E. Jones, Mme Matzanauer and Paul Althouse. The chorus, robed magnificently in blue, stood on a dais a little to the left of the stage and clustered around the soloists. The unseen speaker opened the proceedings : "Without knowing it, Oedipus is at cross-purposes with the forces which spy on us from the further side of the grave. From the day of his birth they have been watching him, to set a snare for him into which he shall fall." As the music disclosed its dark, petrified vision of the cruel Powers, a gaunt, twelve-foot effigy of Oedipus the King soared into view, dominating the luminous upper half of the scene. The production must have seemed to many present like some bizarre nightmare as other garish and ghostly puppets, representing Creon, Tiresius, Jocasta and the remaining protagonists took their places beside it. At the chilling peak of the drama, when news came of Jocasta's suicide, the huge effigy vanished; then, as the singers and instrumentalists proclaimed their revulsion at the savage gods, a hideous image of the blinded, naked and outcast Oedipus rose high above the scene, finally sinking into oblivion beneath the titanic pressure of a tragic destiny.

Raimund Herincx, the bass singer, who created one of the great stage triumphs of the century with his portrayal of Nabucco for the Welsh National Opera, filled the role of Creon in a performance of *Oedipus Rex* at the Herodes Atticus Theatre, Athens, only a few years before the composer died. During rehearsals for the production, Herincx, a superb mime with a Puckish sense of humour, established a friendly and intimate relationship with Stravinsky, whose kindness touched him deeply. When Raimund spoke to me about this manifestation of kindness in a man whom misguided people so often regarded as waspish and intolerant, I detected a sincere ring of hero-worship in his voice. One incident, in particular, rooted itself in his memory.

The choosing of a tenor for the title role was causing grave concern, since each of the four men already suggested—Ronald Dowd, John Mitchinson, Gerald English and Alexander Young—had to refuse because of a previous engagement. Finally Herincx put forward the name of Stuart Burrows, then a young, comparatively unknown singer with a few B.B.C. television and Covent Garden appearances to his credit. Stravinsky, who had previously discussed the capabilities of this Welsh tenor with Charles Mackerras, the conductor, pretended to be surprised at the nomination, but, with a guileful show of innocence, readily approved it.

At the first rehearsal he noticed Burrows, pale and unhappy, standing alone, waiting for instructions. Stravinsky, switching on one of those huge, fatherly grins that seemed to reach both his ears, approached Burrows and asked in a reassuring voice "Why are you looking so nervous?" The singer fidgeted in silence, then, gathering courage, stared Stravinsky straight in the eye. "Well, you see, Mr Stravinsky, I'm a little afraid of you—such a great composer." Stravinsky placed a hand on his shoulder. "You have no need to be," he replied. "It is I who am afraid of you—such a fine, healthy tenor."

For the actual performance a large audience, including prominent critics and other distinguished people, filled the splendid old amphitheatre. Intimidated by this clearly knowledgeable assembly, and with the most important composer of the age on the rostrum, Burrows, understandably, shook with fright as he rose to his feet. Once again Stravinsky's face wrinkled into a vast, warm, reassuring grin. He nodded encouragement to the singer, continuing to smile at him as if to a much-loved brother, and, enveloped by the sunshine of his personality, Burrows became transformed, acting and singing the part of Oedipus so magnificently that the audience cheered him enthusiastically after the performance.

"Stravinsky, by his kindness, quite literally made Stuart what he is today—a front-rank, international tenor," Raimund told me. "I had never before encountered such gentle compassion on the stage or the concert platform. It was a beautiful and moving experience."

He also spoke feelingly about the composer's impish humour. Stravinsky had seen the Sadler's Wells production of *Oedipus Rex* and, referring to this, he suddenly began a voluble discussion about the correct way to perform his own music. On an impulse, he seized Herincx's arm and said "Please sit down beside me, and I'll *show* you how my music ought to be played." The singer did so. Nothing happened. Stravinsky merely squatted there, with shoulders hunched, in a mysterious aura of silence. A few minutes passed, then he looked at his puzzled companion and, with a twinkle in his eye, exclaimed "Oh, forgive me, but you're sitting on my right, instead of my left. Come over here." Herincx changed sides, and instantly became aware of something he had not been able to see before —Stravinsky had his tongue in his cheek, which bulged as if he had a large toffee there. The composer, watching Herincx's dawning comprehension, laughed aloud. "There, *now* you understand how my music ought to be played."

One afternoon Stravinsky, pointing to the score of *Oedipus*, remarked playfully to Herincx, "At this point Creon has galloped all the way from Delphi, having consulted the Oracle. We *know* that the god spoke to Creon because he arrives at the exact moment he is needed for the drama to continue, and he also tells Oedipus what the god said." The composer wagged a finger at his companion. "Now then, what do I, Stravinsky, do for him at this moment? Why, I make him sing in common time, in C major." Then he added, with a sly chuckle, "But not for long!"

During rehearsal the tenor who played the part of the shepherd sang the first phrase a note too high. The singer repeated his mistake three times, and from Stravinsky, three times, came a loud, digruntled "No!" Finally, he shrugged his shoulders in a whimsical gesture of defeat and, turning to one of the musicians, remarked "Oh, well, I suppose he knows best!" A similar incident, related by Laszlo Krausz, occurred during a recording of the *Pulcinella* suite by the Cleveland Orchestra. At one point the solo clarinettist stood up and said, apologetically, "Maestro, in bar — I played an F sharp instead of an F." Stravinsky smiled. "You did? I like it. Let's leave it there, shall we!"

Six days after the Athens performance of *Oedipus Rex* the production moved to Lisbon in Portugal, where Gerald English took over the title role. He and Herincx had a touching demonstration of Stravinsky's humility when, approaching him one afternoon with the remark that he would probably need them at rehearsal, they received the prompt reply, "No, I don't. You two go for a swim; after all, you know the work much better than I do." At the end of the Lisbon performance the President of Portugal decorated Stravinsky on the spot. The audience applauded so loudly and demonstratively that it seemed as if the frail little composer might be swept off his feet and carried away in triumph like some Cup-winning football captain. He stood there, his eyes filled with tears, drinking in this visible token of success and affection.

During those creative years the character of Stravinsky assumed a sharper, clearer, more colourful aspect. That great pianist Harriet Cohen found him "more like an exotic plant than a man". Discussing interpretation and performance with the Russian master, she found that the strength and logic of his ideas influenced her own. "What is your attitude, your mood when you start to play?" Stravinsky asked her. "Head of ice, heart of fire," she told him. "Exactly," he said, with a nod of approval. "You'll do."[8]

Stravinsky's first collaboration with Balanchine was in *Apollo* originally (*Apollon Musagète*) which the choreographer described as "the turning point in my life", and which he intended for that superb dancer Lifar. The beautiful score which Stravinsky wrote for this ballet, a strange compound of disciplined restraint and tender lyricism, brought Balanchine the amazing discovery that, by reducing all the possibilities of a project to the one inevitable and inherent possibility, he could clarify his stylistic art to the point of perfection. This brilliantly perceptive man suddenly realized that, like the tones in music, the tints in painting, and the curves of linear groupings in sculpture, choreographic gestures have a 'family' relationship which imposes inescapable laws.

Diaghilev received the score of the new ballet, then without a name, in September 1927, and praised it highly. He described it as being "full of majestic themes, all in the major key". Diaghilev embraced the composer, who said: "Try to do it well, and make Lifar do all kinds of flourishes."[9] He also urged the impresario to find a good title for the ballet. This amused Diaghilev, since the subject of the work had not yet presented itself; but soon both materialized, and a new masterpiece, *Apollon Musagète*, was born.

The ballet was prepared at Monte Carlo in the spring of 1928. Nicholas Nabokov, the gifted young composer whose Ode, choreographed by Massine, delighted audiences during the Diaghilev season there, described in *Old Friends and New Music* some of the events in the rehearsal hall. On entering it, looking for Diaghilev, he saw the huge figure of André Derain leaning against the upright piano. Diaghilev sat to his left, and next to him a grotesque, dishevelled little man with thick glasses and a straggling goatee beard giggled away in a bleating voice. This oddity was André Bauchant, the primitivist painter, whom Diaghilev, seeking to avoid 'a false Hellenism', had commissioned to design the sets. His pockets bulged with photographs of his own work, which he showed to anyone he could coax into a discussion, urging them to buy the originals. In the centre of the rehearsal hall, as Nabokov entered, three ballerinas were clustered around and over a male dancer. The ballerinas were Tchernicheva, Doubrovska and Nikitina; the male dancer was Serge Lifar. That group's pose has since become famous in the annals of choreographic classicism : Lifar knelt between the three ballerinas, who dipped forwards, with their necks stretched upwards, so that they looked like three drinking swans whose precarious balance was maintained by a trembling hand clutching Lifar's shoulder. In front of the group stood its inventor, the smiling and very young-looking George Balanchine—Diaghilev's recent discovery—his new choreographic genius.

The première of the ballet took place at the Théâtre Sarah-Bernhardt, Paris on 12th June 1928, with Stravinsky conducting. Lifar appeared as Apollo and so moved Diaghilev that, backstage after the performance, the impresario knelt down and kissed his leg in homage. "Remember it, Seriozha, for the rest of your days," Diaghilev said to him. "I am kissing a dancer's leg for the second time in my life. The last was Nijinsky's, after *Le Spectre de la Rose*."[10] Shortly afterwards he presented Lifar with a beautiful lyre made of gold. The audience applauded rapturously at the final curtain, and Gordon Craig subsequently wrote that he found the ballet so wonderful that he left the theatre during the interval that followed it, without seeing the rest of the programme, because he wanted to preserve its loveliness in his memory as long as possible.

Apollon Musagète was an indisputable triumph, and Diaghilev described it in these words : "Stravinsky's new ballet is a great event in the musical word. I consider it as one of his masterpieces, the product of true artistic maturity. It has a majestic serenity about it. . . ." The dance critic B. H. Haggin, writing in the *Hudson Review*, a famous American journal, contributed probably the best of all the reports on the première of the ballet : "*Apollo* amazes one with what it produced at the beginning—the visually exciting and touching dance and pantomime metaphors that express Apollo's growing consciousness of his powers and describe his involvement with the three Muses : the soaring leaps around them that express his wonder and delight; the leaps that frighten them in the coda; the turns with which, fascinated, he follows Terpsichore's playful little hops; the exquisite episode in which he and Terpsichore sink to their knees, facing each other, he holds out his open hands, she places her elbows on them and opens her hands, and he lays his cheek on them."

Balanchine collaborated with Stravinsky in other major projects—

Card Game : *A Ballet in Three Deals, Balustrade, Danses Concertantes, Elegie, Reynard, Orpheus, Agon, Ragtime, Monumentum Pro Gesualdo, Noah and the Flood, Movements for Piano and Orchestra*. Throughout the years that saw these ballets created and performed, Stravinsky and Balanchine, both Russian emigrés, schooled in the subtle artistic ferment that was Paris after World War I, and both settled in America, became firm friends. One of Balanchine's associates remarked : "The only time Balanchine loses that air of calm, complete authority he has is when he is with Stravinsky. Then he's like a boy with his father. The two can respect each other's opinions, be gay and playful together, work together— but they never forget who is the father, and who the son." Balanchine summarized his own feelings about their relationship in these words : "It's a pleasure to be with Stravinsky, because he's a happy man."[12]

Happy the composer may have been, but Serge Diaghilev, provoked by what he regarded as increasingly rapacious raids on his balletic pre- serves by the dancer Ida Rubinstein, felt completely miserable and almost worked himself into a teeth-baring rage. Rubinstein, having at the begin- ning of 1928 started to form a dance company of her own, now cast her covetous gaze in the direction of Diaghilev's own wonder-child Igor Stravinsky. She wanted initially to include Stravinsky's new ballet *Apollon Musagète* in her repertoire; but, on being told by his publisher, Paichadze of the Edition Russe de Musique, that Diaghilev owned the European rights, she offered to commission a new work. Benois submitted two plans, one of them for a ballet to be set to music by Tchaikovsky; and Stravin- sky, aware that the première of the new work would coincide with the thirty-fifth anniversary of Tchaikovsky's death, swallowed the tempting bait. He decided, after a brief search, that one of Hans Andersen's longer stories, *The Ice Maiden*, would be an ideal subject for the ballet.

Stravinsky intended Andersen's appealing tale as an act of homage to Tchaikovsky, and took as his starting point a number of pieces by that composer. The scenario of the ballet was directly based on the story, which Stravinsky described thus : "A fairy imprints her magic kiss on a child at birth and parts it from its mother. Twenty years later, when the youth has attained the very zenith of his good fortune, she repeats the fatal kiss and carries him off to live in supreme happiness with her ever after- wards. . . ."[13] The composer pictured all the fantastic parts danced in fluffy white ballet skirts, and for the rustic scenes a tourist-thronged village set against a lovely Swiss landscape.

Stravinsky composed most of the music for the new ballet, entitled *The Fairy's Kiss*, at Encharvines on Lake Annecy during the summer of 1928, completing the instrumentation at Nice in the autumn. The orchestration of the score took up so much of his time that he could not supervise Nijinska's choreography, and, inconsequence, found, when he directed the final rehearsal in Paris, that he disapproved of much that she had done. He had brought great imagination and sincerity to his treatment of the 'borrowed' melodies, and, indeed, *The Fairy's Kiss* illustrates with profound eloquence his love for Tchaikovsky's music. It was based on what he described as "the cut of its phrases and their ordering", although subsequently he dismissed it rather contemptuously as "saccharine salon music". The première of the ballet, with sets by Alexandre Benois, given by the Ballets Ida Rubinstein, took place at the Opera House, Paris on 27th November 1928.

The following day, after seeing the performance, Diaghilev wrote that the new ballet, particularly Stravinsky's music, had given him a terrible headache. He described it as being "more like a bad suite by Tchaikovsky than anything else, tearful and monstrous", and condemned the music for its "dull harmony and dead execution".[14] During the performance, he said, everybody pretended there was nothing wrong, and Stravinsky got his two curtain calls; but, claimed Diaghilev, "the ballet is still-born". And, suddenly becoming aggressive, he asked, "What is the point of it all? We need someone, either Napoleon or the Bolsheviks, to come and blow up these hovels, with their public, their p—— who think themselves dancers, their millions spent on buying musicians. . . ."[15]

Diaghilev's anger vented itself upon the unfortunate Ida Rubinstein with still greater fury after he had attended another of her performances in the company of Stravinsky. He described what he saw as "a ghastly experience". According to him, Rubinstein, who danced the principal role, was a bent, ridiculous figure, with dishevelled red hair, who wobbled on her points and presented "an enormous gaping mouth with close-set teeth trying to grimace a smile".[16] She wore a coffee-coloured toga, which Diaghilev venomously suggested might have cost "1,000 francs a metre",[17] and she looked "as old as the devil".[18] He classed her performance as "shocking"[19] and noted—with fiendish satisfaction—that, when Ida disappeared into the wings, hunched up and ashamed, nobody clapped.

Whatever the artistic merits of Rubinstein may have been during that performance, she had, at the peak of her fame, been a superb dancer. She took the title role in Fokine's and Bakst's masterpiece *Schéhérazade* during the first Paris season of the Russian Ballet, and Romola Nijinsky wrote of her: "Rubinstein, tall, with movements of a great plastic beauty, was admirable as Scheherazade. Her gestures were a combination of dignity and sensuality, and expressed the essential languors of a woman who demanded sexual satisfaction . . . this pale, marvellous woman whom he (the slave) so desired with every nerve and muscle in his body quivering."[20]

Stravinsky clearly supported Diaghilev in his harsh judgement of Rubinstein, since he telephoned the impresario next day to convey his regret and indignation at what they had both seen. Yet, according to Argoutinski, the composer went into Ida's dressing-room after the final curtain and whispered urbanely, "delightful, from the bottom of my heart I tell you it's enchanting".[21] Diplomacy and dishonesty sometimes make strange bedfellows.

As the months passed, Diaghilev saw Rubinstein more and more as a dangerous rival who had taken from him all his former colleagues—Stravinsky, Sauguet, Benois, Wilzak, Schollar, Massine, Nijinska, Unger—and the mere mention of her name kindled his wrath. He expressed his feelings about Stravinsky's defection in the biting remark "Notre Igor aime seulement l'argent!";[22] and he suggested cuttingly that the 'or' in Igor stood for gold. Diaghilev felt the instability of his position keenly, not only because of ill-health, of which he was soon to die, but also because his financial resources had been evaporating for some time. What money he could spare now went into the collection of rare books and manuscripts by great Russian writers, and the genius which had once blazed inside him seemed to be shrinking into a small, pitiful flame.

Stravinsky was deeply troubled at the dissolution of his friendship with Diaghilev, since he felt both gratitude and affection for him. In May 1929, entering the Gare du Nord *en route* to London, he unexpectedly met Diaghilev and Boris Kochno; the startled impresario spoke to him with embarrassed kindness, but the barrier still towered between them. Soon, however, the composition of a new work, the *Capriccio* for piano and orchestra, occupied Stravinsky's mind and, after concentrating throughout the autumn on its instrumentation, he finished it in September. With himself as the soloist, the première took place on 6th December 1929, in the Salle Pleyel, Paris, at a concert of the Paris Symphony Orchestra, conducted by Ansermet. A brilliant, whimsical, staccato piece in the style of a Weberian *Konzertstück*, it carried its audience back to the lustres and *décolletages* of an early Victorian-type drawing room.

At the beginning of August in that year, while Stravinsky was working on his *Capriccio*, which La Scala subsequently commissioned Massine to choreograph, the inimitable Serge Diaghilev, now a very sick man, went to the Lido to recuperate, hoping that the rest and change of air would restore him to health. Alas, his condition grew worse, puzzling his doctors, who suspected from his temperatures that he might have typhoid, but could not be certain. Diaghilev had, in fact, suffered an attack of diabetes, his old, neglected illness. The sallow, wasted colour of his face, puffy, with the glazed yellow quality of diabetes, the tired, frightened eyes, with dark, heavy bags beneath them, flashed a warning light for that final and most awe-inspiring of curtains. Diaghilev sank into a coma some time before the end, but rallied fitfully to say a few cheerful words to his visitors, who included Serge Lifar and Coco Chanel. On 19th August 1929, about five in the morning—that hour when the frail cobweb of life so often disintegrates—the death agony seized him; he gasped for nearly an hour, then suddenly expired. He spoke his last words to the Baroness d'Erlanger, a faithful friend who stayed at his bedside: "Ah,

Catherine . . . how beautiful you look . . . I am very ill, very ill, indeed . . . I feel so hot . . . light-headed." This incomparable man was only fifty-seven years old.

Many people who knew him intimately have contributed enough descriptive anecdotes to create a reliable portrait of Diaghilev. He carried a cane as Boris Godunov a sceptre—with an air of regality dispelled only when, with a debonair flourish, he whistled it around to illustrate some flight of oratory. Diaghilev used to chew tiny, violet-scented candy and, in consequence, a faint odour of violets hung almost permanently around him. His haughty bearing, reinforced by a high-pitched, nasal, and capricious tone, could be intimidating; yet his warm smile and generous heart quickly dispelled resentment and hostility. He held dominion over others, not so much by implacable opposition—though he could be ruthless—as by suave, impetuous arguments, capped by often infallible judgements. He could discern the whole crystal-clear outline of a situation when it seemed to comprise only scattered, irreconcilable fragments.

In some matters, particularly as regards religion and superstition, Diaghilev was as naïve and circumspect as a convent-reared schoolgirl. His relationship with the Almighty did not appear to be a recognizably intimate one; yet he periodically left a visiting-card at the paradisal gates. On one occasion, when Diaghilev, who had an almost hysterical terror of ocean voyages, travelled by ship to New York and a storm arose, he instructed his servant Vassily to kneel down and pray for them both. While the intercession rose Heavenward, Diaghilev himself lay comfortably on a bunk. Yet if kindness and generosity have any value, then Diaghilev communicated regularly with his Creator.

He took pride in the large salaries that he paid, and exhibited signs of distress when, during a financial crisis, he had to delay handing over the money. Unexpected gifts—substantial sums—reached many of his dancers and technical, or artistic staff; the recipients did not solicit these, and Diaghilev made them spontaneously, depositing the money in the respective bank accounts. Most of his artistes never requested, or needed, a contract; he gave his word and though institutions might crumble and decay that for Diaghilev represented the enduring and unbreakable.

Whilst during a lean period he showed generosity to others, he often deprived himself of even the visible tokens of respectability. Julian Braunsweg, director-general of Festival Ballet for so many years, described how, in 1926, as a budding impresario, he went to Diaghilev after negotiating an engagement for the Russian Ballet at the Deutsches Künstlertheater in Berlin and diffidently raised the delicate mater of the expenses he had incurred. Diaghilev listened gravely, then remarked "Young man, why do you think you will make money in ballet? Look at my shoes . . ." and, uncrossing his legs, he displayed the sole of one shoe—it was in holes! "You see? I have never made any money in ballet, and you never will!"[23]

I

His fear of the evil eye, dominated his life like an African witchdoctor's curse. He carried amulets, invested, so he believed, with magic powers, pronounced talismanic formulas, with the first two fingers of his right hand upraised as if in exorcism, avoided black cats or walking under ladders, counted paving stones and studied the esoteric trends of astrology. When Arnold Haskell, the writer, visited Diaghilev at a hotel, the impresario greeted him thus : "Come in and sit down. No—for God's sake don't put your hat on the bed, it's unlucky! It means death; no—no—not on the table, either—that means poverty."[24]

Diaghilev has often been portrayed as a cold, self-centred egotist, capable of praise and encouragement when a performance sated his artistic hunger, but devoid of any real warmth or human feeling. Such caricatures do him a grave injustice. Certainly Tamara Karsavina, whom I visited in 1971, saw him differently. This grave and gentle old lady, who, though incapacitated by her age, still had the slim, aristocratic legs of a *prima ballerina assoluta*, described Diaghilev as displaying an almost childlike sensitivity. We sat drinking vodka in a room crowded with souvenirs of her great past, including a large, sad-faced doll in a fluffy white tutu who looked as if she was only waiting for some unseen orchestra to begin tuning-up before floating across the carpet towards me. The thought occurred to me that perhaps Diaghilev had had more than a professional fondness for the lovely girl who brought his, and Stravinsky's, *Firebird* to life.

Diaghilev always insisted that Karsavina's name went at the top of posters outside theatres where she was appearing. On one occasion, Tamara told me, the manager of a small theatre deliberately placed the name of his wife, who had a minor part in a production, above her own. Diaghilev was furious. He rushed into the manager's office, shaking with anger and white to the lips; seizing the culprit and swinging him to and fro, he flung him against a wall, with enough force to break every bone in his body. "I thought Diaghilev meant to kill him," said Karsavina. "He stood there, towering over the manager, who lay on the floor, staring up with terror, and cried out in a slow, twisted voice, 'Never, never do that again'. Then, turning towards me with tears streaming down his face, he took my hands in his own and whispered 'Forgive me, forgive me . . .' again and again, as if the fault had been his own."

On another occasion, as previously narrated in this book, Diaghilev learned that Lifar had fallen in love with Karsavina; red-faced and shouting at the top of his voice, he called the astonished young man a debaucher. Admittedly, the impresario regarded any breath of romance in his company as an ill wind, since it meant the possible defection, or at least the reduced efficiency, of the artistes concerned; but his rage over the Lifar incident, and his violent assault on the erring theatre manager, seemed utterly disproportionate to the issues involved. Diaghilev's bisexuality, which he openly professed, has been grossly exaggerated by morbid writers incapable of understanding the ambivalence of the creative psyche. He had the capacity to nurture and sustain an intense love; but, recognizing his own physical shortcomings, did not openly display it. When I gently conveyed to Karsavina my suspicion that this very sensitive, warm-hearted man might have been secretly in love with her, she wrinkled her face in a sweet, madonna-like smile—almost like that of a shy young schoolgirl suppressing a blush—and whispered, "Do you really think so? Perhaps. . . ."

Diaghilev did not, contrary to the claims of some misguided people, seduce or possess Nijinsky like some demoniac Svengali; he loved and helped him, encouraging his rare gifts until, through encroaching madness and the dancer's own waywardness, he could do no more. Mr Dobrecki, manager of the Russian Ballet over many years, revealed the fact that Diaghilev "paid important sums to the artist's current account at the bank" and that, at a time when the dancer could no longer fend for himself, "he was keeping Nijinsky entirely; paying for his first-class hotels, first-class tailor's bills, and generally assuring him a life of luxury".[25]

Diaghilev was broken-hearted at the news that Nijinsky had suffered a complete mental collapse. Once, frantic with joy at some reported improvement, he raced to Paris, only to face disillusionment. He sought diligently for some means of healing that pathetically sick mind—now, alas, damaged irreparably. One readily forgives Romola Nijinsky for her harsh criticisms of Diaghilev, since they were activated largely by grief and the immense, blinding love she bore her husband. Kyra, the dancer's daughter, put the matter into perspective with these words : "I remember one day Diaghilev coming to our flat in Paris. I must have been about nine at the time. Father was already very ill, and Diaghilev hoped to awaken something in him. He came up to father, spoke a few quiet words, but father only stared into space beyond him, looking at nothing. There was no trace of recognition. I could see how Diaghilev suffered, and I felt infinitely sorry for him. Then he spoke to me. . . . Immediately I felt all his charm, and I loved him. Now that I am old enough to understand, I am infinitely grateful to this great man for my father's sake. I honour and respect his memory. He understood him as no-one else ever could; he gave him the chance to develop and show his wonderful creations to the world, yes, I am truly grateful."[26]

The news of Diaghilev's death shocked and saddened Stravinsky. Since the première of *The Fairy's Kiss* the two men, who really had a profound affection for each other, had drifted apart, Stravinsky feeling that the impresario, extolling 'modernism' at any price, cared only for the sensational; now death had widened the gap, but perhaps had also, in a sense, closed it, for healing comes with remorse and understanding. The composer, writing of Diaghilev's death, remarked that everything that is original is irreplaceable—an epigram which, in a singularly fine phrase, the painter Constantine Korovine expressed differently: "I thank you," he said to Diaghilev shortly before his death, "I thank you for being alive."[27]

Walter Nouvel, in a letter to Stravinsky, praised the dead impresario in these words: "We are sharing the same sorrow. I am bereft of a man to whom I was tied by a friendship for forty years. But I am happy today that I never failed to be faithful to that friendship. Many things united us, and many things separated us. Often I suffered from him, often I was revolted by him, but now that he is in the grave all is forgotten and all forgiven. And I understand now that no ordinary measure of the conduct of human relations could be applied to so exceptional a man. He lived and died 'one of the favoured of God'. But he was a heathen, and a Dionysian heathen, not an Apollonian. He loved all earthly things: earthly passions, earthly beauty. . . . Such a man must be loved by Christ."[28]

As befitted one who had claimed direct descent from Peter the Great, the passing of Diaghilev, in its final stages, had the splendour and the sadness of a Viking funeral rite. Serge Lifar prepared the body for burial, according it the reverence given to a dead king. Those enigmatic eyes that once harboured wonderful balletic visions were closed forever; the face that had changed so often from raging anger to sweet serenity looked young and handsome. The following night, as he lay in his darkened room, surrounded by flowers, a violent storm swept across Venice, churning up the lightning-streaked canals and providing a Wagnerian requiem for Diaghilev, as dramatic and spectacular as he himself would have had it. At dawn, reposing in a coffin with a crucifix in one hand, and smothered in tuberoses, tea-roses, and carnations, he was carried from the hotel across a thick green carpet of leaves laid by the storm and placed upon a gondola.

The slender boat, seeming like a proud black swan with its wings furled, glided across the lagoon, taking with it the strangely diminished body of probably the most remarkable man who had ever transformed and irradiated the mystique of stage dancing. One can almost imagine the ghosts of dead ballerinas skimming on their points beside the barge; in three accompanying gondolas a Russian priest and the choir of San Giorgio dei Greci sang the plaintive chant of the Slavic funeral service. Diaghilev, with his superb artistic taste, could not have wished for a nobler, more picturesque departure. On the little island of San Michele, among the whispering cypress-trees, they buried him and wept over him; and there until the year 1971, when his friend Stravinsky lay down beside him, Diaghilev slept alone. On a simple stone are engraved these words:

Venice, l'Inspiratrice Éternelle
de nos Appaisements.
Serge de Diaghilev
1872–1929.

GIDE HELPS TO CREATE "PERSÉPHONE"

Stravinsky was upset by Diaghilev's death, but also, in a sense, emancipated by it, since he now faced the future dependent solely on himself. In 1928 he had completed the re-instrumentation of his Three Pieces for String Quartet and the Study for Pianola, which, performed in Berlin on 7th November 1930, now bore the title Four Studies for Orchestra. As the creative sap rose inside him again, he started work on one of the most important compositions of his life, the *Symphony of Psalms*, one of the pieces commissioned by Koussevitzky to celebrate the fiftieth anniversary of the Boston Symphony Orchestra. In this work Stravinsky showed once more a genius for renewing and enriching his own art by the cultivation of that historical awareness which, largely through his leadership, became a dominant feature of twentieth-century music. The verses he used came from Psalms XXVIII, XXXIX, and CL in the Vulgate. Writing choral passages bare of chromaticism, which sometimes exploited the voices in unison, and stripping his orchestra of violins, violas and clarinets, he created a work in the grand style whose bold, craggy architecture proclaimed a new-found strength. The score is curiously rigid and hieratic, yet the simplicity and sombre colouring of the three movements contrast wonderfully with the final radiant Alleluia, which glows like the mosaics in a Byzantine church.

The use of the word 'hieratic' to describe a particular aspect of Stravinsky or his music appears elsewhere in this book. One of the meanings of the word is 'priestly', an adjective which, with its flavour of ritualism or traditional orthodoxy, seems to fit a composer who, in his constant search for more original, but simpler forms of expression, drew upon traditional styles of art, reaching far back into the past to achieve what might be termed 'art by privation'. Stravinsky needed the atmosphere of the stage to bring out his best and, since the vivid unity of action which a theatrical setting provides was not always available or suitable for a subject, he found a substitute in works like the incantatory Mass, the cold, stern oratorio *Oedipus Rex*, the Canticum Sacrum, with its impersonal use of the dead Latin tongue, and the solemn, but uplifting Requiem Canticles. His liturgical idiom strikes a slightly chilling, but impressive note in the chorus of ghosts in Act III of *The Nightingale*, in the fourth Russian Song, in the closing movement of the Symphony in C, and in the graveyard scene of *The Rake's Progress*, where strange passages of bass instrumental chanting occur. Even in so early a work as *The King of the Stars* the listener is aware of a kind of transcendental mysticism that marks its creator as a hierophant or propounder of sacred mysteries.

Various concert tours in Europe, during which Stravinsky performed his *Capriccio*, interrupted the composition of the *Symphony of Psalms*, but he completed the work on 15th August, writing the last two movements partly at Nice and partly at Charavines on Lake Paladru, subsequently finishing the orchestration. He inscribed it "to the glory of God and dedicated to the Boston Symphony Orchestra on the occasion of its fiftieth anniversary". Ansermet conducted the first European première on 13th December 1930, in a Société Philharmonique de Bruxelles concert at the Palais des Beaux-Arts, Brussels, and six days later Koussevitzky directed the first American performance at Boston. Stravinsky himself thought highly of the *Symphony of Psalms*, and when he conducted it in later years invariably presented it with deep insight and affection.

During a series of visits to Mainz and Wiesbaden the composer became friendly with Willy Strecker of Schott's, the music publishing firm, who, at the beginning of 1931, introduced him to the young American violinist Samuel Dushkin and suggested that he should write a special work for him. Dushkin was the discovery of Blair Fairchild, a wealthy American who, dazzled by the musical eloquence of the violinist when he first heard him as a child, sponsored his training and career thereafter. Stravinsky hesitated at first when Strecker made his bold request, but, finding Dushkin to be a sincere, unattitudinizing player, and not the type of temperamental virtuoso he detested, agreed to accept a commission from Fairchild for a violin concerto. He stipulated that Dushkin should collaborate over the solo part.

Characteristically, he first examined the standard violin concertos and reached the conclusion that not one, including those of Mozart, Beethoven and Brahms, could be classed as among its composer's best work. The concerto he wrote did not conform to any example, yet, for all its explicit elements of pastiche, it was brilliantly scored, intriguing in the manner in which the soloist caught the textures of the other instruments in conversation. Stravinsky composed the first two movements and part of the third movement at Nice, completing the concerto at La Vironnière, a splendid *château* near Voreppe, which he rented from a country lawyer who, in his own words, looked like Flaubert. Although from his attic studio in the *château*, he had a breathtaking view of the Val d'Isère, the slightly primitive aspects of country life and the need to drive into Grenoble for provisions irked him and, on finishing the score, he gladly departed. The poor rendering of the concerto by the Berlin Radio Orchestra at the première given in Berlin on 23rd October 1931, with Stravinsky conducting and Dushkin as the soloist, so enraged Paul Hindemith who was present, that speaking of the performance afterwards he castigated the players with a verbal fury.

Stravinsky and Dushkin subsequently appeared together in a number of violin and piano recitals. The programmes included, not only arrangements of earlier works (excerpts from *The Firebird, Petrushka* and *The Nightingale*, for example) but also the Duo Concertante, which Stravinsky created after writing his Violin Concerto. The composer had never really liked the combination of violin and piano, and confessed that he "took no pleasure in the blend of strings struck in the piano with strings set in vibration with the bow"; yet, in this instance, he decided that the union of the two instruments would serve his purpose—that of writing a "lyrical composition, a work of musical versification". Perhaps because of the uncertainty he felt at this marriage of convenience, much of the music is pedestrian and rarely comes to life. Stravinsky finished the Duo Concertante on 15th July 1932; he and Dushkin gave the first performance at the Berliner Rundfunk on 28th October the same year.

During a visit to Rome in 1932, he conducted some Debussy pieces. Mussolini sent for him after the concert, and Stravinsky entered that notoriously huge and ugly office in the Palazzo Venezia, where the *Duce*, dressed in a dark business suit, greeted him with an Italianate "Bonjour, Stravinsky, asseyez-vous."[1] Mussolini treated the composer with a dictatorial condescension. On being told that the *Duce* played the violin, Stravinsky, droll as ever, suppressed with great difficulty the temptation to mention Nero. He remembered afterwards that Mussolini had cruel eyes and he tried to avoid returning to Rome, in case he had, once again, to suffer the indignity of meeting the tyrant whom Cassandra of the *Daily Mirror* so fittingly described as "the swollen bullfrog of the Pontine marshes".

From mediocrity to the heights of glory; so, not infrequently, runs the life of a great man. Thus, after completing the Duo Concertante, an opportunity came to the composer at the beginning of 1933 when Ida Rubinstein commissioned him to set to music a poem by André Gide based on the Homeric *Hymn to Demeter*. After travelling to Wiesbaden to discuss the project, Gide showed Stravinsky the manuscript on 8th February, and both men agreed on how to discharge their respective tasks. The poetry of Gide's text, largely a reworking of material "more than twenty years old", did not arouse much enthusiasm in Stravinsky and he wrote it, denigratingly, as *vers caramel*, classing Gide himself as an "anti-poet". He also raised his eyebrows at such directions in the libretto as "sounds of joy in the orchestra" and "Pluto must be a bass, the deepest possible". No-one, at this stage of his career, told Igor Stravinsky what to do without dropping sparks into a gunpowder keg.

Gide, whose novel *La Porte Etroite* was described by Apollinaire as the finest of its decade, wrote with a purity and harmony of style that surely give him an immortal place amongst the great masters of French literature. When the First World War ended there were three other leading French writers—Claudel, Valéry and Proust—but while each of them excelled in one literary form, Gide spread his moralizing genius over a wide area, dominating the entire literary scene in the year following the war. Gide considered that, in attempting to conform to man-made principles and customs, the individual was compelled to develop a counterfeit personality which crippled him and which must, at all costs, be rejected. Considering the originality of thought and strength of character which he always displayed, his differences with Stravinsky were inevitable. Gide's undistinguished appearance and his manner of dressing like a *petit bourgeois* betrayed nothing of the spiritual ferment inside him. He had a thin, slightly ironic smile (or was it, Stravinsky wondered, a sign of inner torment?) and when he spoke only his lips and mouth moved, his body and the rest of his face freezing into immobility. Described by Curtius as "The Voice of the European Mind", he became the spokesman for the new *mal du siècle*, the symbol of the *angst* of the post-war generation.

One of Gide's first letters to Stravinsky explained that the source and inspiration of *Perséphone* had been the Homeric *Hymn to Demeter*, according to which, in Andrew Lang's fine translation :

> Persephone, daughter of the Earth-Mother Demeter, was by Hades snatched away. . . . (She) was playing with the deep-bosomed maidens of Oceanus, was gathering flowers—roses, and crocuses, and fair violets in the soft meadow, and lilies and hyacinths, and the narcissus which the earth brought forth as a snare to the fair-faced maiden. . . . Wondrously bloomed the flower, a marvel for all to see, whether deathless gods or deathly men. . . . The maiden marvelled and stretched forth both her hands to seize the fair plaything, but the wide-eyed earth gaped and up rushed the Prince. . . . (Against) her will he seized her, and drove her off weeping in his golden chariot; but she shrilled aloud, calling on Father Cronides, the highest of the gods and the best.

Elevated in style and mood, reserved and silvery in atmosphere, *Perséphone* has, at times, a kind of religious ecstasy that transcends the banality of much of the poetry. Gide admired some of the music that Stravinsky wrote for the libretto no more ardently than the Russian enthused over the verses. Where Gide, in the opening scene, gave Stravinsky an opportunity for graceful and voluptuous music, the composer produced music (the *Ländler* of the nymphs, for example) that seemed to the French poet uncouth and mediocre. Stravinsky could certainly write a beautiful melody, but he showed, so often, a fierce contempt for the senses and, in preserving a religious atmosphere in *Perséphone*, refused to make any transparent appeal to them. In this attitude he was undoubtedly correct. The score bristles with severe and ascetic instrumental groupings (oboe and tuba; flute, tuba and timpani) but it pulsates with thrilling, even awe-inspiring music, of which Perséphone's new vision of the light, and the gorgeous Russian barbaric chorus hailing the reborn queen and threaded by festive drumbeats are shining examples.

The unstaged preview performance of *Perséphone* at the home of the Polignacs appears, in Stravinsky's own words, to have been rather explosive : "I can still see the Princess's salon, myself groaning at the piano, Suvchinsky singing a loud and abrasive Eumolpus, Claudet glaring at me from the other side of the keyboard, Gide bridling more noticeably with each phrase." Stravinsky completed the orchestration on 24th January 1934, and conducted the première of this great work, given by the Ballets Ida Rubinstein at the Paris Opera House on 30th April, with Rubinstein herself in the title role. In this production Kurt Jooss arranged the dances, and André Barsacq designed the scenery and costumes.

In *Le Ménestrol*, after the première, the critic Jean Chantevoine wrote : "The music of *Perséphone* is dry, glum, lacks individual accent and expansion, and strikes me as a symbol of those abstract theories which would deprive man of all in him that is not 'social'—or in other words all that is his own self : love, joy, caprice, preferences." As against this, *La Revue Musicale* praised the music unstintingly : "The score is splendidly balanced, the choruses are superb, and some of them stand among the greatest things Stravinsky has given us. The austere, powerful music rises at times to great heights of noble emotion."

The mood of religious ecstasy which inspired Stravinsky throughout the composition of *Perséphone* found a new, if humbler manifestation in the short *Credo* and *Ave Maria*, written in 1932 and 1934 respectively. Scored for unaccompanied S.A.T.B. choir, they were intended for use in the Russian Orthodox Church service; although, as mentioned previously, he subsequently, as a token of his transfer to the Roman Catholic faith, replaced the original words with Latin texts.

Although Stravinsky became a naturalized Frenchman on 10th June 1934, and a year later, with typical aplomb, applied unsuccessfully for membership of the Académie Française, a vacancy having been created by the death of Paul Dukas, he made an increasing number of visits to America. After the Paris production of *Perséphone* he toured the United States for the second time. He had gained tremendous confidence and status as a conductor, and while some critics cavilled at his 'unromantic' approach to his own early music, others welcomed him as a refreshing breeze in a hot-house of over-ripe tradition. Throughout the next few years Stravinsky thrust his roots deeper and deeper into the American way of life. He had a certain personal magnetism, with the power to evoke, not only respect, but a deep, instantaneous affection in others. William Roerick, who took the part of Laertes in Sir John Gielgud's production of *Hamlet* in the winter of 1936 at the St James Theatre in New York, met the composer and invited him to attend a performance, then go backstage. The company included Lillian Gish, the great 'star' of the silent cinema screen and the ideal interpreter of D. W. Griffith's frail, romantic heroines. When their illustrious guest appeared, they fussed over him; but he immediately asked to see Miss Gish, who greeted him nervously in her dressing-room. Stravinsky, about the same height as the pocket-sized tragedienne, chatted to her first in a rather threadbare English, then in French, rattling off, with the enthusiasm of an inveterate admirer, the titles and merits of *Birth of a Nation*, *Hearts of the World*, *Broken Blossoms*, *Way Down East*, and other films in which she had appeared. Suddenly with the manner of a Spanish grandee paying homage to his queen, he seized one of her hands and, bending low, kissed it. Not to be outdone, Miss Gish planted, on an impulse, a kiss on Stravinsky's bald head. He gave her a warm, understanding and boyishly responsive smile.

The peripatetic Stravinsky usually returned home from his travels with pungent comments about the places he had visited. "Miami might at least be expected to possess a first-rate orchestra. But nothing in the city seems to be propitious to the arts, apart from the hotel I stayed in, which had a Venus de Milo with the arms restored. . . ."[2] At a Midwestern hotel he suffered some characteristically American automation and described the incident in these words :

I called to order my *petit déjeuner* before going to bed and was answered by a recorded Mother Superior voice—'This is your breakfast robot. After you hear the dial tone, please give your name, room number, breakfast order, the time you wish it served . . . beep.' A silence followed, just long enough—it was sealed by a terminal 'beep'—to encompass a statistically averaged recitation of the requested facts from a properly organized customer. But I could not remember the sequence of the questions, did not *know* my room number, neglected to say how to prepare the eggs, forgot to specify the time of service. Moreover, that final 'beep' so exasperated me that when I did get 'organized' I promptly recorded an order for two hundred pieces of burned toast to be sent to the three-hundredth floor at 4.0 a.m.[3]

Stravinsky was interested in people, although he sometimes antagonized, or deeply offended them, and this is clear from *Chronicle of My Life*, the autobiography which he planned in 1934 and which, published in Paris the following year, contains many graphic comments about famous personalities. This book and Stravinsky's other writings, the *Poetics of Music* and the volumes of *Conversations*, are not endearing works. Their self-righteous tone and sometimes pedantic self-justification, flavoured by his original legal training, tend to irritate rather than attract, as do his highly idiosyncratic generalizations about music; but they are invaluable for the light they throw on Stravinsky himself.

It was in 1934, the year of Elgar's death, that Stravinsky came to Britain with Samuel Dushkin, and they visited Liverpool on 23rd February to give a recital in the Rushworth Hall, a fine, acoustically perfect music room in a building now demolished. The Sandon Studio Society fortified the recitalists with a splendid lunch in Bluecoat Chambers, where Stravinsky, smiling broadly at the prospect of food, asked for steak and claret. During the meal, Patrick Abercrombie, the Chairman, was called from the room; he returned, pale and distressed, to announce that Sir Edward Elgar had died. Stravinsky then rose, or rather bounded from his chair and, speaking rapidly in French, delivered a scintillating and intensely rhetorical tribute to Elgar, prefacing it with an autobiographical fanfare about his own early music. "Our paths went in different directions," he remarked, "but Elgar was a supremely great composer of whom the English should be proud." Stravinsky asked his fellow-guests to stand for a minute in respectful silence.

Gordon Green, himself a distinguished concert pianist at the time and one of the most thrilling exponents of Liszt's *Totentanz* I have heard, sat close to Stravinsky at lunch and carefully noted his boyish enthusiasm, his delight in the spellbinding effect of his own words, and his childlike sincerity. He also admired the composer's athletic musculature. There were no steps up to the platform of Rushworth Hall on that day, and at rehearsal the agent Wilfred van Wyck, poised on the higher level, stooped down to help Stravinsky, already handicapped by his short stature, to climb from the floor to the platform. Stravinsky impatiently brushed him aside and, executing a gazelle-like leap, landed almost effortlessly on the platform. The astonished agent touched the muscles of the composer's right arm and exclaimed "Mon Dieu—Monsieur Carnera!" (Carnera was a gigantic heavyweight boxer.)

Before the concert, Stravinsky, who carried a camera, photographed his companions outside the Adelphi Hotel, then, remembering that he had mislaid a white tie, dashed into a store to purchase another. Gordon turned the pages of the score at the recital and observed that the composer-pianist's fingers, as he placed them tentatively on the keys, trembled with nervousness. Stravinsky, who had insisted on the lid of the grand piano being down, whispered his concern that the instrument should produce a satisfactory tone. He used to pontificate about the correct way of rendering his own music, cautioning others to "play all the notes as they are written—no more and no less". It amused Gordon, turning the pages of the score during a performance of the Duo Concertante, to perceive that Stravinsky ignored this edict. "When he reached the difficult passages he either left out notes, or filled in with some nice chording!"

Speaking vigorously in French and German at a reception following the concert, which was given before the Liverpool Music Society, the composer made a spirited defence of himself against common criticism and misunderstanding. There was a habit, he said, not of saying Stravinsky has "done this well", or "Stravinsky has done this badly", but of asking "Why has Stravinsky done it at all?" This attitude he contemptuously dismissed. What mattered was that he had done it, and that he had tried to do it in a way that completely satisfied his own criteria. He regarded musical composition as a problem, or as a series of problems to be solved. There were the instruments, the materials in his own mind, and his own powers; with these he worked out the difficulties facing him. To do this, a man must acquire the *habit* of writing music, and acquire it by diligence and daily practice. He himself composed every morning, except when travelling, and considered it wise not to wait for inspiration before composing; but rather to sit down at his desk and work at the music, resolving the problems as they arose.

Stravinsky's business-like approach to the mystique of composition finds confirmation, if any were needed, in what Alexei Haiev said of him: "Stravinsky cannot imagine separating the task of composing from that of providing for the needs of, say, his cat. He will provide nourishment for his cat by composing. For his hobbies, flowers, books, wines, he 'arranges' time around his composing. Other men arrange time to compose."[4]

Stravinsky denied vehemently what some people said of him, that he had progressed by jumps. Indeed, nothing in nature moved at all except by greater or smaller jumps—it was only necessary to examine any organism through the microscope to see that. Sometimes people asked why a new work did not continue the line of the old one. "What is the line?" he enquired. "Nobody replies!" The composer also remarked, during his speech, that the public should consider itself a partner in musical performance. He thought that the radio made listening to music very much a habit,—"the young lady who might have increased her musical understanding by playing the piano now eats cakes and listens to the radio!"

Returning to Paris after an American tour, Stravinsky started work on a new piano concerto, which he planned as an imposing large-scale composition. His second son, Soulima, an outstandingly brilliant pianist, had, under his father's baton, performed the solo parts of the Piano Concerto of 1924 and the *Capriccio* at Barcelona in November 1933, and, with the memory of these triumphs fresh in his mind, Stravinsky decided to create a Concerto for Two Solo Pianos, without orchestra. He and Soulima gave the first performance at the Salle Gaveau, Paris, on 21st November 1935.

An intriguing composition in which the two piano parts miraculously dovetail, it has many original features, which include the quasi-cymbalom-like repetition of a single note, the faint, drum-like ostinato figures, and the diversified unity of the variations. The diamond-bright, crystalline structure of the fugue reminds one of Myra Hess's description of Busoni's playing as a marble sculpture which one felt one could touch.

Stravinsky's fondness for jazz found new expression in his *Preludium*, which, at the time of writing, has not been published. Written partly in Paris in December 1936 and partly in New York, the following year, the music, scored for jazz band, and re-arranged by the composer in 1953, received its first performance at an Evenings-on-the-Roof concert, conducted by Robert Craft at Los Angeles on 18th October 1953.

Balanchine admired Stravinsky tremendously. "All of Stravinsky's music can be danced," he said, "every single note he has written."[5] The choreographer was never so happy as when he and his illustrious friend set out to create a new ballet, and the chance came when Edward Warburg and Lincoln Kirstein, directors of the newly-formed American Ballet, commissioned the composer to write *Card Game : A Ballet in Three Deals* for a Stravinsky-Balanchine festival to be presented at the Metropolitan Opera House, New York in the spring of 1937. The punctilious nature of their collaboration may be realized from the stinging rebuke which Stravinsky flung at Balanchine when they first began to work on *Orpheus*. The composer asked Balanchine how long he thought the *pas de deux* of Orpheus and Eurydice should run, to which the choreographer replied "Oh, about two and a half minutes." Stravinsky snapped at him "Don't say 'about'—there is no such thing as 'about'. It is two minutes, two minutes and fifteen seconds, or something in between. Give me the exact time, please, and I'll come as close to it as possible."[6] From that moment the two men understood each other perfectly.

Card Game, sharing the festival with *Apollo* and *The Fairy's Kiss* at the Metropolitan Opera House on 27th April 1937, proved an indisputable success, the critics hailing the event as the most brilliant evening of ballet ever seen in New York. *Card Game* is scored for double woodwind, four horns, two trumpets, three trombones, tuba, timpani, bass drum and strings, the three movements (or deals) being played without interruption. Shortly before the performance, Stravinsky, basking in a golden blaze of publicity, had himself photographed by the Press playing poker with Balanchine and Warburg. With his glasses pushed up on his forehead, his eyes gleaming in the flashlight, a smile of devilish cupidity on his face, and a fan of cards held jauntily in one hand, he might have been a showboat professional about to rook some gullible millionaire from the big city. At the première Stravinsky conducted a seventy-piece orchestra hired for the occasion.

During the creation of *Card Game* the composer always arrived punctually for a six-hour rehearsal, then, in the evening, took the pianist home with him and worked on the tempi. Meticulously apparelled in suède shoes, marvellous checked suits and beautiful ties, he looked, according to Kirstein, "the small but perfect dandy, an elegant Parisian version of London tailoring". At rehearsal he would clap his knee like a metronome for the dancers, then, abruptly stopping the run-through, rise and, gesticulating rapidly to emphasize a point, suggest a change. Never tyrannical or capricious, he helped the dancers in a practical, kindly way.

Modern Music reported on *Card Game* in these words :

> The scene is a card table at a gaming house, and dancers are members of the pack. . . . The musical opening of each scene is a short processional . . . which introduces the shuffling of the pack. For the card play . . . there are group dances, solo variations and finales. . . . The music is dry, brilliant, melodic, and extremely complex in its rhythmic pattern, a synthesis of purely creative yet evocative passages, balanced by fragments definitely reminiscent of Rossini, Délibes, Johann Strauss, Ravel, Stravinsky's *Capriccio* and jazz in general.

Shortly after the première of *Card Game* the composer was commissioned by a Mr and Mrs Bliss to produce a new work, and he set about writing a Concerto in E flat major for fifteen instruments, which took the name of their Washington D.C. estate 'Dumbarton Oaks'. Although resembling in style the Bach Brandenburg Concertos, it does not consist of *concertino* and *ripieno* groups, all the instruments being treated as equals. The music, to some extent, illustrated what Constant Lambert once said about Stravinsky : "He is essentially a decorator, not a builder, and he must always find new shapes to decorate." Completed early in 1938, the 'Dumbarton Oaks' Concerto had its première at Washington D.C. on 8th May the same year, with Nadia Boulanger conducting.

In 1938 Walt Disney Enterprises asked Stravinsky for permission to use *The Rite of Spring* in a cartoon film to be called *Fantasia* and, according to him, gave a gentle hint that if he did not agree they would use it, anyway, since the music had no copyright protection in the United States. He did consent, and accepted a fee of $5,000 from the Disney office. A year later he saw the film with Balanchine in a Hollywood studio and discovered to his annoyance that the score had been changed, one alteration being 'Dance of the Earth', in which the horns played their glissandi an octave higher, and another the 'reshuffling' of the different episodes. Stravinsky described the musical performance as execrable. His resentment burned like a slow fuse over the years, reaching explosive point early in 1960 in a letter published in the *Saturday Review* :

> Sir,
> A letter printed in the *Saturday Review* for 30th January 1960, quotes Mr Walt Disney as follows : "When Stravinsky came to the studio . . . he was invited to conference with the conductor . . . and the commentator . . . was shown the first roughed-out drawings, said he was 'excited' over the possibilities of the film . . . and agreed to certain cuts and rearrangements and, when shown the finished product, emerged from the projection visibly moved . . . and we paid him $10,000 not $5,000."
> In fact, my contract, signed and dated 4th January 1939, by my then New York attorney, states that the Walt Disney Enterprises paid the sum

of $6,000 for the use of *Le Sacre du Printemps* and that $1,000 of this fee was to be paid to the publisher for the rental of the material. My *cachet*, gross, was, as I said, $5,000. This contract further states that the *Sacre* was to be recorded between 25th March and 20th April 1939. At this time I was in a tuberculosis sanatorium near Chamonix. I did not, indeed could not, have consulted with the musical director and commentator of the film and, in fact, I left the sanatorium only once in a period of several months, and that was to conduct *Perséphone* in the Maggio Fiorentino. The allegation that I visited the Disney Studios on two separate occasions, once to see preliminary sketches and later to see the final film, is also false. I appeared there for a single time only, as I wrote. I was greeted by Mr Disney, photographed with him, shown drawings and sketches of the already finished film, and, finally, the film itself. I recall seeing a negative film of *The Sorcerer's Apprentice* and I recall that I was amused by this and said so. That I could have expressed approbation over the treatment of my own music seems to me highly improbable—though, of course, I should hope I was polite. Perhaps Mr Disney's misunderstanding was like that of the composer who invited a friend of mine to hear the music of his new opera. When the composer had finished playing the first scene and the time had come for comment, all my friend could think of to say was "then what happens?" whereupon the composer said "Oh, I am so glad that you like it."

IGOR STRAVINSKY

In 1938 Stravinsky, with the co-operation of Charles-Albert Cingria, paid a warm and graceful sixtieth-birthday tribute to his friend Ramuz with the *Petit Ramusianum Harmonique*. He contributed three quatrains with words and music, intended to be sung, unaccompanied, by a single voice or by several voices in unison, and these he interpolated in a poem with short rhyming lines written by Cingria.

Stravinsky, in 1939, again toured America as a pianist and conductor, arriving there in the S.S. *Manhattan*. The ship was packed to the scuppers, like a Chinese ferry, and although he had paid for a private cabin, Stravinsky had to share with six other people. Toscanini, similarly placed, refused to be treated as if he were a sardine in a tin; irate and moody, he slept in the lounge, or roamed the decks in a cold, but seething fury.

One of the highlights of Stravinsky's visit to America was the commission he received to compose a symphony to celebrate the fiftieth anniversary of the Chicago Symphony Orchestra. No sooner had he tackled this project than the Chairman of the Harvard University Charles Eliot Norton Professorship Committee invited him, through the good offices of Nadia Boulanger, to accept the chair of poetry for the academic year 1939–40. A strange invitation it must have seemed, for Stravinsky's anti-romantic tendencies and suspicious attitude to any sensuous appeal possibly inhibited his poetic sympathies; but Mr Chauncey Stillman, who created the professorship, had extended the definition 'poetry' to include the visual arts of painting, sculpture and architecture. as well as archaeology, literature and music.

Stravinsky, flattered by this tribute to his universality of spirit, accepted, and arrangements were made for him to live in Boston or Cambridge from October 1939 to the following May, with a break of two months for his concert engagements. The lectures which he delivered, sometimes illustrated by analysis and performance of one or other of his own works, brought eager audiences to the public meetings or student assemblies, where they served as highlights of the academic year. Stravinsky spoke in French. An English translation of his lectures in book form, entitled *Poetics of Music*, appeared in 1947. It contains the very quintessence of Stravinsky's reactions to the phenomenon of music. His reasoning, a constant odyssey of questions, draws answers completely outside our restricted thought patterns. Like a cool detached surgeon demonstrating to a class of initiates the correct use of the scalpel, Stravinsky strips away irrelevancies. The six lectures that make up the *Poetics* form an 'explanation of music' that runs incandescently through a complex pattern of confession, dogma, investigation and polemics.

Stravinsky's daughter Ludmila had died on 30th November 1938, and on 2nd March 1939 his wife followed her. Then on 7th June 1939 his mother died. These losses, coupled with the outbreak of the Second World War, persuaded him, after he had spent some months in a sanatorium at Sancellmoz, to settle in America. Stravinsky had grown to love the country and its people. On 9th March 1940, in Bedford, Massachusetts, he married Vera de Bosset, formerly the wife of the Russian painter Serge Soudeikin, who designed the scenery for the ballet *The Tragedy of Salome*. Stravinsky and Vera became United States citizens on 28th December 1945. He should have had the film actor Edward G. Robinson as his witness during the naturalization ceremony; but, alas, the authorities discovered that, through a technicality, Robinson himself had been an illegal immigrant for the past forty years!

Stravinsky concentrated throughout the summer of 1940 on completing his Symphony in C for the Chicago Symphony Orchestra. Performed by the same orchestra for the first time in the United States at Chicago on 7th November 1940, this important work, scored for normal symphony orchestra, with double woodwind, bore the dedication "Composed to the glory of God and dedicated to the Chicago Symphony Orchestra". The refinement of the instrumentation and the melodic simplicity of the four movements indicate Mozart as a possible source of inspiration. Stravinsky composed a Tango for piano solo in the same year.

In 1941, at the invitation of a pupil, he made an arrangement of that venerable and venerated symbol of American patriotism, "The Star Bangled Banner". He sent a copy of the score to Mrs Franklin D. Roosevelt, doubtless expecting her to signify her delight at being so honoured;

but the inclusion of a major seventh chord in the second strain of the piece must have ruffled the feelings of some highly placed official. Back came the score with a hasty note of apology. Stravinsky, subsequently selling the arrangement through Klaus Mann, performed it with the Boston Symphony Orchestra in the winter of 1944. Those who attended the concert seemed confused and bewildered. "Only a few of the first bars had been played," said a reporter in one Boston paper, "when voices began to falter, eyebrows lifted, and nearly everybody stopped singing, to let the orchestra finish alone its dissonant rendition of the well-known music."

Next day, after numerous amateur lawyers had telephoned complaints, a police commissioner visited the composer and acquainted him with a Massachusetts law forbidding anyone to 'tamper' with national property —Chapter 264, Section 9 of the General Laws demanding that the anthem be played "as a whole or separate composition or number, without embellishment or addition in the way of national or other melodies". He also told Stravinsky that he had detailed policemen to remove the offending piece from the music stands.*

Stravinsky restored himself to favour by conducting the Boston Symphony Orchestra in the approved version of "The Star Bangled Banner" at a subsequent concert; whereupon a squad of twelve police, including a captain, sergeant and members of the radical squad, who had gathered in the hall to preserve the *status quo*, nodded to each other that 'everything is O.K.', and departed. Next morning a Boston newspaper carried the banner headline, "Stravinsky foils arrest by playing anthem O.K."

The aura of greatness which surrounded the composer, coupled with an uncompromising frankness of judgement that provoked hostility in others, sometimes made it difficult even for illustrious colleagues to approach him. Thus, when Rachmaninov, whom Stravinsky once referred to as "a six-and-a-half-foot scowl", was touring America in 1942 and wanted to meet him, he wrote to Serge Bertensson, subsequently one of his biographers : "As I know how much Igor Fyodorovich has always disliked my compositions, even though he respects me as a pianist, and he must know my attitude to modern music, I am not sure whether I could invite him and his wife to my house—which I'd love to do—because I don't know how he would receive my invitation. Would you be so kind as to send out a feeler to gauge his reaction to such an idea?"⁷ Bertensson telephoned Vera Stravinsky, who replied "Delighted" to the invitation. Before dinner and during it at Rachmaninov's house, the two giants skated diplomatically around, but never close to, the subject of music—discussing mana-

* Heaven forbid that comedy of this kind should infiltrate into Britain; if it ever does, that great and warm-hearted conductor John Pritchard, who has concocted many delightful variants of the British National Anthem (he and Fritz Busch devised a particularly engaging one during a rainy afternoon at Glyndebourne) will doubtless be prosecuted with the full vigour of the law.

K

gers, concert agencies, royalties and other matters; but not a word about compositions. On the topic of food, Stravinsky mentioned a fondness for honey. A few days later Rachmaninov procured a huge jar of the finest honey and delivered it personally at the Stravinskys' home.

One would like to think that this gift sweetened the relationship between the two men, but, at subsequent meetings, they suffered each other in a constrained, uneasy silence. Rachmaninov's wife talked volubly while he, almost as if henpecked, sat with his shoulders hunched, enveloped in a soulful, melancholy introspection. On learning that Stravinsky carried out exercises designed for him by a Hungarian gymnast, she reproved her husband for his cowardice in shirking an early morning cold shower. Poor Rachmaninov—in the light of this incident the savage fury with which he sometimes attacked a piano keyboard at a concert is comprehensible.

Rachmaninov, like Stravinsky, was an exile from his native land, and the Soviet ideologists condemned him as vehemently as they did the creator of *The Rite of Spring*. The Kremlin, speaking in 1931 through the oracular voice of *Pravda*, the official news organ, flung vicious censure at Rachmaninov. His music, they declared was "that of an insignificant imitator and reactionary : a former estate owner, who, as recently as 1918, burned with a hatred of Russia when the peasants took away his land—a sworn and active enemy of the Soviet Government". Hearing this tirade of hate, and facing a subsequent boycott of his own music in Russia, Rachmaninov replied with characteristic contempt : "I am quite indifferent."[8] But the attack hurt him deeply.

Not even Stravinsky's music—the Concerto for Violin and Orchestra —could redeem *Balustrade*, a ballet which Balanchine choreographed in 1941 and which, staged at the Metropolitan Opera House, ran for only three performances. The brilliant sets and costumes by Tchelichev commanded respect, but the critics ridiculed the whole enterprise. John Martin complained bitterly that "while gifted American artists are starving in the effort to bring their work before the public, there is money available for the production of European importations of this calibre". *Balustrade* was danced by the American Ballet, the cast including William Dollar, Lew Christensen, Annabelle Lyon, Charles Laskey and Leyda Anchutine.

The following year Stravinsky wrote his *Four Norwegian Moods*, comprising Intrade, Song, Wedding Dance and Cortège, originally intended for a Broadway revue, but subsequently scored for medium-sized orchestra. The first performance of the new version was given on 13th January 1944 by the Boston Symphony Orchestra, with Stravinsky conducting. Another small, but appealing work, the orchestral triptych *Ode*, came from his pen in 1943 and consisted of Eulogy, Eclogue and Epitaph. He dedicated it to the memory of Natalia Koussevitzky, wife of the conductor.

In 1942 Stravinsky composed his *Circus Polka* for a ballet of elephants in the Barnum and Bailey Circus. Eric Walter White related an amusing story of Stravinsky's reaction to the assignment: "The original commission for this ballet came to George Balanchine from Ringling Brothers of the Barnum and Bailey Circus, and he was entrusted with the choice of music. It is said that he immediately telephoned Stravinsky. 'What kind of music?' asked the composer. 'A Polka?' 'For whom?' 'Elephants.' 'How old?' 'Young.' 'If they are very young, I'll do it.' "[9]

The ballet, performed by a troupe of fifty elephants in tutus and fifty circus starlets, with costumes by Norman del Geddes, probably made the ghosts of Barnum and Bailey green with envy; but, regrettably, it did not arouse any Terpsichorean spirit in the trunk-waving dancers. "The elephants," wrote Balanchine, "trumpeted their annoyance at the choreography I gave them, although I tried to keep it as elementary as possible, and they flapped their ears in pain at the Stravinsky music. Their trainer was much relieved when the circus, after cashing in for a season on the publicity the number had received, dropped it from the show; he had been muttering from the start that if they kept on making his beasts do things like this he would end up with a herd of neurotics on his hands." Stravinsky later prepared a symphonic version of the *Circus Polka* and in 1944 the Boston Symphony Orchestra gave the first performance of this.

People who telephoned Stravinsky's home must occasionally have felt like dazed travellers in some Alice-in-Wonderland dimension. When Joseph Szigeti telephoned in 1943 a Russian voice answered him: "Sorry, Mr Stravinsky out. Please call again; he will be back an hour ago."[10] Understandably, at times, the conviction grew that the master, immured in his Pentagon of a study, protected by its forbiddingly closed door and sound-proof walls, was 'in retreat' and not likely to be back for many hours ago!

From 1933 onwards the Russian Ballet of Monte Carlo—the company Balanchine had been fired from by de Basil after helping to start it—had been touring America under the sponsorship of Sol Hurok. Serge Denham controlled the company, then in a run-down condition, in 1944, and persuaded Balanchine to help him to revitalize it. Balanchine came, like a wizard with a magic watering-can, to irrigate the parched earth of the Russian Ballet of Monte Carlo and, almost overnight, fresh green shoots pushed their way into the sunlight—young dancers transformed by his brilliance and enthusiasm, seeking to create new artistic triumphs. So they did; one of them being *Danses Concertantes*, choreographed by Balanchine to Stravinsky's crisp and resilient music, which had been first performed by the Werner Janssen Orchestra in Los Angeles on 8th February 1942.

The ballet had its première at the New York City Centre on 10th September 1944, with Alexandra Danilova and Frederic Franklin as principal dancers. Eugene Berman designed the scenery and costumes. Danilova, for more than twenty years the *prima ballerina assoluta* of her era, had at one time a deep romantic attachment to Balanchine; but it ended, with a touch of *opera buffa*, one day when the choreographer, rejoining Danilova after a prolonged absence, tendered a bottle of toilet water as a gift. With flashing eyes and a neck arched like a hissing swan, Danilova, who had expected some more costly token of his esteem, said haughtily "Toilet water? . . . How very kind of you—I can see you've been thinking of me night and day!"[11] Then, in a magnificent rage, she flung the bottle at his head. Poor Balanchine! In those days he sometimes lived like a prince; sometimes like a pauper—the bottle of toilet water was all that he could afford.

The Symphony in Three Movements, first performed by the New York Philharmonic Orchestra on 24th January 1946, was completed the previous year, and Stravinsky declared that each of its episodes was linked in his imagination with specific cinematograph images of the war, with the square march beat of the finale, its grotesque band effects, conjuring up the goose-stepping soldiers and paraphernalia of destruction. The indignation he felt at the war-mongers was increased by a grim, but typical instance of Nazi brutality of which he wrote a graphic description. It happened in 1932 at Munich. The composer, hearing a scuffle beneath the balcony of his room in the Bayerische Hof, looked down and saw a squad of Brown Shirts beating up a group of civilians. When the victims tried unsuccessfully to protect themselves with street benches, they were battered mercilessly. By the time the police arrived the cowardly thugs had disappeared. Stravinsky related how the same night he accompanied Vera and the photographer Eric Schall to a small restaurant. During the meal a gang, sporting swastika armbands, entered the room. One of them spat out insulting remarks about Jews, hurling his abuse at Stravinsky and his party. When the composer rose with his companions to leave, the shouting Nazi and his "myrmidons", as Stravinsky described them, rushed after the party and, when Schall protested, viciously assaulted him. Schall was bloody and bruised by the time he could be rescued and the incident reported to the police.

The choice by a great man of a particular word to describe something about which he feels deeply is always revealing, and the lip-curling contempt that attached to Stravinsky's use of the word "myrmidons" impregnated his report of this ugly happening. One senses, not only his righteous anger at the barbaric treatment of the unfortunate Jews and of Eric Schall, but his revulsion at everything connected with the Third Reich. To Igor Stravinsky the preservation of human dignity was tremendously important.

II

STRAVINSKY BECOMES AN AMERICAN CITIZEN

Nineteen forty-five was a particularly bright year for Stravinsky, since it saw the fulfilment of his ardent wish to become an American citizen. In that year he also composed the *Ebony Concerto*, one of his Cooks-tour expeditions into the unfamiliar realm of jazz. It was hearing Woody Herman's band in pieces like "Caledonia", "Bijou" and "Goosey Gander" that inspired him to write this work, although he succumbed not to their style, but to their instrumentation. It must be said of the *Ebony Concerto* that only momentarily, in the introduction to the finale, is there any flavour of jazz. Fascinated, as always, by instrumental groupings Stravinsky seized on the idea of using brass mutes (the closely muted passage at the lead-back to the second movement repeat—probably derived from the opening chorus of "Caledonia"), but he misapplied the principle of riffs of "Goosey Gander"—as revealed in his own rather niggling first movement—and failed to capture the fundamental jazz feeling. There have been numerous attempts at a *rapprochement* between jazz and 'straight' composers. Few have achieved any notable success.

Methodical as ever, Stravinsky studied recordings by the Herman band and also learned fingering from a professional saxophonist. Some weeks later he conducted the recording of his *Ebony Concerto* in Los Angeles; a work which, in his old age, he regarded as 'remote' from the rest of his creative output. Stravinsky grumbled about the smoke in the recording studio, the atmosphere reminding him of Pernod clouded by water. The players alternated between blowing horns and blowing smoke.

During this period Stravinsky wrote a few 'conversation pieces' which illustrated the diversity of his interests. One of these was the Sonata for Two Solo Pianos, composed from 1943 to 1944 and comprising three movements bursting with fertility. He created for the Blue Network Programme the bright and resilient *Scherzo à la Russe*, which the Paul Whiteman Band performed in 1944; and he produced the Elegy for Solo Viola, dedicated to the memory of Alphonse Onnou, the enigmatic *Babel*, a cantata for reciter, male chorus and orchestra, and *Scènes de Ballet*, intended for Billy Rose's revue *The Seven Lively Arts*, which flourished on Broadway from 1944 to 1945. *Babel* formed part of a cycle of biblical episodes called *Genesis*, organized by Nathaniel Shilkret at Los Angeles in 1944, with Schoenberg and five other composers participating, and the first performance of it, as a separate entity, was given by the Werner Janssen Orchestra in the same city the following year. Only fragments of *Scènes de Ballet*, a classical ballet, were used in Rose's revue, but in the winter of 1945 the New York Philharmonic played the complete work, with Stravinsky conducting.

After the première Stravinsky received the following telegram : "Your music great success stop could be sensational success if you would authorize Robert Russell Bennett retouch orchestration stop Bennett orchestrates even the works of Cole Porter." The composer, greatly amused, did telegraph back, but only to say, characteristically, "SATISFIED WITH GREAT SUCCESS, IGOR STRAVINSKY."[1]

He not only enlivened and enriched the musical life of America, but also stimulated thought and discussion by his provocative writings and speeches. The restraint which Stravinsky exercised in his work rarely appeared in his verbal expression, which, often spiced with biting humour, witty epigrams and ferocious irony, found many vulnerable targets. Not only did he detest critics of his music, but he delighted in spotlighting individual reviewers, calling them "dunce" or "simpleton" and making other derogatory remarks. When the Hollywood composer Vernon Duke (who wrote serious music under his real name Vladimir Dukelsky) published an article headed "The Deification of Stravinsky", he pounced on the author, rending him with a barbed satire. Having been referred to as I.S. in the article, Stravinsky, in his reply, reduced Vernon Duke to the letters V.D. At regular intervals he described Duke, who wrote *April in Paris,* as the composer of *March in Malibu, June in Jutland, Autumn in New York, Leapyear in London, February in Fujiyama,* and *Christmas in Caracas.* Swept along by the sheer eloquence of this riposte, Stravinsky ended his letter to *Listen* magazine with the postscript, "Kindly send me whichever future issue of your sheet happens to contain notice of the *completed* vital statistics of V.D., so that I may send an appropriate wreath."

Stravinsky launched many withering attacks on the critics he so detested. In reply to Robert Craft's question "What do you mean when you say that critcs are incompetent?" he said, "I mean that they are not even equipped to judge one's grammar. They do not see how a musical phrase is constructed, do not know how music is written; they are incompetent in the technique of the contemporary musical language. Critics misinform the public and delay comprehension. Because of critics, many valuable things come too late. Also, how often we read criticisms of first performances of new music in which the critic praises or blames (but usually praises) performance. Performances are of something; they do not exist in the abstract, apart from the music they purport to perform. How can a critic know whether a piece of music he does not know is well or ill performed?"[2]

The music critic of a national newspaper, faced with a première, has to swallow the whole meal at a brief sitting and then try, in the half hour or so before his deadline, to digest it. A new composition may bristle with subtleties of key relationships, cunning rhythmic and melodic figures, involved complexities of tempo, accentuation, and dynamics; polyphonic relationships; and vocal or instrumental colour groupings. Scores of new works are not always available to a critic, so that he can nourish and illuminate his mind before and during a concert. He does the best he can. If he is an honest critic, he will be emphatic in his impressions, but reserved in his judgements. He will also confine any comments about performance largely to appraisal of its tonal characteristics and general expressiveness, perhaps summarizing his reactions in a sentence like "It seemed to me, at a first hearing, that the playing did justice to the music."

Stravinsky liked publicity that served his interests as much as any other composer and would certainly have resented a new composition of his being performed in a vacuum of secrecy, with nothing more than a programme note—and what cryptic, unintelligible notes he himself wrote! —to guide the perplexed, sometimes dismayed music lover. His naïve belief in the ignorance of critics bore little relationship to the true facts: critics who write for reputable papers are usually expert in their subjects and, not infrequently, musicians themselves.

Paul Rosenfeld, a distinguished American musicologist and essayist, who died of a heart attack in 1946, interviewed Stravinsky at Carnegie Hall, after the composer had rehearsed a programme which included *Reynard* and *Ragtime*. He described the composer, who strode rapidly on to the stage from the wings, as "looking like a metallic insect, all swathed in hat, spectacles, muffler, overcoat, spats and walking stick; and accompanied by three or four secretarial, managerial personages". Rosenfeld, overwhelmed by the sparks of vitality that exuded from this apparition, assessed him as "an electric shock".[3] During the rehearsal of *Reynard*, speaking alternately in German, French, Russian and English to the players and members of his entourage, Stravinsky coaxed everyone into the spirit of the animal comedy, miming and singing to bring the characters alive; sometimes dancing a little on the rostrum, or leaping in the air with his feet together, or grinning ferociously from behind his glasses as, pretending to be Reynard, he plucked a feather from the silly, vain old cock.

After rehearsal, and seated in the parterre, Stravinsky neatly turned the tables on Rosenfeld, who found that it was he, and not the composer, who was being interviewed. A look of disgust passed over Stravinsky's face at the suggestion that he might impose an intellectual theory upon himself when he created a new work. He snorted his utter and contemptuous renunciation of this heresy, and the equally abhorrent notion that he might be influenced by personal emotion. On the subject of romanticism, he scoffed at those who, seeking to escape from it, committed the most grotesque errors. "Take Schoenberg, for example. Schoenberg is really a romantic at heart who would like to get away from romanticism. He admires Aubrey Beardsley! It's unbelievable, isn't it?"[4]

Discussing his own music, Stravinsky declared "What interests me most of all is construction. What gives me pleasure is to see how much of my material I can get into line. I want to see what is coming. I am interested first in the melody, and the volumes, and the instrumental sounds, and the rhythm. It is like making love to a woman. You find yourself—without knowing how—in possession of, say, four bars of music. Well, the real musician is the one who knows what there is to be done with those four bars; knows what he can make out of them. Composition really comes from the gift of being able to see what your material is capable of."[5]

At the close of the interview, a young man rushed up to Stravinsky, stated that he greatly admired his work, and solicited the honour of shaking his hand. The composer, bowing like some Indian prince, granted the favour, basking unashamedly in the brightest of sunshine—the adulation of the young.

In 1946 Stravinsky composed the Concerto in D for Strings, known as the 'Basle' Concerto, at the invitation of Paul Sacher, who wanted it to celebrate in 1947 the twentieth anniversary of the foundation of his Basler Orchestra. Basle, situated on both banks of the Rhine in the north-west corner of Switzerland, has a glorious intellectual past that commanded Stravinsky's respect. Founded in A.D. 374 by the Roman Emperor Valentian, the town boasts one of the oldest and proudest universities in the world—Pope Pius II created it in 1460, and the illustrious men who have taught there since include Bonifacius Amerbach, the jurist, Erasmus of Rotterdam, the humanist, Oecolampadius, the reformer, the philosopher Jacob Burckhardt, the painters Hans Holbein the Younger and Arnold Böcklin, and the physicist Christian Friedrich Schönbein. The town itself is a treasure-house of noble buildings, rich in history, its museums overflowing with magnificent tapestries, costumes, stained glass, banners, fine sculptings, and all the accumulated glory of the past.

The warmth of Stravinsky's response to Sacher's invitation to write the concerto may have been generated partly by his gratitude to Mrs Maja Sacher, a great patron of the arts. It was in the splendid library of her house at Schönenberg that Stravinsky, Bartók, Hindemith, Rainer Maria Rilke and Bohuslav Martinu found, for a time, peace and contentment, during the troubled years immediately prior to the outbreak of the Second World War. Presided over by a lady of infinite grace and wisdom, the lovely house had an idyllic setting, and the deer used to come, unafraid, right up to the doors and windows. Martinu, in one of his essays, wrote of Stravinsky's creative work : "It is positive and spontaneous; life around him is full of beauty; not imaginary beauty, transmuted, mysterious, but the simple, natural beauty of individual things." He felt in his music "the almost primitive touch, the core of the problem denuded of all veils . . . music complicated, but not subtle. It coalesces with life and avoids nothing in life which is manifest".

Stravinsky never dwelt in the past, although he drew inspiration from it, but, looking progressively forward across his Unknown Country, deliberately turned his back on his own compositions. In 1946, in a California city, a famous violinist told the composer Carlos Chaves a story which vividly illustrates this. The violinist wished to enlarge his repertoire, but felt discouraged when he examined the recent concertos for the instrument. He approached Stravinsky and suggested that, in the literature for the violin, there ought to be a work corresponding to the admirable music of *The Firebird*, *Petrushka*, and *The Rite of Spring*. The creator of those magnificent pieces gazed at him enigmatically, then replied, "Sorry,—I am not interested in decadent music !" Understandably, he did not receive a commission from the astonished violinist.

The composer loved to honour those he held in affection or esteem, and in September 1947, to mark Nadia Boulanger's birthday, he wrote his 'Little Canon' for two tenors, the score of which, at the time this book is published, has not, to my knowledge, been printed.

His occasional *bonnes bouches* antagonized some critics who seemingly wanted him to function as a conveyor-belt of great and noble music, not realizing that the trifles he created were like the experimental carvings which Leonardo da Vinci tossed on to a dusty shelf high up on the wall of his workshop, one of which—a sad, mystical Christ—found its way into the hands of Gordon Craig centuries later. André Hodeir, for example, asked "How could a man who had written a masterpiece as convincing as *The Rite of Spring* stoop to signing scores like the Concerto for Strings or *Ballet Scenes*? Is he a prankster at heart—and even at times a parodist— or did the genius who composed *The Wedding* simply resign himself to doing stylistic exercises because he found himself in a creative impasse?" Stravinsky brushed such remarks aside as being unworthy of his verbal swordsmanship.

It must have been gratifying to the composer, separated by a large span of years from the halcyon days when *The Firebird* and *Petrushka* dazzled the world, to realize that through the brilliance of Balanchine new ballets, irradiated and enlarged by his own music, continued to dominate the stage. And in 1947 Stravinsky wrote the austere, but powerful *Orpheus* to a commission from Lincoln Kirstein's Ballet Society. Although, generally, the music is restrained, the dynamic flame of the old Stravinsky sometimes bursts into blinding radiance, and a movement like the 'Dance of the Bacchantes', swept along by savage syncopations, is as harshly disruptive as the 'Ritual Dance' in *The Rite of Spring*.

A few months before the première of this great work, Nicholas Nabokov visited Stravinsky at his Hollywood home. During the afternoon of the day after his arrival, Nabokov asked to see *Orpheus*. The composer took him to the study, sat down at the piano with the score, carefully wiped his glasses with a 'Sight Saver' and, emitting occasional humming sounds and explanatory asides, began to play. At a passage in the 'Epilogue', where a solo harp interrupts the slow progress of the fugue, Stravinsky, clipping the air with his fingers, announced "Here, you see, I cut off the fugue with a pair of scissors, and introduce this short harp phrase, like two bars of an accompaniment. Then the horns go on with their fugue as if nothing had happened. This is repeated at regular intervals." Nabokov asked him why he had done this—it seemed pointless. Stravinsky smiled mischievously, as if disclosing a highly professional secret. "You must have heard?" he enquired. "It is a reminder of this"—pointing to a page in the score—"the song of Orpheus . . . Orpheus is dead, the song is gone, but the accompaniment goes on."[6] Months later, in a blinding flash of comprehension, Nabokov, listening to the first performance of *Orpheus*, suddenly apprehended the uncanny insight and artistry of its creator.

The première took place at the New York City Centre on 28th April 1948. It was given by the Ballet Society, with a scintillating cast headed by Nicholas Magallenes, Francisco Mencies, Maria Tallchief, Herbert Bliss and Tanquil LeClercq. The décor and costumes, created by Isamu Noguchi, had a beautiful simplicity, Maria Tallchief wearing a head-piece with a filmy veil floating behind it and a flesh-coloured body stocking relieved by vertical twists of material and three 'modesty' discs. She danced divinely, achieving incredible feats of equilibrium. Three weeks before the première, Stravinsky, ready to conduct *Orpheus*, arrived in New York, looking, in the words of Balanchine, "compact, dapper, authoritative, with his spectacles much of the time pushed up on his forehead like a racing-driver's goggles, and only in intervals of repose being returned to their perch on his large nose".[7] Those intervals were all too rare, for, assisted by Balanchine, he toiled unremittingly to make *Orpheus* a great success. No-one harboured any illusions about the facilities and atmosphere of the City Centre, a depressing hall with pseudo-Oriental decorations, poor acoustics and an orchestral pit so narrow and dirty that Stravinsky, with a characteristic touch of acerbity, likened it to a men's lavatory. The stage, looking from the rear stalls barely larger than a handkerchief and raised much too high for people in the front seats, tested the navigational skill of members of the Ballet Society, who, as they disappeared into the wings, ran the risk of colliding with stage hands clustered in the confined space.

Yet *Orpheus*, magnificently conducted by its composer, proved to be a shining success. The long, mysterious *pas de deux* for Orpheus and his

Dark Angel had a mystical gravity and tenderness that touched everyone who saw it, as did the unutterably poignant *pas de deux* for Orpheus and Eurydice where, after being rescued from Hell, she clings to him imploringly, while he struggles against the temptation to look at her. As Stravinsky, stooping slightly, directed in the pit, and the dancers coordinated their supple movements to the pulsating beauty and drama of the score, Morton Baum, chairman of the City Centre's finance committee, sat in the stalls, watching a performance and hearing music unlike anything he had seen or heard before. So staggered was he by the miracle being enacted on the stage that, after the final curtain, he raced around the building in search of Ben Ketchum, the house manager. His eager questions to Ketchum elicited two facts : firstly that the performance had been given by a group called the Ballet Society, and secondly that their promoter, fund-raiser and general provenance was Lincoln Kirstein.

Bubbling with enthusiasm, Baum located Kirstein and learned that the impecunious Ballet Society was on the verge of collapse; then, like a bulldozer rumbling into action, he went to his own committee and, against a fusillade of protests and objections, persuaded them to finance his newly discovered wonder-child. In the autumn of 1948 the Ballet Society's performing group, taking the title of The New York City Ballet, became the first ballet company in the United States to be classed as a public institution. With Balanchine as artistic director and Kirstein as general director (unsalaried positions) the New York City Ballet achieved many triumphs and a distinctive identity of its own.

Stravinsky admired the company and its choreographer so much that he even permitted Balanchine to tamper with his *Firebird*, reducing it in length and streamlining some of its more romantic episodes. When the revised version took to the stage of the New York City Centre on 27th November 1949, with marvellous designs and costumes by Marc Chagall, the *Firebird* was Maria Tallchief, a splendid dancer with black hair, olive skin and lustrous, dark eyes, who married Balanchine in 1946 and, on the grounds that she wanted children and he did not, was granted an annulment five years later. The critics praised the performance warmly. Yet, in the following year, when the company visited the Royal Opera House, London, *The Times* critic described this *Firebird* as "a poor emaciated creature" and, commenting on the new choreography, asked wistfully "Where are the golden apples of yesteryear?" Alone of all the London critics, Richard Buckle, then writing for *The Observer,* rushed to the defence of Balanchine's new production, describing it as "an exciting ballet with dancing in it". Marc Chagall executed a fine gouache to commemorate this new version of *The Firebird* and fittingly—since he admired Stravinsky tremendously—it came into the possession of Martin Riskin, who acquired it from the composer's wife.

It was in 1948 that Stravinsky's association with the young American conductor Robert Craft began, lasting until his death twenty-three years later. Craft, who had been Schoenberg's research assistant, became the unofficial custodian of the Stravinsky image, his rehearsal conductor, literary collaborator and close friend, contriving through his own brilliance as writer and orator to keep the composer's pungent personality before the public. On the occasion of his seventy-fifth birthday, Stravinsky co-operated with Craft in a series of question-and-answer "conversations" covering various episodes in his life, commenting on distinguished composers or other creative artists, and discussing contemporary music in general. These conversations are dealt with in Chapter Thirteen of my book.

Nineteen forty-eight also saw the completion of Stravinsky's nobly conceived Mass for chorus and double wind quintet. His choice of instrumentation might have seemed rather odd to those traditionalists who favoured huge orchestral tuttis for the more dramatic aspects of the Mass; but it serves, magically, to throw the choir into bold relief by providing a sharp and effective tonal contrast. It also freshens and sweetens the atmosphere of the music, giving it a hard, clean edge reminiscent of the most splendid medieval church music. The genesis of the Mass dates back to 1942, when Stravinsky, rummaging through a second-hand book shop in Los Angeles, came across some of the Mozart Masses. He subsequently wrote : "As I played through these rococo-operatic sweets-of-sin, I knew I had to write a Mass of my own, but a real one."[8] He composed the work, not for concert programmes, but for use in the church, making it liturgical and almost without ornament. Ernest Ansermet conducted the première of the Mass in Milan on 27th October 1948; the first American performance took place in the Town Hall, New York on 26th February 1949, with the composer conducting the Chamber Art Society.

While composing the *Kyrie* and *Gloria* of the Mass in 1944, Stravinsky associated with the distinguished poet and dramatist Franz Werfel, who tried to persuade him to write music for his film *The Song of Bernadette*. Although Stravinsky did compose music for the 'Apparition of the Virgin' scene (this piece became the second movement of the Symphony in Three Movements) he shied away from the idea of a commission, since the business and artistic conditions attaching to it largely favoured the producer. Stravinsky admired Werfel, a man of tremendous courage, finding his large, magnetic eyes strangely beautiful. His death, shortly after their meeting, shocked and troubled Stravinsky.

During a chance visit to the Chicago Art Institute in 1947 the composer caught sight of the famous Hogarth paintings, *The Rake's Progress*, which immediately suggested a series of operatic scenes to him. Hogarth took enormous interest in the music of his time, introducing musicians into his pictures whenever possible, so that it is perhaps fitting that Stravinsky should have gone to him for inspiration. He loved, when drawing a scene, to include well-known figures of the day : the singer and the flautist in the fourth picture of his great series *The Rake's Progress* have been identified as leading artists of the period.

On the advice of Aldous Huxley, he invited W. H. Auden to write a libretto. There are few flickers of human warmth in Stravinsky's score (the Rake's cavatina in praise of love is one of them), but the work becomes what the listener chooses to make of it—from a moral tract to a razor-edged satire, and from a series of musical tableaux to a symbolic music drama. *The Rake's Progress* is an extraordinarily skilful presentation of twentieth-century music in eighteenth-century fancy dress, compelling admiration by its technical brilliance and those few moments of lyrical tenderness in which the composer slips off the hieratic mask which he wears in most of his later works.

Auden, a superb craftsman in words, resisted the temptation to produce a highly romanticized, overblown libretto. In the words of Karl-Birger Blomdahl, the Swedish composer, "lyrical poetry, by virtue of its self-enclosed perfection, does not lend itself to composition. To do so would be to add an undesirable redundancy and to impose limitations". There is no redundancy in the libretto of *The Rake's Progress*; only the flawless dovetailing of words and music.

When Stravinsky invited Auden to tackle the text of his opera, all he knew of the poet's work was his commentary for the film *Night Train*; but the softly grating voice of Huxley, the finely-shaped sentences rippling musically through pursed lips, constituted powerful advocacy for anyone he might care to name. He had, to anyone who had not seen him before, an awe-inspiring aspect; his alabaster features included a slightly hooked, slightly haughty nose and a right eye clouded by a milky film. He talked like a human but immensely enthralling encyclopaedia, and expounded such rare subjects as the stimulation of erotic sensibilities through breathing exercises, the significance of Baudelaire's Latin poems, the sexual customs of the American utopias, the hallucinatory 'realism' of mescalin-induced trances, and the possibility of flights to the moon within the twentieth century. Huxley, a skilled masseur and natural healer, cured Stravinsky of insomnia.

When Stravinsky wrote to Auden about his opera, the poet modestly replied that since the librettist must satisfy the composer, rather than the converse, perhaps he might be given some idea about character, plot and other kindred matters. He suggested that between the acts there should be a choric parabasis as in Aristophanes. Finally, he described the chance of working with Stravinsky as the greatest honour of his life. The poet subsequently brought in as collaborator Chester Kallman, who, although well-known in America, must have been excited at the prospect of sharing a commission from the most illustrious living composer, thereby gaining universal renown. Kallman wrote the following parts of the libretto : Act I, the second half of Scene I and Scene III; Act II, Scene II; Act III, Scene I and the first half of Scene II.

Auden, a compound of reason and superstition, fascinated Stravinsky. The cold crystalline logic of his arguments found a strange contradiction in his credulous remarks about black magic, graphology, the telepathic powers of cats, predestination and similar matters. Auden scarified Society, yet staunchly defended and upheld its precepts. He was outraged at the failure of Stravinsky and his wife to vote.

The poet stated that when Stravinsky looked at the Hogarth paintings he noticed, in the one depicting Bedlam, a blind beggar playing a one-stringed fiddle; this kindled his imagination and, although in the opera he denied the presence of such a figure, it existed as a tiny flame applied to his combustible intellect.

Auden told me that Stravinsky set the libretto exactly as it was delivered, although he requested a *reprise* of a chorus. The fact that the composer wanted to create a more-or-less traditional opera, with fixed numbers, recitatives, and an orchestra of Mozartian dimensions, pleased Auden and Kallman, since it is technically simpler to write a libretto for such a work than for a music-drama of Wagnerian scale. Yet they viewed the task with misgiving, and Auden explained to me the problems which he and his partner faced in fulfilling their obligations.

Hogarth had treated the Rake, not as a person with identifiable characteristics that appealed in some degree to the spectator, inviting compassion or condemnation, but as a passive, almost symbolic figure whose role it is to succumb to the temptations which the Devil dangles before him. As the Rake moves from one scene to another, his friends and associates vanish and he appears in entirely new company. Hogarth's bloodless and satirized Rake filled the two writers with dismay, for passive characters cannot sing. Auden summarized the situation in these words: "So far as a story was concerned, all we had to start with was the basic premise of a young man who inherits a fortune, is corrupted by it, and ends in penury and madness; and of the scenes in the series only the Brothel and Bedlam seemed obviously usable."

Auden and Kallman therefore had to invent a history for their hero Tom Rakewell, to establish a permanent and interesting relationship for him with a few other characters, male and female. Tom should yield to temptation, but he must also resist it; and the temptations, like those which plagued poor Becket in T. S. Eliot's *Murder in the Cathedral*, must be of appreciably different kinds. The two writers, concerned to give Tom a mythical resonance, realized, too, that although settings, costumes and speech might be pure, unadulterated eighteenth-century, the Rake must personify Everyman and the libretto be a compound of fairy-tale and medieval morality play.

To show his spiritual conflicts on stage, they needed two characters—

one to tempt and one to be tempted. "As Faust is accompanied by Mephisto, we gave Tom Rakewell a servant, Nick Shadow," explained Auden. "Tom does not, like Faust, know the identity of Nick from the beginning. On engaging Nick, Tom asks him what wages he wants; Nick replies evasively, saying that he will tell him when a year and a day have passed. Tom agrees to this and, of course, when the time is up Nick Shadow reveals himself as the Devil and asks for his soul. Now we had at least continuous roles for the two singers."

To compensate for Tom's passivity, and to add musical variety to his role, the librettists made him a mercurial manic-depressive, now bubbling with gaiety, now wallowing in despair. As a structural device, following the fairy-tale analogy, they gave Tom three wishes :

> I wish I had money
> I wish I were happy
> I wish it were true

Whenever Tom makes a wish, the blood-chilling Nick Shadow pops into sight like some demoniac Jeeves; the first time to announce that an uncle has left him a fortune, the second time to suggest a strange marriage, and the third time with a spurious machine (about which Tom has just been dreaming) for transmuting stones into bread. Tom utters a final poignant wish when, thanks to Ann Truelove's miraculous intervention, he wins a card game with Shadow, saving his soul, though not his reason :

> I wish for nothing else

Auden and Kallman introduced this girl as a wholesome foil to the brimstone-reeking Nick Shadow, and Tom, engaged to her when the opera begins, cherishes her sweetness and devotion through all his inane debaucheries. She, loving him for better or—decidedly—worse, saves the frightened hero from damnation. Auden admitted that, although Stravinsky wrote beautiful music for Ann to sing, she could not be called an interesting character,—"for this defect we are, of course, responsible; but I doubt if, given the subject, another librettist could have done much better".

Of the three roles for female voices Auden and Kallman created, they found Mother Goose, the Madam of a brothel, an easy assignment, since she could appear in only one scene. The other major female role, that of Baba the Turk, shocked some of the critics, who foolishly read into the text obscene sexual innuendoes. Auden and his partner dreamed up this hormone-freak with nothing in mind but the Hogarth engravings, in which the Rake marries an ugly old heiress for her money. Having already shown Tom succumbing to the temptations of wealth, they decided to be fashionably modern "and make him commit an act *gratuit*". In order to assert his freedom of will from the compulsions of Passion and Reason he marries this "lady from the circus with a magnificent Assyrian beard . . . in her own eyes as much a *grande dame* as the Marschallin in *Rosenkavalier*, immensely proud of her beard as a visible sign of her genius, that which gives her a high status in the circus world".

Auden made a wise choice in conscripting Kallman to collaborate in the libretto of *The Rake's Progress*. A gifted poet, Kallman subsequently achieved great distinction with his verse. One of his most famous creations with Auden was *Elegy for Young Lovers,* staged in 1962, with music by Hans Henze. He displayed a phenomenally detailed and reliable knowledge of opera. Auden told me "It was Kallman who introduced me to that art."

The letters that passed between Auden and Stravinsky are illuminating. In one epistle, the poet sent his love to Vassily the cat, the "illness-loving Fraulein" (Stravinsky's housekeeper, Eugenia Petrovna), and Popka the parrot. There were, in fact, forty parrots and lovebirds in the ménage at that time, and Auden, striving at one of his visits to co-ordinate the poetic text with arias, ensembles and choruses, must have felt like some disciple of Messiaen in a typical ornithological setting. One of the verses for the libretto which he sent to Stravinsky contained the words "Soon dawn will glitter outside the shutter, And small birds twitter. . . ."—a subconscious response, perhaps, to the Stravinskian aviary! Another letter, dealing with the propensities of Baba the Turk, shrewdly suggested that, to differentiate her character and emotion from that of the two lovers, her rhythm should be more irregular and her tempo of utterance faster. Auden informed Stravinsky that, in consequence, he had given any line of Baba's twice the number of accents as compared with the equivalent line of Ann's or Tom's. One is made aware, by these letters, as by the text itself, of the fastidious care and craftsmanship which Auden, like Kallman, applied to his task.

The première of *The Rake's Progress* in the autumn of 1951 was an event of international significance. Given at La Fenice, Venice, as part of the Venice Festival, which acquired the performance rights for $20,000, it attracted music lovers from all parts of Europe, as well as America, and thousands of disappointed Stravinsky-ites failed to secure tickets. Before a year had elapsed, performances of *The Rake's Progress* took place in Paris, Antwerp, Brussels, Copenhagen, Monte Carlo, Stuttgart, Cologne, Düsseldorf, Hamburg, Frankfurt, Milan, Munich and many other places.

La Fenice, the opera house in Venice, is a magnificent building with a fine portico in the style of Palladio. It is what the Italians call *carina*— lovable. The very beautiful entrance, as Stravinsky knew it, gave an impression of light. In this white marble and gold setting stood a major-domo wearing a white wig and resplendent in cocked hat, white velvet breeches and a coat richly trimmed with gold lace. He carried a staff of office with a huge golden knob. If anyone dared to puff a cigarette, this immensely dignified and statuesque figure took up a menacing attitude, waving his great staff and pointing majestically to the notice *"Vietato di Fumare"*.

From the roof of the auditorium, whose radiant colours never seemed garish, hung superb chandeliers made in Murano, one of the Venetian islands. Between the tiers of white-painted boxes, each decorated with a gay motif of flowers, fruit and knots of ribbon, were plaques commemorating famous musicians. The spacious rooms, through which members of the audience drifted during the lengthy intervals, had inlaid cabinets and silk-covered chairs that gave patrons the feeling that they were in the palace of some Venetian noble. 'Fenice' means 'phoenix', the legendary bird which, when burnt, rose in new splendour from its own ashes. The theatre did, indeed, 'rise from the ashes' in 1836 when, after the destruction by fire of its predecessor, the San Benedetto, it was rebuilt and took its present name of La Fenice.

On the day following the first performance of *The Rake's Progress* in Venice there was a magnificent reception at the Palazzo Loredan, where the Mayor praised the composer as the last of a line of illustrious visitors to the city going back to Caesar, Attila and Charlemagne. Stravinsky, not immune to flattery, but with his mind focused on practical things, caught sight of his publisher Ernest Roth and whispered anxiously "Have you got the cheque?" The story reminds me of the incident in which Samuel Goldwyn, striving to persuade Bernard Shaw to sell him the film rights of *St Joan* cheaply on the grounds of cultural advancement, received the tart comment, "All *you* think about, Mr Goldwyn, is art; all *I* think about is money."

There have been many fine performances of *The Rake's Progress*, but Alexander Young's poetical account of the sad hero which I saw in Islington in July 1965, and to which Stravinsky gave his blessing, stand out in retrospect. Otakar Kraus, veteran of the world première of 1951, has probably never been surpassed as Nick Shadow. He made Shadow a ghastly and wonderful characterization, with evil make-up like something from a Fritz Lang silent film, and, in moments of passion, so it seemed, had bulging, malevolent eyeballs.

Stravinsky had a strange traumatic meeting with the writer Evelyn Waugh in New York in February 1949. Waugh's cold, popping, fish-like eyes, fixed relentlessly on the composer, made him feel like some oddity, and he soon found that the razor brandished by Waugh in his books had an even sharper edge in conversation. The bright remarks which he volleyed at Waugh ricocheted off the author's rhinoceros-hided exterior. Stravinsky, seeking a common field of parlance, addressed Waugh in French, only to be told (with an embarrassed contradiction by Waugh's wife) "I do not speak French." The composer asked the writer if he would like a whisky, whereupon the eyes popped aggressively—"I do not drink

L

whisky.''⁹ Whatever topic Stravinsky raised was greeted with a disparaging remark or a rebuttal. Finally the composer, driven by Waugh, a garrulous expert on the subject, into a lengthy discourse about United States burial customs, formed the opinion that his companion must be gathering material for a doctorate on mausoleums. After this gruelling encounter, Stravinsky's comment "I much admire Mr Waugh" testified eloquently to his fair-mindedness and sense of humour.

Friendship for Igor Stravinsky was an indissoluble union of kindred souls, and it touched profound depths of affection in his character. Friendship inspired the charming *Greetings Prelude* which he composed for the eightieth birthday, on 4th April 1955, of the conductor Pierre Monteux. The music might never have existed if Stravinsky had not, in Aspen during the summer of 1950, been rehearsing Tchaikovsky's Second Symphony. One of the orchestral players had just become a father and sat at his desk filled with happiness and exultation. Instead of the doleful Russian horn melody which Stravinsky expected, the proud father played a bright and festive little tune. The composer, who was not to be trifled with when on the rostrum, glared balefully at the prankster, but relaxed into a broad grin when someone explained the reason for the joke. He remembered the tune a year later, when a music festival in South Carolina asked him to contribute a fanfare to open their season, and set about composing canons on the piece. Stravinsky felt a certain boyish delight in delivering this unpretentious music as a tribute to Monteux, but sometimes regretted his *Greetings Prelude*, since, thanks to the healthy temperament of various orchestras, it came back, like a boomerang, to celebrate his own birthdays.

In 1950 news of the death of Nijinsky filled Stravinsky with sadness and compassion—perhaps even a twinge of remorse. The unhappy dancer, who had contracted blood-poisoning from an infected tooth, went into a coma on 5th April and did not recover consciousness. Serge Lifar, who had befriended Nijinsky so much in the dark days of his madness, obtained permission to transport the body to France; there, with Lifar, Anton Dolin, Ashton, Karsavina and the devoted wife following the cortège, Nijinsky was buried in the Montmartre Cemetery, not far from the grave of Vestris.

Drawn into the whirlpool of the Russian Ballet without comprehending the nature of the intellectual miracle demanded of him, Nijinsky tried vainly to surface the creative ripples which, growing bigger with every successive triumph by the insatiable Diaghilev, finally engulfed him. He could neither read music nor play an instrument. Did Stravinsky really try to help him, one wonders? This question is not posed as a thin disguise for criticism, but because some of the composer's reported utterances often showed a brisk intolerance with those who mentally came below his shoulder-level. Kindness he could and did exhibit on many occasions; but he rarely suffered either folly or incompetence. Four years after Nijin-

sky's death, Lifar, admittedly with some reason for disgruntlement wrote :
"One should accept any comment by Stravinsky with considerable reserve,
for I have reason not altogether to believe in his sincerity, especially after
his passionate outburst about my own musical sense in 1954, when I was
creating his *Firebird* at the Paris Opéra."

Karsavina, superb dancer that she was at the height of her powers, told
me that she, too, "being poor at counting, musically", had tremendous
difficulty in mastering the steps in *Petrushka*, even though Stravinsky used
to sit at the piano, during rehearsals, and play for her. His genius as a
composer far outshone his ability as a coach, and he seemed throughout
his life to gaze at certain people across an intellectual gulf.

Stravinsky certainly had a poor opinion of Nijinsky's musical ability,
but it is also true that the dancer did not rate his Russian colleague highly
and said of him "He seeks riches and glory . . . Stravinsky is a good composer, but he does not know about life. His compositions have no purpose." He also complained that Stravinsky and his wife declined to look
after Nijinsky's child Kyra while the dancer toured America, implying
what Madame Nijinsky stated emphatically, that the composer was a
cold fish.

Reading Stravinsky's dictum that Nijinsky's choreography for *The Rite
of Spring* was unsuited to the work, revealing complete ignorance of music
and of its proper relation to movement, one must remember that it is con-
tradicted by what Emile Vuillermoz, Jacques Rivière and André Levison
wrote about Nijinsky's treatment of the ballet. Where the composer
detected only "rhythmic chaos", Levison saw that "in their simplified
gymnastics the dancers expressed the respective duration and force of the
sounds; they bend their knees and straighten them again, they raise their
heels and fall back on them; they stamp in place, insistently marking the
accented notes. . . . An all powerful restraint dominates them, disjoints
their limbs, lies heavy on the necks of their bent heads".

Diaghilev, who in 1914 replaced Nijinsky with Massine, after sending
him a telegram "Russian Ballet no longer needs your services", has been
harshly and, I think, unjustly condemned for placing Nijinsky on the
heights, then tossing him brutally aside. Perhaps a degree of blame attaches
to him for over-estimating Nijinsky's capabilities; but when a star dancer
fails, at the peak of a triumphant season, to realize the particular hopes
and aspirations of his producer, then the hateful decision has to be made
to replace him with someone else. Diaghilev did, in fact, show more kindness to Nijinsky than Stravinsky, and never abandoned hope of seeing
his reason restored. It is true that Romola Nijinsky attributed her husband's madness to Diaghilev's curt dismissal; but the Tsar's doctor, Bot-
kine, had already diagnosed certain glandular anomalies in the dancer,
and no-one could prevent or influence the tragedy.

Lifar related a touching incident which occurred in 1929, when madness had seized Nijinsky and turned his soaring leaps and superb arabesques into stony rigidity or palsied twitchings. Lifar and Diaghilev visited Nijinsky at the Swiss nursing-home where he was then living; a place impregnated with a hospital atmosphere, where white-coated attendants flitted silently along the corridors. Entering his dungeon-like room, they saw a half-naked man sprawled across a divan; his hands moving ceaselessly to and fro as he stared at them with eyes of a hunted beast. Yet presently a look of childlike innocence crossed his face.

Some time later, when Nijinsky was incarcerated in a sanatorium in a dingy Parisian suburb, Diaghilev, with typical compassion, had the idea of taking the dancer to the Opera to see *Petrushka*—one of his favourite roles. Karsavina, his former partner, would be there. Lifar enthused over the suggestion, as did Nijinsky's sister-in-law, Walter Nouvel, Grigoriev and Boris Kochno. They called for Nijinsky and persuaded him to dress. He rewarded them with mingled grimaces and smiles. His legs, that had once set female hearts fluttering, shocked them; huge and flabby, they seemed incapable of supporting his body.

The good Samaritans transported the bald-headed, greyish little man to the theatre, saddened by the sick, hopeless look on his face. During the performance of *Petrushka* he sat in a box, watching intently, his face flushed. The rumour spread that Nijinsky was in the theatre; friends and admirers flocked around him, seeking in vain to draw him into conversation. During one of the intervals they took him on to the stage to be photographed with Karsavina, Diaghilev, Lifar, Grigoriev and others, while a crowd of painters, designers, dressmakers, stage hands and ballet mothers watched compassionately from the wings. He stood there, staring intently, as if he heard, once again, the cheers of a great audience, sated with the magic of his dancing, echoing around him. Karsavina kissed him, and for a fleeting moment he smiled; then his face darkened into sadness. . . . After the performance, when it was time to go home, Nijinsky refused to leave and had to be carried away.

A far cry from the glorious day when he had dazzled Paris with his unsurpassed rendering of the role of Petrushka. The nuances of his dancing —the lithe jumps, the poignant tilt of the head, the seemingly effortless turns—conveyed the most tender and complex emotions. He brought memorably to life the musical picture which Stravinsky painted of the loving, pathetic and always neglected doll.

12

HOMECOMING OF AN EXILE

If Stravinsky could show intolerance to those who failed to reach his intellectual level—and genius is inseparable from some maladjustments of character—he was, for all the crustacean aspects of his temper, a deeply sensitive man, with a piety that survived the disdain which his own tongue-in-cheek sophisms heaped upon it. Robert Craft wrote an account of Stravinsky attending a Russian Easter Midnight Mass in 1951. The two men, unable to find room in the densely packed white church with the 'blue onion dome', joined an overflow of worshippers outside. Their companions included a White Russian faction with whom Stravinsky and his wife were not on speaking terms; but, from the nostalgic hymn-singing, both clans shared a common homesickness. Shortly before midnight the worshippers in the grounds lit tapers, then at twelve precisely the church doors opened to disgorge a flood of richly-garbed clergy and congregation into the multitude of flickering fireflies outside. The bishop, resplendent in a scarlet, white and gold samite and preceded by a deacon spreading fumes of incense, paused at the top step to sing *"Christos Voskresch"* ("Christ is Risen"), whereupon the crowd intoned *"Vieestinoo"* ("He is Risen, indeed"). Three times around the church moved a stately procession—a priest carrying a tall cross, a cluster of acolytes bearing holy banners or icons, and the globe and sceptre of Christ the King,—followed by the faithful with their dripping candles. The ritual ended with the exchange of Easter kisses between all those present.

Two months later, on his birthday, Stravinsky, making his way to morning service and deprived of his breakfast by it, snarls like a hungry tiger, according to Craft. For two hours, during birthday Confession and Mass, he and his companion kneel on a hard, uncushioned floor. On entering the church Stravinsky prostrates himself before the altar rail and prays there, while an acolyte, rattling his thurible, spreads an odour of sacredness. A priest then confesses him, after eliciting the name of his patron saint. With a partlet suspended over his head and a pectoral cross held to his lips, Stravinsky, now in docile mood, is absolved. After taking the sacraments he prays with his head touching the floor.

What signified the free and spontaneous approach of Igor Stravinsky

to the inborn Christian mysticism of his own nature was not so much his
participation in these ritualistic customs, but the fact that, returning home
from the birthday service to the earthy smell of whisky and cold Russian
cutlets, he prayed once again in his study, watched over by the icon that
served as a talisman as he composed.

The paths of Stravinsky and Dylan Thomas crossed in 1950, when
Auden, arriving late for an appointment, explained that he had been
rescuing an English poet from some kind of difficulty. He told Stravinsky
about Thomas and spoke so eloquently that, shortly afterwards, the composer took the trouble to read his poems. Two years later the English film
producer Michael Powell visited Stravinsky in Hollywood to invite him
to write the music for a short film, *The Doctor and the Devils*, to which
Dylan Thomas would contribute the verse. The proposal came to nothing,
since there was no money to support it.

Then, in May 1953, Boston University expressed a desire to commission Stravinsky to write an opera with Thomas. The two men met in
Boston, and Stravinsky, faced with this pathetic, infinitely gifted caricature
of a human being, decided, with a surge of compassion, that the only
thing to do was to love him. Intensely nervous, constantly puffing ciga-
rettes, Thomas looked like Tom Rakewell at the end of his primrose
dalliance. His nose, set in a face swollen and discoloured by excessive
drinking, was a red bulb, and his eyes were glazed. He drank a glass of
whisky with the composer, praised *The Rake's Progress*, extolled W. B.
Yeats as the greatest lyric poet since Shakespeare, and promised to visit
his companion in Hollywood, so that they could plan the opera together.
On returning home, Stravinsky had a special room built for Thomas, but
in November, before it could be used, a telegram arrived. It told him
that the poet was dead, and Stravinsky, reading it, wept.

During the months following Thomas's death, Stravinsky cherished the
thought of composing a piece of music to his memory, and finally decided
that a poem of Dylan's could better serve his purpose than any other. He
chose the one written by Thomas in memory of his father, which begins :

> Do not go gentle into that good night,
> Old age should burn and rage at close of day;
> Rage, rage against the dying of the light.

Stravinsky used entirely canonic music, requiring a tenor voice and a
string quartet, in setting Thomas's beautiful verses. After completing the
song, he added a purely instrumental prelude and postlude (called dirge-
canons) : these are antiphonal canons between a quartet of trombones and
the string quartet.

In Memoriam Dylan Thomas, conducted by Robert Craft, had its
world première at the Monday Evening Concerts at Los Angeles on 20th
September 1954, when Aldous Huxley delivered the dedicatory address.

Between April 1951 and August 1952 the composer wrote his *Cantata*, dedicating it to "the Los Angeles Chamber Symphony Orchestra, which performed it under my direction and for the first time on 11th November 1952". His great classical period had reached its apogee with *The Rake's Progress*, and in the *Cantata*, scanning new horizons of his Unknown Country, he tackled the problems of setting English words to music in a purer, non-dramatic form. Fascinated by their simple beauty and compelling syllabification, he selected four popular anonymous lyrics of the fifteenth and sixteenth centuries: three are semi-sacred, and the fourth, "Westron Wind," is a love lyric.

Jennie Tourel sang in the first performance of the *Cantata* in New York in the winter of 1952, also singing in the work at the Venice Festival a year later. Like Stravinsky she knew the horrors of war and the pangs of homesickness. When the Nazis overran France in 1940 she was a high-ranking mezzo at the Opéra Comique, famous for her brilliant portrayals in *Carmen* and *Mignon*; but what happened to thousands of others in France of Jewish descent happened to her—the Gestapo hounds began to sniff at her front door and, warned of the danger, she fled the country. It was Tourel who, in the première of *The Rake's Progress* at Venice, created the role of Baba the Turk.

Outside the Metropolitan Opera House, New York, one gusty morning in February 1953, trucks cluttered the kerbside, unloading scenery. On some of the crates labels bore the stencilled words "The Rake's Progress", for this was the first performance of Stravinsky's opera in that fabulous building. Anyone who penetrated inside the closely guarded auditorium, where a rehearsal of the opera was in progress, might have realized for the first time the real meaning of the word 'pandemonium'. In the pit the orchestra flared up with an E major fanfare, as Fritz Reiner conducted from the rostrum. To the left, positioned near the double-basses, Igor Stravinsky, visibly excited and nervous, directed from a music-stand, pausing now and then to dart over to Reiner, whisper a few agitated remarks, then rush back to pick up the beat. An intruder might have supposed that *The Rake's Progress* needed two conductors! Yet the succeeding performance, with its dazzling progression of arias, quartets, recitatives, and a marvellous *cabaletta* with a high C, provided one of the most thrilling events in the entire history of the Metropolitan Opera House.

Other performances, including a splendid one conducted by Stravinsky at Boston University in May the same year, familiarized the American public with *The Rake's Progress*. At the Opéra Comique in Paris, however, the first French production of the work, directed by André Cluytens, wooed the public and the critics in vain. Jean-Claude Rivière, after noting the cold response of the audience, asked "Does Stravinsky actually make fun of his own music in a parody of opera?"

Robert Craft, interviewed by the American journalist John Ardoin in

June 1960, made some remarks about his own relationship with Stravinsky, about Berg's *Wozzeck*, and about *The Rake's Progress*:

I hate the unjust idea that I am supposed to be pushing Stravinsky towards serial music. Stravinsky felt that he was finished with a period after *The Rake's Progress*. I love the music of this period, but he felt he needed to go on to something else. He felt he couldn't do another *Rake's Progress*. He would like to write another opera, but it will be nothing like *The Rake*. *The Rake's Progress* will be alive, fresh and touching when everyone feels *Wozzeck* is stale. Even now the screeching, muted trombones in *Wozzeck* have lost much of their power. With all its faults, and there are many, *The Rake* has the best book possible. It is perhaps some of the best poetry that Auden has written.

In 1951, when Schoenberg died, Stravinsky began studying the little known and largely neglected works that the German composer had written during the forty years since *Pierrot Lunaire*—especially the *Serenade* for seven instruments and voice, and the *Suite* for seven instruments. Inspired by what he read and heard, Stravinsky created his own *Septet*, which, completed in 1953, bears the fruit of this harvesting of Schoenberg's ideas. The evening before Stravinsky was to go into hospital, a group of instrumentalists gathered at the home of the musicologist Peter Yates, to present to the composer the first reading of the *Septet*. At the end of the performance, Stravinsky, clearly excited, sprang to his feet. "It is tonal—strictly tonal," he exclaimed. His very sensitive ear recognized what Yates also heard: that the *Septet* had progressed beyond the rule of the Harmonic Era—tonality was no longer the point at issue.

In 1953 he also composed his *Three Songs from William Shakespeare*, the musical content of which is organically serial. Stravinsky, discussing the songs with Yates, remarked "A good composer does not imitate; he steals." This work, dedicated to a concert foundation called 'Evenings on the Roof', epitomizes his discovery of Webern's music.

A fire which destroyed the Long Island plant of Boosey & Hawkes in October 1954 created an appalling loss to music, when thousands of scores, including whole collections of Stravinsky, went up in smoke. Well might the exasperated composer cry "An enemy hath done this thing".

Against all setbacks and irritations, his output and fertility of invention continued unabated. In 1954, the year of the fire, he completed the instrumentation for an ensemble of harp and guitar of the *Four Russian Songs* which he wrote in 1917.

One of the barbs that penetrated the composer's hypersensitive skin came from an article about him written by Claire Nicolas and published in the magazine *Junior Bazaar*. It was Claire and her sister Sylvia who first introduced Huxley to Stravinsky while lunching in Los Angeles Town and Country Market. After the publication of her article, Claire wrote to Stravinsky complaining that Matthew Huxley had said that the composer did not like it because she had not mentioned the books in his library, and other domestic showpieces; he had also made remarks that might appear to disparage the illustrious man. Stravinsky's feelings were considerably ruffled by the incident, and it took all Aldous Huxley's tact and sweetness to mollify him.

Stravinsky, concluding a European tour which began in Rome, visited Britain in 1954 to conduct, in the Royal Festival Hall, a concert sponsored by the Royal Philharmonic Society. The programme, including *Orpheus* and *Petrushka*, seems from reports to have been brilliantly presented by the Royal Philharmonic Orchestra. Evan Senior, writing in *Music and Musicians*, declared Stravinsky's appeal to be "predominantly for the young" and added "the age-group that set him on his feet nearly half a century ago is still the one that keeps him there". He noted the composer as "lithe, eager, running up and down the steps to the platform, and conducting with a minimum of gesture and a maximum of showmanship . . . in a manner that belied his seventy-two years". At this concert the Royal Philharmonic Society gave Stravinsky its coveted gold medal.

Towards the end of 1944 the immensely gifted Kenneth Macmillan choreographed Stravinsky's *Danses Concertantes* (written from 1941 to 1942) and Nicholas Georgiadis designed the scenery and costumes. Performed by the Sadler's Wells Company on 18th January 1955, this new production used no story or theme, and Macmillan concentrated on providing a succession of dances based on classical ballet techniques to Stravinsky's elegant and scintillating music. Arnold Haskell, the dance critic, wrote of this production : "Here is the music made visual, and here is wit without a stage full of props. The wit is implicit in the movement. That is true choreography."

During the spring of that year, the Hamburg State Opera staged a Stravinsky evening; this included a performance of *Oedipus Rex* in which, according to one reviewer, the producer Günther Rennert created "a miracle of inventiveness". In the foreground the chorus, with dark grey, amorphous faces, stood enveloped up to their necks in sarcophagi; above them, spotlighted, stood Oedipus (Helmut Melchert), clad in a blood-red robe, Creon (James Pease) in grey and Jocasta (Maria von Ilosvay) in sage-green, all wearing masks.

In 1955 Stravinsky completed a new choral work, the *Canticum Sacrum*, dedicating it "to the city of Venice, in praise of its Patron Saint, the Blessed Mark, Apostle". Scored for an orchestra without violins and horns, but with harp and organ, it received its first performance at St Mark's during the Venice Festival staged in mid-September, 1956.

The composer, excited though he might be at the strange new vistas opened up by serialism, did not overlook the fact that in a work of this kind, with no tonal centre to act as a landmark, the average choral singer can easily lose heart. Thus, although the *Canticum Sacrum* has two passages of almost unsupported atonal canon, the rest of the music, in keeping with the dignity of St Mark's, is much more sedate. Stravinsky introduced old devices, with beautiful unison writing, majestic block passages, and antiphony, the choir and orchestra being set against an organ. The composer kept in mind the Chinese adage, "Make haste slowly".

At Ojai, California, during the tenth anniversary of the Ojai Festival held in May 1956, he directed *The Wedding* before an enthusiastic audience. Robert Craft took over the rostrum at this concert to conduct the première of Stravinsky's arrangement of Bach's Chorale and Canonic Variations on "*Von himmel hoch*", originally for organ solo. In this version a brass choir announces the chorale and on subsequent appearances it is sung by a mixed choir. The instrumentation preserves the organ characteristics of the music and the whole work sets forth one of Bach's most complex masterpieces with a pleasing clarity of line.

One of Stravinsky's most glorious achievements in the realm of ballet was undoubtedly *Agon*, which Balanchine, rejoining the New York City Ballet after a year's absence caused by the illness of his wife Tanquil Le Clercq, choreographed in the autumn of 1957. Stravinsky visited Paris in October that year to conduct the Sudwestfunk Orchestra in a performance of the *Agon* music at the opening concert of the *Domaine Musicale* series. Christina Thoresby wrote of his taut and tingling twelve-note score : "There were far more criticisms expressed about the new Stravinsky work than about the works of the new Viennese masters. *Agon* was only finished this year, and many people seem to have difficulty in assimilating Stravinsky's new style. But for those who have accepted the transformation it was obvious that Stravinsky has co-ordinated in a masterly way those parts of the ballet which he wrote as long ago as 1953 with the more recent parts which he finished this year. He has produced a work of extraordinary homogeneity."

Although the concert première of *Agon*, conducted by Robert Craft, took place in Los Angeles on 17th June 1957, the first stage performance was given on 1st December by the New York City Ballet in a Stravinsky-Balanchine programme at the City Centre which included *Orpheus*, *Apollo*, and *The Firebird*. A programme note told the audience that "the *Agon* pieces were all modelled after examples in a French dance manual of the mid-seventeenth century"; they found, however, not a work that transported them back to the world of Louis XIV, but one which, although constructed in a modern style, embodied a profound knowledge of classical forms and procedures. For the new ballet Balanchine assembled a distinguished group of dancers—Diana Adams, Melissa Hayden, Arthur Mitchell, Todd Bolender, Roy Tobiss and Jonathan Watts.

Danced in tights and leotards, without décor or plot, *Agon* depended entirely upon the magic of music and movement for its effect. The score, based on Renaissance dance forms such as the Sarabande, Bransle and Galliard, is pure Stravinsky in its complex rhythms and ingenious orchestration. Balanchine's choreography may have hinted at a period step, but he used traditional forms merely as a springboard for his own brilliant inventions. He characterized the solo Sarabande, which Todd Bolender danced with great suppleness, by a free plastic use of the upper body, curious gliding backward steps, with the front heel brushing the floor, and superb, unpredictable, catlike leaps. Melissa Hayden, presenting a pert, rather whimsical nonchalance, created novel balances and intriguing patterns in the Bransle Gay. There was a magnificent duet between Diana Adams and Arthur Mitchell, in which their twining, weaving bodies displayed beautiful linear designs—one of Balanchine's most inspired concoctions. In the opinion of one critic, they danced this bewitchingly strange and lovely *pas de deux* superbly and he added "The others also performed their fiendish solos and ensembles with élan." He praised the score as a miracle of rhythmic definition and precision.

Two years later, when the Bolshoi Ballet, making its first trip to the United States, arrived in New York, Balanchine staged a special performance of *Agon* for the company at the City Centre. Accustomed to ballets with clearly sketched plots and situations, the visitors reacted to Stravinsky's dodecaphonic music and the cool, abstract orientation of the dance sequences with ill-concealed boredom. It was as if every member of the Bolshoi audience had a nagging toothache.

A concert to honour Stravinsky's seventy-fifth birthday took place on 17th June 1957 as part of the eleventh Los Angeles Music Festival. A huge audience gave the composer a standing ovation as he entered the UCLA's Royce Hall. A greeting from President Eisenhower was read; Aldous Huxley spoke in praise of Stravinsky; and beautifully illuminated scrolls were presented to the composer by representatives of the Los Angeles City Council and the National Association for American Composers and Conductors.

At the Festival Hall, London, on 17th June that year, the Institute of Contemporary Arts gave a special all-Stravinsky concert at which the French conductor Manual Rosenthal directed the London Philharmonic Orchestra, the London Bach Society, and the Elizabethan Singers, with Michel Sénéchal and Madeleine Reynaud, in a programme comprising *The King of the Stars*, *The Rite of Spring*, and *Perséphone*. Dartington Hall Summer School also honoured Stravinsky's seventy-fifth birthday by mounting a 'miniature festival' of his music, and the composer attended this.

Stravinsky dominated a two-day festival of contemporary music staged at Donaueschingen in the Black Forest during the winter of 1957. He again conducted the orchestra of the Sudwestfunk; this time in the first German performance of *Agon*, which drew such a prolonged storm of applause that, to bring it to an end, the composer had to signal the players to leave the platform. In contrast, Luigi Nono's 'atomised' *Varianti* for solo violin, strings and woodwind goaded the Donaueschingen diehards into vociferous protest. The hisses and boos that rose after the rendering of this work were clearly directed at Nono, who remained unperturbed, knowing that the Donaueschingen tradition calls for one good *scandale* at each festival.

On 23rd September 1958, in the magnificent Tintoretto-painted assembly room of the Scuola di San Rocco in Venice, Stravinsky conducted the première of his new thirty-eight-minute-long *Threni—id est Lamentationes Jeremiae Prophetae*, dedicated to Lincoln Kirstein and Balanchine. This work was performed by Ursula Zollenkopf (soprano), Jeanne Deroubdix (contralto), Hugues Cuenod and Richard Robinson (tenors), Charles Scharbach and Robert Oliver (basses) and the choirs of the Hamburg Norddeutscher Rundfunk, with the orchestra of that organization for which *Threni* was written. Stravinsky directed the first performance in memory of Allesandro Piovesan, the young and vital Venetian maestro, who died early in 1958 and who had arranged the three big Stravinsky premières in Venice.

Whereas *Agon* progressively shows Stravinsky's adoption of the twelve-note technique, *Threni* is completely serial. Far from being stuffy and cerebral, however, this setting of the Lamentations of Jeremiah for large orchestra, chorus and six solo singers is a gravely beautiful work. Notwithstanding its greater concentration and apparent break with the composer's earlier styles, *Threni* comes in direct line of descent from *The Wedding*, the *Mass* and the *Canticum Sacrum*, in which Stravinsky expressed the hieratic, 'Byzantine' side of his genius.

In May 1959 he visited the Royal Danish Festival at Copenhagen, where, following a performance of his *Apollon Musagète* in the Royal Theatre, he was presented with a huge laurel wreath by Henning Bronstej, the general manager. After another day spent in sight-seeing, he attended a gala concert at the Tivoli and there, to the accompaniment of thunderous applause, received the Sonning Award of 50,000 kroner (approximately $7,000) from Knudsage Rüsager, director of the Royal Conservatory. The composer was visibly affected and bowed very low, almost as if to hide his tears, as he clasped Rüsager's hand. A performance of his *Octet* was included in the concert, which the King and Queen of Denmark attended.

Before a large audience in the Town Hall, New York, on 20th December 1959, he conducted the first American performance of his *Epitaphium* for flute, clarinet and harp, given by Murray Yanitz, Robert Lostokin and Gloria Agostini. This seven-bar work was composed for the tombstone of Prince Max Egon zu Fürstenburg, patron of the Donaueschingen Festival. It is not one of Stravinsky's most inspired pieces, and I sympathize with the critic who could see no reason for not leaving it on the tombstone. More interesting, musically, was the *Double Canon, Raoul Dufy, Memoriam*, which, written in the same year and scored for two violins, viola and cello, was given its first performance in a Stravinsky Festival at the Town Hall, New York on 10th January 1960.

Stravinsky's thoroughness and love of order, as well as his abundant commonsense, have drawn many tributes, but one of the most unusual came in 1959 from Goddard Lieberson, President of the U.S. Columbia Records, who said "I'd much rather be represented in a business deal by Stravinsky than any lawyer you could name." Stravinsky's deep involvement in the life and structure of his compositions made him painstakingly observant during a performance. B. H. Haggin, the American critic, heard him, at a rehearsal of *The Fairy's Kiss*, say to the Boston Symphony Orchestra basses: "Stronger, you are covered by the trombones, but I don't want to touch the trombones"; then repeat the passage, in which now the basses were not covered by the untouched trombones.

For all his immense erudition, the composer loved the simple pleasures of life. He rejoiced in the soft, gentle air of a Californian night in spring or summer, the roses and carnations in his garden. As Christmas arrived a deluge of greetings-cards covered the mantelpiece of his living-room, while gifts in fancy-coloured paper filled odd corners. Unless something had happened to upset him, friends who called usually found him happy and bubbling over with fun. He loved, during his rare periods of leisure, to wander in hardware stores, examining everything within range, or through the maze of Italian, French and Spanish food counters in some Hollywood lunch market. Sometimes he drove to the ocean, via the interminable Sunset Boulevard, or listened to recordings of *Traviata* and *Aïda*, for which he had a profound affection. He took a boyish delight in all kinds of mechanical gadgets—stop watches, pocket metronomes and the like.

His fondness for household pets resulted in Pópka, a small grey parrot, Lyssaya Dushka (Bald Darling), a bedraggled canary, and a flock of eight lovebirds, two of which, presented by the writer Emil Ludwig, bore the picturesque names Lana Turner and Whit-Whit. There was also a splendid, much-publicized tomcat, Vassily Vassilyevich Lechkin.

Stravinsky contrived, behind closed doors ("I have never been able to compose unless sure that no-one would hear me") to work with the fastidious care and regularity which characterized all his creative output. In a recorded interview he remarked "I like to compose music much more than listen to it," adding wistfully, "listening gives you always surprises. Very rarely good surprises, and very often bad surprises. . . . The activity of composing is everything for me." His wife Vera wrote of him "His managerial cortex is very powerful, and alcohol does not interfere with his work unless, of course, he gets 'squiffed'. In the Swiss years he used to drink white wine while composing, and in the French years red wine. In America it is Scotch and sometimes a bumper of beer."[1]

Nineteen fifty-nine was a busy and exhausting year for Stravinsky, his wife and Robert Craft, his *Eminence Grise*. It included what might be called a Pacific odyssey, of which Craft wrote a brilliant account. In the region around Manila, where people prayed and waited for rain, they saw the great rice fields, scorched and brown; natives, with umbrellas to protect themselves against the polished-copper sun, padded along the cracked, dry roads, fringed by coconut or banana groves, from which projected bamboo huts on stilts. Arriving at Hong Kong the visitors descended upon the Repulse Bay Hotel, where they sat on a terrace overlooking a jade sea dotted with purple sampans and sugar-loaf islands. Stravinsky commented dryly that the *salon-du-thé* orchestra "made a Rossini overture sound like *Chopsticks*".

In Tokyo they dined at the Fukudaya, while in the streets outside moved the jostling procession of varied and exotic types that made up a typical crowd in a Japanese city—girls in Indian saris, or neat Chinese dresses; mothers guiding whole crocodiles of children; Buddhist monks, Roman Catholic priests, Orthodox archi-mandrites, Shinto *kannushi*, Indian *sadhus*, huge *sumö* wrestlers with long hair knotted on top of their heads; sellers of red fish (*kingyo-ya*) or of roasted, sweet potatoes (*yaki-imo*); Buddhist nuns with shaved heads; and a plethora of Tokyo's 80,000 prostitutes. Stravinsky and Craft sat around a low table at the Fukudaya, while pretty geishas trotted in with hot *sake*, replenished their cups, then kneeled submissively beside them to provide more drink when they needed it. One of the geisha's principal functions is to see that the guest is happy and contented, made to feel on the very brink of Paradise—a situation which Igor Stravinsky, with his fondness for good living, found irresistible.

During a visit to the *kabuki* theatre, which enjoys a popular appeal in Japan comparable to that of opera in Italy, the Stravinskys and Craft inspected the wardrobe and 'props' rooms, the offstage music room, and the revolving-stage machinery. The actors included children, one only eleven years old; glistening with grease-paint, they had an easy-going professionalism. One person of great importance in the *kabuki* theatre whom Craft did not mention was the *omuko-san* ('honourable shouter of cries in the gallery'); he it was who demonstrated the success of the performance by shouting praise, admiration or encouragement from the gallery. The *omuko-san* needed a considerable degree of finesse to spring his interjections at precisely the right point in the drama; consequently he gained an almost professional status and belonged to a club, or 'craft', to whom, as if to reputable critics, the manager allotted free seats.

The spectacles which Stravinsky and his party encompassed in Japan included the temple of Sanjusangen-do, which dates from 1251. Its dark hall contains 1,001 large images of the Bodhisattva Kwannon, all shining with gold, brandishing an incredible number of hands, and set in long, straight ranks. The central statue and some of those around it are thir-teenth-century masterpieces by Tankei, one of the greatest Japanese sculptors. Few sophisticates from the West can approach this hieratic forest of bodhisattvas without a chilling sense of something terrifying, gargantuan and unreal. It must have comforted the observant Craft to discover among the blood-freezing array of basilisk-eyed golden heads, erect bodies and grotesquely branching arms, two gentle Sivas playing cymbals and a lute. Stravinsky hated the proliferation of statuesque divinity—"I will have 1,001 sleepless nights," he grumbled.

On 9th February 1960 the Russian-born painter, designer, and art historian Alexandre Benois died in Paris at the age of ninety. After a funeral service at the church of Saint-Christophe de Javel, he was buried on 12th February at the Cimetière des Batignolles. His death must have touched Stravinsky, for Benois stood out in his Unknown Country as a familiar, much-loved landmark, and it probably reminded him of his own vintage years, now withered by the frost of old age. It was Benois, more than any other man, who, with his remarkable gift for evoking period and for capturing delicately but surely the elegance of eighteenth-century France and the charm of nineteenth century St Petersburg, directly influenced the artistic taste of Diaghilev during those glorious, early years of the Russian Ballet.

A further reminder to Stravinsky of the slow erosion of the balletic past came later that year with the news of the death in Venice on 20th September of Ida Rubinstein, then aged seventy-five. This colourful Russian dancer, actress and *animatrice* went to Paris with the Russian Ballet in 1909 to create the role of Cleopatra. Her striking beauty and almost Oriental personality brought her tremendous fame, and the following year her teacher Fokine gave her another exotic role in *Schéhérazade*. She had no great technical ability as a dancer, however, and left Diaghilev's company after the 1910 season, returning for a single charity performance of *Schéhérazade* in Paris in 1920. Yet, having shone in the firmament of ballet as a 'star', Rubinstein determined to remain one. She settled in Paris and staged a series of productions with herself as the chief luminary, dancer or actress. On these she expended huge sums of money, commissioning works from the great choreographers, musicians and writers of the day. As related previously in this book, Rubinstein more than once aroused the anger and jealousy of Diaghilev in the process of doing so.

Stravinsky, in writing about his own music, could be irritatingly obtuse. The cryptic programme note which he penned for the première of his *Movements for Piano and Orchestra*, given at the Town Hall, New York on 10th January 1960 reads more like a chemical formula than a musical analysis : "The fifth movement (which I rewrote twice) was a construction of twelve 'verticals'; the listener has to get down and look up through the series, so to speak. The *gamma* and *delta* hexachords are more important here than the A and B. And five orders are rotated instead of four, with six alternates for each of the five, while, at the same time, I see the six in all directions, as through a crystal."

What did the average music lover, confronted by this claptrap at a concert, make of it all? Perhaps he vowed to bring an astrological chart to his next Stravinsky evening. One almost suspects the composer of having taken up Nietzsche's famous battle cry : "I will put fences around my thoughts and my words, so that swine and herdsmen may not break into my gardens."*

While Stravinsky *père* made adult comprehension more dubious with his programme notes, Stravinsky *fils*, in the person of Soulima, the distinguished pianist, made juvenile understanding much easier with his *Piano Music for Children*, published in the same year as the première of *Movements*. This book, which introduced the pupil in a simple, unpretentious way to classical textures and forms, provided a fruitful oasis in the vast desert of instructional ambiguity through which the young are so often compelled to wander.

Proof of Stravinsky's international prestige included in 1960, a memorable first night in Stockholm of Ingmar Bergman's production of *The Rake's Progress*, when Sweden's usually restrained and placid opera-lovers broke into wildly enthusiastic applause. It was the first time that the great stage and film director had tried his hand at opera, and a Stockholm critic hailed the event as one to go down in the history of the art. While the King and Queen took part in the deafening applause, Bergman, accompanied by Michael Hielan, the conductor, walked across the stage to bow.

An invitation reached Stravinsky in 1960 to compose a hymn for a new English hymnal being compiled by the Cambridge University Press and, at the suggestion of T. S. Eliot, he took his text from Part IV of *Little Gidding*, the last of the poet's *Four Quartets*. A serial work, in which single notes and small note clusters are repeated in a very attractive and characteristically Stravinskian way, this anthem, entitled *The Dove Descending*

* That the art of esoteric programme-note writing still flourishes may be realized from the following analysis by the young *avant-garde* composer Alan McCombie, expounding one of his own works: "Serio-modular formalism in its extreme and most advanced form has shown us the incipient birationalism of total serialism. This dichotomy is explored in the present work through the multiplanar interjuxtaposition of bivalent (quasi-multivalent) tone clusters with neo-aleatoric material arranged in spaced points, occlusions, antipoints and reflexes. The contemporary dilemma concerning the socioeconomic relevance of multiple, i.e., ambidilectic thematism is highlighted by the organic reantiorientation of paraorganic material throughout the work."

The reader may be excused for supposing this "flux of words," as Sir Arthur Quiller-Couch would have described the analysis, to be a practical joke; but the exposition is meant to be taken seriously.

Breaks The Air, received its first performance in one of the Monday Evening Concerts at Los Angeles on 19th February 1962, with Robert Craft conducting.

The continuing influence of both Stravinsky and the dead but still potent Diaghilev could be seen from about 1955 onwards in the productions of the New York City Ballet, which, invigorated with new blood by Kirstein and Balanchine, became one of the youngest, freshest and most vital dance companies in the world. Following Diaghilev's example of keeping abreast of modern ideas in every field, they staged ballets to music by composers ranging from Charles Ives to Webern, from Gesualdo to twentieth-century jazz, from an American neo-classicism to surrealism. One of their most exciting and successful festivals opened at the City Centre, New York in November 1960, when, with other ballets, they presented the *Monumentum Pro Gesualdo*, set to Stravinsky's score of the same name, consisting of three of Gesualdo's madrigals for five voices, transcribed for instruments and celebrating his 400th anniversary.

Gesualdo, like Stravinsky, was not only an astonishingly bold composer, who sounds strangely 'modern' to us in his daring harmonies (his music has been described as "Wagner gone wrong", a term also applied to Schoenberg), but he was also a fascinating man. A neurotically hypersensitive member of an old aristocratic family—one of his uncles having been canonized—Gesualdo showed sado-masochistic tendencies, experiencing a delirious pleasure in being flogged, for which purpose he kept a specially trained servant. Madrigalist and murderer, virtuoso lutanist and Neapolitan prince, he anticipated many of the technical and expressive aspects of music that flourished several centuries after his death. The haunting major/minor ending of his madrigal *Luci serene*, for example, looks forward to the close of the first movement of Walton's *Viola Concerto*, written over 300 years later. His intriguing personal life—he murdered his wife and her lover—have tempted historians into regarding his music as merely sensational; but Stravinsky, by completing *Illumina Nos*, one of Gesualdo's *Sacrae Cantiones*, and 'recomposing' this and two of the other songs, demonstrated his relevance to a composer of the mid-twentieth century.

The ballet *Monumentum Pro Gesualdo* had a distinguished cast. The long, slim, almost flawless body of the luminous-eyed Diana Adams, who shone so lustrously in the ballet *Agon*, served once again as a kind of master-puppet for Balanchine's manipulating genius. Her virtuosity seemed inexhaustible. Lillian Moore, the dance critic, writing of Miss Adams's dancing in this work and the preceding *Episodes*, said "It is not every ballerina who can appear poised and serene while being carried upside down, her bent legs framing the face of her partner, as Miss Adams was in *Episodes*. . . . But *Monumentum* was not as provocative as *Episodes* . . . it is remembered chiefly for a fairly con-

M

ventional, but lovely lift in which Miss Adams, in an arabesque, was lightly tossed by one group of men to another."

In December 1960 Stravinsky conducted *The Nightingale* in a performance sponsored by the Washington Opera Society. On entering the hall he received a standing ovation. The orchestra consisted of members of the National Symphony. Brilliant hues of red, green and blue lit the stage for the opera; the cast wore beautiful, authentic Chinese costumes and the singers, according to Press reports, scaled their voices effectively to the delicacy of the music.

Stravinsky went to Belgrade with the Santa Fe Opera in October 1961, and conducted an excellent ensemble in *Oedipus Rex* and *Perséphone*. Composers from all over Yugoslavia came to the city to greet and honour him.

Paul Sacher, who commissioned the work and to whom it is dedicated, directed the Basler Chamber Orchestra and the augmented Basler Chamber Chorus in the première at Basle in the spring of 1962 of *A Sermon, A Narrative And A Prayer,* with three distinguished soloists—Jeanne Deroubaix (alto), Hugues Cuenod (tenor) and Derrik Olsen (speaker). Shortly before the performance Stravinsky wrote to Sacher :

As *Threni* (Jeremiah's Lamentations) was based on the Old Testament, *A Sermon, A Narrative And A Prayer* is a New Testament cantata—in Faith and Charity the virtue of Hope, this New Testament way to the truth, leads to the first Christian Martyr, St Stephen, to pray for his torturers, thus repeating the deed of his Master. The inspiring beauty of the King James Bible text (*St Paul's Epistles* and the *Acts of the Apostles*) and Thomas Dekker's *Prayer* (of the same period of the English language) were chosen for my new cantata—that's all that should be said to the listener of my music.

During a visit to London in 1962 the composer responded with typical grumpiness to a manifestation of the stolid British indifference to bad weather. About to leave London by air for Australia and New Zealand, via Cairo, he found his travelling plans thwarted, or so he thought, by a heavy yellow fog. Plagued beyond endurance by a series of minor setbacks, Stravinsky entered the lift at his hotel to go up to his room. The lift boy, deciding that the great composer looked a kindly old man, smiled disarmingly. "Lovely day, sir," he chirruped. Stravinsky glared balefully at him. "What," he snarled at his companion, "do these people think a climate is? Lovely day? Indeed! I wonder how bad the weather has to be before they even admit that it's 'not so good !' "

Nineteen sixty-two was a memorable year for Stravinsky. The music-loving community of New York turned out in thousands to celebrate the eightieth birthday of the composer, whilst, at the same time, international attention focused on the birth—symbolized by the opening of the Philharmonic Hall—of the magnificent complex of buildings known as the

Lincoln Centre for the Performing Arts, reputed then to be the largest project of its kind in the world. To commemorate Stravinsky's octogenarian status, the Los Angeles Monday Evening Concerts performed at least one of his works in each of its concerts throughout the year. In January, during ceremonies held at the State Department, the Secretary of State, Dean Rusk, presented the composer with a gold medal. Stravinsky was also invited to the White House as a guest of President John F. Kennedy and his wife. The distinguished company included Mrs Stravinsky, Princess Radziwill, Nicholas Nabokov, the composer, Princess Chav-char-Vadze, Max Isenbergh, the State Department's chief of cultural affairs, his wife and Robert Craft. At dinner the President toasted Stravinsky thus : "You have been through many things in your life. People have thrown sticks and tomatoes at you. Now you are here and we are delighted to have you. You have enriched the world." It would not be long before John Kennedy himself would be a target for hostility; butchered by an assassin's bullet.

Another première of a Stravinsky work came on 14th June, when, on the television network of CBS, who commissioned it, America watched *Noah and the Flood*, one of the most widely publicized events of its kind, and an extremely expensive one. This twenty-five-minute production seemed to John Ardoin, writing in *Musical America*, as a monstrously overblown presentation. What he censured was not the work itself, but the sophomoric preamble which, superficially discussing the flood legend in various cultures from ancient Peru to the biblical story, inflated the whole production into a full hour crammed with hotch-potch padding. He resented the "vicious commercialism" which preceded and followed the prologue; according to him, the nature of the sponsored advertisements deprived the performance—involving a group of famous film actors—of any dignity.

Ardoin also observed that, instead of creating a ballet, Balanchine and Ter-Arutunian had fashioned a hybrid work with trick photography, with hazy superimpositions and overlays. He wrote :

> There were only two real moments of dance (*The Building of the Ark* and *The Flood*) and only the first of these came off with its sharp *Agonesque* movements. The second was virtually chaotic, with dancers writhing under large pieces of slick cloth and darting across the screen. . . . A further distraction from the score was the fussy and uncongenial sets by Ter-Arutunian. Especially irritating was the tawdry Garden of Eden scene, with its trimmings of tinsel and cellophane. . . . It is disappointing not to be able to single out any one aspect of the production as being completely successful or enjoyable, but such was the case.

The distinguished actors in the première included Laurence Harvey (Narrator), Sebastian Cabot (Noah), Elsa Lanchester (Noah's Wife), John Reardon and Robert Oliver (The Voice of God), and Richard Robinson

(Satan), with members of the New York City Ballet, a chorus directed by Gregg Smith, and the Columbia Symphony Orchestra. Stravinsky and Craft conducted.

In September 1962, after a brief sojourn in New Mexico, where the Santa Fe Opera presented all his works for the lyric stage, Stravinsky made his first pilgrimage to Russia in fifty years, stopping on the way to participate in Israel's Music and Drama Festival. Accompanied by his wife and Craft, he travelled in a Soviet TU-104 airplane. The Soviet authorities had invited him in 1960 to return, promising him many honours if he would celebrate his eightieth birthday there. The irony of this belated recognition was intensified by someone finding an entry in a Russian encyclopaedia calling Stravinsky "a composer of no great value whose works are a mixture of simplicity and decadence". This insult, coupled with a rather blunt reminder by Stravinsky that he had never received any royalties from performances of his music behind the Iron Curtain was undoubtedly the cause of the expedition being cancelled, or at least postponed. The composer, however, continued to yearn for his native land, and, although no money reached him from the Soviet strong-hold, the hand of officialdom tactfully changed the denigrating note in the encyclopaedia.

The Kremlin maintained—and indeed still does maintain—an *Index Expurgatorius* of Western and renegade Russian composers whose works are supposed to exemplify the corruption of modern Western music. The list, at the time Stravinsky returned to Russia, was extremely long and included Hindemith, Schoenberg, Berg, Webern, Krenek, Ravel, Honeg-ger, Milhaud, Auric, Poulenc, Messiaen, Britten, Menotti, Cowell and Copland. It could be said of Stravinsky then, as of Abou Ben Adhem, "And lo, his name led all the rest!"

Harshly criticized throughout the Stalinist regime, he was welcomed as a hero when he first set foot on Russian soil on 21st September 1962 and when, in Moscow, on 26th September, he conducted a concert. What were Stravinsky's feelings on revisiting the land of his birth after so long an absence? During a Press interview he subsequently referred to the crusade in these words : "I told them, 'I am as Russian as you are, and not an emigrant.' I left *Tsarist* Russia in 1910 because I couldn't stand what was going on, and because of my wife's ill health. I was more revolutionary than the Bolsheviks, who are very conservative in music. I told them this, but not as loudly as I say it now. Mezzo-forte."[2]

There is a faint flavour of the Arabian Nights about Craft's description of his adventures in Russia with the great composer and his wife. On arriving at the Moscow airport Stravinsky made a profound obeisance. An excited, gift-bearing deputation fussed around the party. A woman, introducing herself as the daughter of the poet Balmont, presented a birch-bark basket containing moss, a twig, a blade of wheat, an acorn, and a

leaf. A telegram of good wishes from Shostakovich was pushed into Stravinsky's hand; someone whispered in his ear that thirty thousand people
had queued for his forthcoming Leningrad concerts.

Next day the conductor Ivanov presented Stravinsky to the Moscow
National Orchestra, who responded with applause and bow-tapping.
When Craft commented on the coolness of this tribute, Alexandra Alex-
androvna, acting as interpreter and guide to the party, explained: "We
have no personality cult here." Craft conducted the orchestra in *The Rite
of Spring*, noting that the sobriety of the performance, which did not
glitter like many given in America, clearly delighted Stravinsky. He also
observed the curious bass drum used by the Russians; open on one side,
almost as if sawn in two, it produced a *secco* articulation from its single
head which made the opening of 'Dance of the Earth' sound like a Calgary
stampede.

After a reception at the Composers' Union, attended by Krennikov,
Shaporin, Dankovich and Kabalevsky, came a tour which embraced St
Basil's and the Kremlin. Moscow, in 1962, had changed in many respects
since the day when the composer had left Russia at the invitation of Serge
Diaghilev; but it must have seemed to him, as he looked once again at the
grim towers and walls of the Kremlin, the vast Red Square and the gay
onion domes of St Basil's Cathedral, that his childhood and youth were
unfolding before his eyes like a ghostly panorama. Most of the familiar
streets had been retitled and now bore the names of Russian poets and
Communist heroes. The famous Metropole, a palace of a hotel when
Diaghilev mingled with the Moscow intellectuals, had lost its nineteenth-
century grandeur; the carpets looked threadbare, the paint flaked from
the walls; the porters, stripped of their gold braid, might have been Orwellian guards; and in the lobby, once filled with princes and grand-dukes,
American business men walked briskly, carrying briefcases. Yet the great
Theatre School, with its massive door, stood there, as majestic as ever,
as did many of the other fine buildings which belonged to Moscow's
cultural heritage.

From the handsomely painted Soviet cupboard, figuratively speaking,
clattered a large and embarrassing skeleton. It happened at the Novodevichy Monastery, an island of old Russia decaying behind ancient walls,
as Craft described it. The party, penetrating further than officialdom
would have liked, encountered some old women in ragged clothing who
knelt and prayed before crosses, graves and the statues of angels. Poor
people in modern Russia, the Utopia of well-fed, happy Comrades . . .? The pretty face of the guide-interpreter froze; the hitherto
warm and friendly atmosphere suffered a chilling drop in temperature.
From that moment it seemed that Stravinsky and his party, though still
treated with all the courtesy of a well-conducted Cook's tour, were *persona
non grata*.

Craft remarked upon Stravinsky's increasing 'Russification' during the visit, and his defence of solecisms or misdemeanours which, in any other part of the world, would have stung him to exacerbation. He commented that, back at Hollywood, a five-minute delay in the serving of dinner ruffled his temper; but that the appearance of a meal in Moscow, after a two-hour hitch, drew the commendation "What a very good service!" Whilst despatching his food, Stravinsky uttered such asides as "the salt is marvellous", ignoring or pretending not to notice the fact that the meat had the consistency of rhinoceros hide. If Craft wished to complain about anything, his illustrious friend hastily silenced him.

A breathtaking round of activities kept Stravinsky and his entourage busy during the next few days. Igor conducted a concert in Tchaikovsky Hall, where the audience, clearly bored or baffled by *Orpheus*, rustled programmes, but also, at the end, clapped joyously over the return of the prodigal. At the Moscow television studios the composer casually mentioned that he was writing a biblical cantata, in Hebrew, for the Israeli Government; a piece of news which, in a country disowning both God and Jesus, understandably aroused no enthusiasm.

The party visited the Scriabin Museum and the Tolstoy house, lunched at the United States Embassy, and attended a reception at the Metropole, where Madame the Minister of Culture and leading Soviet composers greeted and extolled Stravinsky. At the reception Craft noted the sensitive, intellectual face of Shostakovich, who, chewing his fingernails, trembling, stuttering and nervously manipulating his hands, might, from the description given, have been a Jane Austen schoolgirl, rather than a great and mature symphonist; but then, to be self-conscious is only natural in a land where officialdom constantly looks over the shoulder of every creative artist.

A journey to Leningrad, the old St Petersburg, had the semblance of a nostalgic homecoming. Vladimir Rimsky-Korsakov, now pale and wintry, met Stravinsky and, failing to be recognized, burst into tears. The party visited Stravinsky's birthplace (Oranienbaum), sat in the ravishingly beautiful Maryinsky Theatre (now the Kirov Theatre), gazed upon the turquoise palace of Tsarskoe Seloe, now called Pushkin and finally returned to Moscow through a landscape lit by a sky streaked with gold. There was a farewell banquet at the Metropole, preceded by the arrival of gifts —samovar, gold spoon, gold tea-glass holders and inscribed scores; Stravinsky, chatting about post-Mahlerian music, teased poor Shostakovich about his provincial attitude. The party, summoned to the Kremlin for a meeting with Khrushchev, found the pudgy premier affable, but also slightly aggressive and boastful. Finally, at Sheremetievo Airport, on 11th October 1962, the party set off *en route* for Paris.

The weather-vane of the Soviet ideologists, always reacting to prevailing winds of expediency, did so with respect to Igor Stravinsky. Having once denigrated him as a third-rate bourgeois composer unworthy to take his place among the artists of the U.S.S.R., they, suddenly awakening to the fact that the rest of the world regarded him as a genius decided to do likewise. When, in 1970, the composer's niece travelled from Russia, she brought news of an astonishing *volte-face*. The letters which Stravinsky had left in the land of his birth now reposed as venerated relics in the Pushkin House, the Russian Museum, the Institute of Russian Literature, the Rimsky-Korsakov Archives, the Leningrad Public Library and the Leningrad Institute of Theatre and Music. Hero-worship extended even to Stravinsky's father; a firm of publishers, Kutateladze and Gosenpoud, having issued a biography of him. Stravinsky, with a cynical smile, classed the purloining of his letters as a theft characteristic of Soviet officialdom, and commented dryly that the title of the publishing firm sounded like the names of Hamlet's student friends in a garbled translation. He was amused at what he described as the new confidence shown in his music by the U.S.S.R. as revealed in the following story published by *The Sunday Times* :

Most of the West's NATO and scientific secrets were passed to Moscow through Mrs Lindner . . . and Mrs Schultz, the personal assistant to two Bonn Ministers of Science. The third member of the espionage ring, Dr Wiedermann, and the two women frequently dined out together in Bonn, and the last occasion when secret information is alleged to have passed was just over a week ago, during a performance of Stravinsky's ballet *The Firebird*.

At least, Kastchei's evil castle contained nothing quite as sinister as the bloody deeds hatched inside the Kremlin over the post-revolutionary years !

13

THE CHARACTER OF A GENIUS

At the Istra concert-hall at Zagreb, in July 1963, Stravinsky, taking part in the Zagreb Biennale, one of the greatest of Yugoslav festivals, conducted a memorable concert devoted to his music; after first shedding his dinner-jacket and tie, loosening his collar, and apologizing to the large audience in Russian. For a man of eighty he showed amazing stamina, having driven to Zagreb by road from Budapest in one day, attended a concert the night before and, with unmistakable signs of boyish delight, presided over a long and harrowing Press conference. At one of these journalist's *soirées* Stravinsky made some revealing and characteristically droll remarks about the serial aspects of one of the works performed in the festival, his *Movements for Piano and Orchestra*:

I am wholly engaged in the serial system of composition. It is now the only system that I recognize. It has replaced the harmonic system . . . so there you are, then. You understand that I write everything in serialism. The twelve-tone system of Schoenberg interests me less than the serial system. The twelve-tone system would be smaller than a thirteen-tone system,—and why take less when you can take more? I take twelve tones and notes and divide them into two parts, six on the left and six on the right, and I make combinations of all the twelve serially and arrange them like a star with its rays. Thus I have forty-eight notes and tones instead of twelve. So you see I am an extremely rich man. An American millionaire! not in dollars, but in series!

Vivid impressions of great men by people who do not know them intimately are usually more interesting and often have more validity than the affection-inspired assessments of those whose perceptiveness is dulled by familiarity. During a concert of Stravinsky's music in the Zellerbach Hall, University of California, Berkeley, California in 1963, the composer occupied a box with his wife. In an adjacent box sat Gloria Brown, who noted his dehydrated, seemingly lifeless appearance; hunched and frail, he showed no sign of involvement. Then the music began; as it filled the hall, Stravinsky underwent a remarkable change—almost a transmogrification. His body quivered and palpitated with the force of the sensations he experienced. It was as if a powerful drug or electric current had been injected into his system. In a few minutes he ceased to be a tired octogenarian, plagued by illness and responsibilities, and became a young man irradiated by vitality and enthusiasm. Miss Brown, a gifted artist, was so affected by what she saw that, after returning home, she stood before an easel and, reaching into her memory, painted a picture of Stravinsky sitting in the box. This appeared some time later in an exhibition of her work at the Arleigh Gallery in San Francisco.

For many illuminating stories and comments about Stravinsky we are indebted to his friend and advocate, the American conductor Robert Craft, who has frequently been mentioned in previous chapters. Craft, born in 1923, brought up in the modern and not the ancient world of music, is best known through his association with Stravinsky; but, like the composer, he displayed an eager, truth-seeking intellect, without a touch of bigotry or prejudice. He made himself one of the most penetrating and persuasive interpreters of Schoenberg and his two greatest disciples, Berg and Webern. Craft's programme notes for certain Schoenberg performances, taking the listener bar-by-bar, phrase-by-phrase through a passage, showing exactly how the music is conceived and put together, have been models of clarity and percipience. Yet there was much about Stravinsky that perhaps even he failed to comprehend.

The composer, often contemptuous of those who could not understand himself and his music, could spring like an enraged panther on anyone who dared to stalk him. Thus, when Paul Henry Lang, reviewing the first volume of the Stravinsky-Craft *Conversations*, poured out a torrent of hostile abuse, Stravinsky rounded on him with uncontrolled fury. Yet, strangely for him, he remained silent about the most offensive allegation of all—that in these conversations Stravinsky was little more than a puppet perched on a ventriloquist's knee, uttering what Craft, with his loaded questions, had persuaded him to say.

The battle of words between Stravinsky and Lang, centred upon the pages of the *Herald Tribune*, raged with a Samurai ferocity, and the composer sent a vitriolic telegram to the paper after Lang, reviewing *The Flood*, complained aggressively of "the direction of the venerable maestro himself and his amanuensis, librettist and *valet-de-chambre* Robert Craft". It is hardly surprising that Stravinsky, in his telegram, described the review as "suppurating with gratuitous malice". His broadside, however, had little effect upon Lang, who, publishing an article on 11th March 1963, wrote: "In a special appendix, Mr Stravinsky and/or Mr Craft (by now the collaboration has reached a stage where Mr Stravinsky should use the business designation 'A Division of Craft Products Inc.') launches a hysterical attack. . . ." He also referred to Craft as "the 'ventriloquist of God' " and added "I am afraid that when these controversial volumes are finished, we may discover that what protrudes from Mr Craft's head is not Mephistophelean horns, as once suspected, but donkey's ears."

Stravinsky rightly resented this custard-pie abuse, flung by the indefatigable Lang with such obvious relish; but posterity, which dearly loves a whiff of scandal in the public lives of great men, will undoubtedly cherish it.

While the bitterness of Lang's onslaught cannot be condoned, it must be admitted that the clockwork which operates some of these 'conversations' does tick over rather too obviously. It is disconcerting to note, for example, that the preface which Stravinsky supplied to Edward Lowinsky's *Tonality and Atonality in Sixteenth-century Music* reappears unchanged (except for punctuation) as an apparently spontaneous answer to a question, and that an inquiry about new music draws a reply that clearly must have been prepared in advance: "The *newest* music I have seen in the last year is the first volume of lute entablature by Adrian le Roy (1551) (transcribed by my friend André Souris . . .)"[1] It reads like a book-publisher's blurb, or a disarmingly 'spontaneous' advertisement.

These 'conversations' are weighed down by clattering ornaments of preciosity. Stravinsky's reference to the "esurient intermediaries"[2] whose commissions whittled away his fee for the use of *The Rite of Spring* in Disney's *Fantasia* sent me scurrying for a dictionary. The "horripilating"[3] dream in which he found himself a hunchback smacks of the worst kind of Victorian horror-writing. And what, I wondered, were the "tergiversations"[4] which Father Rojdestvensky tried to teach at the Second Gymnasium School which Stravinsky attended as a child; only to learn, from my dictionary, that the word means 'evasions', 'subterfuges' or 'changes of side'.

It is true that Stravinsky was fascinated by language; but surely he never expected anyone to regard as free, off-the-cuff repartee that pretentious remark "No ecdysiast at the moment of the final fall was ever regarded more attentively than Napravnik as he peeled this glove."[5] Most readers will doubtless be astonished to learn that the pompous word 'ecdysiast' means nothing more esoteric than 'stripper'.

The trouble with the 'conversations' that Craft held with his illustrious friend is that, reading them, one glimpses two figures reflected in a mirror, —his own, and Stravinsky's. They seem at times to blend, dissolve, and re-materialize into a single dominating image—but whose? To read Craft's immensely witty and picturesque descriptions of his Marco Polo travels with the Master is to realize that here is no docile, insipid amanuensis, patiently hoarding pearls of wisdom scooped from the oyster-shells of a one-sided friendship, but a brilliant, opinionated man whose eyes, though dazzled by "a vision of the glory of the Lord", are, quite frequently, blinded by his own eloquence. Craft's discourses are spiced with a Johnsonian humour; his perspective is vastly larger than that of any doting

Fenby loyally serving and extolling a handicapped genius. There is, for me, something contrived and artificial in the analysis and projection of a great mind and personality through 'conversations' which never really spark with true spontaneity. They are, of course, revelationary—a fact which many authors, myself included, have gratefully accepted—but the manner of presentation has a slightly theatrical flavour and, to me, smacks of the television studio interview, with its carefully prepared and mutually agreed questionnaire. I would be happier if Mr Craft, having noted the impromptu sayings, the gentle ruminations, the harsh strictures, the sweetness, the anger, the wisdom and the indiscretions of Stravinsky, had conveyed them to posterity in a more conventional way.

One unfortunate side-effect of the 'conversations' is that, like some hallucinatory drug, they both captivate and stupefy the reader, who, hypnotized by the bizarre, pontifical style of the phraseology, may suspend or reject his own judgement. Donald Mitchell, in his book *The Language of Modern Music*, expressed the matter cogently in these words : "It all too often happens that what Stravinsky says or writes, about his own music or musical beliefs, is seized upon and quoted as if it were divine law. Worse than that, his music is 'interpreted' in terms of what he writes about it; the work is made to fit the 'explanation'. (No work has suffered more in this respect than *The Rake's Progress*. How much has been read, for example, into Stravinsky's incautious reference to *Cosi*!). I should be the last to deny that Stravinsky's thoughts about his music do not [*sic*] contain the most remarkable and clarifying of insights. But he often changes, or modifies, his opinions (why shouldn't he?) and, more relevant to our present purposes, leaves much *unsaid*."

An article in the *New York Times* of 4th March 1972, reported Robert Craft as denying emphatically certain charges that he had distorted or misrepresented Stravinsky's ideas. "Stravinsky would talk and I would write down what he said. Later I would face him with the words, and he would throw out a lot. Finally we would decide on a finished version." Craft also repudiated the suggestion that Stravinsky spoke poor English. "He had a better vocabulary than I have. There are forty dictionaries around the house in many languages, and he was always reading them." Refuting the specific charge that he had exploited the composer, Craft remarked that the true story might be exactly the opposite. "Stravinsky saw what I could do for him. He even exploited *me* to some extent. . . . Was I an influence on him? Of course I was."

That influence, according to Lillian Libman, once Stravinsky's personal assistant, extended further than people suspected. She believed, reported the *New York Times*, "that in the end Mr Craft simply got carried away with the excitement of his own increasing virtuosity as a writer and stylist. For me, there is an obvious difference in style and tone between the first two books and the others. . . . All that social awareness and the dazzling vocabulary came later on." Commenting on Stravinsky's frailness after he reached the age of seventy, Miss Libman described him as "a great man who permitted life to be lived for him by others, so that he might hold the love of those around him who were more attached to the world than his creative life allowed him to be".

Perhaps the truth lies between two disparate poles : like the collaboration which soloists enjoy in Brahms's *Double Concerto*, handing over a tune with continuity from one to another, Stravinsky and Craft shared a resilient give-and-take partnership. Nothing that Craft has done in this context deserves censure, indeed, he sacrificed much for the composer he revered. But posterity alone can decide, when the distance of time has put everything into perspective, the precise nature of so intimate a David-and-Jonathan relationship. Indisputable evidence from many unimpeachable sources proves that Stravinsky, even in the winter of his life, indulged in witty and searchingly brilliant repartee; yet ultimately it is not in what we say, but in what we do, that the world judges us. In the final reckoning the colossus that was Igor Stravinsky stands alone, his only champion or advocate the bedraggled, unhappy Petrushka, the sad, delicate introduction to his *Apollo* music, or the splendour that shines through the titanic upheaval of *The Rite of Spring*. A man needs no more, in Heaven or out of it.

Stravinsky, in the full bloom of his maturity, seemed from the many reports written by journalists and others to have been a kind of Superman. In his Hollywood home he worked, not so much like the traditional idea of a Bohemian composer, as like a scientist in a laboratory. His studio, lined with sound-absorbent cork, had double doors which, when closed, indicated to his family that, come what might, nobody must interrupt him. Only if the door stood open could Vera Stravinsky enter.

Every morning, with few exceptions, he rose at eight, swallowed a cup of strong coffee, smoked one cigarette, and carried out a strenuous course of physical culture, which included eye exercises. Then, with only the morning paper for company, he took breakfast. The rest of the day, broken by short intervals for meals, letter-writing and half-an-hour of sleep, consisted of careful, dedicated work, involving some rescoring of earlier pieces. Those compositions which Stravinsky wrote while still a Russian citizen were not, through the perverse laws of that country, protected by international copyright, and only by rescoring them could he be certain of collecting royalties on performances.

In this connection it is amusing to recall what Nikolai Pavlovich Anosov, one of the outstanding conductors of the Soviet Union, said during a visit to Britain a few years ago. "In Russia we publish all our new parts in full, with all orchestral parts available for any orchestra to buy for its own library. But when we want to give a performance of British music, we find that London publishers will not sell us the parts. We have to hire them, and for a limited period, and then return them. To get to know a work properly an orchestra must have the full parts and rehearse it over a long period; and the conductor must have the score for some months to study it and work out his approach to it. You simply can't do this if you can only hire the music for a little while and then have to send it back." While sympathizing with Anosov, who registers a legitimate complaint, I would suggest that the reluctance of British publishers to sell scores to Russian orchestras is directly related to the 'what I have I hold' policy of the Soviet authorities, who, after conceding the claims of the pianist Gerald Moore to be paid a fee commensurate with his high status, impounded the money as he boarded a plane to leave Russia for home.

A deeply religious man, Stravinsky spent the first fifteen minutes of his waking hours in prayer. He also read theology, writing a number of religious works himself and, when he was not travelling, attending services at the Russian Orthodox Church in Los Angeles. His often narcissistic views about his own music contrasted sharply with those he held about the music of other composers. Wagnerian opera he called "rubbish and racket"; Debussy's *Pelléas et Mélisande* he described as "the biggest bore in history," although he warmly praised Verdi, Gounod, Tchaikovsky and others.

For relaxation Stravinsky played solitaire, strolled in the patio at the back of his house, chatted with the gardeners or to Celeste, the *pusspartout* cat, as Vera wittily described it, and listened to recordings,—not, it should be emphasized, of his own music. Afternoon tea, served Russian-style in a glass, provided another break in the routine of work.

The composer suffered from polycythemia and had to undergo a blood test every seventh day and bleedings every two months. At one time he was given capsules of radio-active phosphorus, issued to him in lead-tipped calipers by a medical technician wearing protective clothing, as a means of holding the disease in check; but the doctors decided that continuance of the drastic treatment involved some risk to his constitution. It says much for Stravinsky's courage and humanitarian philosophy that, notwithstanding his debilitating illness and the grim remedy prescribed, he maintained a cheerful, bantering and constructive attitude to life. Igor Stravinsky was not only a very great composer, but a brave, humble, devout and wholly inspiring man.

Various published Press interviews and articles, as well as a letter from Vera Stravinsky to a cousin in Moscow,[6] give a detailed picture of his home life in 1963, shortly after he reached the ripe age of eighty. When not on tour, he and his wife lived in a modest house on North Wetherly Drive in Hollywood. The house, small and low-ceilinged, with only one bedroom, might, according to Vera, be more fittingly styled a cottage or *dacha*. It contained thousands of books of every possible variety and vintage, distributed around every room and categorized by language and content. Stravinsky read assiduously and before visiting Persia steeped himself, with characteristic thoroughness, in the journals of Ibn Battûta!

The house, almost bursting at the seams with its *objets d'art*, books and domestic impedimenta, had a certain theatrical opulence, with posters advertising performances of *Oedipus Rex* and *Perséphone* at the Moscow Opera adorning the walls. The tables overflowed with such treasures as glass obelisks and paperweights from Venice; pre-Columbian idols; *santi* from New Mexico; Russian cups, spoons, samovars; Inca and Coptic textiles; early-American antiques; pieces of coral, lapis lazuli and drift-wood.

Scarcely a vacant space could be found on the walls, which presented a variegated display of paintings, old maps, cartoons (one showed Rossini lifting a huge firecracker), photographs of friends and celebrities, and, in the bedroom and Igor's studio, a number of splendid icons. The pictures were mostly contemporary—by Picasso, Giacometti, Berman, Miro, Kandinsky, Klee and others. The composer and his wife liked to purchase pictures by young painters whose work they liked and whom they wished to encourage.

Vera Stravinsky, with loving tolerance, referred to the bathroom as "looking like the prescription department in a pharmacy", with hundreds of bottles, jars and other containers, all neatly labelled by Igor, providing treatment for, or safeguards against, almost every ill. By the time the post arrived—"enough to fill a laundry basket"—Vera, with female cunning, contrived to be out of the house. Stravinsky answered the letters imme-diately, then filed them away. Many were from autograph-hunters and found their way into a special waste-basket. One can hardly blame Stravinsky, for this deluge of paper left very little time for composing before lunch; although he spent three hours at the task in the afternoon, and three more at night.

Vera, with her tall, splendidly proportioned figure, languidly smiling blue eyes framed by fine Scandinavian features, made a striking contrast to Igor Stravinsky, whose short, spare body, bull-fiddle nose and guitar-like ears were shrewdly, but affectionately caricatured by Cocteau and Picasso. Vera confessed that she knew nothing about what happened when her husband composed. She mentioned, however, that whilst at work on his cantata *Abraham and Isaac* he claimed that his musical enzymes had been charged by his discovery of certain musical potentialities in the Hebrew tongue, so much so that, at eighty, he had the vigour and zest of a brilliant indefatigable youngster.

Stravinsky worked at a small upright piano muted with felt and with a plywood drawing board, bearing quarto-sized strips of manila paper, clipped above the keyboard. Around this paper, which served as the pencil-sketch manuscript, a number of smaller papers acted as charts of serial orders, calculations of permutations and the like. On one side of the piano stood a small table, on which rested coloured pencils, india-rubbers, an electric pencil-sharpener, the stylus which Stravinsky invented himself and used to draw staves, and other implements of his profession.

The composer wrote vituperatively of the process of gramophone recording, as he had experienced it :

> Recording processes have already arrived at the stage at which the manufactured performance has supplanted the true one and at which, on choice, most of us would reject the true. Natural balance, natural dynamics, natural echo, natural colour, natural (and endearing) human error—such as the cracked horn-notes that have disappeared from recorded per-formances, but still occur in concerts—these have been replaced by added echo and reverberation, by a neutralizing dynamic range, by filtered sound, by an engineered balance. The resulting product is a superglossy, chem-fab music substitute that was never heard on sea or land, including Phila-delphia. Fake phonography has overtaken fake photography, and a record-ing nowadays has been so thoroughly 'corrected' technically that it is as unlike a live performance as a painted corpse in a Hollywood mortuary is unlike a living human being.[7]

Notwithstanding this tirade, Stravinsky, who had an exclusive contract with Columbia Records for almost thirty years, participated in more recordings than any other composer of his time. He recorded, and some-times supervised the recording of most of his symphonic, operatic and chamber music.

Stravinsky's reaction to the hero-worshipping people who plagued him with requests for autographs, or the privilege of shaking his hand, was unpredictable. Occasionally, when some dulcet-voiced female, singing the praises of *The Firebird*, gushed all over him, he rounded on her like a hunted tiger with a thorn in its paw, rending her with some barbed witti-cism. As previously mentioned, most of the letters that flooded the letter-box of his home in California found their way into a large waste-basket; not because he was uncharitable or pompous, but because time and res-ponsibility pressed heavily upon him. There were moments, however, when he was kindness itself. Not the least gift he bestowed, when moved to generosity, was the radiance of his smile, which Raimund Herincx, the great bass singer, described to me as "a huge boyish grin that spread across his face from ear to ear, crinkling the flesh with a kind of sweetness and lighting up those tired, but insatiable eyes".

In August 1964, when Stravinsky visited Israel to conduct the world première of his cantata *Abraham and Isaac*, which he wrote as a token of gratitude for the hospitality shown to him by the people of Israel during his previous visit, Junius Rochester, a member of the United States Depart-ment of Commerce, was deeply affected by this very appealing facet of the composer's character. Stravinsky, his wife and Craft sat in the dining-room of the elegant King David Hotel, chatting enthusiastically about music and life. During the meal a fine Israeli wine was served to the composer, who showed visible appreciation of its flavour. Stravinsky was in full voice, gesticulating, grunting and snorting to illustrate various points, and putting the most expressive nuances into his voice. After dinner, the party rose and left. In the foyer an American Jew, bearded and wearing ascetic black, rushed over to Stravinsky and begged for his autograph. The composer granted the favour immediately and with the most beautiful of smiles. Rochester, who had pursued Stravinsky for months to obtain a signature on a photograph of the maestro at rehearsal with the Seattle Symphony Orchestra, felt completely mystified.

At the première Stravinsky, according to Rochester, "trotted onto the platform like a small, bent gnome", and conducted with "jerky, emphatic movements of his arms", keeping the rest of his body absolutely still. He used an extremely large score, studying it intensely as he directed the orchestra. Levi Eshkol, then Prime Minister of Israel, sat in the front stalls, greatly enjoying the performance. Robert Craft conducted the other Stravinsky works in the programme. He and the composer also shared a concert at the Roman ruins which stand, gaunt and dramatic, beside the Mediterranean at Caesarea.

Throughout his life, the 'priest' in Stravinsky dominated his music, and as early as 1907 one finds in the two songs, opus 6, the germ of that hieratic ritualism which, in pieces like *The Wedding*, the *Symphony of Psalms* and the moving tributes in music which he paid to his friends, would one day develop fully. During the final decade of his incredible career, this priestly ritualism manifested itself in works which showed his undiminished powers at an extremely high level. Nineteen sixty-four, for example, saw the publication of his *Elegy for J.F.K.*, a tribute to one of America's great presidents, and of his *Fanfare for a New Theatre*, scored for two trumpets. When he was composing his presidential encomium, Stravinsky was asked if he had in mind "another masterpiece similar to his *Berceuses du Chat*". "Oh no," he replied, "that's a master*puss*". On 17th April 1965, at Chicago, Robert Craft conducted the first performance of the *Variations* (*Aldous Huxley in Memoriam*), probably the most compelling piece which Stravinsky had written since *Movements*, with more easily accessible textures and ideas. In the same year the world took note of the *Introitus* (*T. S. Eliot In Memoriam*).

From 30th June to 23rd July 1966 the New York Philharmonic presented a ten-concerts Stravinsky festival at the Lincoln Centre for the Performing Arts, the programme illustrating the relationship between his music and that of the composers who either influenced him or derived inspiration from him.

During the final short phase of his amazing life Stravinsky showed increasingly not merely the signs of physical dissolution, but also the symptoms of a phoenix-like intelligence striving to keep unsullied that *motus animi continuus* in which, according to Cicero, eloquence resides. Like von Aschenbach in Thomas Mann's *Death in Venice*, he resisted the approach of death and continued to think of himself as 'the youngest one'. Time dissolved through the crack in his bedroom door, said Stravinsky, and he saw again the images of his lost world, feeling, like Aschenbach, a vaulting unrest, a youthfully ardent thirst for distant scenes.

Stravinsky grew wiser and more compassionate as the end drew near. Spending the summer of 1970 at Evian-les-Bains, a year before his death, he studied his companions at that Valhalla of convalescents with the percipience of George Arliss in the film *The Man Who Played God*. The remarks he subsequently made in *Themes and Conclusions*, conveying some of his reflections at Evian-les-Bains, disclosed not only profundity of thought, but an affecting sweetness of character. What we regard as the unfriendly silence of the very old, Stravinsky observed, is more often the consequence of deafness. Those narrow pursed lips—'the lockjaw look'—derive from dental deficiencies and instabilities, rather than from bitterness and enmity. And the fitful speech of old people springs, not so much from ill-humour as from difficulties of enunciation. Many old men and women, immured behind misconception and hostility, would be happier if those around them had the kindness, tolerance and compassion of Stravinsky.

The life-giving and therapeutic value of creative activity formed the subject of a brilliantly perceptive article by Sidney J. Harris published in the *Miami Herald* on 4th August 1971. Mr Harris pointed out that Kant, at the age of seventy-four, wrote his *Anthropology, Metaphysics of Ethics* and *Strife of the Faculties*. Tintoretto, at the same age, painted his awe-inspiring *Paradise* on a canvas 75 by 30 feet. Verdi, when nearly seventy-five, composed *Otello*, one of the supreme masterpieces of native Italian opera. At seventy-eight, Lamarck completed his great work on zoology, *The Natural History of the Invertebrates*. Richard Strauss lived and composed until eighty-five, and Sibelius until ninety; while Titian, at a staggering ninety-eight, painted his glorious *Battle of Lepanto*. Goethe was still writing his tragic and colossal *Faust* at the age of 83. Mr Harris rightly stressed in his article that creative people not only tend to live longer than others, but they also produce to a later age.

And what Stravinsky produced at the ripe age of eighty-four was the *Requiem Canticles*, his final major work and one in which his creative energy was as strong as ever. The significance and size of this great choral *oeuvre* represent one of the loftiest and most powerful contributions to the repertoire of a transcendental yet recalcitrant medium.

N

JOURNEY'S END

Stravinsky had a strange preoccupation with death. He wrote a number of pieces bearing the title *"In Memoriam"*, and also regularly cut out and filed newspaper obituaries. He hoarded portraits of such defunct celebrities as Pope John, President Kennedy, T. S. Eliot, Aldous Huxley and even Celeste, his beloved cat. This facet of his character derived not so much from any inherent morbidity, since he relished life with an omniverous appetite, as from a deep artistic sensitivity to that which, for all its horror, raises drama to supreme heights and, in some instances, opens up awe-inspiring vistas of nobility and courage. Death, whether in *Perséphone* or the *Mass*, was for Stravinsky the beautiful, raven-haired woman of Cocteau's *Orphée*: she who, to the sound of a ghostly lyre, pointed down at the dead stranger and commanded "Levez vous". To Stravinsky death was inseparable from rebirth. Nursing the cold classicism of a dead age, he breathed life into its nostrils until, with fast-beating heart and panting lungs, it danced to the swift, youthful surge of his music.

The composer's fondness for 'the good earth' extended in many directions, as did his reverence for what he once called 'the something beyond nature'. A gourmet and, when his favourite dishes tempted him, the gentlest and best-mannered of gluttons, he dined happily at famous restaurants like the Boule d'Or and the Ami Louis in Paris, where crayfish, *foie gras* and other fine food, set before him as before a Chinese mandarin, brought a sparkle to his eyes. He sipped the wine like a critical and expert taster from Bordeaux. And when, at eighty-four, his liver rebuked him on one occasion for consuming crayfish as avidly as a seal being fed at the zoo, Stravinsky, recalling that he had previously inspected the delectable monsters in the restaurant kitchen, attributed his malaise to divine retribution for the sin of "eating creatures that one has already met socially".

John McClure, an American writer, described Stravinsky as giving the impression of "slightness" and of being "as frail as a bird". Certainly the composer's fragile appearance conveyed nothing of his remarkable strength of character. McClure contributed this portrait of Stravinsky:

His voice is deeply pitched and resonant with a persistent Russian accent . . . Stravinskian is a kind of unblended Esperanto made from English with *subito* French and German spiked with Italian, and the conversation in his polyglot household will switch without warning into any one of them. . . . His use of English is both precise and fresh, and he has the philologist's love of finding and tracing new words and new meanings. . . . Stravinsky's eagerness for the new or the text, whether music or book, concert or country, makes his critics by comparison look like testimonials to the art of taxidermy. . . . He loves to know, to taste, to touch and to see, as much as to hear.

Except in his angry moments—and there were many—he was an incomparable host or guest, whose constant jokes, witty opinions and idiosyncratic ideas made an evening in his company seem, according to his friend Goddard Lieberson, like a session with Voltaire, Morgenstern, Gogol, Ostrowski and George Bernard Shaw, all at the same time. He read books, old or new, with an insatiable hunger, ranging from dignified classics to the titivating periodicals, and watched television whenever he could spare the time. Strolling in the garden of his Hollywood home soothed the irascibility that threatened so often to burst into flame, and the sight of lemons, oranges and avocados on his own tree filled him with pride. His fondness for animals and certain reptiles extended even to the tongue-forking lizards which, in the hot sunshine, darted for cover as he approached.

There was never any pomposity about Stravinsky himself, which explains why he detested it in others. He could be deeply offended, but he did not quickly take umbrage, or assume a pious attitude of outraged morality. Once, a traveller from a firm bearing the Orwellian title of 'The X. Blue Printing Company' called to see him. The visitor, wishing Stravinsky an effusive "Merry Christmas", pressed a gift into his hand and said "Why don't you open it right here, Mr Straw-windsky?" The composer, thanking him politely and ceremoniously, unwrapped the gift, to find one of those commercial calendars with half-naked girls disporting themselves on the pages. "Very nice," remarked Stravinsky. He was shown the *pièce de résistance* on the October page—a superb pair of cream-coloured, female buttocks. The distinguished creator of *The Rite of Spring* gravely signified his pleasure; whereupon the visitor tweaked his ear and addressed him as "You old rascal!" When the salesman had gone, Stravinsky roared with laughter until the tears ran down his cheeks, then shouted at the top of his voice "Vera, Vera! Look what I've received!"[1]

A grateful world heaped many honours on the composer. In 1951 he received the gold medal in music from the National Institute of Arts and Letters; and in 1954 the Royal Philharmonic Society bestowed its coveted gold medal. In 1955 he gained the Sibelius Gold Medal, given every five years for outstanding services to music. Four years later the Sonning

Foundation of Denmark chose Stravinsky to receive its first international music award. And in 1963 the Finnish Fund for Arts and Sciences awarded him an international prize named after Sibelius and valued at 27,000 dollars.

Stravinsky's razor-edged, analytical mind challenged and investigated whatever puzzled or alienated him. When he listened to an unfamiliar work, he usually sat with the score open before him, a magnifying-glass ready to hand; if a difficult or abstruse passage or chord stopped him, he seized the magnifying-glass and closely scrutinized the page, until he had fathomed its mystery.

He treated his fellow artistes with a gay, bantering irreverence. "Stokowski's Bach? Bach's Stokowski would be more like it."[2] After watching a television programme on Pablo Casals, he remarked "*That* was an interesting performance. In one scene the cellist and a sort of Hungarian composer, Zoltán Kodály, are shown together with their great-grand-daughters —or so the viewer supposes until learning a blush later that they are the wives. And what are the two racy octogenarians talking about? Well, they are talking about the trouble with me, which is that I must always be doing the latest thing,—*they* say, who have been doing exactly the same old thing for the last hundred and eighty years. Señor Casals offers extracts of his philosophy, too; for example, playing Bach in the style of Brahms." The conductor Leonard Bernstein he dismissed lightly and with a touch of sarcasm. "Mr Bernstein has made himself well known."[3]

Stravinsky's opinions were often as dogmatic as Wagner's. A powerful and resourceful opponent of the more decadent aspects of the Romantic age, he struck heavy blows against it with both his music and his public utterances. Inevitably other men, spokesmen for particular cults and fashions, attacked this exacerbating genius; as, for example, did the noted composer and exponent of the 12-tone school, Ernst Krenek, who wrote of Stravinsky's "comedy masquerade, in which he hides behind Pergolesi, Bach, Weber and Tchaikovsky for so long that when he finally emerges again as Stravinsky one does not recognize him for himself. His individuality can always be identified in the unmistakable gestures with which his genius animates his figures, but no-one knows what has become of the real personality—perhaps he does not know himself, possibly he does not want to know. In his autobiography, written so coolly and with such conscious detachment, Stravinsky speaks of many people and things, but is silent about the only cardinal fact of his mysterious career; namely, how he journeyed from *The Rite of Spring* to *A Card Game*".

How, indeed! Not by standing still and day-dreaming, or by remaining rooted in a decadent tradition but by travelling incessantly through a changing and resourceful musical territory, travelling with ears attuned to every strange and challenging sound and with an eager, boyish heart full of the miracle and enigma of life.

Stravinsky enjoyed his American citizenship, finding peace of mind, financial security and a place where he could practise his art, undisturbed. He became a familiar figure in American concert halls, as conductor and solo pianist in his own works. A devoutly religious man, he deplored the serious decline in modern church art, especially liturgical music, and on one occasion remarked, with corrosive humour, that in the churches of Los Angeles one heard anything—Rachmaninov and *Tristan and Isolde*.

His love of America and its way of life came near to idolatry, and since settling there he became, in the words of Vera, his wife, "softer and less frequently angry". Stravinsky permitted no criticism of America in his presence and, if anyone dared to offer any, he either changed the topic of conversation or rudely interrupted him. He loathed the ideological dictatorship of Soviet Russia which prescribed what a composer should write, or how he should write it, as much as he detested the obscene, goose-stepping militarism of Hitler. "As far as I am concerned, they can have their generalissimos and Führers," he declared on one occasion. "Leave me Mr Truman and I'm quite satisfied."[4]

Stravinsky's cool, objective business-like approach to the task of musical composition reflected his integrity as well as his inflexible determination. Alexei Haiev, writing in the year 1949, said that he lived by his music as a shoemaker does by his cobbling, or a banker by his strategy with money. "If he were asked to write an *Overture to the Moon*, I feel sure Stravinsky would accept the commission. He would execute it quite honestly. The finished work would represent exactly what he feels and what he can accomplish at this particular moment. He would not try to guess what those who commissioned him might have in mind. Certainly he would not want to imagine what his audience expects to hear about the moon. He does not uplift the public by writing down to it. His approach is simple. As a humble being he will be humble towards his work; as an artist he will do his best—and that is all."[5]

The correspondence which deluged Stravinsky almost every day revealed not only the respect, but also the affection which people from all walks of life felt for him. In 1969, when he was recovering from an illness, a batch of letters reached him from a Long Island school. "You're a real cool guy," one child wrote, "and if you wish you can write me back." Another youngster, concerned that Stravinsky might find hospital life tedious, advised him to "look at the nurses". One child disclosed a nice sense of values with the remark "Sorry a good composer like you is sick. P.S. My father is a doctor." And from a youthful music lover came the wish that he "would get better and compose another operetta".

Stravinsky had a bantering, sometimes barbed wit, sharpened perhaps by a thirty-year-old Ballantyne's Scotch that he consumed in moderate, but stimulating draughts. Leopold Stokowski, he said "must have spent an hour a day trying to find the perfect bisexual hairdo".[6] He described a new Gian Carlo Menotti opera in these words : "It is 'farther out' than anything I've seen in a decade; in the wrong direction, of course."[7] To him the *New Yorker* music critic Winthrop Sargent was known simply as 'W.S. Deaf'. A meretricious conductor, flapping his arms in extravagant gestures, reminded him of "an Oriental belly dance seen from behind".[8] People often irritated Stravinsky by stopping him in a store or on a street corner, saying "Excuse me, aren't you the composer of *The Firebird*?" then pushing an autograph book in his face. "One of these days," he muttered ominously to Nicholas Nabokov, "I'll hire a secretary and call him Mr Firebird, and when people ask me this, I will be able to say 'Oh, no, *this* is Mr Firebird, in person, flesh and bone'."[9]

At a dinner which Stravinsky gave, his son Theodore related how at a lunch of freethinkers a guest insulted the Blessed Virgin and fell down dead. "He was lucky," said the composer, "because he went straight to Heaven." His son asked him why. "Because he died of shame," replied Stravinsky.

He had many touching human qualities; not least that of his love life. Goddard Lieberson wrote of it in simple, sincere words which can scarcely be surpassed. "His love for Vera, his wife, was passionate, tender and abiding. She was his necessity, his reason for living, in short his love. With her he was utterly romantic. It was very beautiful to see, and one can cry to think of it. Just as Robert Craft, whose brilliant intelligence and musical companionship added many years to Stravinsky's life, so Vera, with her beauty, her charm, her wit and (despite her own inevitable great age) her girlish, fun-loving attitudes, gave to Stravinsky a series of emotional rebirths."

The composer hated as ardently as he loved : he hated stupid people, stupid letters, stupid opinions, stuffy rooms and stuffy music, charlatanism and insincerity. Often he used his scathing, pitiless humour, not merely to denigrate, but also to ridicule. If he loathed a piece of music, he usually distorted its title or the name of the composer, or he invented a comic nickname for it. To him Richard Strauss's *Rosenkavalier* was *Sklerosenkavalier*, and the music of Shostakovich he called "the old oyster",[10] as denoting a flabby interior. Stravinsky loved precise, picturesque, or onomatopoeic language, using concrete images rather than abstractions. Explaining how he intended to treat Auden's libretto for *The Rake's Progress*, he said "I will lace each aria into a tight corset".[11]

His fragile, birdlike appearance masked an indomitable zest for living; but harrowing onslaughts of lung congestion, blood clotting, and surgery imprinted on his system the death from arteriosclerotic heart disease which finally descended upon him. Despite all the irrefutable symptoms—the repetitive sickness, the stooping, enfeebled posture, the nurses helping him in and out of wheelchairs, and all the other accoutrements of a declining sovereignty—it seemed to those of us who revered him that this fantastic, lovable legend could not possibly come on an end. But we were wrong.

On 6th April 1971, in the bedroom of a New York hotel, Stravinsky's heart stopped beating. He was eighty-eight years old. Tributes flowed incessantly towards New York; but soon, fulfilling his own wish, an aeroplane flew Stravinsky's body to Venice for burial on the Island of San Michele.

Stravinsky had a special affection for Venice, not merely because he had been associated with it musically for some years, but because the Byzantine origin of its architecture, as reflected in the dome of the Salut, for example, seemed to accord with the hieratic quality of much of his later compositions. As a token of pride at his *squisita amicizia* in choosing Venice for his final resting place, the municipality pictured the cypress trees of San Michele on the posters displayed to mark this universally important event.

The Church of SS. Giovanni and Paolo stands on a canal that leads directly to the Fondamenta Nuova and thence to San Michele. Stravinsky's body, contained in a simple, dark mahogany coffin, rested in the nave before the high altar, surrounded by huge wreaths and flanked by *carabinieri* in full dress. Musically, the service, distorted by the poor acoustics of the church and hampered by the difficulties which an unaccompanied *settecento* work presents to any choir in such an environment, did not reach the lofty standards upon which Stravinsky had always insisted; but perhaps, glancing back across the dim interval between life and death, he smiled indulgently at this, and the splendid over-decorative speech which the Mayor of Venice delivered. The resident Orthodox priest recited the Orthodox Requiem; after which Robert Craft conducted the orchestra of the Fenice Theatre, and a team of soloists, in a performance of the *Requiem Canticles*.

At the close of the service bearers carried the body of Igor Stravinsky down the aisle to the waiting funeral gondola, which soon floated away across the sage-green water.

Sailing from Venice towards Torcello one moves into a haze of sadness as the city sways away southwards and the quayside becomes a shadowy blur. To the left, on the northernmost tip of Venice, one glimpses the Casa degli Spiriti, which used to be a gambling haunt; there, when it flourished as an inn, the corpses spent their last night before being ferried across the water to the cemetery. On the right, halfway to Murano, one sees the Isola di San Michele, the island given over to the dead. A huge wall surrounds this necropolis, hiding the white marble tomb-stones from the sight of passers-by; a silent, inhospitable island where the inhabitants keep eternal siesta.

Yet there is quite a holiday atmosphere about the funerals of San Michele in spite of the sadness of the event; and perhaps, as the gondola bearing that precious cargo glided past the fishermen's boats, with their gay orange sails, the great cultural heritage which Stravinsky created lay invisibly heaped, like flowers of Paradise, upon the hearse. Under the proud gaze of Verrochio's Colleoni, the slender vessel, sweeping in a graceful *glissando* across the sea, carried him away to San Michele, there to lie beside Diaghilev.

> *They told me, Heraclitus, they told me*
> *you were dead,*
> *They brought me bitter news to hear and bitter*
> *tears to shed.*
> *I wept as I remembered how often you and I*
> *Had tired the sun with talking and sent him down*
> *the sky.*[12]

And so Igor Stravinsky, passing through the Unknown Country, reached his final destination.

THE MUSIC

15

PREPARATION FOR THE JOURNEY

Some years ago a critic described Igor Stravinsky as the "Flying Dutch-man" of music, sailing the seven seas in search of a style. It is not, I think, vital that the composer should have found one, or that, finding it, he should have clung to it, forsaking all others. Like a radio signature-tune, a fixed and recognizable style may become the tombstone of that which it seeks to animate. Familiarity deadens receptivity. Too definite a style can be damaging to a creative artist, as G. K. Chesterton illustrated with this piece of rococo alliteration by Swinburne: "From the lilies and languors of virtue to the raptures and roses of vice. . . ."

Stravinsky's great triumph was that, while most of his coevals remained in the post-Wagnerian phase, he pushed boldly on through his Unknown Country. All composers reach those crossroads where they either have to stop writing altogether, like Rossini and Sibelius, or they have to develop anew, like Beethoven and Verdi; but Stravinsky never really paused to make a decision. What he accomplished he did as naturally as breathing or walking. Stravinsky did not 'invent' neo-Classicism; indeed, Busoni, Casella and Hindemith were already thinking along similar lines and the movement, if one may so describe it, existed as a barely perceptible quality in musical thought. He sensed it and gave it not merely life, but also its most perfect expression. His example, reinforced by the prestige of his Russian and *fauve* compositions, created the rallying point and symbol of anti-Romanticism at a time when neo-Romanticism still ruled like a king divested of all but his regal trappings. It is to be hoped that, as the decades pass, our civilization will be judged, not by jet aeroplanes, sky-tilting office blocks and other man-made wonders, but by such brilliant and subtle minds as that of Stravinsky; and that the serious listener of the future will find imperishable truths in the persistent, childlike voice that speaks to us in *Threni, Canticum Sacrum, Agon* and *A Sermon, A Nar-rative And A Prayer*.

Stravinsky played a major part in cleansing twentieth-century music of the luxuriance which threatened to smother it. In assessing his role as a pioneer, it is necessary to consider what type of music was being written between the première of *The Rite of Spring* (1913) and *The Soldier's*

Tale (1918), and to ask where music might be today but for his visionary leadership. In 1917, when Stravinsky toiled over *The Soldier's Tale* (for seven instruments and narrator), Pfitzner's lush, neo-Romantic *Palestrina* was first produced. In 1919 was the première of Richard Strauss's opera *Die Frau Ohne Schatten*; and a year later Stravinsky's *Pulcinella* ballet, 'after Pergolesi', appeared in Paris. In 1924, when Sibelius's Seventh Symphony had its first public hearing, Stravinsky's Concerto for Piano and Wind Instruments was premièred.

The composer's various achievements have sometimes been construed as landmarks of a disastrous journey into the Unknown Country which he explored so diligently : supra-expressionism, neo-paganism, neo-Classicism, neo-Romanticism, neo-jazz, neo-ecclesiasticism, neo-popularism and, in his final phase, post-serialism. Someone likened him, as he approached the age of eighty, to a lost and frantic bird, flitting from one abandoned nest to another. Yet the real truth, as I see it, is that Stravinsky's genius illuminated many facets, distilling so intense a range of colours and tones that one is never bored by familiarity or repetition.

The multiplicity of these facets of his originality has made the perception of the full value and meaning of much of his music a slow process of discovery. Yet, although Stravinsky never founded or belonged to any school or coterie, he became a centre of gravity for the intellectual forces of our time. Ever since those glorious triumphs with the Russian Ballet, this creator of a new aesthetic reigned without a rival in European circles. One of the most subtle and enlightened minds of the day, he regarded every age as an historical unity and, recognizing the imperishability of true values, evolved a living relationship with the past. Stravinsky, absorbing and consuming stylistic influences or openly confiscating that which he admired and coveted, did not hesitate to profit from the achievements of others, and his confession "whatever interests me, whatever I love, I wish to make my own" revealed, as he readily admitted, a rare form of kleptomania. In one of the quiet pages of his early *Fireworks*, for example, he took a generous bite at Dukas's *The Sorcerer's Apprentice*, and also helped himself to the theme of J. F. C. Lanner's Tyrolese Waltz for the musical-box tune of *Petrushka*. Although *Fireworks* reflects the influence of the new French Impressionistic school of Dukas, Debussy and Ravel, it clearly reveals, for the first time, Stravinsky's own distinctive and exuberant personality. Accents are displaced, bar-lines irregular, and the work fairly splutters with dynamic energy.

The barefaced crib from *The Sorcerer's Apprentice* may be excused; for the snippet is none the worse for being given a heady, intoxicating flavour by Stravinsky—and how many people would recall the Lanner theme today but for the musical-box interlude of *Petrushka*? Great art resembles a pearl : the nacreous deposits that create the final dazzling lustre come from sources outside itself. Beethoven's *Hammerklavier* Sonata, as we know it today, draws its profundity, not only from the original manuscript pages, but from the deepening insight and inspiration of a host of front-rank pianists who have performed it, and added to its colossal stature, since he wrote it. "No man is an island",—least of all the creative artist.

Stravinsky was far from being an "island" when he composed his derivative Symphony in E flat (1906–7). This piece, which he subsequently revised, undoubtedly shows technical ability, but not a great deal of originality or sensitive feeling. The opening sonata Allegro pursues the formula of textbook sonata Allegro in a disappointingly anonymous way, looking towards Richard Strauss for its principal theme, which soon acquires a Wagnerian chromaticism. Admittedly the Scherzo, gay and bustling, reveals glimpses of Stravinsky's own personality, but the Largo, coming third in the four-movement scheme, sits down with a bump at every juncture. There is a fine expressive vein threading the piece, but the music is steeped in Tchaikovsky's idioms and flirts unashamedly with "In the fields there stands a birch tree", from the last movement of his fourth symphony. Stravinsky plods along in the footsteps of that paternal trio, Rimsky-Korsakov, Tchaikovsky and Borodin, apart from one episode where he interpolates a folksong which he later used in the 'Dance of the Nursemaids' in *Petrushka*. The Finale shows vitality and imagination, but it soon evaporates like a trickle of water in a sun-baked desert.

The preceding works were a four-movement Piano Sonata (1903–4)—in Stravinsky's own words: "probably an inept imitation of Beethoven"— which was never published; a song for bass and piano called *The Mushrooms Going To War* (1904), also unpublished; and *Faun and Shepherdess* (1906) a song-cycle to poems by Pushkin which, scored for mezzo-soprano and orchestra, contains glimpses of the landscape and spiritual atmosphere of the Hellenic world and also discloses a nodding acquaintance with Dukas, Debussy and Ravel. There is also a suggestion of Tchaikovsky in the music, which reveals folksong connections; and, as one critic shrewdly observed, the first song could well be a party-piece for Olga in *Eugene Onegin*.

After these trifles, and before he dazzled the world with *The Firebird*, Stravinsky wrote the *Pastoral* (1907), *Two Melodies of Gorodetzky* for mezzo-soprano and piano (1907–8), the *Fantastic Scherzo* for orchestra (1907–8), *Fireworks*, a fantasy for orchestra (1908), *Funeral Dirge* for wind instruments (1908), the manuscript of which has been lost, and Four Studies for piano (1908).

Pastoral, a cool, beautifully transparent piece steeped in the rustic atmosphere of an Arcadia, is notable for the diatonic purity of its vocal line, its sparse but glittering instrumental texture, and the intriguing contrast between staccato notes and rich melodic curves. Stravinsky made several transcriptions of this work.

The titles of the *Two Melodies* are 'Spring' ('The Cloister') and 'The

Song of the Dew' ('Mystic Song of the Ancient Russian Flagellants'). A jingling bell accompaniment threads the first song, which contains the lament of a jilted bellringer's daughter about to enter a cloister. The second piece depicts a group of virgins collecting dew at first light as a means of improving their chances of marriage. Both songs, although quite pretty, have a declamatory flavour which does not wholly accord with Gorodetzky's poetic texts.

The *Fantastic Scherzo*, composed under the guidance of Rimsky-Korsakov and borrowing unashamedly (bars 49–50 in the score) from his *Flight of the Bumblebee*, was inspired by Maeterlinck's *Vie des Abeilles*, with the first part conveying the humming activity of the hive, the slow middle Trio suggesting the flight of the Queen bee, set symbolically against the rising of the sun, and the final part, which repeats the first with variation, recapturing the tranquil industry of the hive. Stravinsky confessed in his *Conversations* that bees had always fascinated him. In this work, positing Man as a supra-dimensional spectator, he presents, through his insect tableau, the eternal and compelling cycle of life.

The orchestral fantasy *Fireworks*, which Stravinsky wrote for the wedding of Rimsky-Korsakov's daughter and the composer Maximilian Steinberg, has a clean, incisive quality, the sharp, explosive power of the brass interjections, the pungent contrasting of timbres, and the flashing, spluttering brilliance of the piece heralding the titanic upheaval of *The Rite of Spring*.

The manuscript of *Funeral Dirge*, scored for wind instruments and written in memory of Rimsky-Korsakov, disappeared in Russia during the Revolution. "I can no longer remember the music," Stravinsky said years later, "but I remember the idea at the root of its conception, which was that all the solo instruments of the orchestra filed past the tomb of the Master in succession, each laying down its own melody as its wreath against a deep background of *tremolo* murmurings simulating the vibrations of bass voices singing in chorus."[1]

In the Four Studies for piano one detects, through the irregularity of the metric values, resulting in a breakaway from traditional tonality and rhythm, the questing dissatisfied *wanderlust* of a genius who already stood on the border of his Unknown Country and who, dazzled by the fleeting vision of the *Firebird*, set off across the green pastures that now beckoned him. . . .

16

THE GREEN PASTURES

The Russian sensuousness of *The Firebird* (1909–10), its exotic colouring, strongly reminiscent of the work of Stravinsky's teacher Rimsky-Korsakov, and its fairy-tale fantasy have an irresistible appeal. This music, scored for orchestra, came to life at the beginning of four years of intense creative activity and of astonishingly rapid development, during which he also wrote *Petrushka* and *The Rite of Spring*. In that brief span he penetrated deeply into his Unknown Country : for *Petrushka* has almost as little in common with *The Firebird* as it has with *Coq d'Or*, the glowing, iridescent atmospherics of two years before have given place to the ice-cold brilliance of primary instrumental colours and to the steel-sharp sonorities of polytonality. The rhythmic and harmonic complexity of *The Rite of Spring*, coupled with its savage use of a huge orchestra, expanded these characteristics into a masterpiece of frenzied violence.

One of the few works of the twentieth century to become immediately popular, *The Firebird* bubbles with vivacity. The flickering, nervous brio of the Firebird's Dance, the ferocious and frightening malevolence of the Infernal Dance of Kastchei's Retinue, the magic sleep of the Berceuse, and the final radiant tableau are evocative in every detail. And yet the first recognizable tune does not occur until the Khorovod (Round-dance), which, as Edwin Evans discovered, is not really by Stravinsky at all, but is a popular Russian folksong, "In the Garden", found in the second movement of Rimsky-Korsakov's Sinfonietta. The composer, searching for inspirational sources, ransacked another of Rimsky-Korsakov's treasure-chests in the finale, which is built upon a five-note ecclesiastical tune, a Russian chorale. Creative geniuses do, however, pillage and borrow many times; what is important here is that Stravinsky, like a spinning-maid plagued by a Rumpelstiltskin of ambition, transformed these gleanings into pure gold.

The fairy-tale story of *The Firebird* has the crepuscular magic of some of Walter de la Mare's poetry. There is a wizard-fiend, Kastchei, whose evil soul resides, not in his body, but in the form of an egg hidden in a precious casket. While the egg remains unbroken, Kastchei is immortal, retaining his power over the maidens he holds captive in his enchanted castle and over the knights turned into stone by his wicked spell. A bird with flaming plumage—compound of angel and bird—is caught by Prince Ivan. Unwilling to keep this exquisite creature imprisoned, he releases her. She rewards him with a feather as a talisman against misfortune and promises that, when he needs her, she will fly to his aid. Ivan enters the magic garden of Kastchei's castle, immediately sees the princess of his dreams, Tsarevna, who is held prisoner by the diabolical wizard, and falls hopelessly in love with her. Seized by the monstrous crew of Kastchei's servants, Ivan saves himself by summoning the Firebird, who, revealing the secret of the tyrant's soul, directs him to the casket. Ivan destroys the magic egg, whereupon the fiend and his rabble vanish, and the princesses are set free. Then the Firebird, after joining the hands of Ivan and Tsarevna, flies away.

Stravinsky prepared three different concert suites from his ballet score of *The Firebird*. The first, made in 1911, has the same orchestration as the original. For the second, created in 1919, he used a smaller orchestra, and adopted this for the succeeding version of 1945. He also wrote transcriptions for violin and piano from *The Firebird*, collaborating with Samuel Dushkin in two of these, and in 1965, taking the theme of the finale, he composed a Canon for orchestra. The concert suite of 1919 retains the outstanding music of the ballet.

Steeped in an atmosphere of night and mystery, the introduction contains hardly a single fragment of defined melody; yet the sombre, dark-tinged surge of cellos and double-basses, threaded by splashes of thirds from bassoons, clarinets and trumpets conjures up a mood of tingling suspense. A pianissimo bar for strings alone, with uncanny waves of overtones on open D strings, provides a fleeting glimpse of the Firebird; but not until the listener reaches her Variation, which describes the bird's capture and liberation by Prince Ivan, does the music burst into full brilliance. In the Khorovod, or Round Dance, where Ivan, having penetrated Kastchei's castle, is surrounded by a circle of thirteen dancing maidens, the oboe plays the folk-like theme with a lovely counter-melody on the violins. The simple diatonic tune of the Round Dance contrasts with the whirling chromaticisms of the Kastchei music.

It is the Infernal Dance of Kastchei's Retinue in which, for the first time, Stravinsky shows his thrilling rhythmic mastery. The orgiastic capers of the royal monster, set going by a *sforzando* chord of A minor from the full orchestra, are made vivid, not by the synthetic blending of tone colours, but by the use of raw, unpolished *timbres*, projected in massive, rough-hewn sections. Stravinsky creates a breathtaking acceleration in speed by gradually increasing the number of beats per bar within the same time-scheme. A transition leads to the Berceuse, a nocturnal piece in which the Firebird sings to put everyone, including the wizard Kastchei, to sleep. The closing scene is based on a folk-song "By the Gate" : this, transformed

Karsavina, Diaghilev and Lifar with the unfortunate Nijinsky on the Opéra stage

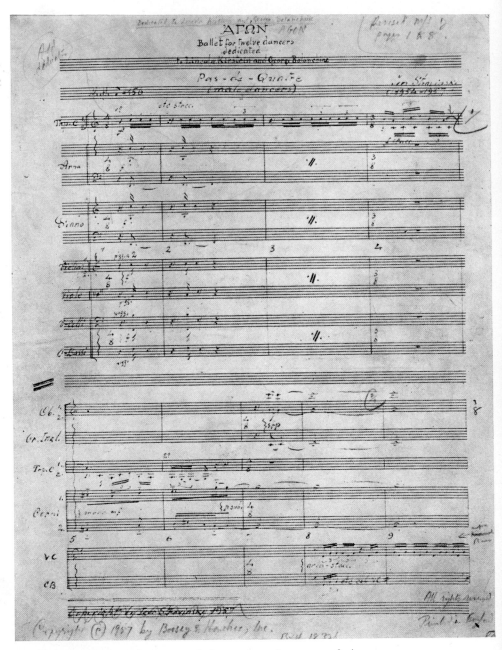

First page of the manuscript score of *Agon*

This was don. by
Laszlo Krausz

Igor Stravinsky

19/64

Drawing of Stravinsky by Laszlo Krausz

Stravinsky at rehearsal

Stravinsky enjoying a joke with the great cellist Mstislav
Rostropovich

Stravinsky being greeted by Ekaterina Furtseva, the Soviet
Minister of Culture

Stravinsky rehearsing the Moscow Conservatory orchestra before a student audience

A painting by Gloria Brown
of Igor and Vera Stravinsky

Stravinsky with his wife
Vera and the choreogra-
pher and dancer George
Balanchine

A water hearse carries Stravinsky's coffin across Canal San Giovanni and Paolo en route to the church for the funeral service. Following it, in a motorboat, are his widow and son

The scene inside the church of San Giovanni and Paolo, Venice, on 15th April 1971, during the funeral service for Stravinsky

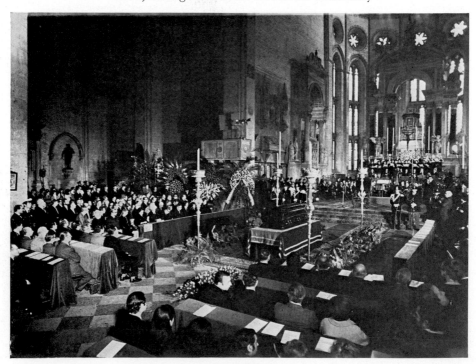

in rhythm to simulate pealing bells, symbolizes the uniting of Ivan and Tsarevna.

There are several different versions of *Petrushka*. The original ballet score dates from 1911, but in 1947 Stravinsky revised it, reducing the woodwind from quadruple to triple and taking out the cornet parts. A version for smaller orchestra, however, existed long before 1947, but some mystery surrounds its origin. There is no special suite for concert performance, the full ballet score being used. Stravinsky did, nevertheless, transcribe the 'Russian Dance', 'In Petrushka's Cell', and 'The Shrove-tide Fair' into Three Movements for Piano Solo (1921), and in 1932, with Samuel Dushkin, he prepared the Russian Dance for Violin and Piano. While arranging the 1947 version of *Petrushka*, the composer, with the dual purpose of copyrighting the score and adapting it to the resources of medium-sized orchestras, introduced a concert ending that omitted the crux of the drama. He did, however, succeed in his task of balancing the instrumental sound more cleanly in some places and in effecting other improvements. Changes apart, there is no doubt that, as a ballet *Petrushka* is not only superior to *The Firebird*, but is one of the greatest achievements in modern music. Stravinsky's use of the chord of C major against F sharp minor was considered in 1911 to be a daring experiment, and probably started the craze for polytonality.

The action of the ballet takes place at a fair in the Admiralty Square of St Petersburg during Easter week in 1830. In a puppet show run by the Charlatan the dolls dance, and it is apparent that both Petrushka and the Moor love the Ballerina. Stravinsky, transporting us behind the scenes, reveals Petrushka's passionate regard for the Ballerina and how, being over-sensitive, he tries too hard and is supplanted by the Moor, who attempts to kill him with his scimitar. In the final scene, filled with the noisy bustle and rejoicing of the fairground revellers, Petrushka comes out of the dark booth, with the vengeful Moor, still brandishing his sword, in pursuit. The sword cuts down the pathetic puppet, who falls to the ground dead. To prove to the horrified crowd that Petrushka was not real after all, the Charlatan holds up a sawdust dummy. They depart, but as the showman drags his dummy into the booth the ghost of Petrushka, heralded by his own fanfare, appears on the roof, shaking his fist at an incredulous world.

Petrushka began as a kind of *Konzertstück* or piano concerto with what is now the second of the four tableaux, 'In Petrushka's Cell', which explains the preponderance of the piano in the first half of the work. Stravinsky himself said that Petrushka was "the eternal and unhappy hero of all fairgrounds and all countries", the tragic clown otherwise immortalized by Pagliacci and Charlie Chaplin. The ballet is more than that. This poignant tale of the puppet in parti-coloured clothes made to dance by its creator before the murderous Moor sends it sprawling in a heap of

o

spilled sawdust, has a theatrical dimension that far exceeds that of its trumpery sets and clockwork instrumentation. *Petrushka* shares, however, modestly, in the tradition of such classical tragedies as *King Lear* and *Oedipus*. Here, in the simple fantasy of Hoffman's doll-world come to life, we glimpse not only a reflection of the ghostly and terrible St Petersburg, gloomy city of the Bronze Horseman, with its indefinable atmosphere of mystery and horror, but the 'tinfoil' magic of the *Commedia dell'Arte*, immortalized in a parody which, for those who look closely enough, is impregnated with compassion.

The scenario of *Petrushka* gave thrilling continuity through the device of a plot within a plot. It comprised four tableaux : the Admiralty Square, St Petersburg, during Carnival Week (*Maslenitsa*); Petrushka's Cell; the Moor's Cell; the Shrove-tide Fair that evening. To match the vividness and the different levels of the scenario, Stravinsky composed 'music within music'. He wrote firstly brilliant national and traditional dances like the dance of the coachman, whose popular appeal, set against a rich background accompaniment, never flags for a single moment, and secondly descriptive music for the protagonists which describes, not only their movements, but also their passions and aspirations. After the sprightly puppet music, for example, a slow chromatic harmony reveals Petrushka's humanity, with all its longing and sadness. Stravinsky uses the solo piano to depict the soul of Petrushka; indeed the instrument *is* the puppet. The picture intensifies as we see Petrushka in his cell; an arpeggio in one key, sounding simultaneously with that of another, displays his split, unhappy personality. Blaring trumpets project his anger and despair. The trumpets ring out again to mock the showman when the ghost of the murdered Petrushka rises above the booth.

Stravinsky, with the deft strokes of a master-painter sure of his craft, used the interval of the augmented fourth to portray the grotesque Moor's obtuseness and vanity, completing the image with "barklike sounds, snarls, and bass *pizzicato*". It is, as Fokine pointed out, a difficult work to choreograph, for in some of the dances—the 'Gypsy Dance' for example— Stravinsky deviated from the rhythmic construction necessary to bring it fully alive. " 'The Dance of the Gypsies' is not like an authentic gypsy dance because the rhythm, the structure of its phrasing, the introduction of a melody, are all without order—as if one gypsy began, then changed her mind; another one started, then also changed her mind."

The music is wilder and coarser than that of *The Firebird* : the bubbling flutes, perky street-tunes, gaudy instrumental colours, and hurdy-gurdy rhythms conjure up the coconut-shies, the shooting galleries, the gypsy tents, and the fun-loving people in their holiday finery much more effectively than conventional scoring could possibly do. "At times," remarked a critic, "one can almost smell the sausages frying."

"I heard, and I wrote what I heard. I am the vessel through which

Le Sacre passed." With this characteristically theatrical remark, Stravinsky launched a fourteen-minute talk for a gramophone recording of that incredible masterpiece; a talk proud, yet without bombast or arrogance, and always illuminating. The composer directed the Columbia Symphony Orchestra for the recording and, in doing so, reminded us of the strange correlation throughout his career between Stravinsky the creator and Stravinsky the interpreter. His evolution as a virtuoso of the baton, and the evolution of his own attitudes *vis-à-vis* his own music, proved as fascinating as the many changes in his compositional style. The first recording of *The Rite of Spring*, which he made in Paris around 1928 —a rather pale reflection of that gargantuan upheaval—discloses a comparatively gentle view of life; whereas, in the taut, crisp, anatomical response which he drew from the Columbia Orchestra in 1961, one detects the influence of his subsequent studies of Gesualdo and Bach, or the blinding light of *Agon*. Both the glorious barbarism of the R.C.A. Monteux version of 1961, and the glowing quasi-romanticism which Ansermet infused into the score, pose interpretative problems.

Does the conductor regard the sacrificial 'Dance of the Earth' as merely a brutal attack on the ear, or does he accept Stravinsky's plea to consider the canonic writing for brasses at the climax, which can be damaged by too savage a performance? *Petrushka*, being relatively simpler music, raised fewer difficulties. Stravinsky himself obtained a tense, microscopically precise rendering of *The Rite*, without the picturesque virtuosity which came from a conductor like Ansermet. Decades after it was written, *Petrushka* has found a fairly settled interpretative level, and in time *The Rite of Spring* will do likewise.

To some extent this great work is what any conductor makes of it. Stravinsky kept it under tight control and never allowed a performance to accelerate into an undisciplined scramble. Under him the quiet sections became sinuous and eerie, the off-beat accents in 'Mystical Circles of the Young Girls' carried just the right degree of savagery. 'Ritual of the Ancients' presented an evocation of unmitigated evil and suppressed horror, and the tamtam crescendos in 'Dance of the Earth' produced an awe-inspiring effect like that of the trumpeting of elephants.

There is, in *The Rite of Spring*, not only the typical Stravinsky sound, but also a residue of late nineteenth-century music—Debussy immediately comes to mind—and some of the music has a smooth finish denied to a number of his later works. What Stravinsky was reaching for in *The Rite* was a stark primitivism, the draining of music to its basic essentials to create an elementary language. "What I was trying to convey," he wrote, "was the surge of Spring, the magnificent upsurge of nature reborn."

To execute this fantastic project he assembled an orchestra of Holbrooke* dimensions : large flutes, flutes in G, four oboes, cor anglais, piccolo, clarinets in E and D, bass clarinet, three clarinets in B flat, four bassoons, eight horns (one more than Mahler used in his first symphony), little trumpet in D, five trumpets, three trombones, four tubas, bass drum, and a huge array of strings and percussion instruments, including a guero, used in Latin American music. The guero is a dried gourd with a notched top, and the player produces the sound by scraping the notches with a stick. Stravinsky bought one for the first time in the spring of 1913, when Ravel introduced him to a percussionist in whose collection were a number of these 'cheese-graters,' as they are sometimes called.

The full ballet score of *The Rite of Spring*, which suffered a few minor revisions over the years, is used for all concert performances. Bearing the sub-title *The Fertility of the Earth*, the first part opens with a solo bassoon playing a theme derived from a Lithuanian folk tune, the astringent sounds transporting one to a remote atavistic past. Mysterious arpeggio trills, and tremolos from the woodwind, suggest the pulsating rhythm of nature, as the sap rises from the burgeoning earth. Seven episodes follow without a pause. In 'Dance of the Young Girls' heavy reiterated chords and bold regular rhythms convey the stamping of men; but gradually girls join them, and the music grows more animated. Finally the girls dance alone, and four trumpets deliver a melody which subsequently figures in 'Spring Khorovod (Round Dance)'. As the dance ends abruptly, to usher in the 'Mock Abduction', flashes of high woodwind melody, set against a flurried string accompaniment and sharp horn interjections, paint the symbolic scene of the rape. In 'Spring Khorovod (Round Dance)' clarinets, crowned by trilling flutes, sing an ancient chant-like melody as each man picks a girl, mounts her on his back, and begins the laborious and difficult Round Dance. After the horns have reintroduced the earlier trumpet tune, the scene fades and, summoned by a plangent figure on the timpani, competitive groups take part in 'Games of the Rival Clans', featuring strenuous gymnastic games. Then comes 'Procession of the Wise Elder', in which the Wise Elder, represented by a tuba, makes his way among the competitors, who fall silent and, in 'Adoration of the Earth', characterized by contra-bassoon, bassoons and timpani, prostrate themselves before him. 'Dance of the Earth', filled with ever-increasing vitality and volume, shows them, revitalized by the mystical communion with the earth, leaping to their feet and whirling to and fro in a wild rhythmic abandon.

---

* Josef Holbrooke (1878–1958) was a British composer who, using a text supplied by the eighth Lord Howard de Walden, achieved fame chiefly through his trilogy of Wagnerian music-dramas *The Cauldron of Annwen*. His music shows an inclination towards romantic – and especially Celtic – legend, although his talents ranged over a wide and varied field. Holbrooke loved to harness vast forces to his highly imaginative scores, an example being the huge orchestra which he demanded for *Apollo and the Seaman* and which sent Beecham searching for that double-reed giant, the sarrusophone, one of its unusual effects.

The introduction to the second part, which carries the sub-title "The Sacrifice", is magnificently atmospheric, with icy sonorities, the cold harmonics of the violins hinting at the restless pubescence of nature, still shrouded by the dark anonymity of night. Presently man appears on the scene and the delicate lyricism of the opening bars is developed in 'Mystical Circles of the Young Girls', a charming 'andante' for strings with a meltingly beautiful theme. As the victim for the sacrifice is chosen— signified by strong reiterated chords for strings and timpani—the other girls, who had temporarily withdrawn, rush forward to surround her. Three dances, each working up to a delirious climax, follow: 'Glorification of the Chosen Victim' which Stravinsky originally conceived as a wild cavalcade of Amazons, 'The Summoning of the Ancients', and 'Ritual of the Ancients'. In the 'Sacrificial Dance (the Chosen Victim)' which ends the second part the elected virgin must dance until she dies of exhaustion in order to ensure the return of Spring. Huge complex chords are hammered out in orgiastic paroxysms. One aggressive chord is beaten out for eight, then nine, and finally for thirty-five bars, each of which has a different metre from that of the bars which precede or follow it. The rhythmic fury accelerates, through indescribable noise and tumult, into a staggering climax which, having raised the blood-pressure of the listener and pounded maddeningly on his ear-drums, suddenly stops, like a giant bass drum burst by flailing strokes, flooding the mind with a sweet, all-enveloping silence. It is infuriating; it is magnificently impudent; it is sheer, unadulterated Stravinsky.

One of the most gripping and vivid commentaries on *The Rite of Spring* as a ballet came from Emile Vuillermoz: ". . . . a secret power brings you back to every performance . . . a kind of barbaric drunkenness seizes you . . . all resistance is useless. At the third hearing you are bound to the music as Mazeppa to the rump of his horse, and forced to gallop, whether you will or not, over mountains and plains. . . . The strange troglodytes who people the place soon become your friends. You are fascinated by the three-hundred-year-old woman who presses a faggot to her heart and . . . pounds her feet down on each note of her theme; you stamp briskly as the little men with cheeks on fire now bend toward the soil, now rear up, their fists high, their heads pressed back and down; you watch for the entrance of the flower gatherers whose thin legs cut the rhythm like scissors; you gasp breathlessly at . . . the procession of elders which advances and recedes like a tide on the strand; you see terrified women thrown, as if by centrifugal force, out of the turning, swarming crowd, lashed by the orchestra's whip, snapped up by the instrumental cyclone".

The years 1910–16, during which Stravinsky left his native Russia to settle first in Switzerland and finally in France, saw a great deal of important music written other than *Petrushka* and *The Rite of Spring*. One thinks immediately of *The Wedding*, an outstanding work of the period, which he commenced shortly after completing *The Rite*. This barbaric and earthy description of primitive Russian wedding customs derives in style and spirit from *The Rite of Spring* itself.

The Wedding, begun in 1914, and virtually complete in 1917 but not scored until 1923, inhabits a peasant Russia which is scarcely more civilized than the pagan land of *The Rite of Spring*. Stravinsky himself created the text from folk material collected by Afanasiev and Kirievsky. This work has a particularly Russian quality which no translation can match. The English language is too strongly stressed to fit into Stravinsky's metres and French is much too liquid in sound to replace the sharp, incisive consonants of the original tongue.

Notwithstanding its ritualistic flavour, *The Wedding* has no definable plot, since the composer intended it to be staged as a *divertissement* or scenic tableau depicting both pagan and Christian aspects of Russian village wedding customs; but the score does present a recognizable sequence of events. At the beginning of the first part, 'At the Bride's House' ('The Tresses'), Nastasia the bride, surrounded by her mother and bridesmaids, is having her hair combed, plaited, and adorned with ribbons. Her companions try to comfort and reassure her. In the second part, 'At the Bridegroom's House', the bridegroom's friends are anointing his hair with sweet-smelling oil. They congratulate the parents on the wedding and invoke a blessing from the Virgin Mary, the Apostles and the Angels. Fetis the bridegroom also asks his parents to bless the happy event. For the final part, 'The Bride's Departure', the scene changes to the house of the bride, who, after seeking a blessing from her own parents, departs in the company of her guests. Both mothers lament the loss of their children.

Part II of the work, comprising one tableau, 'The Wedding Feast', opens with the guests eating and drinking around a table in one of the large rooms in an *izba*. Through an open door can be seen a double bed covered with a huge eiderdown. The guests sing of white and red flowers growing on the branch of a tree, while a tipsy old peasant mumbles an incoherent story about a gold ring with a ruby that someone has lost. Nastasia, after being presented to the guests by her father, is placed in the care of Fetis. A married couple are sent into the bedroom to warm the bridal bed. The bride and bridegroom are toasted in wine and they embrace. When the bed has been properly warmed, Nastasia and Fetis are escorted to it and the door closes behind then. Their parents then sit on a bench in front of the door, facing the guests, while, inside the bedroom, the bridegroom sings of his love.

For all its polyrhythmicality, *The Wedding* is clearly and transparently scored for four soloists (soprano, mezzo-soprano, tenor, bass) a chorus (SATB) and an orchestra consisting of four pianos, timpani, bells, xylophone and percussion. Its twenty-three minutes of music include only one bar for the orchestra alone. Until it reaches four isolated quarter-rests in the last tableau, the singing continues uninterrupted. The different moods —barbarity, gaiety and sadness, tenderness and drunken revelry—are vividly conveyed. A scattering of cloudy pages emphasizes the metallic precision of other passages where bell tones, flat Kremlin chimes, clock strokes, and the bird's-wing vibrations of Chinese temple gongs ring out. In the fourth tableau, the bibulous wedding feast, shouted fragments of speech and falsetto singing impinge upon the tense and gaudy stream of sound, lightening it. There is, as in other works by Stravinsky, an abuse of *ostinato*, but the music, filled with wild, compulsive dancebeats and clangorous chords, flashes with rhythmic fire. Most of the music of *The Wedding* is completely original, although the bridegroom's request for a blessing comes from a collection of liturgical chants for the Octave services and the wedding feast makes use of a popular Russian factory song.

Another work which dates from this period is the cantata *Zvezdoliki* (1911–12), known in English as *The King of the Stars*. Although written at the same time as *The Rite of Spring*, it seems to stand outside the main flow of the composer's art and, indeed, to point in the direction of Scriabin and Schoenberg. Scored for large orchestra and male-voice choir (tenors and basses), this atypical piece, only fifty-two bars long, is a setting in Russian of a poem about mystical events in the cosmos. It contains examples of polytonality pushed to such an extreme degree that occasionally the cracking harmonic structure approaches atonality. Stravinsky dedicated the work to Debussy and sent him the score. Debussy, thanking him for the honour, wrote: "The music from *The King of the Stars* is still extraordinary. . . . It is probably Plato's 'harmony of the eternal spheres' (but don't ask me which page of his!); and except on Sirius or Aldebran I do not foresee performances of this 'cantata for planets'."[2] Debussy had the manuscript of *The King of the Stars* in his possession when he died, and his heirs sold it to an unknown person; but Stravinsky kept a copy in his home at Beverly Hills, California.

In 1913 the composer returned to his opera *The Nightingale*, begun in 1908 and interrupted by *The Firebird*, and completed the work a year later. The first act of the opera, which is based on the Hans Andersen fairy-tale of the same name, was finished during the summer of 1909, but before he could tackle the second Stravinsky received Diaghilev's commission to write *The Firebird* and abandoned the opera. Then, four years later, after he had composed *The Firebird*, *Petrushka* and *The Rite of Spring*, the Moscow Free Theatre persuaded him to write the missing two acts. Aware that, in the intervening years, his style had changed drastically, Stravinsky at first refused, showing reluctance to return, artificially, to his earlier manner. Eventually, however, he alighted upon a solution.

The first act, set on the edge of a forest where the Fisherman and, later, the members of the Emperor's court are waiting to hear the nightingale's song, contains little acting, but the others, framed by the exotic splendours of the court itself, are filled with action and suspense, for they tell the story of the bird's usurpation by her clockwork rival, and her final, glorious reinstatement when she cures the dying Emperor and brings him to the threshold of a new life. Stravinsky, with characteristic shrewdness, realized that the brilliant and fragmentary style which he had evolved by 1913 would, in fact, serve a dramatic purpose, and so it did. The gentle, magical beauty of the Prologue conjures up the stillness and mystery of the forest with haunting effect, while the grotesque fantasy of the Chinese court is vividly conveyed by the dazzling glitter of the second and third act music, so that the listener is untroubled by any stylistic incongruity. Robert Craft, appraising the extraordinary chorus of ghosts in the third act, where, in a rhythmically taut structure, three notes are sung over an *ostinato* of three others, remarked that Gide must have been thinking of this piece when, stimulated by the sounds of nature and the songs of a native chorus, he exclaimed in his Congo book "Oh, if only Stravinsky could hear it!"

The symphonic poem *Song of the Nightingale* which Stravinsky completed in 1917, using Acts II and III of *The Nightingale*, does not compare with similar works of fantasy by Strauss, Sibelius and others, but it constitutes a delightfully exotic and tuneful piece. The delicacy of the orchestration in the opening section magically suggests the tinkling of bell-flowers and the firefly glimmering of lanterns in the palace of the Chinese Emperor. Later on sombre instrumental effects paint the grey atmosphere of the dying Emperor's bed-chamber, until flute and piccolo create a touch of ecstasy that even Death cannot ignore. Harp glissandos interrupt the mock *Cortège solennel* that signifies the sound of courtiers mourning the supposedly dead ruler. Faintly, at the end, we hear the song of the Fisherman greeting the nightingale as he returns from the palace, where his song has restored the Emperor to life. In this fairy-tale scenario the song of the real nightingale is first conveyed by a flute cadenza, then by a solo violin set against the tinkling, rippling figurations of harp, piano and celeste. The artificial bird is characterized by piccolo, flute and oboe.

Stravinsky made very slight alterations to the original score of *The Nightingale* and these appeared in a revised version published in 1962. He also produced, with Samuel Dushkin, in 1932, transcriptions from the symphonic poem entitled *Songs of the Nightingale and Chinese March* for violin and piano.

In 1914 the composer wrote his Three Pieces for String Quartet, whose complex, slightly meretricious scoring not only alarmed performers daring enough to tackle the music, but also prompted George Dyson, in his book *The New Music* (1924) to declare that if the curiously fragmented second piece had any place in the art of the string quartet then the end was near! These little compositions, intended to be contrasting studies in popular, fantastic and liturgical moods (and completely misunderstood when they first appeared) were republished, with new titles, as part of

Stravinsky's Four Studies for Orchestra, mentioned later in this book. In 1915 he wrote the *Souvenir d'une Marche Boche*, a rather brash, unattractive piece of no importance.

It was during these years that Stravinsky composed nearly all his solo songs, including the Verlaine (1910) and Balmont (1911) settings, the *Japanese Lyrics* (1912–13), the *Recollections of Childhood* (1913), the *Pribaoutki* (1914), the *Cat's Cradle* pieces (1915–16), the *Three Tales for Children* (1915–17), the *Berceuse* (1917) and the *Four Russian Peasant Songs* ("Saucers") (1914–17). Simple and direct in expression, they have many attractive facets.

Stravinsky's *Two Poems of Verlaine*, for baritone and piano, are his only settings of French, apart from *Perséphone* a quarter of a century later. There is a flavour of Debussy in the harmonic writing. Verlaine's poems have a natural rhythmic flow of their own and Stravinsky's conception, involving a key signature of five flats, but an indeterminate tonality, does not always dovetail neatly, displaying only fitfully that close relationship between words and music which alone can produce a really fine song. Yet, having written this, I must confess that "Un grand sommeil noir" from *Sagesse* has a quiet, despairing beauty, and that although "La lune blanche" from *La Bonne Chanson* discloses a rather uninteresting vocal line the accompaniment has a mysterious liquid quality that haunts the imagination. Stravinsky completed a version of these songs for baritone and orchestra in 1951.

In the *Two Poems of Balmont*, for high voice and piano, the composer, probably recalling the bitonal success he had achieved in *Petrushka*, partly repudiated the traditionally romantic illustration of the text in favour of a more angular vocal line and varied harmonic character, with some of the phrasing diatonic and some of it bitonal. Based on love poems by Balmont—"The Flower" and "The Dove"—the settings reveal a tenderness and delicacy that presage Acts II and III of *The Nightingale*. The composer re-arranged the songs for high voice and chamber orchestra in 1954.

The *Three Japanese Lyrics*, based on three very short Japanese *haiku* entitled *"Akahito"*, *"Nazatsumi"*, and *"Tsaraiuki"*, have the fragile transparency of a silk painting done in the country of their origin. In these marvellous settings of a Russian translation, scored for soprano and piano, the poet rhapsodizes over spring : not the fierce, animalistic, blood-surging spring of *The Rite*, but the gentle season of white blossoms reflected in a stream like drifting snowflakes. Stravinsky wrote a version of the songs for soprano and chamber orchestra. Here the shrilling little orchestra, with its gurgling flutes and watery violin tone, has the evocative magic of the Japanese or Chinese artists who, in painting a twig or a delicate cluster of flowers, seem to capture the whole of springtime. The music, of an indeterminate tonality, has a splintering, prismatic brightness, abstract melodic line and rhythmic precision that probably derive from Schoenberg's *Pierrot Lunaire*, which influenced Stravinsky greatly when he composed these pieces. It reveals an unexpectedly close relationship with the note-row technique of the Shakespeare songs that came forty years later.

Each of the Three Little Songs (*"Recollections of Childhood"*), scored for voice and piano (or small orchestra), is dedicated to one of Stravinsky's children. The first song, "The Magpie", was for Sviatoslav Soulima; the second, "The Rook", for his daughter Ludmila; and the third, "The Jackdaw", for Theodore. Stravinsky took the words from Russian nursery-rhymes and set them to music which, for all its spontaneous dissonance, has a very appealing and intimate lyricism. He treated the words, not as a syllabic framework on which to drape the music, but as the source of the descriptive, almost onomatopoeic sounds which he used to evoke the cheeky magpie, the hoarse-voiced rook and the impudent jackdaw.

Stravinsky specifically requested the *Pribaoutki*, scored for voice and a small group of string and wind instruments, to be sung by a baritone. These songs have a particular significance for admirers of his vocal music, because, in his own words, "One important characteristic of Russian popular verse is that the accents of the spoken verse are ignored when the verse is sung."[3] He classed the recognition of the musical possibilities inherent in this fact as one of the major discoveries of his life. Having made the discovery, he no longer felt himself bound by verbal stress in setting words to music. Although the vocal line in the songs is fundamentally diatonic, there are many piquant chromatic touches and picturesque effects in the instrumentation. The word '*pribaoutki*' means a form of popular Russian verse, or droll nonsense song, the nearest English parallel to which is the limerick.

The *Cat's Cradle Songs* are scored for contralto and three clarinets (small E flat clarinet, clarinet in A, and bass clarinet), the instruments being used in a sinuous and stealthy way to convey feline characteristics. Epigrammatic in style, with delicate arabesques in the music, the songs have a *Berceuse*-like mood which gives a fairy-tale flavour to their ruminations on the domestic animal world. It is not so much the sense of the words that captivates the listener, as the musical relationship of the vocal line to the ingenious deployment of three clarinets in varied registers and timbres.

Stravinsky, in his *Three Tales for Children*, for voice and piano, again showed his often refuted sensitivity to the poetic values of words. In the first song, "Tilimbom", a little bell rings frantically to warn the farm-yard animals of a fire, cleverly simulated in the piano accompaniment with a vividness that reminds one of Christopher le Flemyng's pastoral vignette *The Bellringer*. The second piece, *"Les canards, les cygnes, les oies"*, uses a flurry of ninths and sevenths to suggest the agitated flight of ducks, swans and geese; while in the third song, *"Chanson de l'ours"*, we catch, through two ponderously alternating notes in the bass, the clumsy, straddling walk of the bear.

The little *Berceuse* for voice and piano, which Stravinsky in his *Chronicle* mentioned in connection with "Tilimbom" and the "Bear's Song" and which, at one time, he intended to publish with them, is a pleasing trifle steeped in the popular Russian idiom which he used during that phase of his life. Stravinsky wrote this lullaby for his daughter Ludmila.

He scored his Four Russian Peasant Songs ("Saucers") for unaccompanied female voices, but in 1954 he re-arranged them for equal voices with an accompaniment of four horns. There is enormous rhythmic interest in the songs, which bear the titles "On Saints' Days in Chigisakh", "Ovsen", "The Pike", and "Master Portly". These pieces, full of dynamic contrast and relief, derive from a tradition of popular music and popular texts, being sung in the past by peasants, while fortune-tellers read their fingerprints on the soot-blackened bottoms of saucers.

The composer wrote another set of Four Russian Songs, for voice and piano, in 1918–19, under the titles *"Canard (Ronde)"*, *"Chanson pour compter"*, *"Le Moineau est assis"*, and *"Chant dissident"*. He rescored them in 1953–54 for an attractive ensemble of voice, flute, harp and guitar, reducing the title to Four Songs. In the first three pieces, written in a dry, brittle style, the melodic line is purely diatonic; but the fourth, a haunting Russian song not unlike a negro spiritual, uses a different kind of idiom—one which looks towards the serial procedures of the Three Songs from William Shakespeare.

In 1917 Stravinsky composed his *Valse Pour Les Enfants*. This charming, fifty-six-bars-long waltz for children confines the bass part of the piano to a five-note *ostinato* stretching across two bars; but the treble introduces a bright thirteen-note tune more ambitiously scored. In the same year he wrote his Canons for Two Horns as a token of gratitude to a Swiss doctor who saved his daughter Ludmila's life, when she was gravely ill with appendicitis, and would take no payment for his services. Stravinsky, in 1917, also composed the Study for Pianola, the main theme of which suggests a Spanish-type vocal *fioriture*, but suffers from the inability of that self-governing instrument to sustain it. A year later he sketched out a Duet for Two Bassoons, a work so far unpublished. Mention must also be made of his *Valse des Fleurs* for two pianos (1914), the manuscript of which disappeared after a concert in 1949.

Although the songs which Stravinsky wrote from 1910 to 1919 revealed a nodding acquaintance with Debussy and Ravel, as well as the technical advances made in the ballets, their character was still recognizably Russian. Two works came to fruition during this productive period, however, which for the first time showed his preoccupation with the music of the past: *Reynard*, begun in 1915 and completed a year later, and *The Soldier's Tale* of 1918. Although these pieces belong to the Russian period, they point a clearly defined path to the neo-Classicism which, in various forms, proved a dominant factor in the music of the next three decades.

Reynard, based on a Russian legend and set to a libretto prepared by Ramuz, is an allegory, and one can almost picture the itinerant side-show, with its atmosphere of birchbark shoes, roughly-dressed peasants, and children with red, grinning faces. Stravinsky called it "A Burlesque in Song and Dance", and included the following directions in the score : "The play is acted by clowns, dancers, or acrobats, preferably on a trestle stage placed in front of the orchestra. If performed in a theatre, it should be played in front of the curtain. The actors remain on the stage all the time. They come on in view of the audience to the strains of the little March, which serves as an introduction, and make their exit the same way. The actors do not speak. The singers (two tenors and two basses) are placed in the orchestra."

There is no preciosity or over-sophistication in this homely tale; two kinds of humour run parallel through it : one the humorous antics of the animals in a barnyard, the other the familiar story of the fox translated into the ironic and satirical terms of modern life. Stravinsky used, in addition to the protagonists, an ensemble consisting of flute, cor anglais, E flat clarinet, bassoon, two horns, trumpet, string quartet, drums and cimbalom. The dominating instrument is the cimbalom, which accompanies the cock, marks the rhythmic accent, and helps to bind the scraps of themes together. The cock, assisted by the cat and the goat, plots to kill the fox, but is twice tricked by the crafty Reynard and is only rescued by the resourcefulness of the cat and the goat, who manage finally to strangle the farmyard pest. Stravinsky illustrates this naïve drama with irresistibly comic effects. There are shrill crowings; flesh-pricking falsetto passages and slides for the voices; drum-rolls as the cock drops from his perch to be caught by the fox; and a cacophony of howls from the quartet of vocalists as Reynard meets his well-merited deserts. Musically a chamber cantata, *Reynard* opens and closes with a march. The voices are placed with the orchestra, singing, with a few slight modifications, exactly the same material; there is, in consequence, an almost micrometric fusion of vocal and instrumental lines.

The Soldier's Tale, written on a shoestring budget when Stravinsky was in dire financial straits, is the ideal choice for those who would provide good entertainment at a low cost. For a performance only seven instruments are needed : clarinet, bassoon, cornet, trombone, violin, double-bass, together with a battery of percussion which includes two side-drums of different size (without snare), drum (without snare), drum (with snare), bass drum, cymbals, tambourine, triangle,—all to be played by one person only. In this work the prophetic movement headed "Music to Scene II", which consists largely of 'lento' melody for clarinet and bassoon, reminds one of the opening of *The Rite of Spring*, yet at the same time it looks forward to the Dylan Thomas and Shakespeare songs. The listener is always conscious in Stravinsky's music of these gestatory cross-currents and 'reminiscences'. Written at a time when Stravinsky had become Parisian by adoption, *The Soldier's Tale* shows him trying out the vogue of flip, penny-whistle tunes cultivated by the group known as Les Six (Milhaud, Poulenc, Auric, and the rest).

The story of this moralistic fable concerns a soldier who sells his violin to the Devil in return for a magic book which provides an infallible answer to every question. He spends three days with the Evil One; but they are, in reality, three years. The soldier returns home, but no-one, including his mother and his sweetheart, recognizes him; so he turns for solace to the riches which the Devil's book helps him to acquire. Finding that wealth brings him no happiness, he throws the book away and goes back to his life of adventure. News reaches him that the King's daughter is ill and, learning that the man who cures her may claim her hand in marriage, he hastens to try his luck. The Devil has the same idea. They meet in the capital. The soldier and the Devil play a game of cards and the former loses his great wealth, but recovers his violin, which his adversary has brought with him. He plays the instrument, and the princess, hearing the sweet music, recovers. The angry Devil swears revenge if the soldier ever sets foot again in his territory. Time passes, and the soldier, pining for his native land, turns his footsteps homeward. Alas, the Devil seizes him and carries him triumphantly away before the gaze of his horrified wife.

Stravinsky and his collaborator Ramuz intended *The Soldier's Tale* for production, not primarily in theatres, but in halls and, whenever possible, the open air. To fulfil this purpose Ramuz wrote a story to be read, played and danced, confining his characters to four, while Stravinsky chose the miniature chamber orchestra already described. The composer related in his *Conversations* how, one night, he dreamt he saw a gypsy girl sitting at the roadside, playing a violin to entertain the child on her lap. On awakening, he succeeded in salvaging the violin tune, which became one of the principal motifs of *The Soldier's Tale*. How Stravinsky loved the slim, silky sound of that long-drawn-out violin bow is evident in the precise direction printed in the score: *"Glissez sur le sol avec l'archet en toute sa longueuer"*. The violin figures prominently in the episodes numbered II, V, VI, VII and XI of the orchestral suite of *The Soldier's Tale*; the cornet and trombone sharing the limelight in those numbered I and IV; the clarinet and cornet flirting with the violin in number V; and the two chorales of numbers VIII and X featuring clarinet, bassoon, cornet and trombone. Thus, within a limited range of instruments, great variety of character and tonal expressiveness is achieved. The score includes a march, a tango, a waltz, the two chorales, and a characteristic splash of ragtime. In addition to the orchestral suite mentioned, Stravinsky, in 1919, arranged a suite for violin, clarinet and piano.

17

THE HILLS AND THE VALLEYS

Pulcinella (1919–20) and the Concertino for String Quartet (1920) marked the beginning of Stravinsky's neo-Classicism, and although his musical style continued to develop during the next thirty years, the whole of his output throughout the period—about forty works in all—comes under that heading. Differences exist between them, and the wonderful Serenade in A of 1925, for example, cannot really be compared with the superb Mass of 1947; yet they share the simplicity, the refinement and the austere dignity which Stravinsky drew from music of the past. His neo-Classicism is wholly integrated—free from the confrontations of a clumsy *pasticheur*—and achieves a timeless, transcendental quality derived from the simultaneous use of the conventions of different eras.

In considering Stravinsky's *Pulcinella*, however, and the plastic surgery which he applied so brazenly to Pergolesi's music, one inevitably asks "Why did he do it?" Certainly he seemed to have no great regard for Italian music of the eighteenth century, described Galuppi and Marcello as "poor composers", and dismissed Vivaldi as a "dull fellow".[1] Admittedly, Diaghilev, who had already commissioned Stravinsky to arrange music by Grieg for *Le Festin* and Chopin for *Les Sylphides*, did thrust into his hands a pile of music by Pergolesi, copied from collections in the British Museum and Naples, and ask him to make a one-act ballet out of it. Yet Diaghilev must have realized that this was a peculiar assignment for the genius who had written the dazzling *Firebird*, the heart-stirring *Petrushka*, the cataclysmic *Rite of Spring*, and the exotic opera *The Nightingale*. Although conscious that the time was ripe for some Classical renaissance, he probably expected nothing more from Stravinsky than a strict, formal orchestration of Pergolesi's cool, sweet, decorative music. And what did the recipient of his commission feel about his task?

The truth of the matter, I suspect, is that his creative faculties, already struggling to escape from the past, needed some vindication to satisfy the faint twinges of conscience—or uncertainty. Did he, I wonder, persuade himself that the music of one age is fundamentally no different from that of another; that the melodies of Pergolesi—or, indeed, of any other 'period' composer—could, as if 'written' for the first time by a living com-

poser in a contemporary idiom, prove as readily accessible and modern
as in their own day? This compromise between rejecting the past completely and bringing it into the conclave of current trends might, subconsciously at least, have seemed to Stravinsky an acceptable solution, or
a period of marking time. If it did, then he undoubtedly saw *Pulcinella*
as a showpiece following the success of *Firebird, Petrushka, The Rite of
Spring* and *The Nightingale*.

Stravinsky, as a child, was told by a schoolmate to observe the skill
of a cat snaring fish. He did so and respected the qualities of order and
calculation ever since, pursuing his instinct as eagerly as any female. "One
has a nose. The nose scents and it chooses. The artist is like a pig snouting
truffles." It mattered not to Stravinsky that the truffles brought to him
by Diaghilev came from Pergolesi's cultivated pasture.

The charming *Pulcinella* suite, of which a revised version was made in
1947, took from the ballet the most characteristic music of its composer;
but it cannot, of course, recapture the historical spirit of the complete
stage production. Stravinsky's fastidious care in marking scores and his
mastery over the mechanics of his craft are manifest throughout the suite,
where one finds, for example, *Tres court et sec mais pas tres fort*, which
Szigeti, the great violinist, whimsically likened to something from a poetic
wine list provided by a restaurant with a superb cuisine and cellar.
"Fruity, but mellow, but with an inner glow", or "Fiery, but with a
velvety unction". There are eight movements: I Sinfonia, II Serenata,
III Scherzino-Allegro-Andantino, IV Tarantella, V Toccata, VI 'gavotta
con due variazioni', VII Duetto, VIII Minuetto-Finale. No phrase in
the music exactly matches or reproduces any by Pergolesi. Without viola-
ting the original, Stravinsky gives the Duet a touch of bantering satire
by permitting music steeped in the love-idiom of the old Italian tradition
to be performed by the grotesque combination of trombone and contra-
bass. There are dissonances in the music, but they are no more obtrusive
than a postage-stamp-sized Picasso would be in an art gallery filled with
canvases by Rembrandt and Rubens.

The music from *Pulcinella* also furnished Stravinsky with material for
two suites for violin and piano; one transcribed in 1925, and the other
(with the collaboration of Samuel Dushkin) in 1933. Piatigorsky assisted
him in 1932 to prepare another transcription for cello and piano. The
suites of 1932 and 1933 each bear the title *Suite Italienne*.

Stravinsky wrote the Concertino for String Quartet for the Flonzaley
Quartet, recasting it in 1952 as an orchestral piece for twelve instruments
(flute, oboe, cor anglais, clarinet, two bassoons, two trumpets, tenor
trombone, bass trombone, violin *obbligato*, and cello *obbligato*). The use
of the word concertino in the title is justified by the fact that the first
violin fulfils a *concertante* role. Comprising a single movement, with an
aloof reference to traditional sonata form, the work opens with the rising

scales of C and C sharp major, coming together in a rather prickly tangle of dissonances, continuing through passages full of searing contrapuntal effects, vague melodic fragments, or pounding rhythms hammered out by paired notes, to a *sospirando* finish which, unprefaced by any dynamic crescendo, is all the more impressive for its unexpected simplicity—a typical Stravinsky effect.

The composer loved the sound of wind instruments and demonstrated this in his Three Pieces for Clarinet Solo, written in 1919 for Werner Reinhart, a Wintertur industrialist and patron of the arts. These pieces do not, like some of Stravinsky's other chamber works, devolve upon rhythmic titillation; they are pure melodies, with a sinuous chromatic curve, developing along three separate, individual paths and reminiscent, in one sense, of Bach's sonatas for unaccompanied violin.

That austerely expressive work, the *Symphonies of Wind Instruments*, written in 1920 for the memory of Debussy and revised in 1947, reveals a masterly perfection of structure. Scored for triple winds, four horns, three each of trumpets and trombones, and tuba, it comprises one brief movement. A piece of absolute music which uses the word 'symphony' not in the conventional meaning, but as a 'sounding together of different instruments', the work ends with a stark dirge, seeming, in its plangent grimness, to echo the final chorus in *Boris Godunov*. As the composer indicated in his *Chronicle*, there is no passionate impulse or dynamic brilliance in the music, which presents "an austere ritual, unfolded in terms of short litanies between different groups of homogeneous instruments"; yet, with its very beautiful transparency of texture, and with the *cantilena* of the softly chanting clarinets and flutes threading the score with a liturgical dialogue, this work must surely captivate any listener.

Mavra (1921–22) is a Russo-Italian comedy in the 1840 tradition and Stravinsky's last composition to use a Russian text. It differs from the Russian and Italian operas of the nineteenth century, however, in that the vocal line, though rarely conveying any feeling of harshness, ranges freely without harmonic dependence upon the orchestra. This *opera buffa* in one act, based on Boris Kochno's adaptation of Pushkin's tale *The Little House at Kolomna*, takes twenty-five minutes to perform. The story concerns two sweethearts, Parasha and Basil. When Parasha's mother bewails the loss of her cook, Basil, disguised as a woman and calling himself Mavra, fills the vacant post at the instigation of the crafty Parasha. Alas, the mother, after leaving the house, returns unexpectedly and encounters her new cook—shaving. She faints. When she recovers, the female impersonator leaps from a window and escapes, as Parasha calls after him.

A gay, scintillating text, it prompted Stravinsky to write a highly inventive score bubbling with humour and irradiated in the love episodes by a lyrical sweetness which, as Paul Collaer shrewdly observed, draws inspiration from four sources: the Russian occidental melody of Glinka and

Dargomijsky, classical Italian melody, and chromatic melody. There is no recitative and the music, involving twelve woodwinds, twelve brasses and some strings, compasses a fascinating stream of melodies for solo voice and ensemble groupings.

Stravinsky makes traditional use of separate arias, duets and ensembles, sometimes accompanied by 'vamped' chords; this, and the fact that the music, for all its atonal flavour, does retain the cadential 'happy ending', probably blinded early audiences to the realization that, in *Mavra*, the composer slyly but affectionately pokes fun at his Russian predecessors, Glinka, Dargomijsky and Tchaikovsky. There are snatches of orchestral melody reminiscent of *Ragtime*, passages treated fugally, and implied modulations which, particularly towards the close of the love duet for Parasha and her Huzzar, reaffirm Stravinsky's mastery of scoring. The *cavatina* style of the Hussar's final aria combines elements of gypsy and Italian music, while its bright use of the trumpet reminds one of Donizetti. With *Mavra* the composer really came of age.

A new score of this attractive work, by Robert Craft, containing the Russian text with an English version, was published in 1969. It is a worthy addition to the Stravinsky archives, but the English text reveals threadbare patches, of which "We've ne—ver had such perfect wea—ther . . ." is a particularly noticeable one.

With Stravinsky's approval, Jack Hylton the bandleader made a curious arrangement of part of *Mavra* about 1930; but the subsequent performance in the Paris Opera House two years later seems to have been a complete fiasco. There are also two fine translations entitled *Chanson Russe* ('Russian Maiden's Song'); one for violin and piano, by Stravinsky and Dushkin, the other, for cello and piano, by the composer and D. Markevich.

According to Stravinsky, the genesis of the Octet of 1922–23 was a dream in which he found himself surrounded by a group of instrumentalists who were playing some very appealing music. He could not recall the music next day, but he remembered that there were eight performers and that they were playing bassoons, trombones, trumpets, a flute and a clarinet. Inspired by this dream, he composed the Octet. Scored for two bassoons, two trombones, two trumpets, flute and clarinet, this work, with its polyglot Parisian idiom of melody and accompaniment, shows his neo-Classical style coming into full flower. The sonorities of the Octet are not as happily blended as those of some of his other compositions, but the whole piece forms a compendium of jovial and solemn moods. A slow introduction leads, in the opening Sinfonia, to an Allegro. Stravinsky wrote the waltz of the second movement ('tema con variazioni') first, and from it he derived the theme which launches the movement and on which the variations are based. There is a *rubans-des-gammes* (ribbons-of-scales)

P

variation which serves as a prelude to each of the others. The final variation, a slow fugato, contrasts brilliantly with the Moderato finale, which has a tingling energy. A revised version of the Octet, involving only minimal changes in the scoring, appeared in 1952.

Between 1917 and 1925 Stravinsky wrote two Suites for small orchestra, which comprise a rescoring of the four-hand piano works entitled Three Easy Pieces (1914–15) and Five Easy Pieces (1916–17). The first of these piano compositions consists of a March, a Waltz and a Polka, each of which has a single, accompanying left-hand figure used as an unvarying *ostinato*. Stravinsky wrote the Polka first as a mischievous caricature of Diaghilev, whom he saw as a smartly groomed circus ringmaster. The ironically simple bass figures poke fun at the impresario's juvenile technique at the piano keyboard. Stravinsky then composed the March for Alfred Casella, and after it the Waltz for Erik Satie. All three pieces, with their sudden tonal shifts and breezy off-key gymnastics, crackle with Stravinskian satire. The titles of the Five Easy Pieces which he wrote as piano exercises for his children, are Andante, Espanola, Balalaika, Napolitana and Galop, in that order. To avoid accidentals as much as possible, Stravinsky chose simple keys, put most of the fingering in the bass, and confined the treble to a light, slowly moving melody. The opening Andante has a charming gravity, but the following numbers are characteristically high-spirited.

While orchestrating these works, Stravinsky transferred the Galop of the Five Easy Pieces to the preceding group of three, thereby creating an even number for each Suite, and he also rearranged the contents. The scores of the two Suites have been used for various ballets. In 1915 the composer transcribed the Polka of the Three Easy Pieces for cimbalom solo—a tribute to that great virtuoso of the instrument, Aladar Racz.

Stravinsky wrote his Four Studies for Orchestra ('Dance', 'Eccentric', 'Canticle' and 'Madrid') between 1918 and 1928. A rescoring, with very slight changes, of his Three Pieces for String Quartet and of the Study for Pianola, which reappears under the title 'Madrid,' they form an attractive suite touched in places by a rich, icon-like colouring and with a fascinating rhythmic differentiation. Slightly reminiscent of *The Soldier's Tale*, which belongs to the same period, the Four Studies display primitive, patterned melodies and time signatures which change almost at every bar without upsetting the prevailing 'tactus'.

The two works of the period for piano and orchestra—the brilliantly dynamic Concerto of 1923–24 with wind accompaniment and the ironic Capriccio of 1928–29—are impregnated with the sophisticated and unorthodox psyche of their creator.

The Concerto for Piano and Wind Instruments, written by Stravinsky for his own performance as a pianist, derived from his belief that, in the Classical concerto, the timbre of the strings absorbs and consumes the metallic sound of a piano. His constant theorizing about music found a comparable echo in the *Symphony of Psalms*, where he resisted the temptation to compose the vocal parts for a team of soloists because, so he argued, the moment they began to sing as individuals, the audience would identify the music with the singer, thus destroying, or weakening its universality.

Scored for a large band of woodwind and brass, reinforced by timpani and double-basses, the Concerto, a product of Stravinsky's uncompromisingly astringent neo-Classic vein, constitutes a splendid, but not wholly convincing synthesis of Bach and ragtime elements. There are three movements : 1. Largo—Allegro, 2. Larghissimo, 3. Allegro. Stravinsky's determination in this work to contrast piano with brass, timpani and string basses is, I think, perverse, and the heavy, lowering introduction, before the piano entry, in the first movement seldom holds together rhythmically in performance, although some wizard of the baton can, with difficulty, make it do so. The tune of the slow movement, with ugly thick brass chords underneath, resembles a parody of middle-period Beethoven piano writing.

A composer's personality may be comprehended as much from his patently flawed achievements as from his lofty triumphs, and one recalls that Bach, Mozart and Haydn, for example, all wrote cardboard music when the spirit inside them did not take fire. At least the Allegro of the Concerto is intriguing, with its continuous and unanticipated slipping of the expected strong beat by adding to or subtracting from the basic two in a bar; and the jazz-flavoured texture of the finale's main theme, as well as the tune in canon after figure 80, are almost as invigorating as anything Stravinsky ever wrote. The composer, in 1924, created a reduction of the Concerto for two pianos, and after certain corrections had been made a definitive version appeared in 1950.

The Capriccio for Piano and Orchestra which he wrote when he was touring the world as a composer-pianist indicate clearly that he was a performer with a big and facile technique, for this music can take all the brilliance a virtuoso can give it. Influenced by the fantasia definition of a *capriccio* expounded by Praetorius, it has three movements : 1. Presto, 2. Andante rapsodico, 3. Allegro capriccioso ma tempo giusto. Chic and very French in character, with a light ironic taste, its *perpetuum mobile* type of outer movements place a heavy burden on the pianist, while the middle movement, including melismas in the manner of Liszt and *à l'hongroise*, presents intricate salon music calling for a front-rank player. After a bold, vigorous introduction, the piano and timpani share a strong, rhythmic idea, with other succinct and, at times, dance-like themes following, after which the introduction returns to provide a neat ending. The rhapsodic, Baroque-style slow movement, whose principal theme looks forward to the manner of *The Rake's Progress* of twenty-two years later, opens with an exchange between piano and woodwinds and displays some cimbalom-like repeated-note effects. A piano cadenza and a flute solo serve as a transition to the finale, whose sprightly dance themes, impregnated with a faint flavour of jazz, give it a scintillating vitality. A revised version of the Capriccio, correcting a few misprints and omissions in the original score, was prepared in 1949.

It is obvious that the resources of the piano during this phase of his life excited and stimulated Stravinsky's imagination. Not only did he cast the instrument prominently as a member of the orchestra, but he wrote four major works for it, in addition to the two concertos already discussed. Two of these are for solo piano—the Sonata of 1924, which masks profound emotion with an austere stylization, and the marvellous Serenade in A which followed a year later.

The Serenade comprises a suite of four vividly contrasted movements for piano. It opens with a massive and stirring 'Hymne', which has a melodic and tonal affinity with Chopin's F major *Ballade*. The 'Romanza' begins and ends with a dry, brightly percussive cadenza in Stravinsky's most invigorating vein. In the two-part 'Rondoletto' some of the off-beat accents produce an effect of tingling vitality, and heavy, closely aligned arpeggios in the bass throw the principal A major theme for the right hand into sharp relief. The work closes with a beautiful, Russian-style 'Cadenza Finale', which, with its delightful 'chiming' theme, unexpectedly weaves an atmosphere of fantasy.

Stravinsky's two other important neo-Classical piano works, both for two pianos, are the oddly named Concerto (there is no orchestra) of 1931–35, and the Sonata written in 1943–44. The serene power of the Concerto and the brilliance of its piano writing, which avoids the commonplace with an almost obsessional determination, show the characteristics of the 'progressive' Stravinsky, particularly his use of 'commas' to give the effect of 'breathing' within the phrase. The baroque figurations have a startling energy and a spirit which, as David Drew pointed out, is derived more from Beethoven than Bach. In the miraculous dovetailing of the two piano parts there are such original features as the quasi-cimbalom-like repetition of a single note, the distant, drum-like *ostinato* sounds and the marvellous final fugue, which includes an inversion of the subject reminiscent of Beethoven's opus 110. Throughout the Concerto we discern the bold, confident hand of the master.

Largely through the contrast between its harmonic astringency and the suave flow of much of its melody, the Sonata has the faint, but distinctively Russian nostalgia which we find more fluorescently in Rachmaninov's music. Indeed, the juxtaposition of disparate tonal centres gives the music an inward spiritual quality that is accentuated in the 'poco piu mosso' of the finale by a recrudescence of Russian lyricism. The burly, peasant-like themes that insinuate themselves into the otherwise Classical texture of the piece create an irresistible, earthy tang.

Stravinsky's fondness for the piano resulted in two minor, but attractive works. One was the unpretentious The Five Fingers, written in 1920–21 and consisting of eight very easy tunes for children on five notes for the piano : Andantino, Allegro, Allegretto, Larghetto, Moderato, Lento, Vivo, Pesante. The composer explained that "The five fingers of the right hand, once on the keys, remain in the same position, sometimes even for the whole length of the piece, while the left hand, which is accompanying the melody, executes a harmonic or contrapuntal pattern of the utmost simplicity."

In the charming Tango for piano solo (1940) an almost unbroken flow of syncopation, sometimes following the tango rhythm, sometimes not, and progressing at a steady 4/4 tempo, presents a dance number characteristic of Stravinsky's *Ragtime* scoring.

Someone remarked that, where ballet music is concerned, Delibes first gave it a heart, Tchaikovsky gave it a soul, and Stravinsky made an honest woman of it. Since the three iridescent scores of Stravinsky's youth had appeared, ballet gained a new dimension, a greater profundity, and he composed much of his finest music, including *Apollon Musagète* (1927–28) and *Orpheus* (1947) for the dance.

One of the greatest of the neo-Classical works, *Apollon Musagète*, with choreography by Adolph Bolm, came to life through a commission by Elizabeth Sprague Coolidge for a modern music festival at the Library of Congress in Washington D.C. This ballet was, in fact, Stravinsky's first link with George Balanchine, who later created *Orpheus*, one of the most important items in the repertoire of the New York City Ballet. It was planned as a *ballet blanc*, founded on Greek mythology and to be danced in the classical style. The ballet has two tableaux, but virtually no plot. The first scene describes the birth of Apollo, while the second relates his association with the Muses Calliope, Polyhymnia and Terpsichore. "After a series of dances," the composer explained, "treated in the traditional style of ballet (*Pas d'Action*, *Pas de Deux*, *Coda*), Apollo, in the Apotheosis, leads the Muses, with Terpsichore at their head, to Parnassus, where they are to live afterwards."

Apollon Musagète, or *Apollo*, as it is more frequently called, is probably Stravinsky's most sweetly beautiful score, with few characteristic discords and staying firmly inside a diatonic key-structure. There are transparent, clear-cut themes, all in the major key, with delicate filigree counterpoint. Much of the music has a transcendental unearthly serenity. Stravinsky published a revised version of *Apollo* in 1947. The changes are few and largely affect directions for the string players.

Apart from *Scènes de Ballet*, composed for Billy Rose in 1944, and the *Danses Concertantes* of 1941–42, created for concert performance and only choreographed by Balanchine in 1944, the period contained three other ballets: *The Fairy's Kiss*, written for Ida Rubinstein in 1928, *The Card Game*, a witty confection of 1936, and, looking much further ahead, the beautiful and poignant *Orpheus* of 1947.

Scènes de Ballet was commissioned for Billy Rose's ill-fated revue *The Seven Lively Arts*, with choreography by Anton Dolin. The composer claimed that his purpose was to write simple, unpretentious music; yet the score has elements of satire and mystery which do not belong to such a category. This lyrical piece, which just misses being in the 'popular' style, comprises an Introduction, ten short, dance-like movements and a concluding Apotheosis—one of the serene, 'coda' episodes at which Stravinsky excelled. *Scènes de Ballet* contains string tremolos of an amplitude quite new to the composer at that time, and presages the fuller symphonic textures of future works. It is typical ballet music, with its inevitable dominant-tonic cadence punctuating the close of a dance phrase or variation, and its bright flourish of arpeggios introducing a concerted dance number. Sir Frederick Ashton used the music for a ballet by the Sadler's Wells Company.

Danses Concertantes is one of the most attractive works that Stravinsky ever wrote. Even away from the stage, the music, scored for chamber orchestra, proves irresistibly enjoyable, whether in the humorous, bustling *Marche-Introduction*, the vigorous and athletic *Pas d'Action*, the richly decorative *Thème varié*, the satirical *Pas de Deux* or the *Marche-Conclusion* which, recapitulating in part the opening section, rounds off the piece with a bravura flourish.

The scenario of *The Fairy's Kiss*, described earlier in the *Life*, was based on a story by Hans Christian Andersen called *The Ice Maiden* and Stravinsky described it as follows: "A fairy imprints her magic kiss on a child at birth and parts it from its mother. Twenty years later, when the youth has attained the very zenith of good fortune, she repeats the fatal kiss and carries him off to live in supreme happiness with her ever afterwards. . . ."

This work may be regarded as an allegory of the romantic artist and his condition, isolated from his fellow men by the gift, or curse, of genius, and deprived of human joys represented by his fiancée, to gain as a reward the final dazzling union with his vision. Stravinsky treated the same theme, years later, in *Orpheus*. His vigorous, anti-romantic public pronouncements, and the 'homage-to-Tchaikovsky' aspect of the score, do not for a moment disguise the delight which he took in concocting the lyrical outpourings of *The Fairy's Kiss*. The voluptuous cello melody of the *pas de deux* or the exhilarating bucolic Swiss Dances in the second scene are in a sense as much Stravinsky as the final Lullaby of the Land Beyond Time and Place. There is, however, more than a touch of bathos in his handling of Tchaikovsky's themes, particularly at the climax where the tune of the song "None but the lonely heart" thunders forth. A saccharine piece to begin with, the song gains nothing but a bizarre flavour when presented by Stravinsky as a superfluous critical gesture. The composer wrote a revised version of the score in 1950; and in 1947, collaborating with Jeanne Gautier, he distilled some of the music into *Ballad*, a transcription for violin and piano. Stravinsky and Dushkin also made a splendid version for violin and piano in 1932. And there is a symphonic suite, *Divertimento*, which Stravinsky authorized as early as 1931.

The Card Game, a ballet "in three deals", was commissioned by the American Ballet. Stravinsky wrote the scenario in collaboration with M. Malaïev, and Balanchine devised the choreography. The characters in the ballet are the cards in a game of poker, and in each of the three deals the action is complicated by the guileful Joker, who believes that he is invincible, because he can assume the identity of any other card. In the final deal a 'royal flush' in Hearts puts an end to his knavish tricks. *The Card Game* has a charmingly lyrical first movement, which contains a *stringendo* passage derived from the Concerto for Two Solo Pianos; the second, consisting of five variations and a coda, has a relaxed, dance-like buoyancy; and the third is a rather skittish parody. In this work Stravinsky flirts unashamedly with Rossini's *Barber of Seville* overture, quotes in his own characteristic way from Ravel's *La Valse*, as well as from the first movement of Beethoven's Fifth Symphony, and, to complete a curiously mixed confection, throws in bits of Delibes and Johann Strauss.

His genius for capturing or creating atmosphere shines with special brightness in *Orpheus*, the scoring of which, for normal-sized orchestra, is restrained, almost austere. Stravinsky composed *Orpheus* to a commission from Lincoln Kirstein's Ballet Society. In the first scene, as Orpheus weeps for Eurydice, the Angel of Death appears and instructs him to enter Hades, where they will both search for her. The second scene shows Orpheus in Hades, with the Angel of Death at his side. The Furies attack him, but the lost souls, dragging their heavy chains, implore Orpheus to play to them. He does so, and the music calms the Furies, who beg him to continue. Pluto, spellbound by the ravishing sounds, releases Eurydice to Orpheus. The Furies blindfold his eyes during the journey back to earth.

Eurydice, following Orpheus, tempts him to turn and look at her. As he plucks the bandage from his eyes, she falls to the ground—dead. This happens during a silent bar in some of the sweetest music of the score—another example of the composer's instinct for doing precisely the right thing at the right time. Wild with grief, Orpheus curses the Bacchantes, Thracian women, and in a rage they tear him to pieces. In the finale, Apollo appears with the lyre of Orpheus and raises it heavenwards.

Orpheus's radiant song, heard about halfway through the work, keeps the music on a subdued level. It is played by harp and two oboes, to which, on a repeat further on, strings, cor anglais and clarinet are added. The harp anticipates the theme which the oboes presently take up. At the entry of the cor anglais it is reiterated in turn by the instruments concerned until, as if growing impatient, they join in a little before their cue, creating the effect of a miniature fugue.

The music, written with simplicity and avoiding ornamentation of all kinds, has a high degree of expressiveness. We experience fear and pity, not so much by spectacle, real or imagined, but from the very structure of the action, which, as Aristotle remarked, is the means used by a good dramatic poet. In the opening bars the 'whiteness of sound' is broken by three Apollonian chords, the third of which the composer regarded as symbolizing the birth of the god. A processional interlude with a thrummed accompaniment ushers in two goddesses to a faster tempo. A solo violin introduces the second scene in which, after a concerted episode, the spotlight falls on each of the Muses. In Calliope's variation, representing poetry, the violins pick out the rhythm of a French couplet and the splendid cello solo draws inspiration from a Russian alexandrine of Pushkin. After this come the solos, or variations of Polyhymnia and Terpsichore, denoting mime and dancing, Apollo's second variation, the lovely, muted *pas de deux*, and the vivacious, intricately scored Coda. A flood of tranquil and expansive music sets the scene of the Apotheosis, where Apollo leads the Muses towards Parnassus.

Stravinsky's magnificent sense of drama allows the orchestra to play forte only once, and this is during the great dramatic episode in Scene II where the Bacchantes attack Orpheus. The music, dying away, seems to hold its breath as the stage is cleared for this tableau of savagery, and when the attack begins the listener might well imagine that Stravinsky had written a postscript to the earth-shaking barbarity of *The Rite of Spring*. The ending of *Orpheus* is a recapitulation of the music from the opening of the ballet, but about half-way through a trumpet begins a fugue-like section with a French horn. One has the feeling of being lifted into space with Orpheus's lyre.

The transcendental character of *Orpheus* derives from the final scene where Apollo, wresting the lyre from an Orpheus torn to pieces, proclaims the timeless power of music. Stravinsky divided the score into dance sections and interludes of serene beauty, with only the dance of the Furies, and later on of the Bacchantes, to shatter its quiet grandeur and dignity of spirit.

In addition to the Symphony in E flat, which he wrote as a student in 1905–7, Stravinsky composed two other purely orchestral symphonies. Both of these works, the delightful Symphony in C of 1938–40 and the powerful Symphony in Three Movements of 1942–45, produced during the first six years of his residence in the United States, may be called inspired.

Stravinsky penned his Symphony in C "to the glory of God" and for the Chicago Symphony Orchestra. In it, as a practical demonstration perhaps of his belief in tradition as a living force which illuminates the present, he tries out his jagged rhythms and pungent harmonies on the framework of the Classical symphony. The first movement has a restless, bird-hopping vitality and a Pulcinella-like complexion. Its two themes are developed in conventional style and then recapitulated, the first being presented by oboe and string accompaniment, the second by oboe and bassoon, repeated by strings. Stravinsky called the second movement 'Aria', and, indeed, it comprises a ravishing song, progressing from a solo for oboe to a fine contrapuntal episode for violins. The florid woodwind lines twist and turn intriguingly. Two classical dances, the minuet and the *passe-pied*, enliven the third movement, which ends in a fugue, with horns replying to the trombone-stated subject. The bite, attack and lithe stride of this piece can be breathtaking in a performance of careful judgement and vivacity. A dialogue, 'largo'—one of the most pellucidly beautiful moments in all music—opens the finale, which continues with sprightly passages that suggest the *concerto-grosso* style.

Stravinsky's Symphony in Three Movements calls to mind Haydn and Mozart, but it nevertheless retains his own striking individuality. Adolf Salazar expressed the view that the work conforms more to the seventeenth-century Italian symphony or concerto than to the Classical type, and added: "It might also be said that it is a skeleton of a symphony: transparent, cold, hard as a diamond, aloof and pure." Presenting a degree of tonal opulence, it has for its three movements an Overture, an Andante, and a 'con-moto' Finale. A strong unity of design, coupled with logical development in well defined textures and intensely rhythmic drive, makes this one of Stravinsky's most significant symphonic achievements.

Apart from the *Duo Concertante* for violin and piano (1931–32) and such minor works as the *Norwegian Moods* (1942), the *Circus Polka* (1942,) the Ode (1943), the *Scherzo à la Russe* (1944) and the little Elegy (1944), the period produced four other instrumental works. These are the Concerto in D for Violin and Orchestra (1931), written for Samuel Dushkin, the Concerto in E flat ("Dumbarton Oaks") (1937–38), the Concerto in D ("Basle"), composed in 1946 and the Ebony Concerto, created for Woody Herman in 1945.

Stravinsky said that the *Duo Concertante* was inspired by his love for bucolic poets of antiquity and for the skilful technique of their art. This theme predominates in all five movements of the work, which, as he intended, form "a musical parallel to ancient pastoral poetry".[2] It is not a wholly endearing piece, mingling passages of grave beauty with garrulous episodes uncharacteristic of the composer. The first movement, styled *Cantilena*, opening in a toccata-like manner, presents a flourish of arpeggio arabesques that usher in a richly scored violin theme, with a *bravura* display of double-stopping. In the Eclogue that follows, a vigorous and harmonic violin part displaces ingenious canonic phrases; it has a cadenza-like role, set against a stream of piano semiquavers. There is a second, more graceful Eclogue, with the violin discarding polyphony and exploring a purely melodic vein. It is the Gigue, full of excitement and dash, but much too discursive and long, that ill accords with Stravinsky's reputation for pithy and succinct utterances. The closing Dithyramb, phrased in the style of a declamation or threnody, with violin and piano plunging into a complex passage of four-part counterpoint, has a touch of mystery and serenity that redeem the more ungracious or perfunctory parts of the score.

Stravinsky composed the *Four Norwegian Moods* in 1942, when he had been domiciled in America for four years. He wrote the piece as incidental music for a film on the war-time landings in Norway, but when the producers insisted that it should be 'arranged' he bluntly refused and published it as an independent opus. The four sub-titles, Intrada, Song, Wedding Dance and Cortège, adequately describe the moods created by the music. This was the first occasion in twenty years when Stravinsky, his imagination kindled by the national character of the work, used folk themes.

An account has been given earlier in this book of how in 1942 the Barnum and Bailey Circus commissioned Balanchine to provide some music for an elephant ballet, and of how, when the choreographer telephoned Stravinsky, the composer, on being assured that the animals were very young, agreed to write it. Stravinsky modelled the music of the *Circus Polka*, scored for wind band, on his own Easy Pieces for Piano Duet. The distinctive rhythm of the traditional polka appears only towards the end of the work, as a counter-subject to a quotation from Schubert's *Marche Militaire*; which may explain why, according to the bandmaster, Merle Evans, the elephants listened to the music "with growing distaste and uneasiness", so much so that "it would have taken very little at any time during the many performances to cause a stampede". In the words of Sir Osbert Sitwell, the animals "turned up their trunks". In October 1942 the composer rescored the *Circus Polka* for symphony orchestra. The music has an exhilarating verve more suited to monkeys than to elephants.

Commissioned by the Koussevitzky Music Foundation to write an orchestral work, Stravinsky composed his Ode, a three-part elegiac chant, as a tribute to the late Natalie Koussevitzky, in appreciation of her "spiritual contribution to the art of the eminent conductor, her husband. Dr Koussevitzky". Some of the harmonies are reminiscent of *The Rite of Spring*, but without the sharp sting of that explosive ritualistic outburst. Instead of gaudy colours, Stravinsky uses monochrome timbres to convey grief; this produces a pungent flavour in the Eulogy, which opens with a sustained song, treated fugally. There is a spring-like touch of lyricism in the Eclogue, which affectionately denotes Tanglewood, home of the Berkshire Musical Festival, where Koussevitzky officiated each summer. The final section, introduced by a theme of great serenity, is melancholy but dignified.

Paul Whiteman commissioned the *Scherzo à la Russe* for a special radio broadcast on the Blue Network programme, and in 1944 the Paul Whiteman Band—choosing too fast a tempo, according to the composer—gave the first performance. Stravinsky wrote the music to the exact specifications of Whiteman's ensemble, then, realizing that it did not possess the intrinsic qualities of jazz, he rescored it for a standard orchestra, experiencing some difficulty, since he found the volume of mandolin and guitar in the first Trio canon of the original version much lighter than that of the proposed harp and piano. Once intended for a war film, and resuscitated in a new instrumental garb for Whiteman's band, the *Scherzo à la Russe* adheres to the Classical form of symphonic scherzo, with its two gay, uninhibited Trios, whose Russian flavour re-affirms the composer's nostalgia for his native land.

Stravinsky's little Elegy, for unaccompanied viola, is a spare, but highly expressive piece which has been used in some productions of the ballet *Orpheus*. The sustained double-stopping of its carefully calculated intervals makes it difficult to perform by anyone but a really accomplished viola player, since, through the transparency of its texture, the slightest lapse of intonation is mercilessly exposed. A beautiful *tour de force*, the *Elegy* exploits through the limited sound-values of one viola all the possibilities of a two-voiced fugue.

It is related that Stravinsky, drawing a single wide-spaced chord on a sheet of paper, asked that renowned virtuoso of the instrument, Samuel Dushkin, if it was playable on the violin. Dushkin at first said no, but later found that it could be accomplished quite easily. The chord, in four different forms, became the starting point for each of the four movements of the Concerto in D for Violin and Orchestra, which Stravinsky wrote for Dushkin. For all its blemishes—and some of the music scratches the sensibility of the listener—this work reveals a patent sincerity of purpose. Once, during the period of its composition, Stravinsky, walking in his garden with Dushkin, suddenly turned to him and said "First ideas are very important. They come from God. And if, after working and working and working, I return to these ideas, then I know they're good."[3]

Stravinsky regarded solo pyrotechnics with contempt and the Concerto therefore has no cadenza, although the 'presto' coda of the final Capriccio provides the soloist with some brilliant double-stopping passages. Much of the work sounds more like chamber music than orchestral. Its movements bear the titles Toccata, Aria, Aria and Capriccio. The first contains three principal themes, which Stravinsky develops with great intricacy, involving the soloist in 'conversations' with the other instruments. The first of the two Aria movements that follow is unmistakably the orchestral counterpart of the arias of *Oedipus Rex*, composed four years earlier, with their strange combination of hinted parody, irrelevant tunefulness and, at the same time, genuine dramatic emotion. A complete contrast comes with the second Aria, whose theme for the solo violin, a beautiful slow *cantilena,* draws added lustre from the rocking bass figure of the string accompaniment. The closing Capriccio forms a dazzling showpiece for the solo instrument. Balanchine used the music of the Concerto for a ballet called *Balustrade* that he produced in New York in 1941.

Composed for a Washington D.C. music lover and named after his estate, the Concerto in E flat ("Dumbarton Oaks")—a work distinctly related to the Bach of the Brandenburg Concertos—can easily see Stravinsky at his driest when performed indifferently; but a rendering of point and elegance makes its bright facets more accessible. The score requires flute, clarinet, bassoon, two horns, three violins, three violas, two cellos and two basses. Passages for full ensemble contrast vividly with others featuring smaller groups. In the *Tempo giusto* first movement—as in the third—fugal writing predominates and reaches a climactic peak. The second movement, *Allegretto,* is a delicious flight of fantasy, with the cloven hoof plainly visible in Stravinsky's delicate, *pointilliste* landscape. This gentle and serene interlude illustrates perfectly his flair for light scoring and the careful punctuation of phrases in a way that makes the musical line stand out in relief against a surrounding background of silence. The music has a spare, Webern-like texture, and the violins, halfway through, sound like balalaikas. In the finale incisive rhythmic attack and splendid string writing, signalled at one point by a C major fanfare on the horns, compel admiration. All three movements are linked together by sustained Brandenburg-style chords.

Stravinsky's *Concerto in D* ("Basle"), written for the conductor Paul Sacher to celebrate the twentieth anniversary of his Basler Kammerorchester, contains lithe, sinewy music of remarkable strength, brightly and pungently scored for strings. The opening Vivace, the longest movement, is lean, muscular and purposeful; and although the following Arioso has a sweetly lyrical tune and harmonies flavoured with Romanticism, the work ends in the mood of its beginning with a tight-lipped, aggressive little Rondo. Stravinsky made a revised version of the *Concerto* shortly after its première in 1947, changing the Rondo slightly by repeating some of the existing material.

Composed for Woody Herman, the bandleader, who gave it its first performance at Carnegie Hall, the Ebony Concerto may not have the stature of some of Stravinsky's greatest achievements, but it is a finer piece than many critics have rated it to be. Much of its early unpopularity was probably caused by indifferent renderings, for, with its uneasy blend of neo-Classical and jazz elements, the Concerto is difficult to bring off successfully. The precariously fragmented texture must be so expertly balanced in performance that the logical development of the music can be clearly recognized. When this is done, the gaiety and humour of the two outer movements are fully appreciated, and the lovely pensive quasi-blues which separates them makes a pleasing impact. The buoyant, though admittedly rather niggling Allegro Moderato movement which opens the Ebony Concerto flirts unashamedly with styles, pretending at one point, by the ambiguously syncopated treatment of a trumpet fanfare, to be true American jazz, and at another reverting, through a traditionally *cantabile* second subject, to a more classical and tuneful form of utterance. There is a gentle, ruminative quality in the succeeding Andante; and a light-hearted spirit to the Moderato finale, which, with a little more sound and fury, would be very effective, indeed.

A chip from the floor of the workshop that produced the Symphony in Three Movements, this vital and stimulating piece has, for all its faults, a highly individual appeal of its own. Scored for French horn, harp and the usual American jazz-band combination of five saxophones, eight brass, and four rhythm instruments, it cleverly anticipated the 'chamber concert jazz' compositional experiments pursued by Macero, Mingus, Guiffre and others a decade later. The sonority of the Ebony Concerto is delicate, yet full and varied. Stravinsky succeeded to a large extent in combining jazz elements with the lighter side of his neo-Classic manner.

In 1937 he completed, with Charles-Albert Cingria, a *Petit Ramusianum Harmonique* as a tribute or gift for C. F. Ramuz's sixtieth birthday. Stravinsky contributed three quatrains with words and music (intended to be sung, unaccompanied, by a single voice, or a number of voices in unison) and these are interpolated in a brief poem with short rhyming lines written by Cingria.

The Ebony Concerto is easily the most successful and convincing of Stravinsky's jazz compositions, and neither *Ragtime* (1918) nor the Piano Rag Music (1919) come anywhere near it for sheer musical appeal. *Ragtime*, scored for eleven instruments (flute, clarinet, horn, cornet, trombone, two violins, viola, double-bass, cimbalom and percussion) is but a pale reflection of the devilish jazz fiddle-music of *The Soldier's Tale* and, with its chilly disdain of any lyrical impulse, its destructive dislocation of rhythm, seems the very antithesis of the jazz idiom. The prominent *concertante* part given to the cimbalom confers a certain panache on this melancholy piece, but, with its clown-like pathos reminiscent of an early Harry Langdon film, it poses, outside the theatre, as a ghostly abstraction of that which it purports to serve. Stravinsky said of the work "It must have sounded to Americans like very alien corn, indeed." He meant the remark as a jest, but for me it constitutes a fair assessment.

The composer also remarked of the Piano Rag Music that he wanted it to appear improvized, a hurly-burly of sound without prearranged order. To create this effect, he notated much of the score without bar-lines, and, with its clusters of 'added notes' clearly derived from the tango and rag in *The Soldier's Tale*, the music, played with a Fats Waller abandon, may possibly suggest the earthy, percussive, vigour of the barrelhouse piano. It compares unfavourably, however, with the piano rag sections in the keyboard music of Charles Ives, which, drawn from his own natural environment, has the lyricism which, in tension with the beat, makes jazz a pulsating, swinging entity. Stravinsky, a cosmopolitan European recoiling from the over-ripe tradition of nineteenth-century Romanticism, strove self-consciously to rediscover the primitive through American jazz; the improvizing American jazzman, on the other hand, found his own primitive vigour within, and as an integral part of, the very harmonic and tonal prison from which the Russian composer sought to escape. That is why Stravinsky failed to capture or apprehend the vitality and spontaneity inherent in the black man's music.

In 1937 he completed an orchestral *Preludium* for jazz band. The composer may have intended it as part of a suite, but, after creating a piano reduction, he rearranged the piece in 1953.

Although his flirtations with jazz did not kindle any recognizable flame of eloquence in his own music, they certainly inspired younger composers, notably in France, where Milhaud experimented with jazz rhythms in the ballet *Le Boeuf sur le Toit* (1920) and his Negro ballet *La Creation du Monde*. A direct jazz influence can be found in Honegger's Concertino for Piano and Orchestra (1925), and in Ravel's Sonata for Violin and Piano (1927), whose second movement bears the title 'Blues'. The first 'jazz' opera, *Jonny Spielt Auf*, came from Ernst Krenek in 1927, and Kurt Weill experimented with jazz for many years, as may be realized from his *Dreigroschenoper*, a modern version of *The Beggar's Opera*, and his light opera *Mahagonny*, phrased in the jazz idiom. Like Stravinsky, these men recognized, in Krenek's words, that "Jazz . . . has revived the art of improvization to an extent unknown by serious musicians since the days of the *super librum cantare*, the contrapuntal extemporization of the fifteenth-century."

Two of Stravinsky's most intriguing creations are his only excursions after *Mavra* into the operatic field : *Oedipus Rex* and *The Rake's Progress*. Despite their stylistic differences—and it must be remembered that *Oedipus Rex* was written in 1926–27 and *The Rake's Progress* completed in 1951—both are neo-Classical in conception.

With the completion of *Oedipus Rex*, Stravinsky, journeying through his Unknown Country, reached his own crossroads, just as Oedipus met his destiny at "the place where three roads meet". He consulted no oracle of fashion, but solved the problem of progression by exploring all the roads available to him. In the dazzling beautiful and diatonic *Apollo*, the serene, dark-tinged *Perséphone* and the nobly austere *Orpheus*, he continued to reinterpret the classical Greek myth. Extending those elements of hieratic ritual which dominate *Oedipus Rex*, he wrote first the eloquent *Symphony of Psalms*, then, as experience produced a finer distillation, the *Mass*, the *Canticum Sacrum*, and *Threni*, works to be discussed later in this book, and all with the Latin tongue illuminated by music not so far removed from it in spirit. As a bridge to his discovery of new expressiveness in serialism, he composed the Concerto for Two Solo Pianos, the Concerto in E flat ("Dumbarton Oaks"), the Symphony in C and the Symphony in Three Movements.

Concerning *Oedipus Rex*, the idea of writing an 'opera-oratorio to a Latin text came to Stravinsky after reading that Saint Francis of Assissi "although he knew French imperfectly, was fond of using it when his heart was too full for him to express himself in the dead language he used for everyday speech". The composer, believing that Latin possessed a loftier dignity than words vulgarized by popular use, asked Jean Cocteau to write a French libretto based on Sophocles's tragedy. This was then translated into Latin. "Cocteau photographed the drama," Stravinsky says in the preface, "as if from an aeroplane." The composer insisted that Cocteau should have the original role of Speaker, and consequently the narrative is in French.

Oedipus is one of the world's greatest tragic dramas, and as such ought to invoke pity and compassion from its audience. It must be readily admitted that the Stravinsky/Cocteau version fails to do so. Here we have a superb story plucked from its context of language and drama, translated by a Frenchman into church-Latin dialogue with its profoundly noble poetry removed, and then set to music by a neo-Classic Russian. There is, about that grim, implacable chorus, not so much the semblance of inhuman gods, as of a cold, basilisk-eyed Gestapo.

Requiring singers of the utmost technical ability, it is not a happy choice of work to present. Cast as an opera-oratorio, it compels the conductor to decide between an essentially dramatic approach and one closer to a liturgical concept. The speeches of the narrator, who describes in the vernacular what is about to be sung in Latin, seem a trifle tasteless and 'clever' in the wrong way. And not even Rossini would have rejoiced over the dreary organ-grinder triolets of Jocasta's second aria.

Stravinsky declared that the words of the text of *Oedipus Rex* are of no importance except for their sonority and rhythm; a statement which Cocteau must have swallowed with reluctance. The composer then stipulated that there should be no action or motion in stage performances of the work. He required the actors to stand as still as pillars, appearing or disappearing with a pantomime efficiency, whenever necessary, by trapdoors or by raised or dropped curtains. These nonsensically 'stylized' directions rest uneasily against the vivid and powerful music of *Oedipus*

Rex, which undoubtedly shocked those of his admirers who looked to Stravinsky for a "return to objectivity".

Nevertheless, for all its faults, the work has many spellbinding moments, touching at its highest peaks the monumental grandeur which Stravinsky sought. The protagonists in the drama are Oedipus (tenor), Jocasta (mezzo-soprano), Tiresias (bass), a shepherd (tenor), a messenger and Creon (both sung by one baritone soloist). A large orchestra, involving triple wind, is deployed. Act I opens with a chorus of Thebans lamenting the plague that has fallen upon the land. They plead with Oedipus to deliver them, and he promises to do so. His brother-in-law Creon returns, after consulting the oracle, to report that Laius's murderer is hiding in Thebes and must be found. Oedipus appeals to Tiresias, the soothsayer, who, persuaded with difficulty to speak, proclaims that the king's assassin is a king. The first act ends with a thrilling *Gloria* chorus.

The first recitative of *Oedipus* is poignant and direct. When the chorus returns with "Save us, save the city", the passionate harmonics are haunting and we hear a superb crescendo based on a steady throb of the timpani. The music shows occasional blemishes, indicative more of Stravinsky's thirst for experimentation than of carelessness. One of these is the tootling woodwind in Creon's first aria, in which the gravity of the sentiments make it sound rather shallow and tawdry. Yet there is a compelling magic in other passages.

Act II opens with a repetition of the chorus which ended the preceding act. Jocasta ridicules the oracle. Laius was killed by robbers at a crossroads—how could her son have committed the foul deed! Oedipus, listening uneasily, recalls that he slew an old man at the crossroads. Was his victim really Laius? After this tense and complicated scene, the narrator speaks over timpani rolls; then the witness to the murder appears. A herald announces the death of Polybe, the supposed father of Oedipus, and reveals that, in fact, Oedipus was merely his adopted son. Jocasta commits suicide, and Oedipus, learning of her death and realizing, with a shocked agony of comprehension, his parricidal guilt and incest, puts out his own eyes. He is hunted, though compassionately, by the sorrowing populace.

The disparate elements of the score give it a parti-coloured appearance. Much of the choral music has a Russian-flavoured severity, but Creon's diatonic aria has a Handelian ring to it, while in Jocasta's chromatic *da capo* aria one hears refulgent echoes of Italian opera. The refinement of Tiresias's aria owes not a little to the rhetorical flights of Richard Wagner; although this dazzling piece, with its melody overleaping intervals of sevenths and ninths, represents the finest page in the score. It is difficult to listen to Jocasta's great tirade *Nonne erubescite* without experiencing goose-pimples, or to the arrogance of Oedipus in *Invidia fortunam odit* without a sense of foreboding. The ominous, fatalistic drum beats, the square chorus, and the stark, unadorned accents are certainly fascinating, and the music effectively sustains the dramatic tension of the work. *Oedipus Rex* has the semblance, if not the full reality of a masterpiece.

After the first performance in Paris on 30th May 1927, Stravinsky revised the score; as a result of this and subsequent revisions, there appeared in 1948 a new edition to which he gave his blessing. Two of the changes he made were added horns and tuba in *Nonne monstrum*. A characteristic alteration came in the spoken narrative right at the end, where the Speaker's personally involved and emotional "Farewell Oedipus, we loved you" became the more detached and unsubjective "You were loved". Stravinsky regarded the original sentence as "a blot of sentimentality wholly alien to the spirit of the work".

Aside from three little *a capella* choruses—*Pater Noster* (1926), *Credo* (1932), *Ave Maria* (1934)—and the brief, comparatively unimportant *Babel* of 1944, the composer used a chorus in only three other works during the whole of his thirty years of neo-Classicism : the beautiful and deeply affecting *Mass* of 1944–47, the great *Symphony of Psalms*, written in 1930, and the wonderfully evocative *Perséphone* of 1933–34.

The *Pater Noster* and *Credo* are simple, solemn pieces which derive from Stravinsky's reminiscences of singing at services which he attended as a boy; using a few mildly dissonant harmonies, they are almost entirely syllabic in setting. Although the *Credo* involves passages of free block chanting, there is no hint of counterpoint. The *Ave Maria* is a four-part setting of a metrically varied four-note melody characteristic of Stravinsky's early popular music of the Russian period. These choruses have Slavonic texts, but the composer also made new versions with Latin words. Babel, commissioned as a contribution to Nathaniel Shilkret's slightly ridiculous *Genesis* suite, makes very small use of a chorus, save for the utterance of the Word of God, which gives it some dramatic force; and certainly the seven-minute work, shaped like a passacaglia in which a fugue serves as one of the variations, has some intrinsic appeal. This partly sung, partly narrated piece exhibits Stravinsky's idiosyncratic lengthening of vowel sounds in words whose traditional stress comes elsewhere.

His noble setting of the Mass, scored for four solo voices, mixed chorus (with boys' voices recommended for the upper parts) and double wind quintet, has a grave, timeless beauty. The score reveals a highly concentrated directness and simplicity which make this music suitable for performance as much in a Byzantine basilica as against the soaring, uncluttered lines of a cathedral of contemporary design. Stravinsky always regarded himself as the heir to all the musical riches of the past, rather than as a 'revolutionary', and the *Mass*, which belongs to the great Flemish contrapuntal tradition, is probably the key to his entire creative development. Although the work rejects large dramatic gestures, it is full of ravishing, even sensuous passages which grow increasingly rewarding with familiarity.

Stravinsky chose his ten-piece wind band wisely, since the comparatively spare accompaniment not only freshens the atmosphere of the music, but also throws the choir into relief, while providing a sharp and effective tonal contrast with it. Although the *Kyrie* opens homophonically, much of the texture, with a directly imitative "*Christe*" passage, is contrapuntal. The *Gloria* begins with a melismatic duet for alto and treble soloists in a manner foreshadowing similar duets in the serial works; a single, highly complex movement, it sets the soloists against quiet *tutti* passages. There is masterly *a capella* writing in the psalmodic *Credo*, which, introduced by the priest's intonation, has a stirring contrapuntal "Amen". The recurring discord on the word "*Crucifixus*" reminds one of the fourteenth-century work of Machaut. The *Sanctus* and *Benedictus* are grouped together in one movement, with related but not identical "*Hosannas*", and with the "*Pleni sunt coeli*" of the Sanctus presented as a fugal exposition. In the antiphonal *Agnus Dei* the vocal and wind choruses alternate, but the voices are always unaccompanied.

The medieval sound of this truly Gothic, completely liturgical *Mass* discloses glimpses of a newer, more austere phase in Stravinsky's career; the sign of that growing interest in the mechanics of composition which finally led him to serialism.

The rarefied rapture and exaltation which lie at the heart of the *Symphony of Psalms*, often suffused with a glowing, more human light, make it a profoundly moving experience. In this work, constructed with the higher contrapuntal forms which he reserved for religious music, Stravinsky allotted the vocal parts to a mixed choir, rather than to a team of soloists, realizing that individual singers would be identified with the music and thus reduce the work from a universal and timeless declaration of faith to one of personal and clearly defined limitations. Since the choral writing never allows a very wide interval between the notes, singers cannot effectively convey their inner emotions. As if anticipating the criticism that such a tonal straitjacket prohibits any free movement, Stravinsky used the orchestra as the principal means of propulsion. Deprived of its upper strings and clarinets, but reinforced in the woodwind sections and the brass, it gathers majesty and strength that suggest the voice of a mighty organ.

The opening Prelude, with its flowing arabesques traced by oboe and bassoon and slashed by a dramatic E minor chord, provides a suitably atmospheric introduction for the chant-like theme sung by the altos. At the start of the second movement, a double fugue for four voices, Stravinsky conjures up from his collection of wind instruments some of the most ravishing sounds imaginable; here, with characteristically wide leaps in the melody, the oboe sings the major subject. A sober and deeply affecting "*Alleluia*" opens the third movement and is followed by an Allegro full of dance-like measures. A long and beautiful coda, built up on a bass *ostinato*, concludes the *Symphony of Psalms*. Supporting a swaying motif for the choir, timpani and pianos swing pendulum-fashion from B flat downwards to F, up again to B flat, on to E flat, and again, in a downward plunge, to B flat. The sequence, repeated through a duration of forty-two bars, while a treble harmony from the wind instruments gradually filters into the texture, seem to glow, as if a tiny flame, fanned by the softest of breezes, burst finally into a burning, blinding C major radiance, with shining major thirds in the heights contrasted against bare, single octaves for voices and instruments below. The *Vulgate* verses used by Stravinsky are highly dramatic. Most of the prosody conforms to ordinary stresses, but there are characteristic exceptions, one being the remarkable *um* in the "*Dominum*" of the last dirge.

Stravinsky wrote the *Symphony of Psalms* "for the glory of God" and to commemorate the fiftieth anniversary of the Boston Symphony Orchestra. He made a revised version in 1948; it contains not only corrected phrasing marks, accents and accidentals, but some new tempi markings for the finale. There is also a piano reduction by Stravinsky's son Sviatoslav, published in 1930.

Perséphone, a melodrama in three parts, is a setting of André Gide's poem on the Homeric *Hymn to Demeter*. One of Stravinsky's most transparent and exquisitely fashioned scores, it is neither parodic nor brittle, but has beautifully classical proportions. The chorus "*Ivresse-matinale*" is delightfully mischievous in its capricious melodic and rhythmic charm; and the portrayal of Perséphone in the Underworld summons up the noble gravity of a Poussin.

A superb combination of flute, harp and solo string quartet accompanies all Perséphone's words, giving them a bright-edged poignancy and, often, a delicate, almost ghostly unreality.

Stravinsky arranged the poem in three scenes: 1. The Abduction of Perséphone. II. Perséphone in the Underworld. III. Perséphone Reborn. He then published a manifesto proclaiming that in this work he had finished with "orchestral effects" and that he had long since renounced "the futilities of brio". Effects or not, *Perséphone* is filled with lovely atmospheric touches which, though delicately applied, have a penetrating magic, and only twice do we hear the full orchestra: to accompany the appearance of Mercury in the second part, and in the introduction to Part III.

The opening choruses conjure up a vista of sunlight filtering down from a cloud-flecked sky and of Perséphone strolling with her companion through fields bright with flowers. Her abduction is precipitated by her discovery of the sweet and deathly narcissus. To gaze into the sepals of this flower is to look, as in a mirror darkly, upon Hades itself. She does so and sees "a people wandering hopelessly, sad, restless, discoloured". Persuaded by Eumolpus that "her youth will lighten their distress, her spring charm their endless winter", she bids her nymphs farewell and departs with Springtime from the earth. In this poignant episode Stravinsky makes the delicate scene-painting more vivid by the rhetorical use of contrast. He clarified the music by separating and punctuating notes and phrase, turning silence into a musical device.

The second part of the melodrama shows us Perséphone in Hades as, clasping the narcissus, she sees the doomed, unhappy people who "recommence without end the incompleted motions of life". Eumolpus advises her to discard pity and fulfil her destiny as ruler of the Underworld. He urges her to drink a cup of water from Lethe. Shades from Pluto's palace tempt her with rich treasures, which she rejects. Finally, taking a ripe pomegranate from Mercury, she bites it, and the taste brings back a desire for the world she had lost. Gazing once more into the narcissus, Perséphone sees the world gripped by eternal Winter and her mother disconsolate and in rags. Yet the darkness thins as Eumolpus describes the birth of Demophoon, destined to be Triptolemus, and his upbringing by Demeter. When this child grows up he will save the world. Perséphone, hastening towards the radiant Triptolemus, her 'earthly spouse', returns to the sunlight, where Demeter also waits with outstretched arms.

Deep-registered passages paint the Byzantine gloom of Hades and the icon-like glow of the jewels offered to Perséphone in homage. Yet here is no heavy Wagnerian chromaticism. The music sways backwards and forwards as gently as rushes in a slow-moving stream.

At the beginning of the final episode a chorus, including children's voices, hails the returning queen. This is a gorgeous, Russian, barbaric piece of music, with festive drum beats that accentuate, by contrast, the starry brilliance shining faintly through the score. It is the spiritual light that triumphs in the end, for Perséphone, upholding the precept of unselfishness, returns of her own free will to Hades and its afflicted people. In doing so, she perpetuates the mystery of life : "For Spring to be reborn, the grain must first consent to die beneath the earth".

Stravinsky stated that for Perséphone he wanted nothing but syllables —beautiful, strong syllables—and an action; which he acknowledged Gide as having given to the text. He himself created a musical score predominantly in E minor and superbly balanced in its tonality; the work closes in that key and, in each of its three parts, a reference to Homer appears, sung by Eumolpus each time with the same E minor phrase. In its structural, rather than its decorative use of ornaments, the music has a Baroque flavour.

This deeply affecting tale, framed in a timeless dimension by Stravinsky's music, has much of the sweet innocence, as well as the sad tinge of the old French story of Nicolette whose white skin, as she ran barefoot through the meadow grass towards her lover Aucassin, made the snow-drops appear dark in comparison. Indeed, this is a work of naïve, but unerring contrasts, of facets that set off and complement each other. The silvery brightness and austerity of the music gains a focal point of humanity from the speech-recitative, which resembles the aria-like delivery of Racine at the Comedie-Française. In later years the composer described the use of melodrama in *Perséphone* as "a sin that cannot be undone, only forgiven". There is, I think, very little to forgive.

At the world première of *Perséphone*, given in the Opera House, Paris, on 30th April 1934, the title role was taken by Ida Rubinstein, who commissioned the work, with choreography by Kurt Jooss and costumes and décor by André Barsacq. Stravinsky conducted. A revised version of *Perséphone* appeared in 1949, but the changes are microscopic. There is also a piano reduction by Sviatoslav Stravinsky.

The composer loved to bestow gifts upon his friends, and in 1947, as a present to Nadia Boulanger on her birthday, he wrote the Little Canon for two tenors, which has not so far been published.

The Rake's Progress was Stravinsky's last neo-Classical work, coming between the *Mass* (1947) and the Cantata (1952). One critic called the libretto of this opera "coy, naïve and exasperating". but his was a shallow, myopic appraisal of a protean masterpiece which has many interpreta-tive facets. Three times the length of *Oedipus Rex,* the opera can tran-scend arbitrary notions of time and style to become what the listener chooses to make of it; for here, deliberately using the closed forms of recitative, aria and chorus, Stravinsky has created a wholly artificial con-cept of musical drama. It seeks neither to engulf the audience in the manner of Romantic opera, nor to alienate it as some post-romantic theatre techniques do, but to allow listeners to react to it with complete independence of spirit and feeling.

Set in three acts, with an epilogue, *The Rake's Progress* was Stravinsky's first full-length opera, with a libretto, inspired by eight of Hogarth's drawings, written by W. H. Auden and Chester Kallman. In the plot, illustrated by music of gaudiness, tenderness, simplicity, wit and incisive brilliance, we see Tom Rakewell abandon his sweetheart, Anne Trulove, squander a newly-inherited fortune on lust and revelry, then surrender his soul to Shadow (the Devil). The bargain he has made with Shadow brings him to the brink of perdition, but he persuades the Evil One to gamble for his pledged soul. Tom wins, but in doing so loses his reason and is put into Bedlam. The poignant ending shows the faithful Anne reunited with her pathetic lover, just before his death. In the epilogue the four principal characters appear in front of the curtain to pinpoint the moral of the opera by saying "For idle hearts and hands and minds the Devil finds work to do".

The musical structure of *The Rake's Progress,* entrusted to a chamber orchestra (no trombones) deploys arias, recitatives, choruses and extended finales for grand ensembles in a way that recalls the Classical patterns of Mozart. Bubbling with bright lyrical episodes, yet presenting what the American critic Ronald Ewer describes as "wide-striking and craggy melody", the score requires a harpsichord to accompany the recitatives. Stravinsky at one time denigrated the sound of that instrument, which reminded him of "peas rattling on a corrugated iron roof", but he overcame his prejudice in *The Rake's Progress.* The composer wrote the music of the opera with a subtle and disarming simplicity which masks a note of parody, as in Anne's virtuoso *cabaletta* in the classical style. Harmonically clear and delightful to sing, it discloses, as might be expected from so inventive a genius, rhythmical and metrical oddities that continually enliven the transparent scoring, with capricious bass phrases and bitonal passages giving the music a piquant flavour.

Lullaby from *The Rake's Progress,* scored for two recorders (soprano and alto) was published in 1960 and is a transcription of Anne's lullaby from the third act.

18

THE FLOWERING DESERT

The next four works, after the completion of *The Rake's Progress* had brought the long neo-Classical period to a close, revealed Stravinsky's growing preoccupation with serialism. Although still tonal, their harmonic and melodic material was organized, more and more, in conformity with serial procedures. Yet these compositions quite often touch the heart and ravish the ear. They are the tentatively atonal Cantata (1951–52), the enchanting Septet (1952–53), the Three Songs from William Shakespeare of 1953, and the poignant *In Memoriam Dylan Thomas*, written in 1954.

After the British première of the Cantata on 17th November 1953, one critic wrote of the work as "a complexity of counterpoint that may look delightful on paper, but which in practice becomes a complete bore", and banteringly described the choral music as the possible source of a sketch for the *Airs on a Shoestring* revue.

The composer was rightly taken to task for his cavalier treatment of the English language in the Cantata, yet there is no denying the strange fascination of these settings of anonymous fifteenth- and sixteenth-century English poems. The oboe's melancholy high A flat at the phrase "Where a spear to my heart did glance" in the long tenor setting of "Tomorrow Will Be Dancing Day" and the sinister quietness of "Mark whom I kiss, the same do hold" are spellbinding. Stravinsky's very avoidance of subjective emotionalism provides a key to the understanding of the medieval scholastic forms, and this I find curious, because Britten's masterly handling of the "Lyke-Wake Dirge" in his Serenade brings out a spine-chilling terror that makes Stravinsky's appear, by comparison, contrived and bloodless.

Stravinsky scored his Cantata for soprano, tenor, female voices and chamber ensemble. He used the four verses of the "Lyke-Wake Dirge" as the basis for a Prelude, two Interludes and a Postlude. Opening with a brief instrumental prelude in the Phrygian mode, the work is written in a free strophic form, making the very attractive tune of the instrumental prelude reappear before the third, fifth and seventh stanzas. A choral 'lament' follows, and between this and its repeat are heard a *ricercare* for soprano and instrumental quintet ("The Maidens Came") in canonic style. The second *ricercare* for tenor, cello, flutes and oboes in pairs, comprising a setting of "Tomorrow Will Be Dancing Day", is followed by a free-form Aria ("Westron Wind") for unaccompanied tenor and soprano. The work ends with an instrumental quintet.

In his love of good technical workmanship—one of the early manifestations of his conversion to serialism—Stravinsky produced some slightly incongruous effects. The small choral part of the Cantata, consisting of a simple strophic setting of the "Lyke-Wake Dirge" for female voices, contrasts rather oddly with the long central tenor solo which is an incredible compound of canonic, inverted and retrograde scoring.

The exploratory twelve-tone path which Stravinsky explored in the Cantata continued its devious, but still indeterminate direction in the Septet. Although in this work the series used by the composer is only a group of six notes in the Aeolian mode, the expressionist use of wide intervals and the *Klangfarbenmelodic* (melody of timbres) show his admiration for Webern, and the work spread uneasy ripples throughout the musical world when it first appeared. Although the Septet rests partly upon serial construction, it is not atonal, but is in A major. A difficult piece to perform, it needs much ingenuity to get precisely the right balance.

Stravinsky scored his three-movement Septet for violin, viola, cello, clarinet, horn, bassoon and piano (or harpsichord). The opening theme, with an octave range developed by imitation, sets an expansive mood. A scintillatingly light episode separates the brilliantly contrasted twelve-measure passage that follows the theme from the closing *fugato*. A transposition of the first five notes of the initial subject of the movement provides the attractive theme of the Passacaglia; it progresses through eight measures and eight variations. For the four-section Gigue which serves as the finale, each section is a fugue based on the subject of the preceding Passacaglia theme.

The Three Songs from William Shakespeare are scored for mezzo-soprano, flute, clarinet and viola. Their musical content is organically serial in structure, note-rows with strong tonal implications effecting a vivid English prosody. Discussing these songs, Stravinsky remarked to the critic Peter Yates, "A good composer does not imitate; he steals". This is a wise, not a cynical observation, for progress depends not a little upon imitation and the stimulus it gives to experimentation. The truly creative mind studies, selects, reassesses, absorbs, digests and perfects. To a large extent, Stravinsky did so in the Three Songs from William Shakespeare.

The path of serialism which he followed was the logical development of exploratory 'surveys' already carried out, not only by Schoenberg, the master of atonality, but by other composers who, though writing in a romantic era, looked adventurously in the same direction. Busoni, as early as 1911, had remarked in *Sketch of a New Musical Aesthetic* : "The tense silence between two movements—*in itself music*, in this environment—leaves wider scope for divination than the more determinate, but therefore less elastic, sound. . . . How important, indeed, are third, fifth, and octave. How strictly we divide 'consonance' from 'dissonance'—*in a sphere where no dissonances can possibly exist*! . . . We have divided the octave into twelve equidistant degrees. . . . Yet Nature created an *infinite gradation— infinite*! Who still knows it nowadays?"

Debussy, through the voice of his Monsieur Croche, proclaimed: "Discipline must be sought in freedom, and not within the formulas of an outworn philosophy only fit for the feeble-minded. Give ear to no man's counsel; but listen to the wind which tells in passing the history of the world."

Stravinsky not only listened to the wind, but rode upon it. One of the first works in which he experimented with twelve-note procedures was *In Memoriam Dylan Thomas*, a setting of the poet's "Do not go gentle into that good night". He intended it to be an elegiac tribute to Thomas, whose tragic death had moved him to tears, and the instrumentation— string quartet and four trombones—has a *dolorosa* sound; but the music itself, rising and falling with mechanical regularity, is anything but dirge-like. Ritualistic grief cannot be separated from dignity, and I do not find in Stravinsky's admittedly original and sometimes poignant music the delicate feeling for words that Britten so often displayed in setting poems. The too easily perceptible emotion of the verse seems in this instance to reject, as in a clumsy heart transplant, the music chosen to illustrate it, and perhaps Stravinsky was wrong to undertake so formidable a task.

The work opens with Dirge-Canons for string quartet and trombone quartet and closes with a similar Dirge for Postlude. In between comes a setting for tenor voice and string quartet of the poem "Do not go gentle into that good night". Admittedly, there is in the Dirges a smoky, plain-chant-like air of mystery, but Stravinsky's exaggerated efforts to follow the inflexions of the English tongue slightly distort the lovely verse.

Perhaps he realized this himself, for in his next work, the *Canticum Sacrum* (1955), scored for tenor and baritone soli, chorus and orchestra, he returned to the setting of a Latin text that had proved so successful, though with some disappointing features, in *Oedipus Rex*. Only by remembering the various influences—Gregorian chant, polytonality, Webern, Byzantine modes, atonality—can the listener reconcile the strange contrasts which the agitated trumpets at the beginning make with the ecclesiastical sound of the organ and choir; yet this is no treasure-house of gilded emotion, but a cold, stately work whose banners are borne aloft by progressive silences and rhythmic subtlety, rather than by deliberately poignant effects. Britten took note of the contrast mentioned when he composed his *War Requiem*.

Mathematical devices abound in the *Canticum Sacrum*, which, written for the Venice Festival in 1955, shows the composer's irrevocable conversion to serial methods. There are two passages of almost unsupported atonal canon, with only a trombone line holding absolute pitch; although the viola parts can be summoned to double the chorus, if necessary. Much of the *Canticum Sacrum* is more sedate, however, and Stravinsky treads cautiously. In this work there is only one short section where the instruments are completely silent while the choir is singing—the *"Et continuo exclamans"* passage at the end of Part IV. The instrumental scoring is for trumpets, trombones, bassoons, organ, violas and double-basses. After the 'Dedication' comes the first section, which is repeated at the close backwards, rather in the manner of Hindemith's *Ludus Tonalis*. In the middle is a twelve-tone section, *"Ad tres Virtutes Hortationes"*, in which, like a musical acrostic, the series of notes turn round on themselves, producing complete circles. The derogatory remark made by one critic that "bleak and cheerless exercises" like this do not create great music falls flat if one remembers the mechanical legerdemain which Beethoven, with his fantastic *cancrizans*, introduced into the last movement of his *Hammerklavier* Sonata. The acid test is the sound and quality of the music itself. There is some beautiful unison writing—notably in the third part of the third movement, to the word "credidi"—and a thrilling use of choir and orchestra against organ. Stravinsky shows what can be achieved with four independent contrapuntal lines and a resilient chorus. I regard the *Canticum Sacrum* as a clean, majestic work that recalls the music of many centuries back.

The *Greetings Prelude*, written in 1955, was a musical telegram 'sent' by Stravinsky to celebrate the eightieth birthday of the conductor Pierre Monteux, which took place on 4th April that year. The music, a gay and perky little piece based on Clayton Summy's "Happy birthday to you", requires no special comment, and Stravinsky himself described it as a fifty-second-long primer of canonic writing for very young children and critics.

In his Choral Variations on *Von Himmel Hoch Da Komm Ich Her*, Stravinsky produced something more controversial than a mere orchestral arrangement of the five variations on his chorale which Bach wrote in 1746–47. His imaginative choice of instruments, excluding all strings—except violas and basses—his addition of a choir, and his highly personal treatment, involving contrapuntal embellishments and rhythmic interpolations, create an effect of inspired scoring which never tarnishes or distorts the original. In transcribing the variations, Stravinsky added the chorale in one of Bach's great settings from the *Christmas Oratorio*. He also transposed variations II, III, and IV to other keys, not only for contrast, but also for the convenience of the instruments deployed.

The music of the ballet *Agon*, written in 1953–57 and choreographed by George Balanchine for twelve dancers, contains passages which are not

organized serially, but they are few, indeed. This one-act work was Stravinsky's first composition for large orchestra since the Symphony in Three
Movements. He modelled the music after examples in a French dance
manual of the mid-seventeenth century. Its fanfare-like, richly percussive
character looks back nostalgically to previous Stravinsky ballets; the
beautiful *pas de deux* is conceived, like a Picasso drawing, as a continuous,
uninterrupted, clearly defined sequence of line and movement and not in
a rythmically free and texturally diffused style. *Agon* is magnificent dance
music, heard to its greatest advantage in the theatre, rather than the
concert hall. Beginning and ending in a firm F major, it combines episodes
based on a serial technique with sections tonal in character and others
embodying Stravinsky's familiar disjunct rhythms. The scoring is largely
in the *concertante* manner, with the extensive use of solo instruments, the
most important being a solo violin which, entrusted with frequent caden-
zas, has a prima-donna role. It serves in a sense as a recapitulation of all
Stravinsky's own styles and practices, with hints of *Petrushka*, *The Soldier's
Tale* and *The Rake's Progress* cheek-by-jowl with passages reflecting his
more recent dodecaphonic phase. The orchestration is of fascinating
subtlety and refinement, its tonal spectrum stretching from tonality over
bitonality and polytonality to atonality and 12-tone procedure. Only
Stravinsky could have blended these gritty ingredients into such fine music.

Mildred Norton, writing in the American journal *The Saturday
Review*, aptly summarized the distinctive qualities of this music as "its
novel and exuberant use of timbres", and added : "Such interludes as
harp staccato against the shimmer of mandolin, of flute configurations
over castenets, or solo violin above trombones, as well as silken harmonics
in the upper strings, are provocative highlights in a tonal palette of characteristic cleanliness and candour."

Although *Threni* (1957–58), that great setting of the Lamentations of
Jeremiah, was Stravinsky's first wholly serial work, it cannot be regarded
as in any sense forbidding and, indeed, has an unforgettable spiritual
power which fully vindicates Donald Mitchell's description of it as "among
the grandest of Stravinsky's masterpieces". Schoenberg frequently pointed
out to friends and foes that the techniques used by a composer are of
minor significance; it is how the composer uses them that determines the
quality of his music. *Threni* illustrates this truth with considerable beauty.
I cannot agree with those who find in the work a profound and touching
penitence; but the composer must have felt deeply when he wrote it.
Although *Threni* is scored for six solo voices, mixed chorus and orchestra,
the music has an affecting delicacy. Even the rhythmic chanting of the
choral passages is never heavy or overblown, and Howard Taubman
rightly classed the music as "a remarkable example of the composer's gift
for saying much and with few notes".

Stravinsky selected his own text for *Threni* from the *Vulgate* and utilized extracts from the first, third and fifth Lamentations of the Prophet Jeremiah. Following the example of his illustrious predecessors of former epochs, he retained the Hebrew letters that figure in exquisitely spaced and coloured episodes at the beginning of each verse of this old Latin translation from the Hebrew. The juxtaposition of these Hebrew letters (Aleph, Beth, Caph, Res(h), Thau, etc.) with the Latin verse, sung occasionally by the soloists and often by the chorus, gives *Threni* a striking, if slightly bizarre effect. We feel in this work the subdued but hostile lashing of Isaiah's tongue. The music is made up of short, distinct phrases which convey an austere, ritualistic impression. Since only a few instruments out of the large orchestra are used at any one time, the work displays no choral or instrumental grandiosity and perfectly illustrates Stravinsky's genius for expressing much in a few notes and voices. There are cryptic references to numbers in relation to the Hebrew characters.

Threni, a totally undramatic and genuinely ritualistic work of symmetrical design and simplicity, does not contain a single tutti, and although Stravinsky deploys a large orchestra, only two or three instruments play individually in counterpoint at any given moment. After an opening monody for the basso profundo, other soloists join in, creating successive canons for two, three and four voices. Occasionally the chorus interpolates a brief, but pregnant phrase. One particularly beautiful passage is the first part of the second section, where the four male soloists sing in canon with the chorus interposing the Hebrew letters at the beginning of the verses. In the closing section, which discards the Hebrew letters, soloists and chorus resolve on a note of unison. Stravinsky could easily have succumbed to the temptation of providing a picturesque but facile ending for this unusual work. Instead, he dissolves the mass note of unison, which is briefly held by the first tenor, then, like a magician pulling a slender pretty girl from a cabinet, he signs the piece characteristically with a short cadence of notes in the orchestra, creating a superbly balanced climax.

Threni was followed in 1959 by the elegiac Epitaphium and Double Canon and by the terse Movements for piano and small orchestra.

The fifty-seven-bars-long *Epitaphium*, written to honour the memory of Prince Max Egon Zu Fürstenberg, the generous and enlightened patron of the Donaueschingen Festival, comprises a twelve-note series in linear exposition (the exposition in the sixth bar is double) and is scored for three instruments : a harp plays the first, third, fifth and seventh bars; flute and clarinet sing a duet in the remaining bars. It has a dignified austere sound, but can scarcely be regarded as inspired.

Stravinsky never met Dufy, the painter, chosen as the subject of his Double Canon, "Raoul Dufy in Memoriam", and wrote the piece in response to a personal request. Its twelve-note theme weaves very ingeniously and never tires the ear. The work, scored for string quartet, has a quasi-vocal aspect, each instrument being allotted a purely melodic line, without any double-stopping.

Movements, tense and highly concentrated, has five movements, separated by four brief sections which serve both as preludes to the music which follows them, and as codas to that which they succeed. This composition may be "anti-tonal", as Stravinsky called it, but the polyrythmic music reveals form, direction, energy, and even a delightful gaiety of spirit that makes one think of a twentieth-century Mozart. The textural shapes evolve and interweave as distinctly as the variants of a dance, while the exquisite scoring helps the listener to apprehend the inventive fantasy and ingenuity of the music.

Stravinsky, at the age of eighty, showed few signs of diminishing powers. While he was writing his *Canticum Sacrum*, the composer had photostat copies made of Gesualdo's *Sacrae Cantiones*, published in Naples in 1603, and finding that the last of the songs, "*Illumina Nos*" (*a sette voci*), had no *sextus* and *bassus* parts, he felt a characteristic urge to complete it by supplying new pages of his own. He offered the work to the Venice Festival, for performance in the concert at which his *Canticum Sacrum* was to have its première; but the authorities refused, not wishing to honour a Neapolitan. Stravinsky did not finish the score until 1957, shortly after completing the ballet *Agon*. He wrote the substitute pages in the spirit of Gesualdo's music.

The composer, in September 1959, also supplied the missing parts of the second and twelfth items from the same set of twenty *Sacrae Cantiones,* and a year later published the three songs under the title *Tres Sacrae Cantiones by Carlo Gesualdo di Venosa (1560–1613), completed by Igor Stravinsky for the 400th Anniversary of Gesualdo's Birth.* In the last two pieces, "*Da pacem, Domine*" and "*Assumpta est Maria*", respectively, he had only to create the missing bass parts.

Having discharged this task, inspired by his profound admiration for Gesualdo, the composer seized upon a project abandoned in 1954, and wrote the *Monumentum*, comprising three Gesualdo madrigals, 'reconstituted' for instruments: "*Asciugate i begli occhi*" (No. 14 in Book V); "*Ma tu, cagion di quella*" (No. 18 in Book V); and "*Beltà poi che t'assenti*" (No. 2 in Book VI). He did not transcribe the originals, but recomposed the musical substance with great subtlety. To vary the tone quality, Stravinsky excluded trumpets and trombones from the first madrigal, used no horns or strings in the second, and deployed the full ensemble for the third. The work bears the title *Monumentum pro Gesualdo di Venosa ad CD Annum: Three Madrigals recomposed for Instruments.*

Another large-scale composition, *A Sermon, a Narrative, and a Prayer,* followed in 1961. The strongly religious meaning of this cantata cannot be ignored. It represents a superb example of twentieth-century religious art and the third movement conveys, without any surface sentimentality, a sense of rapt inner communion, the whole piece impressing by its combined gentleness and power.

The *Sermon* contains passages from the letters of St Paul, the climax of which is a glorious affirmation of faith; they are set for alternating four-part and eight-part choruses. In a dialogue between a speaker and an alto soloist, *A Narrative* proclaims the triumph of this faith over the hideous death of St Stephen the Martyr. And finally *A Prayer*, using the noble words of the English poet Thomas Dekker, provides a radiant view of the eternal state of grace described at the end of the *Revelation of John* : here alto and tenor soloists and four-part chorus participate.

This fifteen-minute-long work demands the utmost concentration by performers and audience alike. In its technical structure may be traced the artistic shock which Stravinsky sustained when he first sampled the music of Anton Webern. A glance at the score reminds one immediately of that master of sparse, Lilliputian tone-patterns : the instruments are used economically, often as soloists (woodwinds in twos; four horns; three trumpets; four trombones; tuba; three tamtams; piano, harp and strings). Yet for all Webern's influence on its twelve-note technique and melodic figurations, the music bears the strong imprint of Stravinsky's own genius.

In the spring of 1962 he wrote the *Eight Instrumental Miniatures*, an orchestral reassessment for fifteen players of the "eight very easy melodies on five notes" for piano published forty years earlier under the title The Five Fingers. The structure of the tunes remains unaltered, although the original sequence is changed; but Stravinsky presents them in different tone-colours, with shifts of register and some thematic filling-out.

Stravinsky's anthem *The Dove Descending Breaks the Air* (1962) is a highly concentrated and technically brilliant setting of T. S. Eliot's poem. The only non-liturgical work he ever composed for unaccompanied S.A.T.B. chorus, it presents a brief, twelve-note study, with each of the four parts following its own serial pattern, except on one occasion, when the tenor and bass exchange rows, and, although not in any sense inspirational, it is quietly moving.

In *The Flood*, a musical play which Stravinsky completed in 1962 and which the Columbia Broadcasting System (CBS Television) televised on 14th June of that year, not a single bar appears directly reminiscent of *The Rite of Spring*, yet the two works are plainly related. Like *Noye's Fludde* by Britten, the text, arranged by Robert Craft, follows the great tradition of the York and Chester Miracle Plays and includes the same comic episode where a recalcitrant Noah's wife slaps the face of a hen-pecked Noah. *The Flood*, which involves five narrators and three solo singers, is a sung or spoken account of the Creation, the Revolt of the Angels, the Fall, the Deluge and the Covenant. The first of the two ballet interludes ("The Building of the Ark") appears to me rather scrappy and tangential, but the second ("The Flood") comprises nearly three minutes of driving, pelting and implacable music for tremolo strings, with hair-raising harmonics on flutter-tongued woodwind and brass. The vocal writing of *The Flood*, a stylistically encyclopaedic and rhythmically dance-affirming piece, follows the same craggy patterns as that of *Threni* and the *Canticum Sacrum*, while the instrumental scoring displays, by turn, the clear line and cohesiveness of *Agon*, and the sparse disjunctiveness of Movements. Described by the composer as a bit of "Igorian chant", it has many appealing facets.

In *The Flood* a chorus without basses sings a setting of part of the *Te Deum* before and after the narration; a bright, incisive piece of writing enlivened by sprightly rhythms and shifting accents reminiscent of *Oedipus Rex*. What reduces the effectiveness of the work is the text, which covers only a tiny patch of time, from the Creation through the building of the Ark and the Flood. A strange collation of biblical, contemporary, metaphysical and fifteenth-century literary sources, it seems too highly compressed for the magnitude of the subject, and the ingredients do not, I think, cohere quite convincingly. More performances of *The Flood* will be needed before the critic can form any dependable judgement about its ultimate value, but the text is disturbing in its comic naïvety. A passage like the following has a curiously flat, pancake sound :

> Mother, we beg you all together
> Come into the ship for fear of the weather.
> The flood is flowing in full fast
> For fear of drowning we are aghast.

Stravinsky wrote the sacred ballad *Abraham and Isaac* in 1962–63 and dedicated it to the people of Israel—who commissioned it through the Israel Festival Committee—as a token of gratitude for their generosity and hospitality during his tour of their country in 1962. Since the work tells the story of how God tested Abraham by asking him to sacrifice his son Isaac, it was fitting that the première of 23rd August 1964 should have been held in the shadow of Mount Moriah, the place in the Bible where God's angel intervened to stop the sacrifice. Stravinsky began to compose the ballad partly because of the fascinating sound qualities of the Hebrew tongue and partly of the subject, which he also found appealing. Scored for baritone and chamber orchestra, it uses the Hebrew text of Genesis (*B'reshnit*) Chapter XXII; there are five parts, distinguished by changes of tempo and performed without a break. The work comprises nineteen verses and ten musical units.

The composer deploys the orchestra—strings, woodwind, and brass, without percussion—sparingly, as a background for the narration. He makes no attempt in his setting to impersonate the protagonists who, in the Bible, use dialogue, and the baritone-narrator indicates a change of speaker by changes in dynamics. The vocal line is, in Stravinsky's own words, "partly *bel*-Cantor-melismatic and partly an interval-speech of nine syllables". There are seemingly 'expressive' rhythmic devices and canons in the music, particularly in the passages referring to Isaac and the two boys; but the composer denied any intention to give the work a deliberate expressiveness. Repetitions of words appear in this twelve-note ballad; they are never accompanied by exact musical repetitions.

Abraham and Isaac is an interesting piece, but the severe and brisk narration rejects the kind of tenderness and wonder which Britten brought to the same episode, and perhaps for this reason many Stravinsky admirers have found it disappointing. The composer wrote the ballad in strictly atonal style, with concentration of speech and brevity as its primary attributes.

The sense of grief and loss he experienced when President John F. Kennedy was assassinated on 22nd November 1963 resulted in the *Elegy for J.F.K.* (1964), which uses words of a poetic text by W. H. Auden not specifically related to the killing. Using a baritone voice and three clarinets, a grouping for which Stravinsky had a special fondness, in a serial structure of disarming simplicity, the work has a transparent sound texture which highlights with a wonderful delicacy every nuance of the text and achieves a compelling intensity of expression.

Stravinsky wrote his Variations for orchestra (1963–64) in memory of Aldous Huxley. The block structures, faceted with precisely cut details, confirm his mastery at that time of the complex language of serialism. This work is not as fragmented as some of Stravinsky's atonal compositions, and the strongly contrasted block sonorities which delineate the various sections make it immediately accessible. Clive Barnes described the score as being based on "a series of notes making up the melody and grouped in two six-note formations. The halves of this melody are more or less symmetrical, permitting the composer to turn the sections upside down and inside out, and by rhythmic changes and varying sonorities to create a series of continuous variations". George Balanchine made a ballet for the music.

The little Fanfare for a New Theatre which Stravinsky wrote in 1964 touches no appreciable heights, but displays a neat and methodical craftsmanship in the bold unmeretricious use of two trumpets.

Stravinsky wrote his *Introitus* in 1965 as a tribute to the memory of T. S. Eliot. This moving work uses male voices in one and two parts to conjure up a dark, sad sonority. The scoring is for tenors, basses, harp, piano, two timpani, two tamtams, solo viola and double-basses. Much of the elegiac sound of the piece comes from the predominantly low-pitched timbres of the instruments. Stravinsky spoke of Eliot as "that kind, wise and gentlest of men". This grave and beautiful setting of words from the Requiem Mass is a kind, wise and gentle composition; not in any way substantial, but carrying an unmistakable flavour of sincerity.

Such works as the *Introitus* and the serial compositions that preceded it may have provoked many critics by their prickly unconventionality, but they continue to open up fresh byways in the Unknown Country of music. Aaron Copland said of Stravinsky : "It is the rightness of his 'wrong' solutions that fascinates one. The notes themselves seem surprised at finding themselves situated where they are."

Stravinsky's final major work, the *Requiem Canticles*, completed in 1966 and scored for vocal quartet, chorus, and orchestra, is much simpler and more direct in expression than *Abraham and Isaac*, but it also reveals a highly idiosyncratic and personal attitude. After sampling the intense romanticism of Webern's Cantatas, which contain strikingly plain and unaffected choral writing, the listener might regard the *Requiem Canticles* as slightly arid; yet the technique Stravinsky uses is much more traditional and the luminous religiosity of the Latin text has tremendous power. He keeps his musical bass in the orchestra and his vocal basses are consistently deployed in middle and upper registers. The chiselled blocks of sound that make up the imposing structure of the *Requiem Canticles* are so aptly shaped for their purpose, so firm of substance, and so ingeniously varied that they produce an effect altogether disproportionate to their size.

Of the seven main sections of the Mass the composer employs only three : the Introit, *Dies Irae* and Responsory (*Libera Me*), transforming them into six short vocal movements and divided by three sections for the orchestra. The enigmatic Prelude, with its chugging, repeated note canopied by a radiant counter point of intertwining violin lines, makes a purely symbolic introduction to the work and displaces the traditional *Requiem Aeternam*. Here a pattern of five solo strings, with a fresh part added at each entry, rises in melodic appeal over a semiquaver pulsation for the main body of the strings, creating an effect of voices uplifted above a muttered invocation. This is followed by the chant-like *Exaudi*, whose homophonic serenity acquires an unforgettable poignancy from the repetition of a few words and a few intervals, with the orchestra delicately emphasizing the unadorned simplicity of some of the choral writing. In the *Dies Irae* choir and orchestra seem almost to disintegrate in a rocket-like explosion of anger reminiscent in temperament, if not in style, of the Dionysian wrath of *The Rite of Spring*. The *Tuba Miram* and the *Lacrimosa*, both for solo voices (bass and contralto) observe the traditional character of these sections of the Requiem with a masterly expressiveness in no way disparate with the great choral heritage surrounding the Mass; the *Tuba Miram* picking up and bringing into full focus the brass sonorities of the previous section, and the *Lacrimosa* progressing with the dignified punctuation marks that distinguish the entire work. Between these imposing sections, and prefaced by a sombrely meditative Interlude, which provides the pivot around which the whole piece revolves, is the densely contrapuntal *Rex Tremendae*, with episodes of rich instrumental

R

harmony. The final *Libera Me*, a homophonic chorale scored for solo vocal quartet, with the chorus interpolating spoken parts, culminates in a tranquil Postlude and exquisite, bell-like chords.

One of Stravinsky's most inspired works, the *Requiem Canticles* uses several note-rows, all of which have melodic segments in common; but there is no consistent attempt at twelve-note saturation. What makes the music memorable is the clear spacing, juxtaposition, and colouring of distinct melodic or chordal ideas which establish and sustain a readily discernible pattern.

The *Requiem Canticles* was commissioned by Princeton University in memory of Helen Buchanan Seeger, and Robert Craft conducted the world premiére in Princeton on 8th October 1966. This noble work, lofty in scale yet touched by the characteristic sensitivity of its creator, filled the church of San Giovanni and Paolo, Venice, on 15th April 1971, as the body of Igor Stravinsky lay in state before the high altar, his odyssey through the Unknown Country complete.

And in his old age the wisdom of his song shall exceed even the beauties of his youth; and it shall be much loved. (Psellus Akritas of Alexandria, *De Ceremoniis, XIV*, 7.)

NOTES

CHAPTER ONE

1 Humphrey Milford, *Selected Modern English Essays* (Oxford University Press) p. 267
2 Igor Stravinsky, *Chronicle Of My Life*, p. 11
3 ibid., p. 12
4 Igor Stravinsky and Robert Craft, *Memories And Commentaries*, p. 24
5 Ezra Pound, *Canto* LXXVI
6 Stravinsky and Craft, *Memories And Commentaries*, p. 20
7 ibid., pp. 22–3
8 ibid., p. 23
9 Stravinsky, *Chronicle Of My Life*, p. 15
10 *Stravinsky In Conversation With Robert Craft*, p. 160
11 ibid.
12 Matthew Arnold, "The Scholar Gipsy"
13 Stravinsky and Craft, *Memories And Commentaries*, p. 30

CHAPTER TWO

1 Stravinsky and Craft, *Expositions And Developments*, p. 21
2 Adrian Boult, *Thoughts On Conducting*, p. xi
3 From an open letter to Serge Diaghilev, *The Times*, 18th October 1921
4 Gerald Abraham, *Rimsky-Korsakov*, p. 21
5 Walt Whitman, *Leaves Of Grass*
6 Rimsky-Korsakov, *My Musical Life*, p. 295
7 Feodor Chaliapine, *Man And Mask*, pp. 71–2

CHAPTER THREE

1 Stravinsky and Craft, *Memories And Commentaries*, pp. 58–9
2 ibid., p. 59
3 ibid., p. 34
4 ibid.
5 Feodor Chaliapine, *Pages From My Life*, p. 168
6 Gerald Abraham, op. cit., p. 129
7 *Stravinsky In Conversation With Robert Craft*, p. 45
8 Stravinsky and Craft, *Expositions And Developments*, p. 129
9 Serge Lifar, *A History Of Russian Ballet*, p. 236

10 Tamara Karsavina, *Theatre Street*, p. 164
11 Cyril W. Beaumont, *The Diaghilev Ballet In London*, p. 177
12 ibid.
13 ibid., pp. 177–78
14 Harriet Cohen, *A Bundle Of Time*, p. 45
15 Stravinsky, *Chronicle Of My Life*, p. 85
16 Edward Lockspeiser, *Debussy: His Life And Mind*, vol. 2, p. 180
17 Victor I. Serov, *Debussy, Musician Of France*, p. 311
18 Stravinsky, *Chronicle Of My Life*, p. 60
19 Naomi Jacob and James C. Robertson, *Opera In Italy*, p. 207
20 ibid.

CHAPTER FOUR

1 Edward Lockspeiser, op. cit., vol. 2, p. 180
2 Romola Nijinsky, *Nijinsky*, p. 182
3 Stravinsky, *Chronicle Of My Life*, p. 67
4 ibid., p. 69
5 ibid., p. 75
6 Oscar Wilde, *An Ideal Husband*, II
7 Stravinsky, *Chronicle Of My Life*, p, 77
8 Minna Lederman ed., *Stravinsky In The Theatre*, pp. 19–20
9 Doris Monteux, *It's All In The Music*, p. 197
10 Stravinsky and Craft, *Dialogues And A Diary*, p. 132

CHAPTER FIVE

1 *Souvenirs sur Igor Stravinsky.*, (translated by D. P. Charean)
2 Romola Nijinsky, op. cit., p. 110
3 Vera Newman, *Ernest Newman*, p. 77
4 ibid., p. 99
5 Serge Lifar, *My Life*, p. 30
6 Romola Nijinsky, op. cit., p. 306
7 ibid., p. 308
8 ibid., p. 309
9 Stravinsky and Craft, *Expositions And Developments*, pp. 122–23
10 Stravinsky, *Chronicle Of My Life*, p. 115

CHAPTER SIX

1 Pigeon Crowle and Mike Davis, *The Nutcracker Ballet*, p. 33
2 Leonide Massine, *My Life In Ballet*, p. 148
3 Interview with Maggie Teyte, *Music And Musicians*, August 1962
4 Edward Lockspeiser, op. cit., p. 98
5 Donald Mitchell, *The Language Of Music*, p. 22

CHAPTER SEVEN

1   Tamara Karsavina, op. cit., p. 185
2   Bernard Taper, *Balanchine*, p. 72
3   Stravinsky, *Chronicle Of My Life*, p. 154
4   Herbert Read, "Tourists In A Sacred Place"

CHAPTER EIGHT

1   From an open letter to Serge Diaghilev, *The Times*, 18th October 1921
2   Harriet Cohen, op. cit., p. 46
3   ibid.
4   ibid.
5   Nicholas Nabokov, *Of Friends And New Music*, p. 159
6   ibid.
7   ibid.
8   S. L. Grigoriev, *The Diaghilev Ballet*, p. 177
9   Stravinsky and Craft, *Dialogues And A Diary*, p. 39
10 Stravinsky, *Chronicle Of My Life*, pp. 173–74
11 Serge Lifar, *My Life*, p. 26
12 ibid.
13 ibid., p. 32
14 Victor I. Serov, *Serge Prokofiev*, p. 148
15 Richard Buckle, *The Adventures Of A Ballet Critic*, p. 57

CHAPTER NINE

1   Bernard Taper, op. cit., p. 77
2   ibid., p. 83
3   ibid., p. 92
4   Irene Downes ed., *Olin Downes On Music*, p. 95
5   Stravinsky and Craft, *Dialogues And A Diary*, p. 101
6   ibid., p. 26
7   Francis Steegmuller, *Cocteau: A Biography*, p. 358
8   Harriet Cohen, op. cit., p. 139
9   Serge Lifar, *A History Of Russian Ballet*, p. 268
10 Bernard Taper, op. cit., p. 99
11 Serge Lifar, *A History Of Russian Ballet*, p. 269
12 Bernard Taper, op. cit., p. 198
13 Stravinsky, *Chronicle Of My Life*, p. 239
14 Serge Lifar, *A History Of Russian Ballet*, p. 271
15 ibid., p. 272
16 ibid., p. 270
17 ibid.
18 ibid.
19 ibid.
20 Romola Nijinsky, op. cit., p. 112
21 Serge Lifar, *A History Of Russian Ballet*, p. 271

22 Stravinsky and Craft, *Expositions And Developments*, p. 85
23 Pigeon Crowle and Mike Davis, p. 48
24 Arnold Haskell, *Diaghilev*, p. 214
25 ibid., p. 263
26 ibid., pp. 277–78
27 Stravinsky, *Chronicle Of My Life*, p. 255
28 Stravinsky and Craft, *Memories And Commentaries*, p. 47

CHAPTER TEN

1 Stravinsky and Craft, *Expositions And Developments*, pp. 89–90
2 *Stereo*, Autumn 1971
3 Stravinsky and Craft, *Dialogues And A Diary*, p. 64
4 Minna Lederman, op. cit., p. 123
5 Bernard Taper, op. cit., p. 197
6 ibid., p. 199
7 Serge Bertennson and J. Leyda, *Serge Rachmaninov—A Lifetime in Music*, p. 374
8 Victor I. Serov, *Rachmaninov*, p. 184
9 Bernard Taper, op. cit., p. 162
10 Joseph Szigeti, *With Strings Attached*, p. 160
11 Bernard Taper, op. cit., pp. 125–26

CHAPTER ELEVEN

1 Stravinsky and Craft, *Dialogues And A Diary*, p. 50
2 *Stravinsky In Conversation With Robert Craft*, p. 107
3 Paul Rosenfeld, *Musical Impressions*, p. 144
4 ibid., p. 147
5 ibid., p. 148
6 Nicholas Nabokov, op. cit., pp. 152–53
7 Bernard Taper, op. cit., p. 199
8 Stravinsky and Craft, *Expositions And Developments*, p. 77
9 Stravinsky and Craft, *Dialogues And A Diary*, pp. 91–2

CHAPTER TWELVE

1 *Stereo*, Autumn 1971
2 *Music And Musicians*, November 1965

CHAPTER THIRTEEN

1 Stravinsky and Craft, *Expositions And Developments*, p. 109
2 ibid., p. 145
3 ibid., p. 135
4 ibid., p. 17
5 ibid., pp. 57–8

6 Stravinsky, *Themes And Conclusions*, pp. 298–307
7 *Stereo*, Autumn 1971

CHAPTER FOURTEEN

1 Nicholas Nabokov, op. cit., pp. 165–66
2 Stravinsky and Craft, *Dialogues And A Diary*, p. 121
3 *Stereo*, Autumn 1971
4 Nicholas Nabokov, op. cit., p. 151
5 Minna Lederman, op. cit., p. 123
6 *Time*, 19th April 1971
7 ibid.
8 Nicholas Nabokov, op. cit., p. 159
9 ibid.
10 ibid., p. 158
11 ibid., p. 159
12 William (Johnson) Cory, "Heraclitus"

CHAPTER FIFTEEN

1 Stravinsky, *Chronicle Of My Life*, p. 45

CHAPTER SIXTEEN

1 Minna Lederman, op. cit., p. 123
2 *Stravinsky In Conversation With Robert Craft*, p. 51
3 Stravinsky and Craft, *Expositions And Developments*, p. 121

CHAPTER SEVENTEEN

1 *Stravinsky In Conversation With Robert Craft*, p. 76
2 Stravinsky, *Chronicle Of My Life*, p. 278
3 Samuel Dushkin, *Igor Stravinsky*, Edwin Corle ed., p. 185

BIBLIOGRAPHY

Abraham, Gerald, *Rimsky-Korsakov* (Gerald Duckworth, 1945).

Auden, W. H., *Secondary Worlds* (G. P. Putnam, 1940).

Beaumont, Cyril W., *The Diaghilev Ballet In London* (G. P. Putnam, 1940).

Bertennson, Serge and Leyda, J., *Serge Rachmaninov—A Lifetime In Music* (New York University Press, 1955).

Boult, Sir Adrian, *Thoughts On Conducting* (Phoenix House) (J. M. Dent, 1963).

Buckle, Richard, *The Adventures Of A Ballet Critic* (The Cresset Press, 1953).

Chaliapine, Feodor, *Pages From My Life* (Harper & Brothers, New York, 1927).

Cohen, Harriet, *A Bundle Of Time* (Faber & Faber, 1969).

Crosland, Margaret, *Jean Cocteau* (Peter Nevill, 1955).

Crowle, Pigeon and Davis, Mike, *The Nutcracker Ballet* (Faber & Faber, 1958).

Davidson, Gladys, *Ballet Biographies* (T. Werner Laurie, 1952).

Downes, Irene (ed.), *Olin Downes On Music* (Simon & Schuster, New York, 1957).

Ewen, David (ed.), *The World Of Twentieth Century Music* (Robert Hale, 1969).

Fokine, Michael, *Memoirs Of A Ballet Master* (Constable, 1961).

Giliot, Francoise and Lake, Carlton, *Life With Picasso* (McGraw-Hill, 1964).

Grigoriev, S. L., *The Diaghilev Ballet* (Constable, 1953).

Haggin, B. H., *Music Observed* (Oxford University Press, 1964).

Haskell, Arnold in collaboration with Nouvel, Walter, *Diaghilev* (Victor Gollancz, 1935).

Hodeir, André, *Since Debussy* (Martin Secker and Warburg, 1961).

Karsavina, Tamara, *Theatre Street* (Constable) (Readers Union, 1950).

Lederman, Minna (ed.), *Stravinsky In The Theatre* (Pellegrini & Cudahy, New York, 1949).

Lifar, Serge, *A History Of Russian Ballet* (Hutchinson, 1970).

——, *The Three Graces* (Cassel, 1959).

——, *My Life* (Hutchinson, 1970).

Lockspeiser, Edward, *Debussy* (J. M. Dent, 1944).

Mackworth, Cecily, *Guillaume Apollinaire* (John Murray, 1961).

Massine, Léonide, *My Life In Ballet* (Macmillan, 1968).

Mitchell, Donald, *The Language Of Modern Music* (Faber & Faber, 1963).

Montagu-Nathan, M., *Contemporary Russian Composers* (Cecil Palmer & Hayward, 1917).

Montagu-Nathan, M., *Rimsky-Korsakov* (Constable, 1916).
Monteux, Doris, *Monteux: It's All In The Music* (William Kimber, 1966).
Music And Musicians
Nabokov, Nicolas, *Old Friends And New Music* (Atlantic Monthly Press, Boston, 1951).
Newman, Vera, *Ernest Newman* (G. P. Putnam, 1963).
Nijinsky, Romola, *Nijinsky* (Victor Gollancz, 1936).
Rimsky-Korsakov, N. A., *My Musical Life* (Alfred A. Knopf, New York, 1923).
Rosenfeld, Paul, *Musical Impressions* (George Allen & Unwin, 1970).
Safránek, Miloš, *Bohuslav Martinů: His Life And Works* (Allan Wingate, 1962).
Serov, Victor I., *Serge Prokofiev: A Soviet Tragedy* (Leslie Frewin, 1969).
——, *Rachmaninov* (Cassel, 1951).
Stravinsky, Igor, *An Autobiography* (Victor Gollancz, 1936) (Calder & Boyars, 1975).
——, *The Poetics Of Music* (Harvard University Press, 1947).
——, *Chronicle Of My Life* (Victor Gollancz, 1936).
——, *Themes And Conclusions* (Faber & Faber, 1972).
Stravinsky, Igor and Craft, Robert, *Conversations With Stravinsky* (Faber & Faber, 1959).
——, *Dialogues And A Diary* (Faber & Faber, 1968).
——, *Memories And Commentaries* (Faber & Faber, 1960).
——, *Expositions And Developments* (Faber & Faber, 1962).
Szigeti, Joseph, *With Strings Attached* (Alfred A. Knopf, New York, 1947).
Taper, Bernard, *Balanchine* (William Collins, 1964).
White, Eric Walter, *Stravinsky: The Composer And His Works* (Faber & Faber, 1966).

INDEX

ABERJONAIS, RENÉ, 70, 87–8
Abraham and Isaac, 190–1, 255–7
Adams, Diana, 170–1, 177
Afanasiev, 214
Aga Khan, 108
Agon, 170–2
Agostini, Gloria, 172
Ailey, Alvin, 31
Alexander III, Emperor, 22
Allegri, O., 44
Althouse, Paul, 121
Anchutine, Leyda, 146
Andersen, Hans C., 37, 66, 82, 90, 126, 215, 230
Anosov, Nikolai, 188
Ansermet, Ernest, 67, 70–1, 74, 83, 89–90, 111, 128, 134, 156, 211
Apollon Musagètes (Apollo), 124–6, 141, 170, 172, 188, 229, 238
Ardoin, John, 167, 179
Argoutinski, 127
Arliss, George, 193
Arnold, Matthew, 23
A Sermon. A Narrative And A Prayer, 178, 203, 253–4
Ashton, Sir Frederick, 118, 162, 230
Auden, W. H., 157–60, 168, 198, 245, 256
Auer, Leopold, 26
Auric, Georges, 64, 180, 221
Ave Maria, 120, 137, 241

Babel, 149
Bach, J. S., 60, 104, 115, 196, 211
Bakst, Leon, 28–9, 41, 45–6, 54, 74–5, 85, 95, 98, 105, 107, 127
Balakirev, 38
Balanchine, George, 31, 116–18, 124–6, 141–2, 146–8, 153–5, 170–2, 177, 179, 229–31, 234, 236, 250, 256
Balanchivadze, Meliton, 116–17
Balla, 83
Balmont, 180
Barnes, Clive, 256
Barsacq, André, 137, 245
Bartok, 69, 152
Bauchant, André, 125
Baum, Morton, 155
Bax, 104
Beaumont, Cyril, 45
Beardsley, Aubrey, 152

Beethoven, 21, 69, 104, 134, 203–5, 227–8, 231
Beecham, Sir Thomas, 212
Béjart, 31
Belaiev, 27–8, 37
Belloc, Hilaire, 15
Benois, Alexandre, 28–9, 32, 45–6, 50, 52, 67, 85, 98, 127–8, 175
Berg, 168, 180, 185
Bergman, Ingmar, 176
Berman, Eugene, 147, 190
Bertensson, Serge, 145
Bertha (S.'s nurse), 86
Bernstein, Leonard, 118, 196
Berners, Lord, 73
Bischoff, Henri, 70
Bizet, 27
Bliss, Herbert, 154
Blomdahl, Karl-Birger, 157
Blumenfeld, Felix, 27, 37
Bolender, Todd, 170–1
Bolm, Adolph, 118, 229
Borodin, 205
Boughton, Rutland, 50
Boulanger, Nadia, 142–3, 153, 245
Boult, Sir Adrian, 26
Bowen, Vera, 81
Brahms, 25, 134, 188
Braque, Georges, 85
Braunsweg, Julian, 129
Brianza, Carlotta, 104–6
Britten, 21, 180
Brown, Gloria, 184–5
Bruce, H. J., 58–9
Bruckner, 25
Brussel, Robert, 40, 43
Buckle, Richard, 114, 155
Bulgakov, Alexis, 41
Burrows, Stuart, 122–3
Busch, Fritz, 94
Busoni, 112, 140, 248

CABOT, SEBASTIAN, 179
Calmette, Gaston, 55–6
Canons for Two Horns, 85, 219
Cantata, 167, 245, 247–8
Canticum Sacrum, 23, 133, 169–70, 172, 203, 239, 249–50, 253, 255
Capriccio for Piano and Orchestra, 128, 134, 140, 142, 226–9
Card Game, 126, 141–2, 196, 230–1

Casals, Pablo, 196
Casella, Alfred, 65, 72, 203, 226
Catherine the Great, 16
Cat's Cradle Songs, 69, 79, 192, 217–18
Cecchetti, Enrico, 43–4, 51, 53, 74–5, 104
Cézanne, 65
Chabrier, 27
Chagall, Marc, 64, 155
Chaliapine, 26, 34, 37, 72
Chanel, Coco, 128
Chantevoine, Jean, 137
Chaplin, Charles, 119, 209
Chav-char-Vadze, Princess, 179
Chateaubriand, 15
Chavennes, Fernant, 70
Chaves, Carlos, 153
Chesterton, G. K., 203
Cherkassky, Shura, 113
Chopin, 222, 228
Christensen, Lew, 146
Cingria, Alexandre, 70
Cingria, Charles-Albert, 70, 143, 237
Circus Polka, 146–7, 233–4
Cluytens, André, 167
Cocteau, Jean, 43, 61–2, 64, 85, 94–8,
    120–1, 190, 194
Cohen, Harriet, 46, 104, 124
Collaer, Paul, 224
Concertino, 93, 222–4
Concerto in D ('Basle'), 152–3, 233, 236
Concerto in E flat ('Dumbarton Oaks'),
    142, 233, 236, 239
Concerto for Piano and Wind, 112–13,
    115, 118–19, 140, 204, 226–7
Concerto for Two Solo Pianos, 23, 140,
    228, 231, 239
Concerto for Violin and Orchestra, 134–5,
    146, 233, 235
Cooper, Fennimore, 15, 25
Coolidge, Elizabeth S., 229
Copland, 180, 257
Cowell, 180
Craft, Robert, 16, 21, 36, 150, 156, 165,
    167, 170, 174, 177, 179–82, 185–8,
    191–2, 198–9, 216, 225, 254, 258
Craig, Gordon, 125
Credo, 120, 137, 241
Cuenod, Hugues, 172, 178
Cullberg, Birgit, 118

D'ALBERT, EUGENE, 26
Daniélou, Jean, 121
Danilova, Alexandra, 147–8
Dankovich, 181
Danses Concertantes, 126, 147, 169,
    229–30
Dargomijsky, 225
Debussy, 16, 29, 37, 46–8, 53, 57, 61,
    65, 73, 79, 81, 92–3, 96, 189, 204–5,
    211, 215, 217, 219, 224, 249
Dekker, Thomas, 254
de la Mare, Walter, 207
Délibes, 27–8, 142, 229
Denham, Serge, 147
Derain, André, 124
d'Erlanger, Baroness, 128

Deroubdix, Jeanne, 172, 178
Diaghilev, Serge, Édits Mir Iskusstva and
    becomes an impresario, 28–9; youth
    in St Petersburg, 32; commissions
    Stravinsky to compose The Firebird,
    39; establishes the Russian Ballet at
    the Châtelet Theatre, Paris, 42;
    première of The Firebird at the Opera
    House, 41; technical and artistic staff,
    43–5; Karsavina and Nijinsky, 45–6;
    rehearsal and staging of Petrushka,
    50–3; première of L'Après-midi shocks
    Paris, 54–6; Fokine leaves, and Massine
    joins the company, 59–60; première of
    The Rite of Spring causes an uproar,
    61–2; Nijinsky is dismissed, 66;
    resources and company depleted by
    war, 72; tours abroad and fresh
    triumphs, 73–85; Nijinsky rejoins the
    Russian Ballet, 80; Massine succeeds
    Fokine as chief choreographer, 80;
    Nijinsky, stricken by madness, dances
    for the last time, 81; visits to Rome and
    Naples, 82–5; Stravinsky defects from
    the company, but returns to work on
    Pulcinella, 90–2; Cocteau's portrait of
    the impresario, 95; the ballet Parade
    is a ghastly fiasco, 97–8; Stravinsky
    collaborates in a season at the Royal
    Theatre, Madrid, 99; Massine deserts
    the company and others follow, 102;
    Slavinsky becomes chief choreographer,
    102; Bronislava Nijinska rejoins the
    Russian Ballet, 104; Stravinsky helps
    to prepare The Sleeping Princess, 104;
    première of the new ballet in London,
    105–7; visit to Monte Carlo, 107–8;
    Massine, begging to be taken back, is
    coldly repulsed, 109; Serge Lifar joins
    the Russian Ballet, 110; the impresario
    gains a new choreographer in Balan-
    chine; triumph of Apollon Musagetès,
    125; contempt and anger vented on
    Ida Rubinstein, 126–8; the impresario
    succumbs to diabetes and dies, 128;
    character of a great man, his generosity
    and superstition, his dictatorial rule and
    kindness, 129–132; Wagnerian depar-
    ture and burial on San Michele, 132
Dietrich, Marlene, 119
Disney, Walt, 63, 142, 186
Dobrecki, 131
Dolin, Anton, 162, 230
Dollar, William, 146
Donizetti, 225
Dostoievsky, 27
Double Canon, 173, 252–3
Doubrovska, 125
The Dove Descending Breaks The Air,
    101, 176–7, 254
Dowd, Ronald, 122
Dowson, Ernest, 21
Downes, Olin, 118
Drew, David, 228
Drigo, Riccardo, 104–5
Duet for Two Bassoons, 88, 219

Dufy, Raoul, 173, 252
Dukas, 137, 204–5
Duke (Dukelsky), 150
Duncan, Isadora, 31
Duo Concertante, 115–16, 135, 139, 233–4
Dushkin, Samuel, 134–5, 139, 208–9, 216,
    223, 225, 231, 233, 235
Dvorak, 69
Dyson, George, 216

Ebony Concerto, 149, 233, 236–7
Elegy, 126, 149, 233, 235
Elegy for J.F.K., 192, 256
Elgar, 139
Eliot, T. S., 158, 176, 194
English, Gerald, 122, 124
Epitaphium, 172, 252
Essipova, Anna, 26
Evans, Edith, 104
Evans, Edwin, 207
Evans, Merle, 234
Ewer, Ronald, 246

FAIRCHILD, BLAIR, 134
The Fairy's Kiss, 23, 126–7, 131, 141,
    173, 230–1
Falla, 46, 65, 79
Fanfare for a New Theatre, 192, 256
Fantastic Scherzo, 37, 205–6
Faun and Shepherdess, 37, 205
Fedorovich, Sophie, 118
Flemyng, Christopher le, 218
The Firebird, 16, 23, 30, 37, 39–42,
    47–9, 57, 60, 69, 76, 82, 84, 89, 92,
    130, 135, 153, 155, 163, 170, 183, 191,
    198, 205, 207–10, 215, 222–3
Fireworks, 38–9, 59, 64, 82–4, 204–6
Five Easy Pieces for Piano Duet, 81, 226,
    234
The Five Fingers, 103, 229, 254
The Flood, 126, 179, 185, 254–5
Fokine, 20, 29, 39, 40, 44–5, 50–1, 58–9,
    80, 97, 127, 210
Fokina, Vera, 41
Four Norwegian Moods, 146, 233–4
Four Russian Peasant Songs, 69, 85, 217,
    219
Four Russian Songs, 89, 134, 168, 219
Four Studies for Orchestra, 133, 217, 226
Four Studies for Piano, 38, 205–6
Funeral Dirge, 38, 205–6
Franck, César, 41
Franklin, Frederic, 147
Fuller, Loie, 39
Fürstenburg, Prince Max Egon zu, 172,
    252
Furtwängler, 115

GALUPPI, 222
Gauguin, 65
Gautier, Jeanne, 231
Geddes, Norman del, 147
Georgiadis, Nicholas, 118, 169
Gerdt, 104
Gershwin, George, 119
Gesualdo, 211, 253

Ghéon, Henri, 41, 95
Gielgud, Sir John, 137
Gide, André, 95, 135–7, 216, 243–4
Gish, Lillian, 138
Glazunov, 26–7, 36–8, 51, 67, 89
Glinka, 20, 23, 26, 30, 224
Goddard, Paulette, 119
Godet, Robert, 47, 55–6
Goethe, 193
Golovine, 39, 41
Goncharova, 72, 74, 85
Gorsky, 20
Gorodetzky, 38, 206
Gounod, 27, 189
Green, Prof. Gordon, 139
Greetings Prelude, 162, 250
Grieg, 222
Grigoriev, 44, 59, 66, 81, 90, 104, 117,
    164
Guerdt, 20
Guiffre, 237

HAGGIN, B. H., 125, 173
Hahn, Reynaldo, 43
Haiev, Alexei, 140, 197
Harris, Sidney J., 193
Harvey, Laurence, 179
Haskell, Arnold, 130, 169
Hayden, Melissa, 170–1
Haydn, 227, 233
Henze, Hans, 160
Herincx, Raimund, 122–4, 191
Herman, Woody, 233–6
Hess, Myra, 113, 140
Hielan, Michael, 176
Hylton, Jack, 225
Hindemith, 115, 135, 152, 180, 203, 250
Hodeir, André, 153
Hofmann, Joseph, 26
Hogarth, William, 156, 158–9, 245
Honegger, 120, 180, 238
Holbrooke, Josef, 212
Hughes, Spike, 60
Hurok, Sol, 118, 147
Huxley, Aldous, 88, 157, 166, 168–9, 171,
    194, 256
Huxley, Matthew, 168

ILOSVAY, MARIA VON, 169
Imperio, Pastora, 100
In Memoriam Dylan Thomas, 166, 221,
    247, 249
Introitus (T. S. Eliot In Memoriam),
    192, 256–7
Isenbergh, Max, 179
Ives, Charles, 177, 238

JONES, ROBERT E., 121
Jooss, Kurt, 137, 245

KABALEVSKY, 181
Kahn, Otto, 109
Kallman, Chester, 157–60, 245
Kant, 193
Kandinsky, 190

Karsavina, Tamara, 20, 29, 40–2, 45, 51–3, 58, 66, 72, 80, 91–2, 95, 130, 162–4.
Kashperova, Mlle., 21–2
Kennedy, President, 179, 256
Khoklova, Olga, 85
The King of the Stars, 47, 134, 171, 215
King Alfonso of Spain, 99
Kirievsky, 214
Kirstein, Lincoln, 118, 141, 153, 155, 172, 177
Klee, Paul, 17, 190
Kochno, Boris, 105, 107, 128, 164, 224
Kodály, 196
Korovine, 132
Kostov, 118
Koussevitzky, Natalie, 146, 234
Koussevitzky, Serge, 89, 102–3, 109, 113, 133, 234–5
Kraus, Otakar, 161
Krausz, Laszlo, 123
Krenek, Ernst, 180, 196, 238
Krennikov, 181
Krushchev, 182
Kshessinskaya, 72

LALO, PIERRE, 62
Laloy, Louis, 96
Lamarck, 193
Lambert, Constant, 91, 113, 142
Lanchester, Elsa, 179
Lang, Andrew, 136
Lang, Paul Henry, 185–6
Lanner, J. F. C., 204
Larionov, 74, 102
Laskey, Charles, 146
LeClerq, Tanaquil, 154, 170
le Roy, Adrian, 186
Levinson, André, 99, 163
Liadov, 27, 29
Libman, Lilian, 187–8
Lieberson, Goddard, 175, 195, 198
Lieven, Prince Peter, 53
Lifar, Serge, 48, 75, 109–111, 124–5, 128, 130, 132, 162–4
Liszt, 70, 139, 227
Little Canon for Two Tenors, 245
Lopokova, 88, 105–6
Lostokin, Robert, 172
Lowinsky, Edward, 186
Ludwig, Emil, 173
Lyon, Annabelle, 146

MCCLURE, JOHN, 194
Macero, 237
Machaut, 242
Mackerras, Charles, 122
Macmillan, Kenneth, 118, 169
Madrid, 86
Maeterlinck, 37, 206
Magallenes, Nicholas, 154
Mahler, 212
Malaïev, M., 231
Mann, Klaus, 145
Mann, Thomas, 193
Marinetti, Filippo, 63

Markevich, D., 225
Markova, Alicia, 117
Martin, John, 146
Martinu, Bohuslav, 152–3
Mascagni, 83
Mass, 23, 133, 156, 172, 194, 222, 239, 241–2, 245
Massine, Leonide, 58–60, 74, 76, 80, 84, 88, 90–2, 94, 97–9, 102, 109, 128, 163
Matisse, 65, 90
Matzanauer, Mme., 121
Mavra, 72, 107, 109, 224–5, 238
Melchert, Helmut, 169
Mencies, Francisco, 154
Mengelberg, Willem, 118
Menotti, 180, 198
Mentner, Sophie, 26
Messiaen, 64, 160, 180
Meyerbeer, 15
Mikhailovich, Prince Serge, 29, 39
Milhaud, 96, 180, 221, 238
Mingus, 237
Miro, Gabriel, 190
Mitchell, Arthur, 170–1
Mitchell, Donald, 187, 251
Mitchinson, John, 122
Mitoussov, Stepan, 28, 37
Monteux, Pierre, 52, 60–4, 67, 162, 211, 250
Monteverdi, 17
Monumentum, 126, 177, 253
Moore, Gerald, 189
Moore, Lillian, 177
Mora, Jean, 70
Mora, René, 70
Mordkin, 118
Movements, 126, 175–6, 184, 192, 252–3, 255
Mozart, 91, 134, 144, 156, 227, 233, 246, 253
Mugnone, Leopoldo, 84
The Mushrooms Going To War, 27, 205
Mussolini, 135
Mussorgsky, 23, 25, 27, 60, 65, 71
Mustel, Victor, 89

NABOKOV, NICHOLAS, 108, 124–5, 154, 179, 198
Naguchi, Isamu, 154
Napravnik, 17, 26, 186
Nemchinova, 92
Newman, Ernest, 73
Newman, Vera, 73
Nicolas, Claire, 168
Nicolas, Sylvia, 168
Nietzsche, 176
The Nightingale, 23, 28, 37–8, 66–7, 81, 90, 134–5, 178, 215–17, 222–3
Nikitina, 25, 125
Nijinska, Bronislava, 72, 104, 106–7, 109, 111, 126, 128
Nijinsky, Kyra, 77, 131, 163
Nijinsky, Romola, 56, 72, 77, 127, 131, 162–3
Nijinsky, Vaslav, 16, 29, 45–6, 51, 53–5,

57, 61–2, 65–6, 72, 77–8, 80–1, 95, 98–9, 125, 131, 162–4
Nono, Luigi, 172
Nurock, 29
Nossenko, Catherine (S.'s first wife), 36
Norton, Mildred, 251
Nouvel, Walter, 28–9, 48, 132, 164

Octet, 109, 172, 225–6
Ode, 146, 233–4
Oedipus Rex, 120–4, 133, 169, 178, 190, 236, 238–41, 245, 249, 255
Offenbach, 28
Oliver, Robert, 172, 179
Olsen, Derrik, 178
Onnou, Alphonse, 149
Orlov, 53
Orpheus, 126, 141, 153–5, 169–70, 182, 229–32, 235

Pastoral, 38, 205
Pater Noster, 120, 241
Pavlova, 20, 29, 44, 72
Pease, James, 169
Pergolesi, 90–1, 196, 222–3
Perséphone, 135–7, 143, 171, 178, 190, 194, 239, 241, 243–5
Petipa, Marie, 104
Petipa, Marius, 28, 57, 104, 117
Petit Ramusianum Harmonique, 143, 237
Petrushka, 16, 44, 49–53, 57, 59, 64, 69, 74, 81, 99, 135, 153, 163–4, 169, 188, 204–5, 207, 209–11, 213, 215, 217, 222–3, 251
Pfitzner, 204
Piano Duets, 72
Piano-Rag Music, 89, 237
Piano Sonata (1924), 23, 115, 119, 228
Piano Sonata, 32, 205
Piatigorsky, 223
Pierné, Gabriel, 40–1
Picasso, 65, 84–5, 90–1, 94–5, 98, 102, 108, 190, 251
Piltz, Marie, 99
Piovesan, Allesandro, 172
Pleyel, Ignaz, 107
Polignac, Princess Edmond de, 74, 77, 82, 107, 115, 137
Ponchielli, 15
Poulenc, 180, 221
Pound, Ezra, 18
Pourtalès, Princess de, 61
Preludium, 141, 238
Preobrajenska, 117
Pribaoutki, 69, 79, 81, 217–18
Pritchard, John, 94
Prokofiev, 73, 102, 104, 108, 112
Prokovsky, Ivan, 27, 29
Proust, Marcel, 43
Puccini, 29, 52, 74, 83–4
Pulcinella, 90–2, 123, 204, 222–3
Pulsky, Romola, 66
Pushkin, Alexander, 37, 107, 205, 224

RACHMANINOV, 145–6, 197, 228
Racine, 245

Racz, Aladar, 78, 226
Ragtime, 89, 126, 151, 225, 229, 237
The Rake's Progress, 134, 156–61, 166–8, 176, 187, 198, 227, 238, 245–7, 251
Radziwell, Princess, 179
Ramuz, 69, 70–1, 78–9, 81, 87–9, 143, 220–1, 237
Raphael, 17
Rasputin, 72, 82
Read, Herbert, 101
Reardon, John, 179
Reiner, Fritz, 167
Reinhart, Werner, 87, 90, 224
Reisenauer, Alfred, 26
Rennert, Günther, 169
Requiem Canticles, 23, 133, 193, 199, 257–8
Reynard, 74, 77–9, 81–2, 107, 109, 126, 151, 219, 220
Reynaud, Madeleine, 171
Richter, Hans, 26–7
Richter, Nicholas, 38
Rilke, Rainer Maria, 152
Rimsky-Korsakov, Nadia, 38
Rimsky-Korsakov, Nikolai, 21–3, 27–9, 32–4, 36–8, 60, 67, 69, 89, 183, 205–7
Rimsky-Korsakov, Vladimir, 36, 38, 182
Rite of Spring, The, 15–16, 18, 22, 30, 34, 47–9, 54, 56–7, 59–65, 68–70, 83, 92–3, 97, 99, 118, 142–3, 146, 153–4, 163, 171, 181, 186, 188, 196, 203, 206–7, 210–15, 217, 220, 222–3, 234, 254, 257
Riviera, Diego de, 65
Rivière, Jacques, 163
Rivière, Jean-Claude, 167
Robbins, Jerome, 118
Robinson, Edward G., 119, 144
Robinson, Richard, 172, 179
Rochester, Junius, 191–2
Rodin, Auguste, 43
Roerick, Nicholas, 49, 54
Roerick, William, 137
Romanov, 67
Roosevelt, Mrs Franklin, 144
Rose, Billy, 150, 229–30
Rosenfeld, Paul, 151
Rosenthal, Manual, 171
Rossini, 83, 96, 142, 203, 231, 239
Roth, Ernest, 161
Rousseau, 59
Rubinstein, Anton, 22
Rubinstein, Artur, 89, 112
Rubinstein, Ida, 45, 126–7, 135, 137, 175, 230, 245
Rubinstein, Nikolai, 22
Rüsager, Knudsage, 172
Rusk, Dean, 179

SACHER, PAUL, 152, 178, 236
Sacher, Maja, 152
Satie, 72, 94–5, 98, 226
Sauguet, 128
Saint-Saëns, 45
Salazar, Adolf, 233
Sargent, Winthrop, 198

Sayn-Wittgenstein, Countess, 70
Scènes de Ballet, 149–50, 153, 229–30
Schall, Eric, 148
Scharbach, Charles, 172
Scherzo à la Russe, 149, 233, 235
Schmitt, Florent, 46, 48, 61, 65
Schoenberg, 17, 58–9, 68, 75, 119, 150, 152, 156, 168, 177, 180, 184–5, 215, 217–18, 251
Schollar, 128
Schubert, 60, 234
Scriabin, 37, 215
Seeger, Helen B., 258
Senior, Evan, 169
Septet, 168, 247–8
Serenade, 23, 116, 222, 228
Sergueev, Nicolas, 105
Sert, José, M., 46
Sert, Misia, 46, 53
Shaporin, 181
Shaw, Bernard, 161
Shilkret, Nathaniel, 150, 241
Shostakovich, 181–2, 198
Sibelius, 203–4, 216
Siloti, Alexander, 37
Simoni, Renato, 52
Sitwell, Sir Osbert, 234
Slalinsky, 102
Smith, Gregg, 180
Smith, Oliver, 118
Sokolova, 91, 99, 105
Soldier's Tale, The, 87–90, 112, 203–4, 219–21, 226, 237–8, 251
Solokov, 27
Sonata for Two Pianos, 149
The Song of the Nightingale, 90–1, 117, 216
Soudeikin, Serge, 144
Souris, André, 186
Souvenir d'une Marche Boche, 69, 217
Spessivtseva, Olga, 105–6
Stassov, Vladimir, 26
Steinberg, Maximilian, 38, 206
Stepanov, Vladimir, 105
Stevenson, Hugh, 118
Stokowski, Leopold, 63, 121, 196–7
Strauss, Johann, 116, 142
Strauss, Richard, 57, 113, 193, 198, 204, 216
Stravinsky, Catherine (S.'s first wife), 78, 82, 144
Stravinsky, Feodor (S.'s father), 17–19, 28
Stravinsky, Goury (S.'s brother), 17–19, 86
Stravinsky, Ielatchitch (S.'s uncle), 20, 25–6
Stravinsky, Igor, Birth and ancestry, 15–16; early life in St Petersburg, 17–40; lessons in piano and score-reading, 21–2; at school, 22–3; Uncle Ielatchitch's influence, 25–6; University, 28; becomes a pupil of Rimsky-Korsakov and composes, 28, 32–3, 36–8; leaves University and marries Catherine Nossenko, 36; death of Rimsky-Korsakov, 38; first commission from Diaghilev, 39; the Russian Ballet

takes over the Châtelet Theatre, Paris, 42; rehearsals, 40; triumphant première of The Firebird, 41–2; happy relationship with Cecchetti, 43; brilliance of Bakst and Benois, Karsavina and Nijinsky, 45; meeting with Debussy, Ravel, Falla, 46–8; travels to Oustiloug to compose a new work, 54; joins Diaghilev at Bayreuth and mocks the Festspielhaus tradition, 56–7; meets Schoenberg, 58; The Rite of Spring scandalizes Paris, 60–2; ill with typhoid, 65; meets Ansermet at Clarens and composes there, 67; outbreak of the 1914–18 war, 68; daily routine at Morges, 70; première of one of the noblest of ballets, 71; financial and domestic worries, 72; meets Prokofiev and returns to Switzerland, 73–4; joins Diaghilev in Spain, 79–80; visit from the Princess de Polignac, 82; at Naples with Diaghilev, Picasso and Massine, 84–5; death of Bertha, his childhood nurse, 86; collaboration with Ramuz, 87–8; following Debussy's death, he settles in France, 92–3; more triumphs in Paris, 94–9; thrills to the pageantry of Seville, 100–1; helps Diaghilev to prepare The Sleeping Princess, 104–7; more travels, 107–13; association with Balanchine begins, 116; first visit to America, 118; meets Gershwin, 119; creates an opera-oratorio with Cocteau, 120–1; Balanchine choreographs his new ballet, 124; the composer works for Ida Rubinstein and angers Diaghilev, 126–8; character and death of Diaghilev, 128–32; European concert tours, 134; collaboration with Gide, 135–6; visit to Liverpool, 139–40; quarrels with Walt Disney, 142–3; accepts Chair of Poetry at Harvard University, 143–4; death of his wife and his daughter Ludmila, 144; settles in America and marries Vera de Bosset, both becoming naturalized citizens, 144; meeting and relationship with Rachmaninov, 145–6; contempt for certain critics, reviewers and musicians, 150–2; association with Robert Craft begins, 155–6; operatic triumph with Auden and Kallman, 157–60; traumatic meeting with Evelyn Waugh, 161–2; religious observances, 165–6; seventy-fifth birthday celebrations, 171; visits Japan, 174–5; pilgrimage to Russia, 180–3; character and relationship with Craft, 185–8; home life, 189–91; physical dissolution, 192–3; assessment of the composer and the man, 194–8; death, 199; burial on San Michele, 200.
Stravinsky, Ignatievich (S.'s great-grand-father), 15
Stravinsky, Ludmila (S.'s eldest daughter), 85, 144, 218–19

Stravinsky, Roman (S.'s brother), 19
Stravinsky, Sviatoslav Soulima (S.'s
    youngest son), 140, 176, 218, 245
Stravinsky, Theodore (S.'s eldest son), 78,
    120, 198, 218
Stravinsky, Vera (S.'s second wife), 144–5,
    148, 158, 173–4, 179–80, 188–91,
    197–8.
Stravinsky, Youry (S.'s brother), 19, 23
Strecker, Willy, 134
Study for Pianola, 133, 219, 226
Swanson, Gloria, 80
Symphony in C, 77, 134, 144, 232–3,
    239
Symphony in E flat, 36, 205, 232
Symphony in Three Movements, 148, 156,
    232–3, 237, 239
Symphony of Psalms, 73, 133–4, 192, 227,
    239, 241–3
Symphonies of Wind Instruments, 73, 93,
    102–3, 224
Szigeti, Josef, 115, 147, 223

TAGORE, RABINDRANATH, 22
Tallchief, Maria, 154–5
Tango, 144, 229
Taper, Bernard, 117
Tartakov, 19
Taubman, Howard, 251
Tchaikovsky, 20–2, 26, 30–2, 45, 89,
    104–6, 126–7, 162, 196, 205, 225,
    229–30
Tchelichev, 146
Tcherepnin, 27, 76
Tchernicheva, 92, 105, 125
Tenichev, Princess, 54
Ter-Arutunian, 179
Teyte, Maggie, 92
Thomas, Dylan, 166, 221, 249
Thompson, Virgil, 116
Thoresby, Christina, 170
Three Easy Pieces for Piano Duet, 69,
    226
Three Japanese Lyrics, 217
Three Little Songs (Recollections from
    Childhood), 59, 217–18
Three Pieces for Solo Clarinet, 89, 224
Three Pieces for String Quartet, 133, 216,
    226
Three Sacred Songs by Gesualdo, 253
Three Songs from William Shakespeare,
    168, 221, 247–8
Three Tales for Children, 81, 217–18
Threni, 172, 178, 203, 239, 251–2, 255
Tintoretto, 193

Titian, 193
Tobiss, Ray, 170
Toscanini, 44, 48, 51, 143
Tourel, Jennie, 167
Toulouse-Lautrec, 39, 65
Tudor, 118
Two Melodies of Gorodetzky, 38, 205–6
Two Poems of Balmont, 217
Two Poems of Verlaine, 19, 217
Tyrwhitt, Gerald, 73

UNGER, 128

Valse des Fleurs, 69, 219
Valse pour les Enfants, 219
Valz, E., 44
Van Gogh, 65
Variations (Aldous Huxley In Mem-
    oriam), 88, 192, 256
Variations on 'Von himmel hoch', 170,
    250
Vassily (Diaghilev's valet), 43, 46, 129
Vaudoyer, Jean-Louis, 43
Verdi, 189, 193, 203
Verne, Jules, 25
Vuillermoz, Emile, 62, 163, 213
Vivaldi, 222
Vladimirov, 105

WAGNER, 48–50, 56–7, 59, 63, 83, 177,
    197, 240
Walden, Lord Howard de, 212
Walton, Sir William, 177
Warburg, Edward, 118, 141
Watts, Jonathan, 170
Waugh, Evelyn, 161–2
Weber, 196
Webern, 168, 177, 180, 185, 236, 248–9,
    254, 257
The Wedding, 68–72, 74–5, 78, 82, 86,
    110–11, 153, 170, 172, 192, 213–15
Weill, Kurt, 238
Wells, H. G., 71
Werfel, Franz, 156
White, Eric Walter, 146
Whiteman, Paul, 149, 235
Wilzak, 128
Wyck, Wilfred van, 139

YANITZ, MURRAY, 172
Yates, Peter, 168, 248
Young, Alexander, 122, 161

ZOLLENKOPF, URSULA, 172